continued on back

Econometric Analysis
by Control Methods

A Wiley Publication in Applied Statistics

Econometric Analysis
by Control Methods

GREGORY C. CHOW

Class of 1913 Professor of Political Economy and Director, Econometric Research Program

Princeton University

John Wiley & Sons

New York • Chichester • Brisbane • Toronto • Singapore

**To My Father and
My Father-in-Law**

Library of Congress Cataloging in Publication Data:

Chow, Gregory C., 1929–
    Econometric analysis by control methods.

    (Wiley series in probability and mathematical
statistics, ISSN 0271-6356) (A Wiley publication in
applied statistics)
    Bibliography: p.
    Includes index.
    1. Econometrics.   2. Control theory.   3. Stochastic
processes.   I. Title.   II. Series.   III. Series: Wiley
publication in applied statistics.
HB139.C48   330'.028   81-571
ISBN 0-471-08706-8   AACR2

Printed in the United States of America

10 9 8 7 6 5 4 3 2

Preface

Since the early 1970s, economists have become increasingly interested in methods of stochastic control. From 1972 to 1978, a series of annual conferences on stochastic control in economics were held successively at Princeton University, the University of Chicago, the Board of Governors of the Federal Reserve System, the Massachusetts Institute of Technology, Stanford, Yale, and the University of Texas, under the sponsorship of the National Bureau of Economic Research and with financial support from the National Science Foundation. Selected papers from these conferences were published in various issues of the *Annals of Economic and Social Measurement*. In 1979, an international Society for Economic Dynamics and Control was formed with its first annual conference held at Cambridge University. Nineteen-seventy-nine also saw the publication of the new *Journal of Economic Dynamics and Control*.

The author's text, *Analysis and Control of Dynamic Economic Systems* (Wiley, 1975), was an attempt to summarize some of the important methods of stochastic dynamics and control together with economic applications for the students and professionals who wish to learn the subject. Since then, not only have new methods been developed, but many novel and important applications have appeared, as we will report in this book. This book is divided into four parts. Part 1 is concerned with control techniques. Methods for large nonlinear systems of simultaneous equations are discussed in Chapters 1 through 5. When the author's 1975 book was published, it was considered difficult or impractical to control such systems. Now, algorithms have appeared and computer programs are available. In addition, the method of Kalman filtering has been developed further and recognized to be useful for the estimation of econometric models, as we will point out in Chapter 6.

Part 2 of this book, including Chapters 7 through 14, is concerned with economic applications of control methods. Chapter 7 suggests an economic definition of the inflation-unemployment trade-off relationship which is implicit in an econometric model and is derived by stochastic control techniques. Chapter 8 provides a method to evaluate the success or failure of historical macroeconomic policies. Chapter 9 attempts to answer the question, "Has government policy contributed to economic instability?" by studying analytically the dynamic properties of the Michigan Quarterly Econometric Model. Chapter 10 recommends the application of the control framework to estimate the amount of resources available for government investment in Taiwan. Chapter 11 shows how imperfect models can be used for the formulation of stabilization policies. Chapter 12 provides a practical guide for using econometric models in macroeconomic policy formulation. Chapter 13 deals with the applications of control methods to the econometric analysis of Soviet economic planning. Finally, Chapter 14 indicates how control techniques can be used to compare econometric models.

In the late 1970s it was the view of some economists that the use of optimal control for the formulation of macroeconomic policies is inconsistent with the assumption of rational expectations. It has now become evident, however, that the use of control techniques for the evaluation of economic policies and for the derivation of optimal policies is not only possible but is essential under rational expectations. Moreover, control techniques are useful for the estimation of macroeconomic models under the assumption of rational expectations. This theme is developed in Chapters 15 through 17, which form Part 3 of this book. While previous chapters have been concerned with control techniques in discrete time and mainly with the study of aggregate economic activities, the last two Chapters 18 and 19 in Part 4 provide an exposition of stochastic control techniques in continuous time and apply these techniques to the study of problems in microeconomics.

It is hoped that this volume will provide its readers with a fairly broad treatment of the techniques of stochastic control and its important economic applications. This book can be used in conjunction with the author's 1975 text. It can also be used independently because the material is self-contained, its main prerequisite being some basic training in econometrics at the level of, for instance, R. J. Wonnacott and T. H. Wonnacott's *Econometrics* (Wiley, 1979).

In the preparation of this book, I have benefited from the collaboration of Sharon Bernstein Megdal (Chapters 4 and 7), Ettie H. Butters (Chapter 5), Suzanne Heller (Chapter 9), and Donald W. Green (Chapter 13). Pia Ellen and Constance Dixon have provided excellent assistance in typing various drafts of the manuscript. Ms. Ellen, in addition, has helped in editing the manuscript and preparing the index. To them, my sincere thanks.

The publishers of several journals have kindly granted permission to reproduce my previously published articles: Chapter 2 from *Annals of Economic and Social Measurement*, **5** (1976); Chapter 3 from *Econometrica*, **44** (1976); Chapter 4 from *IEEE Transactions on Automatic Control*, **AC-23** (1978); Chapter 7 from *American Economic Review*, **68** (1978); Chapter 8 from *International Economic Review*, **19** (1978); Chapter 11 from *Annals of Economic and Social Measurement*, **6** (1977); Chapter 15 from *Journal of Economic Dynamics and Control*, **2** (1980); Chapter 16 from *Journal of Economic Dynamics and Control*, **2** (1980); Chapters 18 and 19 from *Journal of Economic Dynamics and Control*, **1** (1979). St. Martin's Press, Inc. has granted permission to reproduce Chapter 12 from *Optimal Control for Econometric Models* edited by S. Holly, B. Rustem, and M. Zarrop (1979). Academic Press, Inc. has granted permission to reproduce Chapter 14 from *Evaluation of Econometric Models* edited by J. Kmenta and J. Ramsey (1980). Finally, I would like to acknowledge the financial support from the National Science Foundation for conducting most of the research which is now reported in this book.

GREGORY C. CHOW

Princeton, New Jersey
January 1981

Contents

Part 1
Techniques of Stochastic Control

CHAPTER 1

Introduction

The science of economics, as it is generally acknowledged, is a study of means for allocating scarce resources to satisfy competing and not totally attainable objectives. Mathematically speaking, an optimal control problem is concerned with the determination of the best ways to achieve a set of objectives as indexed by a criterion function when the performance is judged over many periods and when the dynamic behavior of the system is subject to a set of constraints. Therefore, dynamic economics and optimal control are conceptually very similar, if not formally identical. The differences, if they exist, lie mainly in the specification of special assumptions concerning the objective function or the dynamic system made in the optimal control literature for the sake of mathematical convenience. Such assumptions restrict the applicability of certain optimal control techniques to dynamic economics. Hopefully they will be relaxed or modified as the science progresses, but restrictive assumptions yield the benefits of analytical power and insights, and may indeed be relevant in many applications.

The scope of this volume is further limited in its treatment of both techniques and applications. The techniques are mainly, though not entirely, generalizations of the methods used for solving the elementary optimal control problem of minimizing a quadratic loss function subject to the constraint of a linear model. The applications are mainly, though again not entirely, econometric in nature, with due emphasis on statistical measurements. The purpose of this book is to present further developments in methods and applications of stochastic control in economics which the author has pursued since the publication of his *Analysis and Control of Dynamic Economic Systems* (1975). In order to survey its contents, it will be convenient to set up the basic optimal control problem of minimizing the expectation of a quadratic loss function subject to the constraint of a linear

3

model with additive stochastic disturbances. Much of this volume will be concerned with extensions, modifications, and applications of this basic control problem.

1.1 OPTIMAL CONTROL OF A LINEAR MODEL WITH KNOWN PARAMETERS

Let the environment facing the economic decision makers be represented by a linear system

$$y_t = A_t y_{t-1} + C_t x_t + b_t + u_t, \tag{1}$$

where y_t is a vector of p state variables, x_t is a vector of q control variables, A_t, C_t, and b_t are matrices of known constants, and u_t is a random vector that is serially independent and identically distributed. It is understood that state variables have been introduced to eliminate $y_{t-2}, y_{t-3}, \ldots, x_{t-1}$, x_{t-2}, and so on, from the system, and to incorporate x_t as a subvector of y_t so that the loss function (2) need not have x_t as an argument. For example, if there are 50 endogenous variables in the original system and the model includes a variable $y_{6,t-2}$, an identity $y_{51,t} = y_{6,t-1}$ can be introduced. Given this identity, $y_{6,t-2}$ can be written as $y_{51,t-1}$ and the second-order lag disappears. If $y_{6,t-3}$ is present, another identity $y_{52,t} = y_{51,t-1}$ can be used and $y_{6,t-3}$ can be written as $y_{52,t-1}$. Let there be 40 identities of this type to rid the system of second- and higher-order lagged endogenous variables. If $x_{1,t-1}$ and $x_{1,t-2}$ are present, we can define $y_{91,t} = x_{1,t-1}$ and write $x_{1,t-2}$ as $y_{91,t-1}$, and so forth. Let there be 10 identities of this type. We then define $y_{101,t} = x_{1t}$, $y_{102,t} = x_{2t}$ to incorporate x_t as a subvector of y_t. The loss function measuring the preference of the decision makers is quadratic:

$$W = \sum_{t=1}^{T} (y_t - a_t)' K_t (y_t - a_t). \tag{2}$$

The optimal control problem is to find strategies for x_t in order to minimize expected loss.

This elementary linear-quadratic optimal control problem can be solved by dynamic programming. First, we find the optimal policy for the last period T, given all the information up to (the end of) period $T - 1$. Denote by V_T the expectation, conditioned on information up to $T - 1$, of the loss for period T, which is a function of the policy x_T,

$$V_T = E_{T-1}(y_T - a_T)'K_T(y_T - a_T) = E_{T-1}(y_T'H_Ty_T - 2y_T'h_T + c_T), \quad (3)$$

where we have set $K_T = H_T$, $K_Ta_T = h_T$, and $c_T = a_T'K_Ta_T$. Substituting $A_Ty_{T-1} + C_Tx_T + b_T + u_T$ for y_T in (3) and minimizing V_T with respect to x_T by differentiation, we find the optimal policy for the last period

$$\hat{x}_T = G_Ty_{T-1} + g_T, \tag{4}$$

where

$$G_T = -(C_T'H_TC_T)^{-1}(C_T'H_TA_T) \tag{5}$$

$$g_T = -(C_T'H_TC_T)^{-1}C_T'(H_Tb_T - h_T). \tag{6}$$

The minimum expected loss for the last period is obtained by substituting for x_T in V_T,

$$\hat{V}_T = y_{T-1}'(A_T + C_TG_T)'H_T(A_T + C_TG_T)y_{T-1}$$

$$+ 2y_{T-1}'(A_T + C_TG_T)'(H_Tb_T - h_T)$$

$$+ (b_T + C_Tg_T)'H_T(b_T + C_Tg_T) - 2(b_T + C_Tg_T)'h_T$$

$$+ c_T + E_{T-1}u_T'H_Tu_T. \tag{7}$$

To obtain the optimal policies for the last two periods, we observe that $\hat{x}_T$ is already found that would yield the minimum loss $\hat{V}_T$, and that, by the principle of optimality of dynamic programming, we need only to find x_{T-1} to minimize

$$V_{T-1} = E_{T-2}\left[(y_{T-1} - a_{T-1})'K_{T-1}(y_{T-1} - a_{T-1}) + \hat{V}_T\right]$$

$$= E_{T-2}(y_{T-1}H_{T-1}y_{T-1}' - 2y_{T-1}'h_{T-1} + c_{T-1}), \tag{8}$$

where, using the expression (7) for $\hat{V}_T$, we have defined

$$H_{T-1} = K_{T-1} + (A_T + C_T G_T)' H_T (A_T + C_T G_T), \tag{9}$$

$$h_{T-1} = K_{T-1} a_{T-1} - (A_T + C_T G_T)'(H_T b_T - h_T), \tag{10}$$

$$c_{T-1} = a'_{T-1} K_{T-1} a_{T-1} + (b_T + C_T g_T)' H_T (b_T + C_T g_T)$$

$$- 2(b_T + C_T g_T)' h_T + c_T + E_{T-1} u'_T H_T u_T. \tag{11}$$

Because the second line of (8) is identical with the last expression of (3) with T replaced by $T - 1$, the solution for $\hat{x}_{T-1}$ is identical with (4) with T replaced by $T - 1$, where G_{T-1} and g_{T-1} are defined by (5) and (6) respectively with a similar change in time subscripts. Accordingly, $\hat{V}_{T-1}$ will be given by (7) with the subscripts T replaced by $T - 1$.

When we attempt to solve the problem for the last three periods, we observe that $\hat{x}_T$ and $\hat{x}_{T-1}$ have been found that would yield the minimum expected loss $\hat{V}_{T-1}$ for the last two periods and that, by the principle of optimality, we need only minimize

$$V_{T-2} = E_{T-3}\left[(y_{T-2} - a_{T-2})' K_{T-2}(y_{T-2} - a_{T-2}) + \hat{V}_{T-1}\right]$$

with respect to x_{T-2}, and so forth. At the end of this process, we find $\hat{x}_1 = G_1 y_0 + g_1$ as the optimal policy for the first period, and the associated minimum expected loss $\hat{V}_1$ for *all* periods (or from period 1 onward). Computationally, we solve (5) and (9) with t replacing T for G_t and H_t backward in time, for $t = T, T - 1, \ldots, 1$. We then solve (6) and (10) with t replacing T for g_t and h_t backward in time, for $t = T, T - 1, \ldots, 1$. Finally, solution of (11) with t replacing T backward in time yields c_1 which is used to evaluate $\hat{V}_1$ given by (7), with 1 replacing T.

Note that the expression $\hat{V}_t$ given by (7) can be used to obtain the values (shadow prices) of the initial resources y_{t-1}. The vector of the shadow prices of these resources is simply the derivative of $-\hat{V}_t$ (negative loss or benefits) with respect to y_{t-1}, namely,

$$-\frac{\partial \hat{V}_t}{\partial y_{t-1}} = -2(A_t + C_t G_t)'\left[H_t(A_t + C_t G_t)y_{t-1} + H_t b_t - h_t\right]. \tag{12}$$

1.2 TECHNIQUES OF STOCHASTIC CONTROL

The previous brief summary of the theory of optimal control for a linear stochastic model and a quadratic objective function provides a convenient setting to introduce the remaining chapters of this book, which is divided into four parts. Part 1 deals with basic techniques of stochastic control. Chapter 2 applies the method of dynamic programming to find a nearly optimal policy for controlling a nonlinear simultaneous-equation model in econometrics and illustrates the method with an application to the Klein-Goldberger model of the U.S. economy. The method of the previous section is thus generalized to deal with a system of nonlinear simultaneous equations. A number of interesting characteristics of the Klein-Goldberger model are uncovered when it is used to perform the optimal control exercise. In particular, it has been found that according to this model, there is no need to trade a higher price level for an increase in real GNP or in total employment. That is, a Phillips curve does not exist for this model. By manipulating the policy variables, the government can achieve any combination of the general price index and real GNP (or total employment) it wishes. This characteristic of the model is to be contrasted with the natural rate hypothesis or a vertical Phillips curve; it implies that the Phillips curve can be shifted at will by government policy. It is also to be contrasted with the negatively sloping Phillips curves uncovered in Chapter 7 for the St. Louis model and the Michigan Quarterly Econometric Model.

Although Chapter 2 has a brief section on the control of nonlinear systems of simultaneous equations with unknown parameters, it deals mainly with the case of known parameters. The problems associated with unknown parameters are treated more thoroughly in Chapter 3. Chapter 4 is concerned with problems associated with large-scale nonlinear econometric models, discusses the computational problems in some detail, and illustrates the method of approximately optimal feedback control by the use of the Michigan Quarterly Econometric Model. Chapter 5 is a guide for a prospective user of a computer program for performing the approximately optimal control calculations using a nonlinear econometric model based on the method as described in Chapters 2 and 4. The computer program itself (written in Fortran) is available in the Econometric Research Program of Princeton University upon request.

Today, the ability of the method presented in Chapter 2 using an algorithm described in Chapter 5 to solve optimal control problems involving over two hundred nonlinear simultaneous equations is taken for granted. The author has used it to control the model of Fair (1976) and a 1977 version of the MIT-Penn-SSRC model which contains about 250 simultaneous equations. However, as late as 1978, it was exciting to discover that the algorithm actually works for such large systems. Furthermore, the algorithm produces as a by-product a linearized version of the model for each time period. From these linear models one can derive analytically the important dynamic properties of the system. The dynamic properties include various multipliers measuring the effects of changes in current and/or past exogenous variables (taking place in one period or in several consecutive periods) on the current endogenous variables. They also include the autocovariance matrix and the spectral density matrix which measure, in the time domain and in the frequency domain respectively, the cyclical properties of the individual time series and the cyclical relationships between time series generated by the model. These concepts are discussed in Chow (1975). Until recently, it was common practice for econometricians to compute multipliers from a nonlinear model by computer simulation. The simulation process amounts to changing the values of the exogenous variable of interest in appropriate time periods, computing the resulting solution paths for the endogenous variables by iterative methods, and measuring the rate of change in the latter with respect to the former. Using the linearized model generated by our algorithm, the multipliers can be easily identified from the coefficients of the model. Similarly, the autocovariance and spectral density matrices can be derived analytically using the linearized model without resorting to expensive simulations.

Chapter 6 presents the method of Kalman filtering and its applications to the estimation of econometric models.

1.3   ECONOMIC APPLICATIONS OF STOCHASTIC CONTROL

Part 2 of this book deals with economic applications of stochastic control techniques. It begins, in Chapter 7, with an econometric definition of the inflation-unemployment trade-off relation implicit in an econometric model. It is argued that such a relation can be ascertained only by optimal control techniques. Economists have tried to vary the time paths of certain control variables in an econometric model and observe the resulting paths of inflation and unemployment generated by simulations of the model. High inflation and low unemployment have often been found to associate with expansionary fiscal and monetary policies according to the model used. It is hoped that, by simulations, the trade-off relationship between inflation and unemployment can be ascertained. However, it is quite likely that the policies used in the simulation experiment can be dominated, in the sense that an outcome corresponding to both lower inflation and lower unemployment rates could be obtained. By the use of stochastic control techniques, one can trace out the lowest inflation rate compatible with a given unemployment rate according to the specification of an econometric model and given a set of initial conditions, thus yielding an econometric definition of the inflation-unemployment trade-off. This has been done for the St. Louis model and the Michigan model. The method suggested can also be used to compare the characteristics of econometric models, as will be discussed in Chapter 14.

Chapter 8 provides a theoretical framework to evaluate historical macroeconomic policies formulated in an environment of uncertainty. Uncertainty in the consequences of the policies adopted because of random elements in the economy makes the evaluation of historical policies difficult. Policies should not be judged merely by the ensuing outcomes which were partly due to chance or luck, but by the expected loss or gain calculated at the time when the decisions were made. Following this principle, we provide in Chapter 8 a method to evaluate historical policies using stochastic control techniques.

Chapter 9 attempts to answer the question, has government policy been destabilizing? It provides an answer by studying analytically the dynamic properties of the Michigan Quarterly Econometric Model under three different policy regimes. The first specifies that the policy variables follow their reaction functions as estimated by historical data. These reaction functions are used to represent the policy behavior of the government. The second specifies that the policy variables follow constant rates of change, representing passive behavior of the government. The third consists of optimal control policies obtained by stipulating certain quadratic loss function to measure economic instability. Undoubtedly the third regime is superior to the first two by construction, but it provides a limit as to what could possibly be achieved under idealized, and perhaps unrealistic, conditions. It is interesting to note, however, that the historical policy reaction functions, when combined with the equations of the Michigan model, have produced an economy with a higher measure of stability than a set of passive policies under the second regime.

Whereas the applications of Chapter 7, 8, and 9 are oriented toward the economist who wishes to study or analyze macroeconomic policies from the perspective of an observer, the following three chapters are concerned with possible applications of optimal control techniques to the actual formulation of economic policies. Chapter 10 indicates briefly how total government investment expenditures should be determined using the method of optimal control. The problem was presented to the author when he served as consultant to the Economic Planning Council in Taiwan in

1978 and the solution was later implemented by the Council. Unfortunately, the chapter contains only the method without an accompanying empirical study of the Taiwan economy.

Chapter 11 points out the possible use of imperfect econometric models for the formulation of stabilization policies. It has been suggested that because econometric models are imperfect and different models may yield different economic projections given the same hypothetical time paths for the policy variables, they cannot serve as a guide to produce actual policy recommendations. Chapter 11 argues that this conclusion is invalid, and that imperfect models can be fruitfully employed as an aid to the formulation and analysis of macroeconomic policies. Based partly on the concepts of Chapter 11, Chapter 12 goes further by outlining 12 concrete steps in applying control techniques to improve the formulation of macroeconomic policies.

Chapter 13 suggests three applications of optimal control techniques to the econometric analysis of Soviet economic planning. They involve checking the validity of the constraints specified by the model with respect to production relationships, tracing out the production frontiers including the trade-off relation between consumption and defense, and, third, the estimation of the preference function of the Soviet government for the purpose of forecasting its future behavior and thus the future course of the Soviet economy. Only the first of the three topics is treated in detail in the empirical sections of the chapter by analyzing an econometric model of the Soviet economy.

Finally, in Chapter 14, we turn away from the subject of analysis and formulation of macroeconomic policies and to a comparison of econometric models by the use of stochastic control techniques. A number of tools are suggested, including the inflation-unemployment trade-off relationship implicit in an econometric model discussed in Chapter 7 and the control tools to evaluate historical policies presented in Chapter 8. Furthermore, the stability characteristics of an econometric model subject to different policy regimes as explored in Chapter 9 could also be used to compare different econometric models.

1.4 STOCHASTIC CONTROL UNDER RATIONAL EXPECTATIONS

Recently, there has been much interest among economists in exploring the implications of the hypothesis of rational expectations for the evaluation and formulation of macroeconomic policies. Part 3 of this book contains three chapters on the applications of stochastic control techniques to the evaluation and formulation of economic policies, and to the estimation and control of econometric models, under the assumption of rational expectations. It has sometimes been alleged that economic policy evaluation and optimization are impossible if economic agents form rational expectations. Chapter 15 is an attempt to dispel this mistaken belief by showing how the consequences of given economic policies can be evaluated, and how optimal policies based on economic models can be found by optimal control techniques, under the assumption of rational expectations. Here "rational expectations" simply means that all expectations attributed to the economic agents that are used in an econometric model are identical with the conditional expectations of the corresponding endogenous variables generated by the econometric model itself, and not formed by some process, such as a distributed lag scheme, other than the econometric model itself. This use of the term "rational expectations" requires only that the econometrician and the economic agents use the same model to form their expectations, without necessarily implying that the latter's behavior is based on maximizing some objective function.

If, in addition, we assume that the economic agent's behavior results from maximization, a more powerful theory or model results. The tools of optimal control are extremely useful for the specification of such optimization models under rational expectations. If the economic agents are assumed to maximize the expectation of an objective function over time in a stochastic environment, the tools of optimal control can be used to determine their optimal decision rules. For example, equation 1 of this chapter may describe the stochastic environment facing the economic decision makers, and equation 2 may represent their preference function; equation 4 with t replacing T then represents their optimal decision functions. In most of our previous applications, the decision makers have been identified with the government authorities. In fact, they may represent economic agents of the private sector, such as consumers and producers. Equation 4 then represents the optimal consumption function, investment function, or demand function for inputs, as the case may be. Chapter 16 is concerned with the statistical estimation of such models using optimal control techniques. It is important to note that the parameters to be estimated include not only the parameters of (1), with time-invariant coefficients A, C, and b, but the parameters of the preference function (2), with $K_t = \beta K$ (β being a discount factor) and $a_t = a$. Methods of maximum likelihood and two-stage least squares are proposed to estimate these parameters. Having estimated the parameters of (1) and (2), which correspond to the "structural" parameters of simultaneous-equation models, one can ascertain how the behavioral equations (4), with time-invariant coefficients G and g (which correspond to reduced-form parameters), will change when government policy changes.

To make explicit the effect of government policy on the environment facing the private economic agents, consider two sets of decision makers, one representing the private sector which controls x_{1t} and the second representing the government which controls x_{2t}. The econometric model (1) with time-invariant coefficients can be written as

$$y_t = Ay_{t-1} + C_1 x_{1t} + C_2 x_{2t} + b + u_t. \tag{13}$$

If the government follows a rule $x_{2t} = G_2 y_{t-1} + g_2$, the environment facing the private agents will be

$$y_t = (A + C_2 G_2) y_{t-1} + C_1 x_{1t} + (b + C_2 g_2) + u_t$$
$$= A_1 y_{t-1} + C_1 x_{1t} + b_1 + u_t, \tag{14}$$

which shows how government policy affects the environment facing the private agents through $A_1 = (A + C_2 G_2)$. Because the latter obtains its optimal policy $x_{1t} = G_1 y_{t-1} + g_1$ by maximizing the expectation of its objective function subject to the constraint (14), one can apply the theory of optimal control to deduce the behavior of the private agents when the government's policy changes. Chapter 17 is concerned with a dynamic game model involving two players. It provides a method to find the optimal policy for the second player (the government) who anticipates that its policy $x_{2t} = G_2 y_{t-1} + g_2$ will affect the behavior of the private sector. This is the solution to a dynamic game with the government as the dominant player. A solution is also provided when the game is assumed to be in a Nash (or Cournot) equilibrium. Furthermore, methods to estimate the parameters of (13) and of the preference functions of the two players will also be provided, under the assumption of a dominant player or a Nash equilibrium.

1.5 OPTIMAL CONTROL METHODS FOR STOCHASTIC MODELS IN CONTINUOUS TIME

Part 4 of this book contains two chapters. Chapter 18 provides an elementary exposition of the model of stochastic differential equations where the random disturbance is driven by a Wiener process or Brownian motion, and of the method of optimal control applicable to this model. The exposition is built upon concepts of dynamic systems and of optimal control in discrete time by showing what the model and the method of dynamic programming would become when the time interval between successive observations is made very small. Applications to microeconomics will also be provided, including the determination of consumption and portfolio selection over time, the theory of mutual funds and capital asset pricing, and the pricing of stock options. Chapter 19 studies the optimum consumption and exploration of a limited natural resource. Although the subject matter of Part 4 is different from the remainder of this book, the methods employed are quite similar. In fact, the methods of stochastic control in continuous time are also applicable to the study of macroeconomic problems when the macromodel is formulated in continuous time. See Gertler (1980) for an example. Like the previous chapters, Part 4 presents a set of powerful tools for dynamic analysis and control, and addresses important economic problems using these tools. Such are the main purposes of the studies contained in this volume.

CHAPTER 2

An Approach to the Feedback Control of Nonlinear Econometric Systems

In this chapter I present an approach to perform approximately optimal feedback control to minimize the expectation of a quadratic loss function given a system of nonlinear structural econometric equations. The method is explained for simultaneous equation systems with given or unknown parameters (Sections 1 and 2). The usefulness of having a solution in feedback form is discussed (Section 3). The Klein–Goldberger model is used as an illustration (Section 4).

2.1 FEEDBACK CONTROL FOR KNOWN ECONOMETRIC SYSTEMS

The solution presented in this section for the feedback control of a nonlinear econometric system with known parameters has been obtained in Chow (1975, Chapter 12) and Chow (1976c). The former reference applies the method of Lagrange multipliers whereas the latter applies the method of dynamic programming to the control of an econometric system with unknown parameters and deduces the solution as a by-product. The exposition in this section applies dynamic programming to the case of known parameters directly. It attempts to relate the theory of control for nonlinear systems to linear theory and emphasizes the computational aspects of the solution more than the previous references.

The ith structural equation for the observation in period t is

$$y_{it} = \Phi_i(y_t, y_{t-1}, x_t, \eta_{it}) + \varepsilon_{it}, \tag{1.1}$$

14

where y_{it} is the ith element in the vector y_t of endogenous variables, x_t is a vector of control variables, η_{it} is a vector of parameters *and* exogenous variables not subject to control, and ε_{it} is an additive random disturbance with mean zero, variance σ_{ii} and distributed independently through time. In this section, the elements of η_{it} are treated as given, leaving ε_{it} to be the only random variables. Section 2 will deal with uncertainty in η_{it} which may also incorporate nonadditive random disturbances if necessary. Lagged endogenous variables dated prior to $t - 1$ will be eliminated by introducing identities of the form $y_{kt} = y_{j,t-1}$. Control variables will be incorporated in the vector y_t for two purposes. First, by defining $y_{kt} = x_{jt}$, one can write welfare loss as a function of y_t alone. Second, lagged control variables can be eliminated by identities of the form $y_{mt} = y_{k,t-1} = x_{j,t-1}$. The system of structural equations (1.1) can be written as

$$y_t = \Phi(y_t, y_{t-1}, x_t, \eta_t) + \varepsilon_t \qquad (1.2)$$

with Φ denoting a vector function, and with $E\varepsilon_t\varepsilon_t' = \Sigma$.

We assume a quadratic loss function for a T-period control problem,

$$W = \sum_{t=1}^{T} (y_t - a_t)'K_t(y_t - a_t) = \sum_{t=1}^{T} (y_t'K_ty_t - 2y_t'K_ta_t + a_t'K_ta_t),$$

$$(1.3)$$

where a_t are given targets, and K_t are known symmetric positive semidefinite matrices. The problem is to minimize the expectation E_0W conditioned on the information available at the end of period 0. Following the method of dynamic programming, we first solve the optimal control problem for the last period T by minimizing

$$V_T = E_{T-1}(y_T'K_Ty_T - 2y_T'K_Ta_T + a_T'K_Ta_T)$$

$$= E_{T-1}(y_T'H_Ty_T - 2y_T'h_T + c_T) \qquad (1.4)$$

with respect to x_T. In (1.4) we have defined

$$H_T = K_T; \qquad h_T = K_Ta_T; \qquad c_T = a_T'K_Ta_T \qquad (1.5)$$

for the sake of future treatment of the multiperiod control problem. Given past observations y_{T-1}, y_{T-2}, and so on, the problem for period T is solved in the following steps.

1 Starting with some trial value $\tilde{x}_T$ for the control, we set ε_T equal to zero and linearize the right-hand side of (1.2) about $y_{T-1} = y_{T-1}^0$ (given),

$x_T = \tilde{x}_T$, and $y_T = y_T^*$ which is the solution of the system

$$y_T^* = \Phi(y_T^*, y_{T-1}^0, \tilde{x}_T, \eta_T),\qquad(1.6)$$

where y_T^* can be computed by some iterative method such as the Gauss–Siedel. The linearized version of the structure (1.2) is

$$y_T = y_T^* + B_{1T}(y_T - y_T^*) + B_{2T}(y_{T-1} - y_{T-1}^0) + B_{3T}(x_T - \tilde{x}_T) + \varepsilon_T,$$

$$(1.7)$$

where the jth column of B_{1T} consists of the partial derivatives of the vector function Φ with respect to the jth element of y_T, evaluated at the given values y_T^*, y_{T-1}^0, $\tilde{x}_T$ and η_T, and similarly for the jth column of B_{2T} and B_{3T}. Computationally, if the structural functions Φ_i are listed in Fortran, each column of B_{1T} can be evaluated numerically as the rates of change in Φ_i with respect to a small change in the jth element of y_T from y_T^*, and similarly for B_{2T} and B_{3T}. In econometric applications, B_{1T} is very sparse, each row typically consisting of very few elements corresponding to the other current endogenous variables in the equation.

2 By solving (1.7), and without resorting to numerous iterative solutions of the nonlinear model in order to evaluate the required partial derivatives as is commonly practiced, we obtain the linearized reduced form

$$y_T = A_T y_{T-1} + C_T x_T + b_T + u_T,\qquad(1.8)$$

where

$$(A_T \quad C_T \quad u_T) = (I - B_{1T})^{-1}(B_{2T} \quad B_{3T} \quad \varepsilon_T),$$

$$b_T = y_T^* - A_T y_{T-1}^0 - C_T \tilde{x}_T.\qquad(1.9)$$

Note that, because all the identities used to reduce a higher-order structure to first-order and to incorporate the current and lagged x's into y_t are already reduced-form equations, the matrix $I - B_{1T}$ takes the form

$$I - B_{1T} = \begin{bmatrix} I - B_{1T}^* & 0 \\ 0 & I \end{bmatrix},\qquad(1.10)$$

where the order of B_{1T}^* is the number of simultaneous structural equations excluding these identities. Thus only $I - B_{1T}^*$ has to be inverted for the computation of A_T, C_T, and b_T in (1.8).

3 We minimize (1.4) with respect to x_T, assuming that y_T is governed by (1.8). This is done by differentiating (1.4) with respect to x_T and interchanging the order of taking expectation and differentiation:

$$\frac{\partial V_T}{\partial x_T} = 2E_{T-1}\left[\left(\frac{\partial y_T'}{\partial x_T}\right)H_T y_T - \left(\frac{\partial y_T'}{\partial x_T}\right)h_T\right]$$

$$= 2E_{T-1}\left[C_T' H_T(A_T y_{T-1} + C_T x_T + b_T + u_T) - C_T' h_T\right] = 0,$$

$$(1.11)$$

where (1.8) has been used to substitute for $(\partial y_T'/\partial x_T)$ and y_T. The solution of (1.11) for x_T is

$$\hat{x}_T = G_T y_{T-1} + g_T, \qquad (1.12)$$

where

$$G_T = -(E_{T-1}C_T' H_T C_T)^{-1}(E_{T-1}C_T' H_T A_T)$$

$$g_T = -(E_{T-1}C_T' H_T C_T)^{-1}(E_{T-1}C_T' H_T b_T - E_{T-1}C_T' h_T). \quad (1.13)$$

By the linear approximation (1.8), A_T, C_T, and b_T are not functions of ε_T and are thus nonrandom. Therefore, the expectation signs in (1.13) can be dropped, but we retain them for future discussion.

4 Using the solution $\hat{x}_T$ of (1.12) to replace the initial guess $\tilde{x}_T$ in step 1, we repeat steps 1 through 4 until convergence in $\tilde{x}_T$. Observe that the solution, even when converging, is not truly optimal because we have used the approximate reduced form (1.8) with constant coefficients A_T, C_T, and b_T. To obtain an exactly optimal solution, one would first compute $\tilde{y}_T$ as the solution of the stochastic structure (1.2) *with ε_T included*, rather than y_T^* as a solution of (1.6). Thus $\tilde{y}_T$ is a random vector depending on ε_T. Second, (1.7) would be replaced by

$$y_T = \tilde{y}_T + B_{1T}(y_T - \tilde{y}_T) + B_{2T}(y_{T-1} - y_{T-1}^0) + B_{3T}(x_T - \tilde{x}_T).$$

$$(1.14)$$

The derivatives B_{1T}, B_{2T}, and B_{3T} in (1.14) which are evaluated at $\tilde{y}_T$, and hence the matrices A_T, C_T, and b_T in the resulting reduced form corresponding to (1.8), will be dependent on ε_T. The matrices G_T and g_T in the solution for $\hat{x}_T$ will be calculated by (1.13) with the expectation signs retained. Such a four-step iterative procedure would be optimal because when the solution $\hat{x}_T$ converges the value y_T given by the linearized structure (1.14) and its reduced form would be exactly equal to $\tilde{y}_T$, the solution value from the original structure (1.2); the second line of (1.11) would be exactly equal to the first line and not be merely an approximation. The earlier approximate solution amounts to replacing (1.14) by (1.7), that is, linearizing the structure about the nonstochastic y_T^* rather than the stochastic $\tilde{y}_T$, thus making the derivatives B_{1T}, B_{2T}, and B_{3T} nonstochastic. The first $\tilde{y}_T$ in (1.14), which equals $\Phi(\tilde{y}_T, \dots) + \varepsilon_T$ by (1.2), is replaced by $\Phi(y_T^*, \dots) + \varepsilon_T$ or $y_T^* + \varepsilon_T$ in (1.7). This approximate solution is the same as the certainty-equivalence solution obtained by minimizing (1.4) subject to the constraint (1.2) with $\varepsilon_T = 0$, as is shown in Chow (1975, Section 12.1).

5   Using (1.8) for y_T and (1.12) for x_T, we compute the minimum expected loss for period T from (1.4), yielding

$$\hat{V}_T = y'_{T-1} E_{T-1}(A_T + C_T G_T)' H_T (A_T + C_T G_T) y_{T-1}$$

$$+ 2 y'_{T-1} E_{T-1}(A_T + C_T G_T)'(H_T b_T - h_T)$$

$$+ E_{T-1}(b_T + C_T g_T)' H_T (b_T + C_T g_T)$$

$$+ E_{T-1} u'_T H_T u_T - 2 E_{T-1}(b_T + c_T g_T)' h_T + E_{T-1} c_T. \quad (1.15)$$

To generalize the solution to T periods, consider next the two-period problem of choosing x_T and x_{T-1}. Because the optimal $\hat{x}_T$ and $\hat{V}_T$ have already been obtained, we apply the principle of optimality in dynamic programming and minimize with respect to x_{T-1} the expression

$$V_{T-1} = E_{T-2}\left(y'_{T-1} K_{T-1} y_{T-1} - 2 y'_{T-1} K_{T-1} a_{T-1} + a'_{T-1} K_{T-1} a_{T-1} + \hat{V}_T\right)$$

$$= E_{T-2}\left(y'_{T-1} H_{T-1} y_{T-1} - 2 y'_{T-1} h_{T-1} + c_{T-1}\right), \quad (1.16)$$

where, after substitution of (1.15) for $\hat{V}_T$,

$$H_{T-1} = K_{T-1} + E_{T-1}(A_T + C_T G_T)' H_T (A_T + C_T G_T)$$

$$= K_{T-1} + E_{T-1}(A'_T H_T A_T) + G'_T(E_{T-1} C'_T H_T A_T), \quad (1.17)$$

the second line of (1.17) having utilized (1.13) for G_T,

$$h_{T-1} = K_{T-1}a_{T-1} + E_{T-1}(A_T + C_T G_T)'(h_T - H_T b_T)$$

$$= K_{T-1}a_{T-1} + E_{T-1}(A_T + C_T G_T)'h_T - E_{T-1}(A_T' H_T b_T)$$

$$- G_T'(E_{T-1}C_T' H_T b_T), \qquad (1.18)$$

$$c_{T-1} = E_{T-1}(b_T + C_T g_T)'H_T(b_T + C_T g_T) - 2E_{T-1}(b_T + C_T g_T)'h_T$$

$$+ a_{T-1}'K_{T-1}a_{T-1} + E_{T-1}u_T' H_T u_T + E_{T-1}c_T. \qquad (1.19)$$

Because the second line of (1.16) has the same form as (1.4), we can repeat the steps in the solution for x_T with $T - 1$ replacing T, yielding an optimal $\hat{x}_{T-1}$ in the form (1.12) and the corresponding minimum two-period loss $[\hat{V}_{T-1}$ from (1.16)]. The process continues backward in time until $\hat{x}_1$ and $\hat{V}_1$ are obtained.

Computationally, we suggest the following steps for the T-period optimal control problem. (1) Start with initial guesses $\tilde{x}_1, \tilde{x}_2, \ldots, \tilde{x}_T$, solve the system (1.2) with $\varepsilon_t = 0$ for $y_1^0, y_2^0, \ldots, y_{T-1}^0$, using the Gauss–Siedel method. (2) For $t = T, T - 1, \ldots, 1$, linearize the structural equations as in (1.6) and (1.7), noting that $y_t^* = y_t^0$ has been computed in step 1. Compute the reduced-form coefficients A_t, C_t, and b_t by (1.9). (3) Using (1.13) and (1.17) alternately, compute G_t and H_{t-1} for $t = T, T - 1, \ldots, 1$. Use (1.18) to compute h_{t-1} and (1.13) to compute g_t backward in time. (4) Using the feedback control equations $\hat{x}_t = G_t y_{t-1} + g_t$ and the system (1.2) with $\varepsilon_t = 0$, compute successively $\hat{x}_1, y_1^0, \hat{x}_2, y_2^0$, and so on. The $\hat{x}_t$ will serve as the initial guesses $\tilde{x}_t$ in step 1. The process can be repeated until the $\hat{x}_t$ converge. (5) Use (1.19) to compute c_{t-1} backward in time. $\hat{V}_1$ will be computed by (1.15) with 1 replacing T.

Recall that by our linearization of the structure about y_t^* (rather than about $\tilde{y}_t$, which depends on ε_t) all the coefficients A_t, C_t, and b_t become constants, and the expectation signs in all calculations above can be dropped. We only retain the expectation $E_{t-1}u_t' H_t u_t = \text{tr}(H_t E u_t u_t')$ in the calculation of c_{t-1} by (1.19), which, by virtue of (1.9), equals $\text{tr}\, H_t(I - B_{1t})^{-1}\Sigma(I - B_{1t})^{-1'}$.

2.2 FEEDBACK CONTROL WITH UNKNOWN PARAMETERS

The exposition of Section 1 has paved the way for introducing randomness in the parameters η_t in the system (1.2). In principle, random η_t can be treated in the same way as random ε_t. To obtain an exact solution to the last-period control problem by the method of Section 1, it is necessary to linearize (1.2) about $\tilde{y}_T$, the solution value of y_T which depends on the random ε_T and η_T. Accordingly, the coefficients B_{1T}, B_{2T}, and B_{3T} in (1.14) and A_T, C_T, and b_T in the resulting reduced form are all random functions of η_T. The approximate method we propose to solve the multiperiod control problem with unknown parameters also follows the five steps described at the end of Section 1, except that all the expectation signs have to be kept in the calculations.

To evaluate the expectations such as $E_{t-1}(A_t'H_tA_t)$ in (1.17), two approximations are made. First, all time subscripts of the expectation signs are replaced by zero. Thus information on the probability distribution of ε_t and η_t as of the beginning of the planning period is used for the calculation of the optimal $\hat{x}_1$; possible future learning about the unknown parameters is ignored. Second, we linearize the structure about y_t^* which is the solution of (1.2) with $\varepsilon_t = 0$ and η_t set equal to its mean $\bar{\eta}_t$, obtaining the structural coefficients $\bar{B}_{1t}$, $\bar{B}_{2t}$, and $\bar{B}_{3t}$; we then compute the $i - j$ element of expectation $E_0(A_t'H_tA_t)$ by the identity

$$E_0(A_t'H_tA_t)_{ij} = (\bar{A}_t'H_t\bar{A}_t)_{ij} + \operatorname{tr} H_t E_0(a_{jt} - \bar{a}_{jt})(a_{it} - \bar{a}_{it})', \quad (2.1)$$

where $\bar{A}_t = (I - \bar{B}_{1t})^{-1}\bar{B}_{2t}$, and the covariance matrix for any two columns a_{jt} and a_{it} of A_t can be approximated by the appropriate submatrix in $D_t\operatorname{cov}(\eta_t)D_t'$, D_t being the matrix of the partial derivatives of the columns of A_t with respect to η_t. Numerically, the kth column of D_t is computed as the rates of change of the columns of A_t with respect to a small change in the kth element of η_t from $\bar{\eta}_t$. For a more thorough discussion of this method, the reader may refer to Chapter 3.

2.3 USEFULNESS OF FEEDBACK CONTROL

If we treat the parameters η_t as known constants and set $\varepsilon_t = 0$, the method of Section 1 provides a solution to the optimal control of a nonlinear deterministic system. Currently, a popular way to solve such a deterministic control problem is to treat the multiperiod loss W as a function of $x_1, \ldots, x_T$ and minimize it by some gradient, conjugate-gradient, or another standard computer algorithm, as in Fair (1974), Holbrook (1974), and Norman, Norman, and Palash (1975). It may be useful to point out the possible advantages of the method of this chapter as compared with the alternative approach.

1 From the very narrow viewpoint of computing the optimal policy under the assumption of a deterministic model, the method of Section 1 compares favorably with the alternative method when the number of unknowns in the minimization problem is large. The number of unknowns equals the number T of planning periods times the number q of control variables. If we are dealing with 32 quarters and 4 control variables, there will be 128 variables, creating a formidable minimization problem. Our method, being based on the method of dynamic programming with a time structure, converts a problem involving T sets of control variables to T problems each involving only one set of control variables. Its computing cost increases only linearly with T. For each period t, we solve a minimization problem involving q controls; the matrix $C_t'H_tC_t$ to be inverted is $q \times q$. Also, if q is increased from 4 to 8, we have to solve an 8-variable problem 32 times, whereas the alternative method has to deal with 256 variables simultaneously.

On the other hand, our method is perhaps more constrained than the alternative method by the number of simultaneous equations (the order of the matrix $I - B_{1T}^*$ in equation 1.10) in the econometric system because our linearization requires the inversion of $I - B_{1t}^*$. However, by exploiting the bloc-diagonality and the sparseness of this matrix, it may be possible to deal with some 150 to 200 simultaneous equations. More computational experience is required to shed light on this question.

2 Once we leave the realm of purely deterministic control, the advantages of our approach are numerous. First, after incorporating the random disturbances ε_t in an otherwise deterministic model, one can no longer regard as optimal the values of $x_2, \ldots, x_T$ obtained by solving the deterministic control problem. Only the value of x_1 for the first period constitutes an approximately optimal policy. In contrast with the method of deterministic control, the method of Section 1 yields the approximately optimal $\hat{x}_t$ $(t = 2, \ldots, T)$ as a function of the yet unobserved y_{t-1}. It provides analytically an estimate $\hat{V}_1$ of the minimum expected loss associated with the nearly optimal strategies. Using the alternative method, one would have to calculate y_1 from $\hat{x}_1$ and ε_1, solve a multiperiod control problem from period 2 to T to obtain $\hat{x}_2$, calculate y_2 from $\hat{x}_2$ and ε_2, and so on, and repeat the T-period simulations many times to estimate the expected loss from such a strategy. Such computations are extremely costly, if not prohibitive.

3 Our method yields a linearized reduced form at each period as a by-product. The reduced-form coefficients are extremely useful for computing the various dynamic multipliers of y_t with respect to current, delayed, and cumulative changes of x_t, and for exhibiting how nonlinear the system is and how the various partial derivatives change through time.

4   The feedback control equations are useful as a basis of policy recommendations. They can be used to compare different econometric models. They can be incorporated into the econometirc model to study the dynamic properties of the system under control. Once the model is linearized, its dynamic properties can be deduced by spectral and autocovariance methods, as described in Chow (1975, Chapters 3, 4, and 6). Not only the mean paths of the variables from periods one to T, but their variances, covariances, autocovariances, and cross-covariances can be deduced.

5   The value of having improved information (a smaller covariance matrix) for a subset of parameters can be ascertained by comparing the minimum expected losses computed by varying the covariance matrix of η_t using the method of Section 2. As a special case, the comparison of $\hat{V}_1$ computed by varying the covariance matrix of ε_t using the method of Section 1 helps to evaluate the importance of the stochastic disturbances in the expected welfare loss. In short, by our method, the rich theory of optimal control for linear systems can be applied to the control of nonlinear systems. Parts of this theory will be illustrated in Section 4.

2.4   A NUMERICAL EXAMPLE USING THE KLEIN–GOLDBERGER MODEL

To illustrate our method, the Klein–Goldberger model as adopted by Adelman and Adelman (1959, pp. 622–624) is used. The equations are listed below.

Consumer expenditures in 1939 dollars $= C =$

$$y_1 = -22.26 + 0.55(y_6 + x_1 - y_{19}) + 0.41(y_{14} - y_{21} - y_3)$$
$$+ 0.34(y_9 + x_3 - y_{22}) + 0.26y_{1,\,-1} + 0.072y_{11,\,-1} + 0.26z_2 \tag{4.1}$$

Gross private domestic capital formation in 1939 dollars $= I =$

$$y_2 = -16.71 + 0.78(y_{14} - y_{21} + y_9 + x_3 - y_{22} + y_5)_{-1}$$
$$- 0.073y_{16,\,-1} + 0.14y_{12,\,-1} \tag{4.2}$$

Corporate savings $= S_p =$

$$y_3 = -3.53 + 0.72(y_4 - y_{20}) - 0.028y_{17,\,-1} \tag{4.3}$$

Corporate profits $= P_c =$

$$y_4 = -7.60 + 0.68y_{14} \tag{4.4}$$

Capital consumption charges $= D =$

$$y_5 = 7.25 + 0.05(y_{16} + y_{16, -1}) + 0.044(y_{13} - x_1) \tag{4.5}$$

Private employee compensation $= W_1 =$

$$y_6 = -1.40 + 0.24(y_{13} - x_1) + 0.24(y_{13, -1} - x_{1, -1}) + 0.29z_6 \tag{4.6}$$

Number of wage-and-salary earners $= N_W =$

$$y_7 = x_4 - (z_4 + z_5) \div 1.062 + (26.08 + y_{13} - x_1 - 0.08y_{16} - 0.08y_{16, -1}$$
$$- 2.05z_6) \div (2.17 \times 1.062) \tag{4.7}$$

Index of hourly wages $= w =$

$$y_8 = y_{8, -1} + 4.11 - 0.74(z_3 - y_7 - z_4 - z_5)$$
$$+ 0.52(y_{15, -1} - y_{23, -1}) + 0.54z_6 \tag{4.8}$$

Farm income $= A =$

$$y_9 = 0.054(y_6 + x_1 - y_{19} + y_{14} - y_{21} - y_3) + 0.012(z_1)(y_{10}) \div y_{15} \tag{4.9}$$

Index of agricultural prices $= p_A =$

$$y_{10} = 1.39y_{15} + 32.0 \tag{4.10}$$

End-of-year liquid assets held by persons $= L_1 =$

$$y_{11} = 0.14(y_6 + x_1 - y_{19} + y_{14} - y_{21} - y_3 + y_9 + x_3 - y_{22})$$
$$+ 76.03(1.5)^{-0.84} \tag{4.11}$$

End-of-year liquid assets held by businesses $= L_2 =$

$$y_{12} = 0.26y_6 - 1.02(2.5) - 0.26(y_{15} - y_{15, -1}) + 0.61y_{12, -1} \tag{4.12}$$

Gross national product $= Y + T + D =$

$$y_{13} = y_1 + y_2 + x_2 \tag{4.13}$$

Nonwage nonfarm income $= P =$

$$y_{14} = y_{13} - y_{18} - y_5 - y_6 - x_1 - y_9 - x_3 \tag{4.14}$$

Price index of gross national product $= p =$

$$y_{15} = 1.062y_8(y_7) \div (y_6 + x_1) \tag{4.15}$$

End-of-year stock of private capital $= K =$

$$y_{16} = y_{16, -1} + y_2 - y_5 \tag{4.16}$$

End-of-year corporate surplus $= B =$

$$y_{17} = y_{17, -1} + y_3 \tag{4.17}$$

Indirect taxes less subsidies $= T =$

$$y_{18} = 0.0924 y_{13} - 1.3607 \tag{4.18}$$

Personal and payroll taxes less transfers $= T_w =$

$$y_{19} = 0.1549 y_6 + 0.131 x_1 - 6.9076 \tag{4.19}$$

Corporate income tax $= T_c =$

$$y_{20} = 0.4497 y_4 + 2.7085 \tag{4.20}$$

Personal and corporate taxes less transfers $= T_p =$

$$y_{21} = 0.248(y_{14} - y_{20} - y_3) + 0.2695(y_{15,\,-1} \div y_{15})(y_{14} - y_{20} - y_3)_{-1}$$
$$+ 0.4497 y_4 - 5.7416 \tag{4.21}$$

Taxes less transfers associated with farm income $= T_A =$

$$y_{22} = 0.0512(y_9 + x_3) \tag{4.22}$$

$$y_{23} = y_{15,\,-1} \tag{4.23}$$

The control variables or instruments are

$\quad\quad x_1 = W_2 =$ Government employee compensation

$\quad\quad x_2 = G =$ Government expenditures for goods and services

$\quad\quad x_3 = A_2 =$ Government payments to farmers

$\quad\quad x_4 = N_G =$ Number of government employees.

The exogenous variables not subject to control are

$\quad\quad z_1 = F_A =$ Index of agricultural exports

$\quad\quad z_2 = N_p =$ Number of persons in the United States

$\quad\quad z_3 = N =$ Number of persons in the labor force

$\quad\quad z_4 = N_E =$ Number of nonfarm entrepreneurs

$\quad\quad z_5 = N_F =$ Number of farm operators

$\quad\quad z_6 =$ time $= 0$ for 1929 ($= 24$ for 1953).

In the control experiments that will be reported, 1953 was chosen as the first year of the planning period. Initial values of the endogenous variables y_0 and extrapolation formulas for the uncontrollable exogenous variables z_t (part of η_t in the notation of Section 1) are given by Adelman and Adelman (1959, p. 624). The four control variables have been listed in the last paragraph. When imbedded in the vector y_t in the notation of (1.2), they become respectively y_{24} to y_{27}. Three runs have been tried. Run 1 uses endogenous variables 7 (number of wage-and-salary earners), 13 (real GNP), 14 (real nonwage nonfarm income), and 15 (price index of GNP) as targets, with the value 1 specified for each of the corresponding four diagonal elements of the matrix K_t in the welfare function. These target variables are steered to grow at 2, 5, 5, and 1 percent per year respectively from their initial values at 1952. Run 2 uses variables 13, 15, 26 (government payments to farmers), and 27 (number of government employees) as target variables. The target for y_{26} is to remain at its historical 1952 value 0.1187, and for y_{27} is to grow 3 percent annually from its estimated 1952 value 9.393. Run 3 uses variables 7, 15, 26, and 27 as target variables. In effect, runs 2 and 3 tie up two instruments and use the remaining two instruments to control real GNP and the price index, or employment of wage-and-salary earners and the price index.

A major motivation behind these experiments is to find out whether the relationship between the general price index and real GNP (or employment) can be shifted at will by government policy according to the Klein–Goldberger model. The answer is definitely yes. The specified targets for the price index, real GNP, and/or employment of wage-and-salary earners are met exactly by the optimal control solutions of the three runs, ignoring random disturbances. Thus the government can choose any price-GNP or price-employment combination at any period it pleases by applying government employee compensation and government expenditures for goods and services as the control variables.

As pointed out by Chow (1975, pp. 167–168), if the number of target variables (the number of nonzero elements in the $p \times p$ diagonal matrix K_t) equals the number $q \leq p$ of control variables, the time path $\bar{y}_t$ generated by the deterministic system (which is obtained by ignoring the random disturbances in a linear econometric model) under optimal control will meet the targets exactly and the deterministic part W_1 of the minimum expected welfare loss will be zero, provided that the submatrix C_{1t} of the matrix C_t in the reduced form whose rows correspond to the target variables is of rank q. In the three runs, the number of target variables equals the number of control variables, and the matrix C_{1t} for all t in the linearized reduced form has rank 4. Thus the targets are met exactly. This illustrates the application of control theory for linear systems to nonlinear econometric systems by the approach of this chapter. Note that, in the theory for controlling known linear systems, Chow (1975, Chapters 7 and 8), it is useful to decompose the solution vector y_t into its deterministic part $\bar{y}_t$ (obtained by ignoring ε_t) and its stochastic part $y_t^* = y_t - \bar{y}_t$ due to the random disturbances. The same decomposition can now be achieved by our method for nonlinear systems. The autocovariance matrix of y_t^* provides the variances and covariances of the variables under control from their mean path $\bar{y}_t$. It can be derived analytically as in Chow (1975) once the system is linearized by the method of this chapter.

To better appreciate the reason government policy can shift the relationship between the general price index and real GNP (or employment), consider the "aggregate demand curve" and the "aggregate supply curve" implicit in the Klein–Goldberger model. The aggregate demand curve relating price to real GNP can be obtained by solving the aggregate demand sector consisting of 16 equations: (4.1)–(4.4), (4.9), (4.10), (4.13), (4.14), (4.17)–(4.22) of the *IS* sector, and (4.11) and (4.12) of the *LM* sector. The aggregate supply curve is obtained by solving six equations: (4.5)–(4.8), (4.15), and (4.16). We refer to the short-run aggregate supply curve, holding all lagged dependent variables constant. Equation 4.8 gives wage w as a linear function of employment N_W. Equation 4.7 gives N_W as a function of real GNP, capital stock K, and government employee compensation W_2. Equations 4.16 and 4.5 explain K by capital consumption charges D (investment I being predetermined by equation 4.2) and D by K, GNP, and W_2, yielding K as a function of GNP and W_2. Both w and N_W thus become functions of GNP and W_2. By (4.15), price $p = 1.062wN_W/(W_1 + W_2)$, where the private employee compensation W_1 is also a function of GNP and W_2 by virtue of (4.6). Hence the resulting aggregate supply curve relating p to GNP and W_2 can be shifted by manipulating the control variable W_2.

If the aggregate supply function relating price to real GNP or to employment contains no variables that are subject to government control, government policy can only shift aggregate demand and trace out the rigid relation between price and real GNP, but cannot achieve more real output or employment without inflation. A case in point is the relation between the wage rate and employment as given by (4.8). No government policy can shift this rigid relationship for the current period, given the predetermined variables. In terms of control theory, no two instruments can steer wage and employment to specified target values as they are linearly related by (4.8). The matrix C_{1t} has two linearly dependent rows and has rank smaller than the number of instruments.

We have computed the optimal control solutions for the three runs described previously, and some other related runs, using $T = 5$ and $T = 10$ as the planning horizon. To start the iterations, we arbitrarily let the initial $\tilde{x}_{it}$ be the 3 percent annual growth path for each of the four control variables beginning from its historical value as of 1953; these initial paths are given in Table 1 for x_1 and x_2. For the first period 1953, we use the values of the endogenous variables as of 1952 as starting values for the Gauss–Siedel iterations to solve for y_{1953}^0, given $\tilde{x}_{1953}$, and use y_{1953}^0 as starting values to iterate for y_{1954}^0, given $\tilde{x}_{1954}$, and so on. Table 1 shows the values of selected target and control variables for run 1 at the three rounds of linearizations (three "passes" through step 1 of the method of Section 1) required for the convergence of the target variables to five significant figures. Note how rapidly these variables converge to the solution, the first pass already near the optimum.

In terms of computing time using the IBM 360-91 computer at Princeton University, each pass took slightly less than 4 seconds, and the total computer time for three passes was about 12 seconds. When we ran the experiments for 10 periods instead of five, the time merely doubled, taking

Table 1   Values of Selected Variables at Three Successive Passes for Control by the Klein–Goldberger Model—Run 1 ($y_7, y_{13}, y_{14}, y_{15}$ as Targets)

Variable	Pass	1953	1954	1955	1956	1957
x_1	0	15.70	16.17	16.66	17.16	17.67
(government	1	21.15	25.60	29.41	32.95	36.35
employee	2	21.21	26.03	30.63	35.35	40.28
compensation)	3	21.21	26.03	30.64	35.38	40.35
x_2	0	33.50	34.50	35.54	36.61	37.70
(government	1	39.96	45.42	49.68	53.59	57.60
expenditures	2	39.95	45.40	49.74	53.85	58.11
for goods	3	39.95	45.40	49.74	53.85	58.11
and services)						
y_{13}	0	171.24	171.85	174.41	178.12	182.31
(real GNP)	1	180.60	189.64	199.13	209.10	219.58
	2	180.60	189.63	199.11	209.07	219.52
	3	180.60	189.63	199.11	209.07	219.52
y_{15}	0	204.75	209.28	215.81	223.35	231.26
(price index)	1	204.52	207.10	210.23	213.80	217.68
	2	204.42	206.47	208.55	210.66	212.82
	3	204.42	206.47	208.53	210.62	212.72

about 24 seconds for three passes to convergence. These would be minimization problems involving 40 variables in the alternative approach to deterministic control. Imagine a 120-variable problem with four controls and 30 periods using a quarterly model of similar size. The alternative approach would be almost prohibitive, but our method would take about 3×24 or 72 seconds. By our method, increasing the number of control variables from four to five would not require much more computing time, because a 5×5 $C_t'H_tC_t$ matrix is still easy to invert and the hard computing work is performed in obtaining the linearized reduced form. By the alternative method, a 120-variable problem would become a 150-variable problem. (For the same reasons, increasing the number of target variables from four to five or six while keeping the same four control variables in our example has produced almost no effect on the computing time.)

We next examine the coefficients G_t and g_t in the feedback control equations for the optimal solution of run 1 with $T = 5$. Of the 27 variables in y_{t-1} (including four control variables), only 18 appear in the reduced form, the matrix A_t having nine columns of zeros. Table 2 exhibits coefficients of selected lagged variables in the feedback control equations for government expenditures x_2. Note that the coefficients of the lagged expenditure, income, and price variables are all negative, showing that government expenditures should respond negatively to recent signs of economic expansion. The feedback coefficients are practically identical for periods 1 through 5 for two reasons. First, because the number of instruments equals the number of target variables and the matrix C_{1t} has full rank, we have $K_t(A_t + C_tG_t) = 0$ and $H_t = K_t$, as shown in Chow (1975, pp. 168–169). This means that the matrix H_t in the quadratic loss function V_t to be minimized in each future period is identical. Second, because the linearized reduced from coefficients A_t and C_t vary only slightly through time, the solution $G_t = (C_t'H_tC_t)^{-1}C_t'H_tA_t$ will also be stable through time. The intercept g_t, however, is increasing in order to meet the growing targets as we have specified.

It may be interesting to exhibit parts of the matrices A_t, C_t and b_t for $t = 1, 3, 5$ to show how time-varying they are. Table 3 shows selected

Table 2   Coefficients of Selected Lagged Variables in the Feedback Control Equations for Government Expenditures—Run 1 ($T = 5$)

Period	Lagged Variable								Intercept
	1	3	5	8	9	12	14	15	g
1	− 0.260	− 0.109	− 0.768	− 0.053	− 0.768	− 0.138	− 0.659	− 0.015	124.4
3	− 0.260	− 0.109	− 0.768	− 0.054	− 0.768	− 0.138	− 0.659	− 0.014	137.0
5	− 0.260	− 0.109	− 0.768	− 0.055	− 0.768	− 0.138	− 0.659	− 0.014	151.0

**Table 3   Reduced Form Coefficients for Consumption
from the Optimal Solution—Run 1**

Period	a_{11}	a_{13}	a_{15}	a_{16}	c_{11}	c_{12}	b_1
1	0.3305	0.1425	0.2036	0	0.3005	0.2712	33.84
3	0.3311	0.1428	0.2053	0	0.2997	0.2736	35.58
5	0.3315	0.1429	0.2064	0	0.3005	0.2750	37.42
Goldberger	0.3219	0.0297	0.2834	0.1027	0.3355	0.2380	

coefficients of the reduced-form equation for consumption expenditures y_1 from the optimal control solution of run 1. Their stability through time is apparent. The last row of Table 3 reproduces the corresponding coefficients from the study by A. S. Goldberger (1959, pp. 40–41) on impact multipliers of the Klein–Goldberger model, although for numerous reasons, including the differences between the two versions of the Klein–Goldberger model, the coefficients given by Goldberger should be different from ours.

If we were to pursue a dynamic policy analysis using the Klein–Goldberger model or any other nonlinear econometric model by the method of this chapter, it would occupy a substantial volume. Once the model is linearized and the approximately optimal linear feedback control equations obtained, the methods of dynamic analysis as described in Goldberger (1959), Adelman and Adelman (1959), and Chow (1975) can be applied to study numerous important and interesting questions of macroeconomic theory and policy. The main purpose of this chapter has been to show that, using our method of feedback control, the theory and techniques for controlling linear econometric systems can be made applicable to nonlinear econometric systems. This chapter has recommended the feedback approach, because it appears to be much more useful than the computation of optimal time paths for the deterministic version of a stochastic control problem and helps to tie together a significant part of stochastic control theory in economics.

CHAPTER 3

The Control of Nonlinear Econometric Systems with Unknown Parameters

3.1 INTRODUCTION

In this chapter, I present an approximate solution to the optimal control of a system of nonlinear structural equations using a quadratic welfare loss function when the parameters of the system are unknown. This is a generalization of the solution given in Chapter 12 of Chow (1975) for the control of nonlinear econometric systems with known parameters. It is also a generalization of the solution given in Chow (1973) for the control of linear econometric systems with unknown parameters. The method of dynamic programming is applied to solve an optimal control problem involving a nonlinear econometric system with unknown parameters. As it turns out, the solution amounts to linearizing the nonlinear model about some nearly optimal control solution path and then applying a method for controlling the resulting linear model with uncertain parameters.

This chapter advances the state of the art in the control of nonlinear econometric systems as it improves upon the certainty-equivalence solution which is obtained by replacing the random parameters in a system by their mathematical expectations. It provides for a set of numerical feedback control equations based on a system of nonlinear structural equations in econometrics. It will show that many useful analytical concepts and tools developed in the theory of control of linear systems are indeed applicable to the control of nonlinear systems. Furthermore, in the derivation of an approximate solution using the method of dynamic programming, it will

30

indicate precisely where the approximation takes place and why an exact solution is difficult to achieve.

In Section 2, we set up the control problem and provide an exact solution to the optimal control problem for the last period. In Section 3, we give an approximate solution to the multiperiod control problem using dynamic programming. In Section 4, the mathematical expectations required in the solution of Section 3 will be evaluated approximately to simplify computations. Section 5 contains some concluding remarks.

3.2 AN EXACT SOLUTION TO A ONE-PERIOD CONTROL PROBLEM

The tth observation of the ith structural equation is written as

$$y_{it} = \Phi_i(y_t, y_{t-1}, x_t, \eta_{it}) \qquad (i = 1, \ldots, p), \tag{2.1}$$

where y_{it} is the th observation on the ith dependent variable, y_t is a column vector of p dependent variables, x_t is a vector of q control variables, and η_{it} is a random vector composed of unknown parameters in equation i, a random residual and variables not subject to control. Higher-order lagged dependent variables are eliminated by the introduction of appropriate new dependent variables and identities. Furthermore, a new dependent variable can be defined to be identically equal to a control variable for two purposes. First, elements of x_t do not have to appear in the loss function (2.3) below as they are embedded in y_t. Second, elements of x_{t-1} do not have to appear in the structural equation (2.1) as they are also elements of y_{t-1}. Denoting the column vector of functions $\Phi_1, \ldots, \Phi_p$ by Φ, we write the system of structural equations as

$$y_t = \Phi(y_t, y_{t-1}, x_t, \eta_t), \tag{2.2}$$

where η_t consists of η_{it} as elements.

The structural parameters may be regarded as fixed or random. In the fixed-parameter case, we take the Bayesian view to derive a posterior distribution for the corresponding elements of η_t; this distribution can be approximated by the sampling distribution of the maximum likelihood estimates of the unknown parameters. In any case, we assume that a probability distribution function for η_t is available for policy planning over T periods. We further assume that, when we look ahead in the calculation of the optimal decision x_1 for the first period in a T-period control problem, this probability distribution function will not be revised by future observations. Thus the possibility of learning about η_t is ignored in the calculation of the optimal first-period decision, but the uncertainty concerning η_t as conceived at the beginning of the planning period is taken into account.

To apply the method of dynamic programming to solve the T-period control problem having the loss function

$$W = \sum_{t=1}^{T} (y_t - a_t)' K_t (y_t - a_t) = \sum_{t=1}^{T} (y_t' K_t y_t - 2 y_t' K_t a_t + a_t' K_t a_t),$$

$$(2.3)$$

where a_t are given targets, and K_t are known symmetric positive semidefinite matrices, we first consider in this section the decision problem for the last period T, given all information available at the end of period $T - 1$. In the last period, the problem is to minimize with respect to x_T the conditional expectation (on all information available up to the end of $T - 1$) which is assumed to exist:

$$V_T = E_{T-1}(y_T' K_T y_T - 2 y_T' K_T a_T + a_T' K_T a_T)$$

$$= E_{T-1}(y_T' H_T y_T$$

$$- 2 y_T' h_T + c_T), \qquad (2.4)$$

where, for ease of future generalization, we have defined

$$H_T = K_T; \qquad h_T = K_T a_T; \qquad c_T = a_T' K_T a_T. \qquad (2.5)$$

The expectation in (2.4) is taken over the random vector η_T on which y_T depends according to (2.2). The vector y_{T-1} is taken as constant.

The one-period optimization problem just described can be solved exactly, at least in principle. Given any x_T, the probability distribution of y_T is induced by the probability distributions of η_T by the use of (2.2). If the nonlinear function Φ is complicated, the distribution of y_T may be difficult to express explicitly, but it can always be evaluated numerically, at least by Monte Carlo techniques. Similarly, the expectation of the quadratic function (2.4) of y_T can also be evaluated. This expectation can then be minimized with respect to x_T by some numerical method. The solution $\hat{x}_T$ will depend on y_{T-1}. If this dependence can be expressed explicitly, we can eliminate x_T as an unknown in the optimal control problem for the last two periods T and $T - 1$, and reduce the two-period problem to one involving only one set of control variables x_{T-1} using the method of dynamic programming. If this dependence is not explicitly expressed, one can hardly solve the two-period optimization problem using a closed-loop strategy. It would be possible to find an optimal strategy among the "open-loop" policies which specify both x_{T-1} and x_T simultaneously at the beginning of $T - 1$, because the expectation

$$E_{T-2}\left[\sum_{t=T-1}^{T} (y_t'K_t y_t - 2y_t'K_t a_t + a_t'K_t a_t) \right] \tag{2.6}$$

can in principle be evaluated as a function of x_{T-1} and x_T. However, the truly optimal stategy for the last two periods is of the closed-loop form; it allows for the choice of x_T sequentially after the outcome y_{T-1} at the end of period $T - 1$ is observed.

Therefore, to solve a multiperiod optimal control problem, it is desirable to express the optimal policies x_t for later periods as functions of the initial conditions y_{t-1}. To do so, some approximation is required. Even for a one-period problem, an approximation would be useful because an exact solution as described in the last paragraph can be very costly. To derive the distribution of y_T from the distributions of η_T using Monte Carlo methods, one may have to sample many times from a distribution involving many random variables, and, for each sample of η_T, some numerical method such as the Gauss-Siedel has to be applied interatively to obtain a numerical solution for y_T. In this section, we will give an exact solution to the one-period control problem. In the next section, we will introduce approximations to the solution of the multiperiod control problem.

To obtain an exact solution for the minimization of (2.4) we differentiate with respect to x_T and interchange the order of integration (or taking expectation) and differentiation, recalling that the expectation is over the random vector η_T, given y_{T-1} and x_T:

$$\frac{\partial}{\partial x_T} E_{T-1}(y_T'H_T y_T - 2y_T'h_T + c_T) = E_{T-1}\frac{\partial}{\partial x_T}(y_T'H_T y_T - 2y_T'h_T)$$

$$= 2E_{T-1}\frac{\partial y_T'}{\partial x_T}(H_T y_T - h_T) = 0,$$

$$\tag{2.7}$$

where the chain rule of differentiation has been applied, and $\partial y_T'/\partial x_T$ denotes the $q \times p$ matrix of derivatives of the p elements of y_T with respect to the q elements of x_T. The solution x_T satisfies the last equation of (2.7).

It will be useful to write the solution in a different form for future use. Define $\tilde{y}_T$ as the solution of

$$\tilde{y}_T = \Phi(\tilde{y}_T, y_{T-1}^0, \tilde{x}_T, \eta_T) \tag{2.8}$$

for the given y_{T-1}^0 and some $\tilde{x}_T$; $\tilde{y}_T$ is a function of the random vector η_T as given by (2.8). Perform a first-order Taylor expansion of (2.2) about $\tilde{y}_T$, y_{T-1}^0, and $\tilde{x}_T$:

$$y_T \simeq \tilde{y}_T + B_{1T}(y_T - \tilde{y}_T) + B_{2T}(y_{T-1} - y_{T-1}^0) + B_{3T}(x_T - \tilde{x}_T),$$

$$\tag{2.9}$$

where

$$B_{1T}' = \frac{\partial \Phi'}{\partial y_T} = \left(\frac{\partial \Phi_1}{\partial y_T} \cdots \frac{\partial \Phi_p}{\partial y_T} \right); \qquad B_{2T}' = \frac{\partial \Phi'}{\partial y_{T-1}}; \qquad B_{3T}' = \frac{\partial \Phi'}{\partial x_T};$$

$$\tag{2.10}$$

and all derivatives of Φ are evaluated at $\tilde{y}_T$, y_{T-1}^0, and $\tilde{x}_T$, and are functions of η_T. The reduced form of the linearized structure (2.9) is

$$y_T = A_T(\eta_T) y_{T-1} + C_T(\eta_T) x_T + b_T(\eta_T), \tag{2.11}$$

where

$$A_T(\eta_T) = (I - B_{1T})^{-1} B_{2T},$$

$$C_T(\eta_T) = (I - B_{1T})^{-1} B_{3T}, \tag{2.12}$$

$$b_T(\eta_T) = \tilde{y}_T - A_T y_{T-1}^0 - C_T \tilde{x}_T.$$

Using the linearized model (2.9) or (2.11), we can express the solution of the last equation of (2.7) for x_T in an iterative form.

An iterative solution of (2.7) is as follows. First, start with some $\tilde{x}_T$, and define the random function $\tilde{y}_T$ by (2.8). Second, use the linearized random function (2.9) to replace y_T in (2.7) by the right-hand side of (2.11),

$$E_{T-1}\left[C_T' H_T (A_T y_{T-1} + C_T x_T + b_T) - C_T' h_T \right] = 0 \tag{2.13}$$

and solve the resulting equation for x_T, yielding

$$\hat{x}_T = - (E_{T-1}C_T'H_TC_T)^{-1}\big[(E_{T-1}C_T'H_TA_T)y_{T-1} + E_{T-1}C_T'(H_Tb_T - h_T)\big]$$

$$= G_Ty_{T-1} + g_T, \qquad (2.14)$$

where

$$G_T = - (E_{T-1}C_T'H_TC_T)^{-1}(E_{T-1}C_T'H_TA_T),$$

$$g_T = - (E_{T-1}C_T'H_TC_T)^{-1}(E_{T-1}C_T'H_Tb_T - E_{T-1}C_T'h_t). \qquad (2.15)$$

Third, evaluate $\hat{x}_T$ by (2.14) at $y_{T-1} = y_{T-1}^0$, and use this value of $\hat{x}_T$ as $\tilde{x}_T$ in the first step. Repeat these steps until $\tilde{x}_T$ converges.

We claim that if this iterative process converges, the resulting $\tilde{x}_T$ is an *exact* solution to (2.7) or to our one-period optimal control problem. This claim is justified if, at convergence, the y_T satisfying the linear function (2.9) or (2.11) is identical with the $\tilde{y}_T$ satisfying the original nonlinear structural equation (2.8). When $x_T = \tilde{x}_T$ and $y_{T-1} = y_{T-1}^0$, the linear equation (2.9) is reduced to

$$y_T = \tilde{y}_T + B_{1T}(y_T - \tilde{y}_T) \qquad (2.16)$$

or

$$(I - B_{1T})y_T = (I - B_{1T})\tilde{y}_T,$$

implying $y_T = \tilde{y}_T$, provided $I - B_{1T}$ is nonsingular. Thus, at convergence of our iterative procedure, the y_T given by (2.9) or (2.11) is identical with the $\tilde{y}_T$ given by the nonlinear equation (2.8), and our method provides an exact solution to (2.7).

The reader will have noted that the expectations involved in the computation of G_T and g_T by (2.15) can be difficult to evaluate numerically. The matrices A_T and C_T can be complicated functions of the random variables η_T. We have written the solution to the one-period control problem in a form that facilitates its generalization to the multiperiod case by suitable approximations. Leaving aside the problem of evaluating the expectations in (2.15) until Section 4, we proceed in Section 3 to obtain an approximate solution to the multiperiod control problem by the method of dynamic programming.

3.3 AN APPROXIMATE SOLUTION TO MULTIPERIOD CONTROL BY DYNAMIC PROGRAMMING

We utilize the feedback control equation (2.14) for $\hat{x}_T$. Note that this equation provides an exact solution only when $y_{T-1} = y^0_{T-1}$ because it was derived by using the linear approximation (2.9) or (2.11) for (2.8) and the linear approximation is exact only when $y_{T-1} = y^0_{T-1}$. All the derivatives in the matrices A_T and C_T are evaluated at $y_{T-1} = y^0_{T-1}$. For values of y_{T-1} other than y^0_{T-1}, the solution (2.14) is only approximate as a consequence of the linear approximation (2.9). However, we need this approximately optimal feedback control equation to eliminate x_T in order to carry out the dynamic programming solution.

Substituting the right-hand side of (2.14) for x_T in (2.11) and the result for y_T in (2.4), we have the minimum expected loss for the last period,

$$
\hat{V}_T = E_{T-1}\big[(A_T + C_T G_T)y_{T-1} + b_T + C_T g_T\big]'H_T\big[(A_T + C_T G_T)y_{T-1}
$$

$$
+ b_T + C_T g_T\big] - 2E_{T-1}\big[(A_T + C_T G_T)y_{T-1} + b_T + C_T g_T\big]'h_T + c_T
$$

$$
= y'_{T-1}E_{T-1}(A_T + C_T G_T)'H_T(A_T + C_T G_T)y_{T-1} \tag{3.1}
$$

$$
+ 2y'_{T-1}E_{T-1}(A_T + C_T G_T)'(H_T b_T - h_T)
$$

$$
+ E_{T-1}(b_T + C_T g_T)'H_T(b_T + C_T g_T) - 2E_{T-1}(b_T + C_T g_T)'h_T + c_T.
$$

$\hat{V}_T$ is exactly the minimum expected loss for period T only if $y_{T-1} = y^0_{T-1}$ in which case the linear approximation (2.9) to y_T is exact. We will use (3.1) to approximate the minimum expected loss and treat it as a quadratic function of y_{T-1}. Because y^0_{T-1} is unknown before the end of period $T - 1$, we will have to perform the linearization (2.9) about some guess of y^0_{T-1}, realizing that the matrices A_T and C_T of the resulting derivatives will be affected by this guess.

We proceed to include the period $T - 1$ in our optimization problem. By the principle of optimality in dynamic programming, we minimize with respect to x_{T-1} the expression

$$
V_{T-1} = E_{T-2}\big(y'_{T-1}K_{T-1}y_{T-1} - 2y'_{T-1}K_{T-1}a_{T-1}
$$

$$
+ a'_{T-1}K_{T-1}a_{T-1} + \hat{V}_T\big) \tag{3.2}
$$

because the optimal policy x_T for the last period has been found and incorporated in $\hat{V}_T$. Substituting the quadratic function of y_{T-1} as given by

(3.1) for $\hat{V}_T$ in (3.2), we have

$$V_{T-1} = E_{T-2}(y'_{T-1}H_{T-1}y_{t-1} - 2y'_{T-1}h_{T-1} + c_{T-1}), \qquad (3.3)$$

where

$$H_{T-1} = K_{T-1} + E_{T-1}(A_T + C_TG_T)'H_T(A_T + C_TG_T)$$

$$= K_{T-1} + E_{T-1}(A'_TH_TA_T) + G'_T(E_{T-1}C'_TH_TA_T), \qquad (3.4)$$

$$h_{T-1} = K_{T-1}a_{T-1} + E_{T-1}(A_T + C_TG_T)'(h_T - H_Tb_T)$$

$$= K_{T-1}a_{T-1} + E_{T-1}(A_T + C_TG_T)'h_T$$

$$- E_{T-1}(A'_TH_Tb_T) - G'_T(E_{T-1}C'_TH_Tb_T), \qquad (3.5)$$

and

$$c_{T-1} = E_{T-1}(b_T + C_Tg_T)'H_T(b_T + C_Tg_T) - 2E_{T-1}(b_T + C_Tg_T)'h_T$$

$$+ a'_{T-1}K_{T-1}a_{T-1} + c_T. \qquad (3.6)$$

Observe that (3.3) has the same form as (2.4) with the subscript $T - 1$ replacing T. The steps following (2.4) can therefore be repeated to yield the solution $\hat{x}_{T-1}$ as given by (2.14) with $T - 1$ replacing T. When this solution is substituted in (3.3) and a similar approximation is used, the minimum expected loss $\hat{V}_{T-1}$ for the last two periods becomes a quadratic function of y_{T-2} as given by (3.1) with $T - 1$ replacing T. The process continues until the approximately optimal policy $\hat{x}_1$ for the first period and the associated expected loss $\hat{V}_1$ for the T-period policy are obtained. Our multiperiod control problem is solved.

We will state our solution in the form of an iterative procedure consisting of the following steps.

STEP 1   Choose some initial guess $\tilde{x}_1, \ldots, \tilde{x}_T$ of the vectors of control variables for the T periods. Using the econometric model, with the unknown parameters and disturbances η_t set equal to their expected values, and the above values of control variables, solve for a set of initial values $y_1^0, \ldots, y_{T-1}^0$ of the dependent variable by the Gauss-Siedel method.

STEP 2   For each period $t, t = 1, \ldots, T$, linearize the nonlinear model for y_t about the above values of y_{t-1}^0 and $\tilde{x}_t$ as is done in (2.9), using repeated random drawings of η_t from the given distribution. For each drawing of η_t, and given y^0_{t-1} and $\tilde{x}_t$, there corresponds a linearized structure

$$y_t \simeq \tilde{y}_t + B_{1t}(y_t - \tilde{y}_t) + B_{2t}(y_{t-1} - y^0_{t-1}) + B_{3t}(x_t - \tilde{x}_t), \qquad (3.7)$$

where $\tilde{y}_t$ is the solution of

$$\tilde{y}_t = \Phi(\tilde{y}_t, y^0_{t-1}, \tilde{x}_t, \eta_t) \qquad (3.8)$$

obtained by some iterative method such as the Gauss-Siedel. To recognize the random nature of η_t, we conceive of many linearized structures of the form (3.7) corresponding to different values of η_t. However, for any given η_t, the partial derivatives B_{1t}, B_{2t}, and B_{3t} in (3.7) are easy to compute. Each derivative is the change in the value of Φ from $\Phi(\tilde{y}_t, y^0_{t-1}, \tilde{x}_t, \eta_t)$ with respect to a small change in one element of its first three (vector) arguments. Having computed B_{1t}, B_{2t}, and B_{3t}, we compute $A_t(\eta_t)$, $C_t(\eta_t)$, and $b_t(\eta_t)$ using (2.12).

STEP 3   The expectations $E_{T-1}C'_T H_T C_T$, $E_{T-1}C'_T H_T A_T$, $E_{T-1}C'_T H_T b_T$, and $E_{T-1}C'_T$ are computed by using numerical integration or Monte Carlo methods, the latter by averaging over repeated random drawings of η_T in step 2. Compute G_T and g_T by (2.15) and obtain the optimal $\hat{x}_T$ associated with y^0_{T-1} by (2.14). Replace $\tilde{x}_T$ by this $\hat{x}_T$ and repeat step 2 for period T and step 3 until $\tilde{x}_T$ converges. As we have pointed out in Section 2, the solution $\tilde{x}_T$ is optimal for the last period, *provided that the initial condition is indeed* y^0_{T-1}.

STEP 4   Using the expectations $E_{T-1}C'_T H_T C_T$, $E_{T-1}C'_T H_T A_T$, $E_{T-1}C'_T H_T b_T$, $E_{T-1}A'_T H_T A_T$, and $E_{T-1}A'_T H_T b_T$ and the feedback control coefficients G_T in step 3, we compute H_{T-1} and h_{T-1} by (3.4) and (3.5) respectively. H_{T-1} can be applied to evaluate the expectations $E_{T-2}C'_{T-1}H_{T-1}C_{T-1}$, and so on as in step 3 and to compute $\hat{x}_{T-1}$, G_{T-1}, and g_{T-1} by (2.14) and (2.15), with $T-1$ replacing T. This $\hat{x}_{T-1}$ will replace $\tilde{x}_{T-1}$ and the process is repeated until $\tilde{x}_{T-1}$ converges. Essentially, in step 4 so far, we utilize the H_{T-1} and h_{T-1} obtained from the results of step 3 in order to repeat step 3 for $T-1$. The solution will be an optimal $\tilde{x}_{T-1}$ associated with the given y^0_{T-2}. Similarly, we can utilize the results of step 4 thus far to obtain H_{T-2} and h_{T-2} in order to repeat step 3 for $T-2$. The process continues backward in time until $\tilde{x}_1$ is obtained.

This solution of $\tilde{x}_1$ would be optimal if the y^0_{t-1} in each future period t were the true value to be realized, and provided that future revisions of the distributions of η_t were ignored. Insofar as the future y's are not known exactly because of the uncertainties in our model, the solution is only an approximate one. However, this solution improves upon the certainty-equivalence solution. One version of the certainty-equivalence solution amounts to replacing $E_{t-1}C_t'H_tC_t$, and so on, by $\overline{C}_tH_t\overline{C}_t$, and so on, where $\overline{C}_t$ is the expected value of C_t. An even cruder version would replace $E_{t-1}C_t'H_tC_t$ by $C_t'(\overline{\eta}_t)H_tC_t(\overline{\eta}_t)$, where C_t is evaluated at the expected value $\overline{\eta}_t$ of η_t. Because C_t is a nonlinear function of η_t, $C(\overline{\eta}_t)$ is not the same as $\overline{C}_t$. Our solution takes into account the uncertainty in the parameters by evaluating the appropriate expectations $E_{t-1}C_t'H_tC_t$, and so forth.

STEP 5   If our solution deviates from the truly optimal because the initial value y_{t-1}^0 used in the linear approximation for each future period is not the true one, we can improve upon these values by recomputing them in step 1 using the nearly optimal feedback control equations $\hat{x}_t = G_t y_{t-1} + g_t$ obtained in the above four steps for the given y_{t-1}^0. Given y_0^0, we compute $\tilde{x}_1$ by its feedback equation. The nonlinear model is solved for y_1^0, with $\eta_1 = \overline{\eta}_1$. Given y_1^0, we compute $\tilde{x}_2$, and so forth. Steps 1 through 4 can be repeated to yield a new set of more nearly optimal feedback control equations. And another round of computations will generate another set of feedback control equations using the previous set to provide initial values in step 1.

STEP 6   The minimum expected loss associated with any set of nearly optimal feedback control equations can be computed by our method. The method as described by (3.1) through the paragraph following (3.6) carries with it the minimum expected loss $\hat{V}_t$ for all future periods from t onward. Each $\hat{V}_t$ has the same form as (3.1) with t replacing T. The total expected loss for T periods is given by V_1. It can be computed by applying (3.1) and using (3.6) to compute c_{t-1} backward in time until c_1 is acquired.

Our method has been derived and described computationally. In the process of describing it, we have contrasted it with the certainty-equivalence solutions (in step 4). We have also found that the method yields linear feedback control equations which are useful in the analysis of macroeconomic policies using an econometric model as more fully discussed in Chow (1975). The minimum expected loss associated with the approximately optimal policy can be analytically derived.

3.4 APPROXIMATE EVALUATION OF REQUIRED EXPECTATIONS

In Section 3, and step 3 in particular, the expectations $E_{t-1}C_t'H_tC_t$, and so on, are evaluated by Monte Carlo techniques using random drawings of η_t. This approach can be very costly, and the gain in accuracy may not be worth the cost. We stated that approach in Section 3 in order to single out conceptually one important source of approximation errors in our method, namely, that of using an inaccurate value of y_{t-1}^0 in the linear approximation of the nonlinear structure at each stage of the dynamic programming solution. In practice, we will recommend using the approximate method of this section to evaluate the required expectations $E_{t-1}C_t'H_tC_t$, and so on. This method will eliminate repeated linearizations of the model corresponding to random drawings of η_t.

Let us rewrite the required expectations in a more streamlined notation. Denote by Π_t the p by s matrix

$$\Pi_t = (A_t C_t \ b_t) \tag{4.1}$$

so that the required expectations $E_{t-1}C_t'H_tC_t$, and so on, in step 3 of Section 3 are submatrices of

$$E_{t-1}(\Pi_t'H_t\Pi_t). \tag{4.2}$$

Denote the s columns of Π by $\pi_1, \ldots, \pi_s$ and the column vector consisting of these columns by π. We suppress the subscript t when understood. If Q is the covariance matrix of π, and $\bar{\pi}$ is the mean of π, we have

$$E\pi\pi' = \bar{\pi}\bar{\pi}' + Q = \begin{bmatrix} \bar{\pi}_1\bar{\pi}_1' \cdots \bar{\pi}_1\bar{\pi}_s' \\ \cdots \cdots \cdots \\ \bar{\pi}_s\bar{\pi}_1' \cdots \bar{\pi}_s\bar{\pi}_s' \end{bmatrix} + \begin{bmatrix} Q_{11} \cdots Q_{1s} \\ \cdots \cdots \cdots \\ Q_{s1} \cdots Q_{ss} \end{bmatrix}. \tag{4.3}$$

The i–j element of (4.2) is, with t suppressed,

$$(E\Pi'H\Pi)_{ij} = E\pi_i'H\pi_j = E\,\mathrm{tr}(H\pi_j\pi_i')$$

$$= \mathrm{tr}\,HE\pi_j\pi_i' = \bar{\pi}_i'H\bar{\pi}_j + \mathrm{tr}\,HQ_{ji}. \tag{4.4}$$

Therefore, once the mean $\bar{\pi}$ and the covariance matrix Q of π are known, the required expectations in (4.2) can be computed by (4.4).

We will provide an approximation to $\bar{\pi}$ and Q assuming that the econometric model consists of a set of constant, but unknown parameters θ and a vector of random residuals ε_t. Thus η_t consists of θ and ε_t; η_{it} in (2.1) consists of θ_i and ε_{it}. This assumption applies to most econometric models encountered in practice. We also assume that a point estimate $\hat{\theta}$ of θ, a covariance matrix V of the estimator $\hat{\theta}$, and a covariance matrix S of the residual vector ε_t are all available. We will treat $\hat{\theta}$ as the mean vector and V

as the covariance matrix of the distribution of θ which is a subvector of η_t in (2.2).

To derive the mean vector $\bar{\pi}$ and the covariance matrix Q of π required in (4.4) from the mean vector and the covariance matrix of η_t (which includes θ and ε_t) we use a first-order approximation of the function π_t of η_t. Let the partial derivatives of π_t with respect of η_t be represented by the matrix

$$D_t = \left(\frac{\partial \pi_{it}}{\partial \eta_{jt}} \right). \tag{4.5}$$

Each element of this matrix, evaluated at $\eta_t = \bar{\eta}_t$, can be computed numerically as the rate of change in π_{it}, an element in $\Pi_t = (A_t C_t b_t)$, with respect to a small change in η_{jt}. Once D_t is found, the covariance matrix Q_t of π_t can be approximated by

$$Q_t = D_t W_t D_t' \tag{4.6}$$

where W_t is the covariance matrix of η_t having as submatrices the given covariance matrices of $\hat{\theta}$ and ε_t. The mean vector $\bar{\pi}$ can be approximated by the value of π associated with $\bar{\eta}_t$. (This approximation could be improved by averaging a sample of π's computed from random drawings from the distribution of η_t.)

To summarize, using the approximation of this section, we simplify the method of Section 3 as follows. Step 1 remains the same. In step 2, only one linearization (3.7) corresponding to $\eta_t = \hat{\eta}_t$ is required. In this step, $\tilde{y}_t$ is defined by (3.8) with $\eta_t = \hat{\eta}_t$, and is identical with the initial value y_t^0 already obtained in step 1. In step 3, the expectations $E_{T-1} C_T' H_T C_T$, and so on, are computed by (4.4) and (4.6); the Monte Carlo calculations are avoided. Here, one has the option to iterate on $\tilde{x}_t$ for use in the relinearization of the model by (3.7). Steps 4, 5, and 6 remain the same as described in Section 3.

Before closing this section, it is useful to point out that if there exist exogenous variables z_t not subject to control, they can be treated as a subvector in η_t. Our treatment of η_t allows for the possibility of treating z_t as random but having a given distribution. The randomness in z_t generates uncertainty in the dynamic system in the same way as the randomness in the other parameters. If z_t were regarded as fixed, it is a degenerate random vector; it only affects the mean vector of π_t in our model without contributing to its variances and covariances.

3.5   CONCLUDING REMARKS

A method is proposed for obtaining an approximate solution to the optimal control of a nonlinear econometric system with uncertain parameters. It results from applying the method of dynamic programming. It provides a set of approximately optimal linear feedback control equations. These equations can then be used to study the dynamic properties of the system under control. Insofar as the method is a generalization of the theory of optimal control for linear systems under uncertainty, many of the useful results and concepts from the linear theory can be applied to the nonlinear case. For example, the comparison in Chow (1973) of the optimal feedback control equations and the associated expected welfare loss under uncertainty with the corresponding results under the assumption of constant parameters is valid for nonlinear systems.

As a generalization of the method of Chow (1975, Chapter 12) for dealing with nonlinear econometric models with given parameters, the method as described in Section 4 is computationally not much more difficult. The main complication lies in the computation of $EC_t'H_tC_t$, and so forth, in place of $C(\bar{\eta}_t)'H_tC(\bar{\eta}_t)$, and so forth, in the certainty case. As we have pointed out in Section 4, this amounts to calculating the derivatives of the elements of $\Pi_t = (A_t, C_t, b_t)$ with respect to the elements of η_t, and applying the matrix D_t of these derivatives to form an approximate covariance matrix of the elements of Π_t using (4.6). The jth column of D_t is simply computed by perturbing the jth element of η_t and evaluating the rates of change in the coefficients π_t in the linearized reduced form. These calculations are by no means difficult using the computers available today.

The method of Chow (1975, Chapter 12) for the control of nonlinear systems with known parameters, which is identical with the method of Section 4 with $C(\bar{\eta}_t)'H_tC(\bar{\eta}_t)$ replacing $EC_t'H_tC_t$ and so on, has been programmed, the Fortran code being available at the Econometric Research Program of Princeton University. The limited experience available indicates that the method is not expensive to use. For example, controlling the Klein-Goldberger model with 23 structural equations for 10 periods with five targets and four instruments using our program takes approximately 24 seconds of computing time on the IBM 360-91 computer at Princeton University. The program provides not only the linear feedback control equations for each period but all the matrices A_t, C_t, and b_t of the linearized reduced form at each time period and for each iteration until convergence, the expected welfare loss, and the graph of the expected time path of each of the 27 (23 plus 4 control) variables. It took three interactions in the sense of three rounds of the initial values of the control variables $\tilde{x}_t$ as described in Section 3. Because the incorporation of uncertainty can be achieved essentially by evaluating the numerical derivatives D_t of π_t with respect to η_t (besides some matrix multiplications), it will not be computationally prohibitive. If one does not treat all the parameters in a very large econometric model as random, the method of this chapter can be applied to incorporate uncertainty in a subset of parameters (the remaining ones being treated as fixed), and to study the effect of uncertainty on the optimal control policies.

CHAPTER 4

The Control of Large-Scale Nonlinear Econometric Systems

After pointing out the special characteristics of existing econometric models which form the basis of the application of optimal control techniques for macroeconomic policy analysis and formulation, this chapter surveys the use of econometric models for the projection of the economic consequences of alternative policies and the formulation of optimal policies. It presents both the theory and the computational aspects of a particular approach of applying feedback control to study policy options using large-scale nonlinear systems of simultaneous econometric equations. It then illustrates this approach by solving an optimal control problem using the Michigan Quarterly Econometric Model. Some topics of further research are suggested in the conclusion.

4.1 NATURE OF ECONOMETRIC MODELS

This chapter reports on the techniques of feedback control which are applicable to large-scale nonlinear stochastic models of national economies. At the outset, several important characteristics of the existing econometric models should be mentioned.

Based on "The Control of Large-Scale Nonlinear Econometric Systems" by G. C. Chow and S. B. Megdal published in IEEE TRANSACTIONS ON AUTOMATIC CONTROL, April 1978, Vol. AC-23, No. 2, pp. 344–349. © 1978 IEEE. Reprinted with permission.

First, they are systems of *simultaneous* stochastic difference equations. A system of *structural equations* can be written as

$$y_t = \Phi(y_t, y_{t-1}, x_t, w_t) + \varepsilon_t, \tag{1.1}$$

where y_t is a vector of endogenous variables at time t which is explained by the model, x_t is a vector of control variables, w_t is a vector of exogenous variables not subject to control, and ε_t is a random vector of residuals with zero mean and independently distributed through time. Φ is a vector of functions Φ_i. Because the system is simultaneous, with y_t appearing on the right-hand side of (1.1), it has to be solved to obtain y_t, given y_{t-1}, x_t, w_t, and ε_t. This feature is absent from most of the models used in engineering.

Second, the functions Φ_i are often nonlinear, but are usually monotone. An example from the University of Michigan Quarterly Econometric Model (Hymans and Shapiro, 1973) is the following equation for y_{16}, consumption expenditures on nondurable goods in billions of 1958 dollars (the numbering of the variables is ours):

$$y_{16} = 94.8 + 7.59\left(\frac{x_1}{y_{47}}\right)$$

$$+ 0.140 y_{50} - 74.2\left(\frac{y_5}{y_{47}}\right)$$

$$- 1.22\left[\sum_{i=1}^{3} \frac{y_{30,-i}}{3}\right] + 0.558 y_{16,-1}. \tag{1.2}$$

The second subscript of each variable is omitted if it equals t, and is written $-i$ for $t - i$. This equation includes four current endogenous variables, y_{16}, y_{47} (price index for personal consumption expenditures), y_{50} (disposable personal income in billions of 1958 dollars), and y_5 (price index for consumption expenditures on nondurable goods). The appearance of several current endogenous variables in one equation makes the model simultaneous. y_{30} is the interest rate on Aaa corporate bonds, entering with time lags from one to three quarters. x_1 is government transfer payments to persons in billions of current dollars, being treated as a control variable.

Third, the models are frequently large. The version of the Michigan Quarterly Econometric Model adopted for our control experiments consists of 61 endogenous variables and an equal number of simultaneous equations. Because there are accounting identities relating the endogenous variables, one could eliminate some unimportant endogenous variables using these identities and reduce the number of equations. On the other hand, to write the model as a first-order system for the control calculations, 71 additional variables (taking the form $y_{62} = y_{7, -1}$ for example) are added to the vector y_t to eliminate variables with time lags of two or more quarters. This makes a total of 132 elements in y_t, but a system of only 61 nonlinear simultaneous equations has to be solved to obtain y_t, given y_{t-1}, x_t, and w_t. The Mark III version of the Wharton Quarterly Econometric Model (in use until 1972) consists of 201 simultaneous equations. The MIT–Penn–SSRC Model consisted of 177 simultaneous equations. Although the number of simultaneous equations is large, the number of current endogenous variables appearing in each equation is small. For example, only 4 out of 61 variables actually appear in (1.2) for the Michigan model. If the equations were linear and were to be solved by matrix inversion, the matrix involved is a sparse matrix. This feature can be exploited to economize computations.

Fourth, not only the unknown parameters in the structural equations (1.1), but the specification of these equations are subject to a high degree of uncertainty. The former uncertainty is inherent in the statistical estimation of a large number of parameters using a limited number of time-series observations. The latter uncertainty is due mainly to the insufficiency of economic theory in specifying the time pattern of responses and the suitable degrees of aggregation for different economic variables. Given these two types of uncertainty, econometric model builders have paid less attention to the problem of measurement errors which has been explicitly dealt with by the control engineers. Uncertainty concerning the econometric models has important implications for the application of stochastic control techniques to economic policy formulation, partly to be discussed in Section 4.

4.2   USE OF ECONOMETRIC MODELS FOR POLICY PROJECTIONS AND OPTIMIZATION

Ever since large econometric models were constructed in the 1950s, they have been used to make economic forecasts and to deduce the economic consequences of alternative paths for the policy variables x_t. To make a one-period projection of y_t, given y_{t-1}, x_t, and w_t, the system of equations (1.1) is usually solved by the Gauss–Siedel method, with ε_t set equal to its expectation zero. This iterative method, as explained in (Chow, 1975, p. 136), for example, lists the equations in a certain order, applies the current set of trial values for the endogenous variables y_t to the right-hand side of the ith equation in (1.1) to obtain a new trial value for y_{it}, and continues to use the next equation to revise the next endogenous variable until convergence. A damping factor is introduced if successive trial values of y_{it} oscillate. Experience has shown that this simple method works for nearly all econometric models. To make a projection of y_t for several periods, the system (1.1) is solved several times, and the solution for each period is used as y_{t-1} in the calculation of y_t for the following period.

Although in the 1950s economists began to set up a quadratic loss function for the purpose of policy optimization and discovered that the certainty equivalence solution for the current period policy x_t is optimal for the multiperiod stochastic control problem of minimizing the expectation of a *quadratic* loss function given a *linear* model with additive random disturbances (Simon, 1956; Theil, 1958), multiperiod policy optimization using a large-scale, nonlinear, simultaneous econometric model has occurred only in the 1970s. A popular approach is to convert a T-period stochastic control problem into a deterministic control problem by setting the random disturbances equal to their expectations (appealing partly to the possibly near optimality of the certainty-equivalence solution for nonlinear models). One then solves the deterministic control problem as an unconstrained minimization problem with respect to the policy path $x_1, x_2, \ldots, x_T$ because the multiperiod loss function can be regarded as a function of $x_1, \ldots, x_T$, given the nonstochastic econometric model. The number of unknowns equals the number q of control variables times the number T of periods. Various standard minimization algorithms have been applied (Ando and Palash, 1976; Athans et al., 1975; Fair, 1974; Kalchbrenner and Tinsley, 1976; Norman, Norman, and Palash, 1975). An Econometric Model Comparison Seminar composed of the proprietors of the major U.S. econometric models, chaired by Lawrence Klein and sponsored by the National Bureau of Economic Research with a grant from the National Science Foundation, is currently comparing the deterministic control solutions from the different models (with the disturbances set at their historical values) for the 17 quarters beginning with 1971.1, using the same essentially quadratic loss function with the inflation rate, the unemployment rate, the GNP gap, and the balance of international payments as arguments. This exercise should reveal the differences among the econometric models in terms of their policy recommendations during a crucial historical period.

If the deterministic control solution is used to make recommendations to policy makers, one may appeal to the near optimality of the first-period solution x_1 and apply it to the first period. The policy in period two will be obtained as the first-period solution to a $(T - 1)$-period deterministic control problem formulated at the end of period one after y_1 is observed, and so forth. Such a procedure may work well, but the dynamic characteristics of the system under control are extremely difficult and costly to ascertain because extensive stochastic simulations would be required. If the policy maker wishes to know not only the expected paths of y_t and x_t in the future when the economy is under control, but the covariance matrices of these time series and the expected total loss for T periods, the solution to the original stochastic control problem in the form of feedback control equations will be desirable. This chapter describes and recommends a solution to stochastic control in feedback form using a large, nonlinear econometric model, and assuming the loss function to be quadratic.

4.3 A FEEDBACK CONTROL ALGORITHM

We will describe an approximate solution to the optimal stochastic control problem in feedback form, that is, $x_t = G_t y_{t-1} + g_t$ where y_t incorporates x_t as a subvector, as illustrated in Section 4, in order to omit x_t as an argument in the quadratic loss function:

$$W = \sum_{t=1}^{T} (y_t - a_t)' K_t (y_t - a_t)$$

$$= \sum_{t=1}^{T} (y_t' K_t y_t - 2 y_t' K_t a_t + a_t' K_t a_t). \tag{3.1}$$

The solution consists of the following steps.

1 Starting with a tentative policy path $x_1^0, x_2^0, \ldots, x_T^0$, and given $w_1, w_2, \ldots, w_T$, we apply the Gauss–Siedel method to the model (1.1) with $\varepsilon_t = 0$ for T periods to obtain a solution path $y_1^0, y_2^0, \ldots, y_T^0$ of the endogenous variables. Thus, for each period t, the following system of equations holds:

$$y_t^0 = \Phi(y_t^0, y_{t-1}^0, x_t^0, w_t) \qquad (t = 1, \ldots, T). \tag{3.2}$$

2 Equations (1.1) are linearized about the point y_t^0, y_{t-1}^0, and x_t^0 to yield

$$y_t = y_t^0 + B_{1t}(y_t - y_t^0) + B_{2t}(y_{t-1} - y_{t-1}^0) + B_{3t}(x_t - x_t^0) + \varepsilon_t. \tag{3.3}$$

The i-j elements of B_{1t}, B_{2t}, and B_{3t} are, respectively, the derivatives of Φ_i in (1.1) with respect to the jth elements of y_t, y_{t-1}, and x_t. They are easily computed numerically by changing the jth element of y_t, y_{t-1}, or x_t by a small amount and evaluating the resulting changes in Φ_i. For the illustrative equation (1.2) from the Michigan model, the 16th row of B_{1t} has only three nonzero elements, in the 5th, 47th, and 50th columns.

3   The linear simultaneous equations (3.3) are solved to obtain the linearized state-space model (or the *reduced-form equations* in the economist's terminology):

$$y_t = A_t y_{t-1} + C_t x_t + b_t + u_t, \tag{3.4}$$

where

$$(A_t; C_t; u_t) = (I - B_{1t})^{-1}(B_{2t}; B_{3t}; \varepsilon_t)$$

$$b_t = y_t^0 - A_t y_{t-1}^0 - C_t x_t^0. \tag{3.5}$$

4   Using the linear model (3.4) with additive random disturbances u_t and the quadratic loss function (3.1), we compute the optimal linear feedback control equations

$$\hat{x}_t = G_t y_{t-1} + g_t \tag{3.6}$$

by well-known methods (Chow, 1975, pp. 178–179) given in Chapter 1.

5   A new tentative policy path $x_1^0, \ldots, x_T^0$ and solution path $y_1^0, \ldots, y_T^0$ are obtained by solving (3.6) and (1.2) with $\varepsilon_t = 0$ consecutively for x_t and y_t ($t = 1, \ldots, T$).

6   We go back to step 2 to linearize the model about the new solution path and then compute the optimal feedback solution for the linear-quadratic problem until the process converges. At the point of convergence, the solution vectors y_t and x_t satisfy both the nonlinear system (1.2) with $\varepsilon_t = 0$ and the linearized model (3.3) with $\varepsilon_t = 0$, and thus also the linearized reduced form (3.4) with $u_t = 0$.

7   The stochastic system under control is approximately described by (3.4) and (3.6), that is,

$$y_t = (A_t + C_t G_t)y_{t-1} + (b_t + C_t g_t) + u_t = R_t y_{t-1} + r_t + u_t. \tag{3.7}$$

The mean path of this system is given by $\bar{y}_t = R_t \bar{y}_{t-1} + r_t$, or equivalently by the solution vector y_t^0 in the last iteration which also satisfies (3.6) and (3.4) with $u_t = 0$. The covariance matrix of the system is computed by, for

$$y_t^* = y_t - \bar{y}_t,$$

$$Ey_t^* y_t^{*\prime} = R_t(Ey_{t-1}^* y_{t-1}^{*\prime})R_t' + Eu_t u_t', \tag{3.8}$$

where $Eu_t u_t' = (I - B_{1t})^{-1}(E\varepsilon_t \varepsilon_t')(I - B_{1t})^{-1\prime}$ because of (3.5). The covariance matrix of the random residuals in (1.1) is assumed to have been estimated together with the other unknown parameters in the econometric model. The expected total loss in T periods when the system is under feedback control can be calculated by a well-known formula (Chow, 1975, p. 179) given by (7) of Chapter 1, with the subscript 1 replacing T.

4.4 FURTHER DETAILS CONCERNING COMPUTATIONS

The first step in preparing the model for control using the computer program available at Princeton University (Butters and Chow, 1977) is to write in Fortran code each of the structural equations (1.1). To eliminate endogenous variables lagged more than one period, such as $y_{30,-3}$ in the consumption expenditures equating (1.2), we would introduce *nid* identities of the form $Y(89) = YL(30)$ and $Y(90) = YL(89)$ where YL stands for y lagged one period. These identities enable us to write $y_{30,-2}$ as $y_{89,-1}$ and $y_{30,-3}$ as $y_{90,-1}$. Furthermore, the program automatically makes up an identity of the form $y_{133,t} = x_{1,t}$ for each of the nx control variables, permitting the user to write the welfare loss (3.1) as a function of y, alone. These *nid* + *nx* identities are combined with the original *ns simultaneous* structural equations, making a total of $p = ns + nid + nx$ equations. In addition to the Fortran coding of the model, the user of the algorithm must provide the variance-covariance matrix of the residuals, the weighting matrix K, the values of the vector y_0, and, for each t in the control horizon $(t = 1, \ldots, T)$, the target values a_t, the values for the exogenous variables w_t, and the trial values for the nx control variables x_t.

As described in Section 3, given the initial vector y_0 and the trial solutions for x_t, the Gauss–Siedel method is used to obtain a solution path $y_1^0, y_2^0, \ldots, y_T^0$ about which the model will be linearized. Once this solution path is obtained, the elements of the matrices B_{1t}, B_{2t}, and B_{3t} of (3.3) will be computed. The *i-j* element of B_{1t} is obtained by computing

$$\frac{\partial \Phi_{it}}{\partial y_{jt}} = \frac{y_{it}^{(1)} - y_{it}^{(2)}}{2\delta_{jt}}, \tag{4.1}$$

where $y_{it}^{(1)}$ equals Φ_i evaluated at $y_{jt} + \delta_{jt}$, $y_{it}^{(2)}$ equals Φ_i evaluated at

$y_{jt} - \delta_{jt}$, and $\delta_{jt} = \max(|dy \cdot y_{jt}|, d\min)$. dy and $d\min$ are set by the user. The default value for both is equal to 0.001. Similarly, we evaluate the *i-k* element of B_{2t} by perturbing $y_{k,t-1}$ and the *i-j* element of B_{3t} by perturbing $x_{j,t}$.

Due to the structure of the model, there will be many zero elements in B_{1t}, B_{2t}, and B_{3t}. In particular, B_{1t} will be a block diagonal matrix

$$B_{1t} = \begin{bmatrix} B_{1t}^* & 0 \\ 0 & 0 \end{bmatrix}, \qquad (4.2)$$

where B_{1t}^* is $ns \times ns$, whereas B_{1t} is a $p \times p$ matrix. Only the ns simultaneous equations, and not the identities introduced, have current values of the endogenous variables on the right-hand side. Frequently there will be columns of zeros within B_{1t}^*. This information will be utilized by the program and no derivatives will be computed for these columns. Similarly, the matrices B_{2t} and B_{3t} have many elements known to be either zero or one, which the program recognizes. Because of the special form of B_{1t} as given by (4.2), the inversion of $I - B_{1t}$ requires only the inversion of its upper left-hand $ns \times ns$ submatrix $I - B_{1t}^*$. A sparse matrix inversion routine can be used as an option for this purpose since, as pointed out in Section 1, B_{1t}^* is, in general, a sparse matrix.

Given the linearized reduced-form equations (3.4), core space and computer time are saved by treating a smaller dynamic system formed by excluding those endogenous variables whose lagged values are absent from the original system and whose behavior is of no interest. If there are m such variables, the reduced form can be written as

$$\begin{bmatrix} y_t^a \\ y_t^b \end{bmatrix} = \begin{bmatrix} A_t^a & 0 \\ A_t^b & 0 \end{bmatrix} \begin{bmatrix} y_{t-1}^a \\ y_{t-1}^b \end{bmatrix} + \begin{bmatrix} C_t^a \\ C_t^b \end{bmatrix} x_t + \begin{bmatrix} b_t^a \\ b_t^b \end{bmatrix}, \qquad (4.3)$$

where y_t^a is $(p - m) \times 1$ and y_t^b is $m \times 1$. To compute the feedback control equations (3.6), only the submodel

$$y_t^a = A_t^a y_{t-1}^a + C_t^a x_t + b_t^a \qquad (4.4)$$

is used.

The iterations as described by steps 1 through 6 in Section 3 will terminate if, for each variable i included in the loss function, the proportional change of y_{it} in each time period t ($t = 1, \ldots, T$) between two successive iterations is smaller, in absolute value, than some preassigned number. The default value of this number is 0.001. There are two ways to speed up convergence. First, if the values of y_{it} oscillate in successive iterations, a damping factor between 0 and 1 can be introduced to dampen the change of each $\hat{x}_{it}$ from one iteration to the next. Second, for some control problems, the parameters in the loss function can be changed to facilitate convergence. For example, one may be interested in obtaining the lowest inflation rates y_{2t} ($t = 1, \ldots, T$) that correspond to an unemployment rate y_{1t} equal to 4 percent. In specifying the matrix K in the loss function, a very large weight will be assigned to the unemployment variable whose target is set at 4 percent, and a much smaller weight will be assigned to the inflation variable whose target is set at some unachievably low rate such as 2 percent per year (which could be further lowered if it turned out to be achievable). A weight combination of 10,000 and 1 may make the program converge more rapidly than a combination of 100 and 1.

To complete the optimal feedback control calculations for the Michigan Quarterly Econometric Model for 17 quarters using three control variables, the program takes 116 seconds of CPU time in the IBM 360-91 computer at Princeton University for each iteration or linearization of the model, costing $20.00 at the delay priority rate. It takes three interations to converge. Increasing the number of control variables to six would have almost no effect on the computing time because the matrix $(C_t' H_t C_t)^{-1}$ required to compute the matrix G_t in the feedback control equation (3.6) would merely become 6×6 instead of 3×3. Increasing the number of time periods T would raise the computed time approximately linearly because similar calculations are performed for each period. Doubling the size of the model, as measured by the number ns of simultaneous equations, would increase the computing cost by a factor of about 4, or 2^2.

4.5 APPLICATION TO THE MICHIGAN QUARTERLY ECONOMETRIC MODEL

Analysis of a particular control problem will serve as an illustration of the application of the techniques described above, as well as identify the role optimal control of econometric systems can play in the evaluation of economic policy. The loss function, except for the last term involving UR$, is one used by the NBER–NSF Econometric Model Comparison Seminar mentioned in Section 2. For the 17 quarters, 1971.1 through 1975.1, the objective is to minimize

$$\sum_{t=1}^{17} \left[0.75(u_t - 4.0)^2 + (\dot{p}_t - \alpha_t)^2 + (TB_t - 0)^2 \right.$$

$$\left. + 0.75(\text{GNP gap}_t - 0)^2 + 0.1(\text{UR\$}_t - \gamma_t)^2 \right], \qquad (5.1)$$

where

u = the unemployment rate

$\dot{p}$ = the annual rate of inflation measured by the GNP price deflator

α_t = 3.0 for $t = 1, \ldots, 12$
    7.0 for $t = 13, \ldots, 17$

TB = the trade balance as a percentage of GNP in current dollars

GNP gap = the percentage deviation of GNP in 1958 dollars (GNP58) from capacity output

UR$ = unborrowed reserves in billions of current dollars

and γ represents a smooth expansionary path for UR$. The instruments available to the policy maker are nondefense government purchases of goods and services in billions of current dollars (GFO$) and UR$, representing government fiscal and monetary policy, respectively. The UR$ term in the loss function serves to prevent erratic behavior of the monetary instrument; however, the deviation of UR$_t$ from γ_t will not count as a part of the loss.

The purpose of this control problem is to determine if some politically feasible combination of fiscal and monetary policies could have improved the performance of the economy during the period under consideration by comparing the optimal and historical paths for the target variables and instruments. Examination of the results leads to an affirmative answer. Tables 1 and 2 present the historical and optimal paths, respectively, for certain key variables. Excluding the UR$ term, the historical value of the loss is 703.4, whereas the minimum value is 232.7. The optimal path for GFO$ is considerably more expansionary than the historical path, although it does fluctuate. The optimal path for UR$ is only mildly expansionary for the first eight quarters, but becomes more expansionary in the later quarters. Monetary policy affects the values of the listed variables with a lag; thus, much of the behavior of the variables, especially during the first half of the control horizon, is attributable to the impact of GFO$. For each of the 17 quarters, real output, GNP58, is greater in the optimal control solution. This leads to lower values for the GNP gap throughout and a lower rate of unemployment in all quarters but one, reducing the loss contribution of the gap term by 421.7 and the unemployment term by 37.8. In the early quarters, however, the lower unemployment rate is achieved at the expense of a higher annual rate of inflation. For nine of the first ten quarters of the control horizon, the historical rate of inflation is lower than that obtained under control, although for six of the remaining seven quarters, the historical figure is higher. The overall contribution of the inflation term to the loss is reduced by implementation of the control solution. In the control solution, the trade balance term deviates more

Table 1 Historical Paths of Selected Macroeconomic Variables

	$\dot{p}$	u	GNP Gap	TB	GNP58	UR$	GFO$
1971.1	4.69	5.95	5.01	0.278	737	29.5	24.1
71.2	4.85	5.98	5.27	− 0.006	742	30.1	25.5
71.3	2.58	5.96	5.55	0.009	747	30.6	27.9
71.4	1.90	5.94	4.99	− 0.312	759	31.2	28.5
72.1	5.49	5.84	4.45	− 0.631	771	31.9	29.7
72.2	1.92	5.69	3.44	− 0.602	787	32.9	30.0
72.3	3.32	5.57	3.01	− 0.406	798	32.9	30.1
72.4	4.05	5.29	2.01	− 0.440	814	30.4	30.5
73.1	5.49	5.04	0.75	− 0.006	833	30.1	31.4
73.2	7.29	4.91	1.17	0.033	837	30.6	32.2
73.3	8.26	4.74	1.74	0.515	841	32.3	32.0
73.4	8.64	4.72	2.12	0.696	846	33.8	33.1
74.1	12.11	5.20	4.82	0.832	831	33.7	35.7
74.2	9.36	5.15	6.14	− 0.101	827	33.7	37.7
74.3	11.88	5.49	7.51	− 0.225	823	34.0	38.8
74.4	14.44	6.60	10.54	0.123	804	36.2	40.6
75.1	7.96	8.35	14.06	0.375	780	34.7	42.5
Contribution to Loss	214.2	44.5	441.7	3.0	Total: 703.4		

Table 2 Optimal Paths Based on the Michigan Quarterly Model

	$\dot{p}$	u	GNP Gap	TB	GNP58	UR$	GFO$
1971.1	6.07	5.08	0.48	− 0.182	772	26.4	78.6
71.2	3.69	4.61	1.34	− 0.491	773	26.8	60.6
71.3	2.81	4.56	1.76	− 0.423	777	26.4	61.9
71.4	3.27	4.23	− 0.57	− 0.902	804	26.8	90.9
72.1	5.43	4.51	1.82	− 0.977	792	27.2	55.1
72.2	3.84	4.77	1.16	− 0.847	805	28.2	66.2
72.3	4.21	4.94	1.31	− 0.619	812	29.8	68.2
72.4	4.85	4.96	1.18	− 0.548	821	30.7	64.6
73.1	5.93	4.99	0.45	− 0.108	835	32.4	60.9
73.2	7.61	4.96	0.68	− 0.041	842	34.5	61.0
73.3	8.11	4.69	0.63	0.348	850	36.2	58.6
73.4	8.11	4.54	0.71	0.458	858	38.9	50.2
74.1	11.75	4.88	2.98	0.485	847	40.9	46.9
74.2	9.63	4.08	0.85	− 0.949	874	41.8	94.8
74.3	11.78	3.31	− 0.99	− 1.660	899	41.8	131.3
74.4	12.62	3.70	1.11	− 1.596	889	40.9	118.1
75.1	9.11	4.41	1.18	− 1.931	897	40.3	172.2
Contribution to Loss	191.9	6.7	20.0	14.1	Total: 232.7		

from its target than it did historically, but in neither case is the contribution to the overall loss significant.

In the above calculation, the estimated residuals in the structural equations were included so that the historical values of the endogenous variables would result if the actual values of the instruments were applied. The economist can use this type of analysis in the evaluation of past policies. More importantly, the policy maker can use the stochastic control techniques as described in Sections 3 and 4 to formulate and evaluate current and future policies. A number of objective functions could be minimized and the results compared to determine a policy mix which is politically feasible and would lead to desired values for the endogenous variables. It should be stressed that analyses of both types, for the evaluation of historical policies and the formulation of current policies, are based on the assumption that the model used is a reasonably good approximation of reality. In the next section, we will comment briefly on the methods to deal with uncertainty in the econometric models to be used in optimal control calculations.

4.6   FURTHER RESEARCH

There are three areas of research closely related to the techniques of feedback control as expounded in this chapter. The first is to improve the computational efficiency and capability of the algorithm to deal with larger nonlinear econometric models. The second is to modify the control solution to account for the uncertainty in the statistical estimates of the model parameters. Although a solution to this problem has already been obtained in Chapter 3, we have not completed a computer code for it. One would like to study the effect of parameter uncertainty on the (nearly) optimal policy and the associated expected welfare loss. Third, the problem of misspecification of econometric models has to be attacked by the effective use of two or more models.

The basic framework to deal with two or more models is a payoff matrix whose elements are the expected losses resulting from the different proposed policies when the alternative states of the world, or models, are true. The policies considered may include the (nearly) optimal policies based on the different models, with or without incorporating uncertainty in their parameters, and some passive policies of feedback control. The expected loss in each element of the payoff matrix need not be the expected multiperiod loss when the policy recommendations from one model are followed throughout all future periods. Because the decision maker can change the model employed for policy recommendations after one period, the entry in the payoff matrix corresponding to a given true state or model and a given strategy should be the expected loss resulting from applying the given strategy for only the first period, but the strategies based on the true model for the remaining periods of the planning horizon. This would show the damage of following the incorrect model in the first period only, but not necessarily in the future periods. Such a payoff matrix can form the basis for deriving a Bayesian strategy, a minimax strategy, and some robust strategies in the formulation of macroeconomic policies in the face of incomplete economic knowledge. The use of imperfect models and of two or more models for policy formulation will be discussed in Chapters 11 and 12.

CHAPTER 5

Optimal Control of Nonlinear Systems Program: User's Guide

The optimal control of nonlinear systems program (OPTNL) computes the optimal control policy and the associated welfare cost using a quadratic loss function for an econometric model whose parameters are assumed to be known. The algorithm used is described in Sections 12.1 and 12.4 of Chow (1975), or in Chapter 2 of this book.

5.1   ELIMINATING SECOND- AND HIGHER-ORDER LAGS IN THE MODEL

Let the model be written as a system of simultaneous structural equations.

$$y_t = \phi(y_t, y_{t-1}, x_t, x_{t-1}, w_t) + u_t, \qquad (1)$$

where

y_t = vector of ny endogenous variables

x_t = vector of nx control variables

w_t = vector of nw exogenous variables not subject to control

npd = number of time periods in the planning horizon

u_t = vector of random error terms

ϕ = a vector of possibly nonlinear functions.

This chapter was coauthored by Ettie H. Butters.

Because the program does not accept lagged endogenous variables of order higher than the first, the user should eliminate the variables with lags of two or more periods by introducing identities. For example, let there be 50 endogenous variables in the model to begin with. The number of simultaneous equations ns is 50. If the model consists of $y_{6,t-2}$, an identity $y_{51,t} = y_{6,t-1}$ should be introduced. This identity permits the user to write $y_{6,t-2}$ as $y_{51,t-1}$ and get rid of the second-order lag. If $y_{6,t-3}$ is also present, another identity $y_{52,t} = y_{51,t-1}$ can be used, permitting the user to write $y_{6,t-3}$ as $y_{52,t-1}$. Let 40 additional identities of this kind be required in our example to eliminate all endogenous variables with lags of two or more periods. There will then be 90 endogenous variables in the model, to be included in the vector y_t.

If the model consists of control variables lagged two or more periods, more identities and endogenous variables will be required. Let there be $nx = 4$ control variables in our example, $x_{1,t}, \ldots, x_{4,t}$. To eliminate the variable $x_{1,t-2}$, introduce the identity $y_{91,t} = x_{1,t-1}$ and write $x_{1,t-2}$ as $y_{91,t-1}$. Similarly, to eliminate $x_{1,t-3}$, introduce the identity $y_{92,t} = y_{91,t-1}$ and write $x_{1,t-3}$ as $y_{92,t-1}$. If 10 identities of this type are required, there will be all together 100 variables in the vector y_t. ny, the number of endogenous variables in y_t, will be set equal to 100.

The computer program will automatically make up a vector consisting of the 104 elements of y_t and x_t. This augmented vector will serve as the argument in the welfare function, its last four elements in our example being included to serve the possible need to penalize variations in the instruments or control variables. The expanded model takes the form

$$\left.\begin{aligned} y_{1,t} &= \phi_1(y_t, y_{t-1}, x_t, x_{t-1}, w_t) + u_{1,t} \\ \vdots \quad & \qquad \vdots \qquad\qquad\qquad\qquad \vdots \\ y_{50,t} &= \phi_{ns}(y_t, y_{t-1}, x_t, x_{t-1}, w_t) + u_{50,t} \end{aligned}\right\} \begin{array}{l} ns \text{ structural} \\ \text{equations} \end{array}$$

$$\left.\begin{aligned} y_{51,t} &= y_{6,t-1} \\ \vdots \qquad & \quad \vdots \\ y_{100,t} &= y_{99,t-1} \end{aligned}\right\} \begin{array}{l} nid \text{ identities} \\ \text{of lagged values} \end{array} \qquad (2)$$

$$\left.\begin{aligned} y_{101,t} &= x_{1,t} \\ \vdots \qquad & \quad \vdots \\ y_{104,t} &= x_{4,t} \end{aligned}\right\} \begin{array}{l} nx \text{ identities of} \\ \text{control variables} \end{array}$$

There are ns simultaneous structural equations, nid identities of lagged values, and *nx* identities for the control variables; altogether the aug-mented *y* vector has *p* elements, with $p = ny + nx$, and $ny = ns + nid$. u_t is a random vector with mean zero and covariance matrix V, to be supplied by the user. The program calculates a linear approximation of the model explaining the augmented *y* vector shown in (2)

$$y_t = A_t y_{t-1} + C_t x_t + b_t,$$

from which it derives a feedback control equation

$$x_t = G_t y_{t-1} + g_t$$

so as to minimize the expectation of the welfare loss

$$E_0 W = E_0 \sum_{t=1}^{npd} (y_t - z_t)' K_t (y_t - z_t),$$

where *npd* is the number of periods, z_t is a vector of targets, and $K_t = K \cdot \text{EXKCAP}^t$ is the weighting matrix. *npd*, z_t, EXKCAP, and K are to be specified by the user.

The model in the form shown in (2) is coded in FORTRAN statements in two subroutines provided by the user. The first subroutine, named MODELS, consists of FORTRAN statements of the *ns* simultaneous structural equations; the second, named MODELI, consists of FORTRAN statements of the *nid* identities of the lagged values. The last *nx* identities of the control variables are not coded by the user, but are "remembered" by the program. Some knowledge of basic FORTRAN is therefore re-quired by the user. A description of the two user-supplied subroutines is contained in Section 4.

5.2   DESCRIPTION OF THE PROGRAM

The general logic of the program, represented in the flow diagram of Figure 1, is taken directly from Section 12.1 of Chow (1975). A description for some of the steps follows.

1   Each iteration starts at A of the diagram, and depends on the optimal path computed in the previous iteration. To provide a tentative path of y_t for the first iteration, the program starts with the given trial values of x_t, $(t = 1, \ldots, npd)$ and solves the nonlinear system using the Gauss-Siedel method which is described in Section 6.6 of Chow (1975). For

60

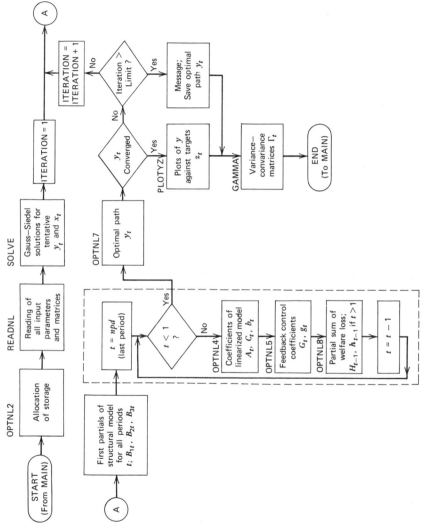

Figure 1. Flow diagram of mainline logic for the nonlinear optimum control program.

the model of (2), let $y_{it}^{(k)}$ be the values of y_{it} at the kth iteration of the Gauss-Siedel process. The iterating process continues until y_{it} converges

$$\left| \frac{y_{it}^{(k+1)} - y_{it}^{(k)}}{y_{it}^{(k)}} \right| < \varepsilon \qquad \text{for } i = 1, \ldots, ns.$$

The method requires the user to supply an initial y_0 vector, trial y_1 and x_1 vectors in period 1 for the first Gauss-Siedel iteration, the maximum number, r, of iterations permitted, and the convergence criterion ε.

2   Instead of computing the tentative path by the Gauss-Siedel method, the program can, if so directed by the user, accept a set of y_t and x_t from an output device as the tentative path to be used for the first iteration. These y_t and x_t are optimal solutions from a previous job, and are being used now to continue the iteration process. At the end of each iteration cycle, the program automatically saves the solutions y_t and x_t in an output device, regardless of whether y_t has converged. The purpose is to safeguard against losing all the results of the iterative process before the job is completed such as when the job is terminated because the estimated time is exceeded or the system crashes. What has been saved can then be used for the next iteration in a later job.

3   The program computes the first partial derivatives of ϕ_j numerically. For example, the derivative of ϕ_j with respect to the variable y_{it} is

$$\frac{\partial \phi_j}{\partial y_{it}} = \frac{y_{it}^1 - y_{it}^2}{2\, dy_i},$$

where

$$y_{it}^1 = \phi_j(y_{1t}, \ldots, y_{it} + dy_i, \ldots, y_{ny,t}; y_{t-1}; x_{t-1}; x_t; w_t)$$

$$y_{it}^2 = \phi_j(y_{1t}, \ldots, y_{it} - dy_i, \ldots, y_{ny,t}; y_{t-1}; x_{t-1}, x_t; w_t)$$

$$dy_i = \max(|\text{FDFRAC} \cdot y_{it}|, \text{FDMIN}).$$

FDFRAC, FDMIN are provided by the user.

5.3   DESCRIPTION OF TIME- AND SPACE-SAVING PROCEDURES

The nonlinear model is constructed in the particular form shown in (2) in order to save both computation time and core space. In that form the matrices B_{1t}, B_{2t}, and B_{3t} of the model's first partial derivatives

$$B'_{1t} = \left(\frac{\partial \phi_1}{\partial y_t} \cdots \frac{\partial \phi_p}{\partial y_t} \right)$$

$$B'_{2t} = \left(\frac{\partial \phi_1}{\partial y_{t-1}} \cdots \frac{\partial \phi_p}{\partial y_{t-1}} \right)$$

$$B'_{3t} = \left(\frac{\partial \phi_1}{\partial x_t} \cdots \frac{\partial \phi_p}{\partial x_t} \right)$$

take the following form:

$$B'_{1t} = \left(\frac{\partial \phi_1}{\partial y_t} \cdots \frac{\partial \phi_{ns}}{\partial y_t} \quad 0 \cdots 0 \right)$$

$$B'_{2t} = \left(\frac{\partial \phi_1}{\partial y_{t-1}} \cdots \frac{\partial \phi_{ns}}{\partial y_{t-1}} \quad d_1 \cdots d_{nid} 0 \cdots 0 \right)$$

$$B'_{3t} = \left(\frac{\partial \phi_1}{\partial x_t} \cdots \frac{\partial \phi_{ns}}{\partial x_t} \quad 0 \cdots 0 \ I \right),$$

where d_k is a vector of all zeros except a single element of one, and where I is an identity submatrix of dimension nx. Because all except the first ns columns have only zeros or ones, the program computes the partial derivatives only for the ns structural equations. The location of the element one in each d_k column of B'_{2t} is informed by an input vector named IDENTVEC, where IDENTVEC$(k) = j$ indicates that the d_k column has an element one in its jth row, the rest of the column being zero.

Some more time may be saved by the program in computing the partial derivatives for the ns structural equations $\phi_1, \ldots, \phi_{ns}$. If a variable such as $y_{8,t-1}$ is not in any of the equations $\phi_1, \ldots, \phi_{ns}$, the program will not waste time in computing the numerical derivative with respect to that variable, provided that it is known in advance that the derivative is zero. Such variables are identified by an input vector named VARBLVEC, supplied by the user. VARBLVEC has $ns + p + nx$ entries, each being either zero or nonzero, corresponding to the following variables:

$$y_{1,t}, \ldots, y_{ns,t}; y_{1,t-1}, \ldots, y_{ny,t-1}; x_{1,t-1}, \ldots, x_{nx,t-1}; x_{1,t}, \ldots, x_{nx,t}.$$

Derivatives of $\phi_1, \ldots, \phi_{ns}$ with respect to these variables are computed to form the matrices B_{1t}, B_{2t}, and B_{3t}. If a variable in the list appears nowhere in the model $\phi_1, \ldots, \phi_{ns}$, the user enters the value zero in its entry in VARBLVEC; otherwise he or she enters a nonzero value as described in Section 5.4. The program computes and utilizes the partial derivatives with respect to only those variables with nonzero values in their corresponding entries in VARBLVEC; it automatically treats the remaining columns in B_{1t}, B_{2t}, and B_{3t} as columns of zeros.

Another procedure used by the program to save time and core space is "compressing" the linearized approximation of the first ns equations of the model. The user does not need to be concerned with this process, because it is done entirely within the program without the user's intervention. The program rearranges the endogenous variables in y_t^s, the first ns elements of y_t, into two categories which we shall call y_t^a and y_t^b. y_t^b consists of variables that have the following characteristics:

1   They are not targeted in the weighting matrix K.
2   They have no lagged values in the model.

Because of these two characteristics, it is unnecessary to compute the optimal path for y_t^b. y_t^a consists of all the remaining variables of y_t^s. In this arrangement the linearized reduced-form equations become

$$\left[\begin{array}{c} y_t^a \\ \hline y_t^b \end{array}\right] = \left[\begin{array}{cc} A_t^a & 0 \\ \hline A_t^b & 0 \end{array}\right]\left[\begin{array}{c} y_{t-1}^a \\ \hline y_{t-1}^b \end{array}\right] + \left[\begin{array}{c} C_t^a \\ \hline C_t^b \end{array}\right][X_t] + \left[\begin{array}{c} b_t^a \\ \hline b_t^b \end{array}\right].$$

The program computes only A_t^a, C_t^a, and b_t^a of the compressed model; it computes the feedback control coefficients G_t and g_t and the welfare loss based on the compressed model, as shown in the flow diagram of Figure 1 where these steps are enclosed by the dotted rectangle.

5.4   USER-SUPPLIED SUBROUTINES

To run the nonlinear optimal control program three subroutines must be provided by the user. They are the main program, MODELS, and MODELI.

5.4.1   Main Program

The main program has to be coded by the user in order to allocate the right amount of space for his model. It calls in the optimal control program package and should be coded as follows:

```
    DIMENSION MAINAR(m)
    REAL*8 DWORD
    COMMON/IOBLK/INPUT,LIST,LCNT,NPG,INOUT2,INOUT3,
1        INOUT4,INOUT5
    EQUIVALENCE (DWORD,MAINAR(1))
    INPUT = 5
    LIST = 6
    INOUT2 = n2
    INOUT3 = n3
    INOUT4 = n4
    INOUT5 = n5
    LCNT = 99
    NPG = 0
    NDIM = m
    MAINAR(2) = 2
    MAINAR(1) = NDIM
    CALL OPTNL1(MAINAR,NDIM)
    STOP
    END
```

All capital letters and numbers must be coded as shown; the lowercase letters represent variables whose values are to be supplied by the user. The following explains some of the symbols:

MAINAR   is an array from which the program assigns all storage space.

m is the dimension of MAINAR; its formula is given in Section 6; note that the number m appears in two places: DIMENSION MAINAR(m) and NDIM = m.

INPUT = 5   device unit 5, which usually refers to the card-reader, is assigned to the input data set INPUT. If the input data is on tape or disk instead of in cards, another unit number should be assigned to INPUT.

LIST = 6   device unit 6, which usually refers to the printer, is assigned to the output data set LIST. If the printed output is to be first stored on tape or disk, another device unit should be assigned.

INOUT2   the program writes in this data set the optimal solutions y_t and x_t at the end of each iteration; each new set of y_t and

x_t replaces the one from the previous iteration. This data set should be kept by the user in case the iteration process is to be continued in a later job.

Three temporary data sets are used by the program to store intermediate results which are to be read by a later part of the program; they are INOUT3, INOUT4, and INOUT5 and they should be deleted at the end of each job.

INOUT3	stores the first partial derivatives B_{1t}, B_{2t}, and B_{3t}.
INOUT4	stores G_t, g_t for each period t to be used in the feedback control equation $x_t = G_t y_{t-1} + g_t$.
INOUT5	stores $A_t + C_t G_t$ and V_t for each period to be used for the computation of the covariance matrices Γ_t.
$n2, n3, n4, n5$	are device unit numbers for the temporary data sets assigned by the user; they should be single digit numbers other than 5, 6, or 7.
LCNT $= 99$	initialize line count and page number.
NPG $= 0$	
NDIM	the dimension of the main array MAINAR.
OPTNL1	the mainline logic subroutine of the nonlinear optimal control package.

5.4.2   MODELS

As described in Section 1 the nonlinear model is coded in two subroutines MODELS and MODELI. MODELS contains the ns simultaneous equations of the model, and it should be coded as follows:

```
SUBROUTINE MODELS(NY,NX,NW,D,Y,YL,XL,X,W,*)
IMPLICIT REAL*8(A-H,O-Z)
DIMENSION D(NY),Y(NY),YL(NY),XL(NX),X(NX),W(NW)
D(1) = φ₁(Y,YL,XL,X,W)⎫
D(2) = φ₂(Y,YL,XL,X,W)⎬ ns simultaneous equations
   ⋮                    ⎭

RETURN
END
```

$$D(1) = \phi_1(Y,YL,XL,X,W)$$
$$D(2) = \phi_2(Y,YL,XL,X,W)$$

where NY, NX, and NW are defined in Section 5.1, and where

D   is the array that contains the new values of the endogenous variables resulting from the calculations.

Y   is the vector of endogenous variables.

YL   is the vector of lagged endogenous variables.

X   is the vector of contról variables.

XL   is the vector of lagged control variables.

W   is the vector of exogenous variables; if there are no exogenous variables in the model, W and NW should nevertheless be coded as dummy parameters.

The right-hand side of the equations, represented by $\phi_1, \phi_2, \ldots$, are the algebraic FORTRAN statements; for example,

$$D(1) = Y(5) + DLOG(YL(1) + XL(3)) - 100.*W(4)/Y(6) + 0.085$$

The following rules should be observed in coding these statements:

1   All mathematical functions should be written in double precision because the program is written in double precision.

2   The order of all lags should be one.

3   If the lagged endogenous variable $y_{6, t-3}$ is in the original structural equations, then as illustrated in the example of Section 1, two variables of lagged values are defined to eliminate this higher-order lag: $y_{51, t} = y_{6, t-1}$ and $y_{52, t} = y_{51, t-1} \cdot y_{6, t-3}$ should then be coded in the subroutine as YL(52) which stands for $y_{52, t-1}$.

4   If $y_{6, t-2}$ is in the original structural model, it should be coded as YL(51) and *not* as Y(52). In the right-hand side of the structural equations the subscripts of the Y vector should be confined to the range from 1 to *ns*; in our example, the range is 1 to 50.

The * as it appears in the last argument of SUBROUTINE MODELS is an optimal facility for nonstandard return, and may be used in the following way. For example, let 10^{-6} be a poor value for the variable D(2), and if it is reached, then the trial solution is considered too far out. If we would like to terminate the program at this point, we can add the statements below the listing of all the equations in the SUBROUTINE MODELS:

$$\vdots$$

```
      IF (D(2).LT.1.D-6) GO TO 31
      RETURN
   31 RETURN1
      END
```

MODELS is called by two subroutines in the nonlinear program: SOLVE, which solves for y_i by the Gauss-Siedel method, and FP, which takes the first partial derivatives of ϕ. SOLVE requires that new values of y_i be used for the calculation of y_j, $j > i$; thus it provides one array, Y, for the two dummy variables D and Y in MODEL. FP, however, solves for each y_i after a variable on the right hand side of a structural equation is perturbed, using the old Y vector, thus providing separate arrays for the dummy variables D and Y in MODELS, and it expects the solution from D. To accomplish the double purposes required by SOLVE and FP the MODELS subroutine must be compiled by the FORTRAN G compiler.

5.4.3 MODELI

The second subroutine for the nonlinear model, named MODELI, consists of all the identities of lagged values as shown in (2); it should be coded as follows:

```
SUBROUTINE MODELI (NY,NX,NW,D,Y,YL,XL,X,W,*)
IMPLICIT REAL*8 (A–H,O–Z)
DIMENSION D(NY),Y(NY),Y(NY),YL(NY),XL(NX),X(NX),W(NW)
```

$$D(ns + 1) = YL(i_1)$$
$$D(ns + 2) = YL(i_2)$$
$$\vdots$$
$$D(ny) = YL(i_{nid})$$

```
RETURN
END
```

The actual values for $ns + 1, \ldots, ny$ and for $i_1, \ldots, i_{nid}$ will be supplied by the user. For example, using the illustration from Section 1,

$$D(51) = YL(6)$$
$$D(52) = YL(51)$$
$$\vdots$$

All parameters are the same as defined in MODELS, as is the use of the * feature. MODELI is used by only one subroutine of the program, SOLVE. As was explained earlier for MODELS, MODELI should be compiled by the FORTRAN G compiler.

For an illustration of the listing of equations in **MODELS** and **MODELI**, the reader may refer to the appendix of Chapter 13 where an econometric model of the Soviet Union will be presented and analyzed.

5.5 DATA REQUIREMENTS

The program accepts data in the sequence represented by the following diagram:

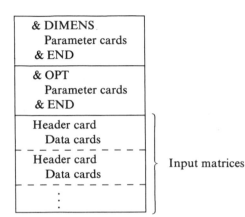

& DIMENS and &OPT are names for two blocks of parameters to be read in by the NAMELIST feature of FORTRAN. To illustrate the use of this feature, consider the following example, taken from the model discussed in Section 1:

$$\_\ \& \text{DIMENS} \_ NS = 50, NY = 100, NX = 4$$
$$\_\qquad\qquad\ NW = 40, NPD = 5$$
$$\_\ \text{END}$$

All input cards for a NAMELIST block must start at a column to the right of column 1. The first card must start with the name, in this case &DIMENS, followed by the parameters for that list. The parameters are separated by commas; spaces are allowed between parameters, but no space is allowed on either side of the " = " sign. A parameter not included in the input is given its default value by the program, therefore it may not be necessary to list all the parameters for a NAMELIST block. The block ends with an &END card. Note in the example "＿" means one or more blanks.

The input matrices are read in blocks, each being preceded by a header card which has the following format:

cols. 1–8   name of the matrix, left justified. The name must be spelled
               exactly as given in Section 5.3 later.

cols. 9–40:   optional format in FORTRAN convention for the data
               following this header card. The default format is 8F10.4.

cols. 41–80:   optional comments describing the matrix.

All data matrices except V and KCAP are to be read in row-wise, following the format specified in their respective header cards. Detailed description for each input matrix will be given in Section 5.3. The following example illustrates an input matrix:

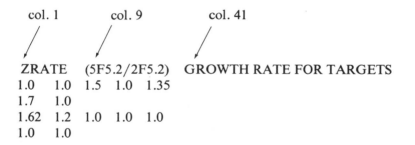

```
col. 1        col. 9          col. 41
  /             /               /

ZRATE   (5F5.2/2F5.2)   GROWTH RATE FOR TARGETS
1.0    1.0   1.5  1.0  1.35
1.7    1.0
1.62   1.2   1.0  1.0  1.0
1.0    1.0
```

5.5.1   &DIMENS

The NAMELIST &DIMENS consists of the following parameters:

NS = number of structural equations in the model; default = 1.
NY = number of endogenous variables of the vector y_t in (2); that is,
       NY = NS + the number of identities of lagged values; default = 1.
NX = number of control variables in the vector x_t in (2); default = 1.
NW = number of uncontrollable exogenous variables in the vector w_t in
       (2); default = 0.
NPD = number of time periods for the plan; default = 1.

5.5.2 &OPT

The &OPT list consists of parameters that are options for the program; they are:

OSUP = 0
　　for full print-out of $A_t, C_t, b_t, G_t, H_t, g_t, h_t$ at every time period. [These symbols are defined in Chow (1975) and in Chapter 1].

= 1
　　for print-out of G_t, H_t, g_t, h_t only at every time period.

= 2
　　for print-out of G_1, H_1, g_1, h_1 at time period 1 only; all other time periods have no print out.

= 3
　　same as in OSUP = 2 except that the program will also omit printing H_1 and h_1.

GAUSS = 0
　　will omit the printing of the Gauss-Siedel solution for y_t used for the first linearization of the model (default value).

= 1
　　will print the above Gauss-Siedel solution.

= 2
　　will print and save the Gauss-Siedel solution and the program will terminate at that point.

GAMMA = 0
　　will omit the calculation of the covariance matrices Γ_t (default value).

= 1
　　when the optimal solution y_t converges[1] the program will calculate the covariance matrices Γ_t of the variables y_t. The program will not print the entire Γ_t but will print only those rows of Γ_t that correspond to the variables targetted in the weighting matrix K.

= n
　　where $2 \leq n \leq ns + nx$. As in GAMMA = 1 the program will calculate Γ_t when the optimal solution y_t converges[1]; the print-out of Γ_t is controlled by the input vector GAMVAR, which is to be supplied by the user; n indicates the number of entries in GAMVAR.

PLOT = 0
　　will plot the values of the means of y_t against target values z_t only for those variables that have nonzero diagonal weights in the K matrix; the means of the control variables x_t are also plotted (default value).

= 1
　　will plot the means of all the variables of the

---

[1] The program will also compute Γ_t when the iteration limit ITERL1 is reached.

optimal solution y_t as well as the control variables x_t against their targets z_t.

UGZ $=T$ if the targets z_t are to grow at constant percentage rates; in this case the user will supply the initial z_0, the Z0 vector, and the rate of growth, the ZRATE vector, and the program will compute $z_t = $ Z0·(ZRATE)^t.

$=F$ if the targets z_t for all periods are to be supplied by the user in the input matrix Z (default value).

OFDIAV $=T$ if the covariance matrix V of the random vector u_t in (2) have nonzero off-diagonal elements; in this case the user must supply the lower triangle of the symmetric V.

$=F$ if the off-diagonal elements of V are zero; only the diagonal elements of V are required for input (default value).

OFDIAG $=T$ if the K matrix in the loss function have nonzero off-diagonal elements; in this case the user must supply the lower triangle of the symmetric K matrix.

$=F$ if the off-diagonal elements of K are zero; only the diagonal elements of K are required for input (default value).

EXKCAP $=$ discount factor for modifying the K matrix for each time period t according to the formula $K_t = K\cdot(\text{EXKCAP})^t$, where K is supplied by the user; default $= 1.0$.

NROUND $=1$ if the tentative path for y_t required in the first iteration is to be computed by the Gauss-Siedel method; this marks the first job run in the iterative process to calculate the optimal path y_t which might require more than one job run (default value).

$=2$ (or 3, 4, etc.) marks the second (or third, fourth, etc.) job run in the iterative process to find the optimal path y_t; the solution for y_t and x_t from the previous job will be read from an output device named INOUT2, to serve as the tentative path for the first iteration of the current run. All other input data remain the same as in the previous job. (See Section 7 on the use of more than one job run.)

ITERL1 =   the maximum number of times the model will be linearized for calculating optimal control path; default = 1. Our method starts with a guess for $x_1, \ldots, x_{npd}$, which, by the use of the Gauss-Siedel method, if NROUND = 1, implies a solution for $y_1, \ldots, y_{npd}$. Around this tentative path the model is linearized and an optimal control path is obtained for the linearized model. This optimal path becomes the initial guess of $x_1, \ldots, x_{npd}$ in the next linearization. ITERL1 refers to the maximum number of times the model will be linearized.

ITERL2 =   the maximum number of iterations allowed for solving the model by Gauss-Siedel; default = 10.

EPS1 =   the convergence criterion for optimal policy; default = 0.001.

$$\text{When } \left| \frac{y_i^{(k)} - y_i^{(k-1)}}{y_i^{(k-1)}} \right| \leq \text{EPS1},$$

for each $i = 1, \ldots, ns$ that corresponds to a nonzero diagonal element of the K matrix, k being the iteration count, the program terminates. The solution y_{it} will be plotted against their targets z_{it}. If the convergence criterion is not met another iteration will be performed.

EPS2 =   convergence criterion for the solution of the nonlinear model by the Gauss-Siedel method; default = 0.001. Gauss-Siedel solves the system of equations (1) until

$$\left| \frac{y_i^{(k+1)} - y_i^{(k)}}{y_i^{(k)}} \right| \leq \text{EPS2}$$

for $i = 1, \ldots, ny$, k being the iteration count.

FDFRAC =   parameter for computing step sizes in evaluating the first derivatives; the step size for the variable y_{it} is $dy_i = \max(|\text{FDFRAC} \cdot y_{it}|, \text{FDMIN})$; default = 0.001.

FDMIN =   minimum step size allowed in the above formula; default = 0.001.

DAMP =   a factor used to dampen the changes in successive
                               iterations of the Gauss-Siedel solution.

$$y_t^{(k+1)} = y_t^{(k)} + \text{DAMP} \cdot \left(y_t'^{(k+1)} - y_t^{(k)} \right)$$

where $y_t'^{(k+1)} =$ solution obtained at iteration $k + 1$,
                               and
$y_t^{(k+1)} =$ solution actually used to compute y_t
                               in the $(k + 1)$th iteration.
"DAMP" may be made small if solution tends to
oscillate from iteration to iteration; default $= 1.0$.

DAMPX =   a factor used to dampen the changes in successive
                               iterations of the control variables x_t.

$$x_{t,}^{(k+1)} = x_t^{(k)} + \text{DAMPX} \cdot \left(x_t'^{(k+1)} - x_t^{(k)} \right)$$

where

$x_t'^{(k+1)} =$ solution obtained at iteration $k + 1$, and

$x_t^{(k+1)} =$ solution actually used to compute the
                               optimal path y_t for the $(k + 1)$th iteration.

"DAMPX" may be made small if the optimal path
y_t tends to oscillate from iteration to iteration;
default $= 1.0$.

5.5.3   Input Matrices

The input matrices described below must appear in the input deck in the
order given; the name of the matrix must be spelled correctly in the header
card. IDENTVEC, VARBLVEC, and GAMVAR are the only vectors
whose elements are integers; all other vectors have floating-point numbers
as elements. The dimension p is defined as $p = ny + nx$.

Name	Dimension	Description
IDENTVEC	(nid)	A vector in which elements are the variables that appear in the identities of lagged values in the model; its construction will be described in Section 5.4.

Name	Dimension	Description
VARBLVEC	$(ns + p + nx)$	A vector that identifies those variables with respect to which the first partial derivatives are computed by the program; its construction will be described in Section 5.4
V	(ns) if OFDIAV = F $[ns(ns + 1)/2]$ if OFDIAV = T	Variance-covariance matrix of u_t in (2); if OFDIAV = F, only the diagonal of V is entered in the input; if OFDIAV = T, the lower triangle of V is entered by columns, starting with the left-most column of ns elements each succeeding column has one less element than the previous one.

ns

The lower triangle
is entered as data
if ODFIAV=T

Name	Dimension	Description
KCAP	(p) if OFDIAG = F $[p(p + 1)/2]$ if OFDIAG = T	The weighting matrix K in the welfare function; if OFDIAG = F, only the diagonal of K is entered as input; if OFDIAG = T, the lower triangle is entered by columns, as described for V above.
Z0	(p)	Initial values of targets for y_t and x_t; required only if UGZ = T.
ZRATE	(p)	Growth rate for targets which the program will compute based on Z0 and ZRATE; required only if UGZ = T.
Z	(npd, p)	Targets to be read in *row-wise* for all periods; required only if UGZ = F.
Y0	(p)	Initial values for the vectors y_t and x_t in period $t = 0$.
W	(npd, nw)	Exogenous variables for all periods, to be read in *row-wise*; required only if $nw > 0$.

Name	Dimension	Description
X	(npd, nx)	A tentative policy for all periods, to be read in *row-wise*. This policy will be used to compute the tentative path y_t by Gauss-Siedel.
Y	(ny)	A trial solution of the y vector for the first period, to be used in the first iteration of the Gauss-Siedel solution for period 1; this vector may take the same value as Y0.
GAMVAR	(n)	A vector whose elements are the row/column numbers of Γ_t to be printed; required only if GAMMA $= n$, where $2 \leq n \leq ns + nx$ and is the dimension of GAMVAR.

5.5.4   Construction of IDENTVEC and VARBLVEC

The use of IDENTVEC and VARBLVEC is discussed in Section 4. Before constructing IDENTVEC, the user must first eliminate all higher-order lags in the nonlinear model by adding identities of lagged values to the model, as discussed in Section 1. To illustrate, we will use the example from Section 1. In this example the model has 50 simultaneous structural equations, 50 identities of lagged values, and four control variables; that is, $ns = 50$, $nid = 50$, $ny = ns + nid = 100$, and $nx = 4$, and the identities of lagged values are:

$$y_{51} = y_{6, t-1} \qquad\qquad 6$$

$$y_{52} = y_{51, t-1} \qquad\qquad 51$$

$$y_{53} = y_{52, t-1} \qquad\qquad 52$$

$$\vdots \qquad\qquad\qquad \vdots$$

$$y_{91} = x_{1, t-1} \qquad\qquad 101$$

$$y_{92} = y_{91, t-1} \qquad\qquad 91$$

$$y_{93} = x_{3, t-1} \qquad\qquad 103$$

$$\vdots \qquad\qquad\qquad \vdots$$

$$y_{100} = y_{99, t-1} \qquad\qquad 99$$

The numbers listed on the right are the variable numbers that will appear in IDENTVEC: for $y_{k,t-1}$ in an identity, the number listed is simply k; for $x_{k,t-1}$, the number listed is $ny + k$. The IDENTVEC for this model will look like this:

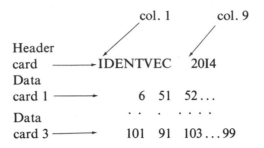

Note that the data entered are right-justified because the format is I, and that the dimension of IDENTVEC is nid, the number of identities of lagged values.

The construction of VARBLVEC is a bit more involved, but the user should not have too much trouble if the steps listed are followed:

1   List the integers from 1 to $ns + p + ns$. In our example from Section 1, the numbers would be from 1 to 158.

2   Above this list of numbers write the following variables in order, with one variable corresponding to one number:

$$y_{1,t}, \ldots, y_{ns,t}$$

$$y_{1,t-1}, \ldots, y_{ny,t-1}, x_{1,t-1}, \ldots, x_{nx,t-1}$$

$$x_{1,t}, \ldots, x_{nx,t}.$$

In our example, we would have:

$$\begin{array}{ccccc} y_{1t} & y_{2t} & \cdots & y_{50,t} \\[4pt] 1 & 2 & \ldots & 50 \end{array}$$

$$\begin{array}{cccccc} y_{1,t-1} & y_{2,t-1} & \cdots & y_{100,t-1}, x_{1,t-1}, \ldots, x_{4,t-1} \\[4pt] 51 & 52 & \ldots & 150 \qquad 151 \quad \ldots \quad 154 \end{array}$$

$$\begin{array}{ccc} x_{1t} & \cdots & x_{4t} \\[4pt] 155 & \ldots & 158 \end{array}$$

3 Look through the right-hand side of each structural equation of the model. Whenever one of the variables listed in step 2 appears, circle the number underneath the variable in the list. In our example, we might obtain

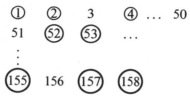

Any number in the list not circled means the variable above it appears *nowhere* in the right-hand side of the structural equations; any variable of the list in step 2 that appears *somewhere* in the right-hand side of the structural equations should have its corresponding number circled. In our example, $y_{3t}, y_{50t}, y_{1,t-1}, x_{2,t}$ are some of the variables not in the structural model.

4 VARBLVEC is simply the list of integers from step 2, with the uncircled numbers replaced by 0; thus VARBLVEC has $ns + p + nx$ entries. In our example, VARBLVEC would look like this:

	col. 1	col. 9			col. 40
Header card	VARBLVEC	10I4			
Data card 1	1	2	0	4 ...	... ...
Data card 5	...	...	...	0	
Data card 6	0	52	53		... ...
Data card 16	...	...	... 155	0	157	158

It is vitally important that IDENTVEC and VARBLVEC be constructed correctly because the program depends on them to calculate the optimal solution y_t. If the econometric model is not very large or the saving of computer space and time is not essential, the user may simply fill in the vector VARBLVEC with all nonzero elements.

5.6   SPACE REQUIREMENTS

5.6.1   The Dimension of MAINAR

The program parcels out all its work space from the array MAINAR. Because the amount of work space depends entirely on the size of the model and the number of periods in the plan, the dimension of MAINAR is provided by the user in the main program. Following is a formula for calculating the dimension, NDIM, of MAINAR, assuming OFDIAV = F and OFDIAG = F:

$$
\text{NDIM} = 100 + 2 \times \left\{ \begin{array}{l} 5p + 2ns + ns(p + nx) + nx + nx^2 + nid \\ + p^*(nx + 1 + nxp) + 2p^{*2} - p^*(p^* - 1) \\ + npd(3p + nw) + 1 \end{array} \right\}
$$

where

$$p = ny + nx = ns + nid + nx$$
ns = number of structural equations in MODELS
nx = number of control variables
nid = number of identities in MODELI
npd = number of periods
nw = number of exogenous variables
$nxp = \max(2, nx) - 1$
p^* = dimension of the "compressed" model which
     is discussed in Section 3
   = number of entries in TABL3, as printed.

The user may find it difficult to determine p^*. p^* should take the same value as p in the very first time the model is run, which will produce a print-out of TABL3; the number of entries of TABL3 (always $\leq p$) can then be used for the value of p^* in the later runs of the model.

Add to the expression within the brackets the following:

$$(ns^2 - ns)/2 \qquad \text{if OFDIAV} = \text{T, and}$$

$$(p^2 - p)/2 \qquad \text{if OFDIAG} = \text{T.}$$

5.6.2   Region Size

The region (or core) size needed to execute the optimal control program is determined by the following factors:

1   Size of the optimal control program $\approx$ 146K.
2   Size of I/O buffers $\approx$ 16K.
3   Size of MODELS and MODELI subroutines = MOD("bytes").
4   Dimension of MAINAR = NDIM("words").

The formula to obtain the value for the REG parameter is

$$REG = \left(\frac{4 \times NDIM + MOD}{1024} + 146 + 16 \right) K.$$

To obtain MOD in bytes, the user should first compile MODELS and MODELI (to debug coding errors as well as to determine the size), and the size of each subroutine can be found at the end of its compilation listing, printed after the words "PROGRAM SIZE."

5.7   THE USE OF TWO OR MORE JOB RUNS

Figure 2 is a schematic diagram showing the input and output of the optimal control program and the relationship between two continuous job runs. Recall from Section 2 that if a model requires a large number of iterations in the optimal control calculation before the optimal solution path y_t is reached, the user may break up the iterating process into two or more job runs. At the end of the first job run, where NROUND = 1 and assuming ITERL1 = 3, the program writes the solution path y_t and x_t obtained from the third iteration onto the data set INOUT2. If the printed output from this job shows that the solution path y_t obtained from the third iteration did not converge, the user may then continue the iterating process by feeding into the program the same input deck with one change—setting NROUND = 2. The program will read y_t and x_t from INOUT2 and use them as the tentative path for the fourth iteration. A third or a fourth job run may be required before the solution path y_t will converge. One may of course obtain the optimal solution y_t in one job run by setting ITERL1 (and the estimated computer time) to a high value, because the program will not terminate until the solution path converges or until the iteration limit is reached (see Figure 1). However, the user is recommended to break up a possibly long iterating process into several job runs, each with a small iteration limit ITERL1. The advantage is that the user may examine the

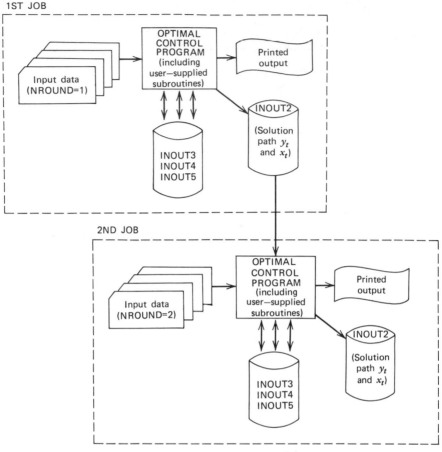

Figure 2. Job diagram showing two job runs.

printed output at the end of each small job, to determine if any parameter, such as DAMPX, should be changed to speed up the convergence or to generate more efficient runs; whereas by giving a high value to ITERL1 the user may look at a printed output only after a lot of computer time has been used, and possibly wasted.

During the first few times that a model is run, many of the input parameters such as ITERL2, EPS1, EPS2, and DAMPX are probably given values on the basis of trial and error. It then makes sense to keep these runs small in order to determine what better values to give these parameters without wasting too much computer time. Moreover, the coding of MODELS and MODELI and the construction of the vectors IDENTVEC and VARBLVEC are subject to errors that can be very easily committed. By setting GAUSS = 2, the user terminates the program immediately after the Gauss-Siedel solution for y_t is obtained, printed, and saved on INOUT2, and he/she may then decide what might be wrong with the model subroutines or with the input data. A good set of Gauss-Siedel solutions can be used as the tentative path for the first iteration in a later run, with NROUND = 2. By running small jobs one does not lose except possibly a small amount of labor.

5.8 OUTPUT AND ERROR MESSAGES

The program prints the following on SYSOUT = A for each job:

1 A list of the &DIMENS and &OPT NAMELIST options, including the default values if they have not been overridden.

2 All the input matrices in the order they are read in.

3 If GAUSS = 1 or 2, the values of the Gauss-Siedel solution for y_t used for the first linearization of the model.

4 The A, b, C, G, g, h, H matrices, starting with the last period. Their frequency of print-out from period to period depends on the value of the OSUP parameter (see Section 5.2).

5 The values of the optimal solution y_t.

6 Total welfare cost and its deterministic and stochastic components.

7 If the convergence criterion EPS1 is met before the number of iterations becomes greater than ITERL1, a plot of the values of the optimal solution y_t against the target values z_t. Whether all of the y_t variables or only those that have nonzero weights in the diagonal of the K matrix are plotted depends on the value of the PLOT parameter (see Section 5.2). The control variables x_t are always plotted against their targets.

8 TABL1 and TABL3. The only useful information these two tables give to the user is the number of entries in TABL3, which should be used as the value for p^*.

9 The Γ_t matrices if GAMMA > 0. If GAMMA = 1, the rows of Γ_t corresponding to those elements targetted in K are printed; if GAMMA $\geq$ 2, the input vector GAMVAR controls the printing of Γ_t.

The following is a list of messages that may be printed in SYSOUT = A:

"PROGRAM TERMINATING BECAUSE GAUSS-SIEDEL FAILED TO CONVERGE FOR VARIABLE I, PERIOD T, IN K ITERATIONS"

—In calculating the Gauss-Siedel solution for y_t, if any variable $y_{i,t}$ does not converge after ITERL2 iterations, this message appears and the program terminates with a condition code of 29.

"PROGRAM TERMINATING BECAUSE OPTIMAL SOLUTION FAILED TO CONVERGE IN K ITERATIONS, ROUND NO. N"—If the optimal solution y_t does not converge after ITERL1 iterations, this message appears and the program terminates with a condition code of 29. In addition, the optimal solution y_t and x_t are saved on the output device assigned by INOUT2 of the main program (see Section 5.2).

"STORAGE ALLOCATION TO THIS POINT = XXXX WORDS OUT OF YYYY (ZZK UNUSED)"—This message appears throughout the printed output, the user may reduce the value of NDIM in the main program accordingly.

"***INSUFFICIENT MEMORY AREA TO ALLOCATE WORK ARRAYS, XXXX WORDS ALLOCATED TO STORAGE BY MAIN PROGRAM, YYYY WORDS REQUIRED SO FAR, INCLUDING THE FOLLOWING ZZZZ WORDS CURRENTLY REQUESTED AT THE POINT INDICATED BELOW"—A trace table follows this message showing the subroutine that led to it. The program will continue and allocates more space when required but will eventually terminate after messages like the one following are printed.

"STORAGE ALLOCATION TO THIS POINT = XXXX WORDS OUT OF YYYY (ZZK REQUIRED)"—When several messages of this type appear before the program terminates, the user should set NDIM in the main program equal to the greatest value of XXXX in these messages for the next job.

"LOOKING FOR 'AAAA' DATA, FOUND THE FOLLOWING: ..."

"LOOKING FOR 'AAAA' DATA, FOUND END-OF-FILE"

"END-OF-FILE WHILE READING DATA FOR 'AAAA'"—These messages appear when the user fails to suppy enough data for the matrix named AAAA or when the entire matrix has been omitted from the input deck. The program terminates with a condition code of 130, 131, or 132.

5.9   JCL REQUIREMENTS

The JCL given in this section applies only to the IBM 360 or 370 computers. Users of other computers must make up their own JCL to run the program and to assign device units for the four sequential data sets used by the program INOUT2, INOUT3, INOUT4, and INOUT5; these data sets are described in Section 4.

Suppose the nonlinear optimal control program (excluding the three user-supplied subroutines) has been compiled and linked-edited to a load module named OPTCN as a member of a catalogued partitioned data set named OPTLIB, then the following JCL may be used to compile and link-edit the user-supplied subroutines, link them with OPTCN and execute the program:

```
// __ EXEC __ FORTGCLG
//FORT.SYSIN __ DD __ *
  ┌ Main Program ┐
  │ MODELS       │
  └ MODELI       ┘
//LKED.SYSLIB __ DD __ DSN = OPTLIB,DISP = SHR
//             DD __ DSN = SYS1.FORTLIB,DISP = SHR
//LKED.SYSIN __ DD __ *
__ INCLUDE __ SYSLIB(OPTCN)
__ ENTRY __ MAIN
//GO.FTOn2F001 __ DD __ DSN = INOUT2,DISP = (NEW,KEEP),
//            UNIT = xxxx,VOL = SER = nnnnnn,
//            DCB = (RECFM = VS,BLKSIZE = 1608),
//            SPACE = (CYL,(2,1))
//GO.FTOn3F001 __ DD __ UNIT = xxxx,VOL = SER = nnnnnn,
//            DCB = (RECFM = VS,BLKSIZE = 1608),
//            SPACE = (CYL,(5,4))
//GO.FTOn4F001 __ DD __ UNIT = xxxx,VOL = SER = nnnnnn,
//            DCB = (RECFM = VS,BLKSIZE = 1608),
//            SPACE = (CYL,(2,1))
//GO.FTOn5F001 __ DD __ UNIT = xxxx,VOL = SER = nnnnnn,
//            DCB = (RECFM = VS,BLKSIZE = 1608),
//            SPACE = (CYL,(5,4))
//GO.SYSIN __ DD __ *
     [Input data]
//
```

Of the four disk data sets, only one, FTOn2F001, is a nontemporary data set; in this data set the program stores the solution path y_t from each job run. DISP = (NEW,KEEP) is used for the first job run with NROUND = 1, and it should be replaced with DISP = OLD in the jobs with NROUND ≥ 2.

The digits $n2$, $n3$, $n4$, and $n5$ in the ddnames should correspond to the same numbers in the main program provided by the user, where INOUT2 = $n2$, INOUT3 = $n3$, INOUT4 = $n4$ and INOUT5 = $n5$. (See Section 4.1). All four data sets are created by unformatted WRITE statements; therefore they must have RECFM = V or VS. Their SPACE parameters may take different values depending on the model. Tape units may replace disk units for these data sets. If GAMMA = 0, the last DD statement, with ddname FTOn5F001, can be eliminated, because no intermediate output associated with computing the Γ_t matrices will be written by the program.

The user might wish to compile the user-supplied model subroutines separately and save the load modules in the same partitioned data set as the one containing the optimal control program (OPTLIB in our JCL example). Suppose MODELS and MODELI are link-edited together as a member named MODELA in OPTLIB, then the following changes should be made in the JCL:

1 Delete the MODELS and MODELI source statements that had been placed after the //FORT.SYSIN ___ DD ___ * card.

2 Replace the INCLUDE card with ___ INCLUDE ___ SYSLIB(OPTCN,MODELA).

CHAPTER 6

Applications of the Kalman Filter to the Estimation of Econometric Models

6.1 INTRODUCTION

The most common application of the Kalman filter in the literature of stochastic control theory is to the estimation of the unknown state vector z_t in a linear dynamic model

$$z_t = A z_{t-1} + C u_t + b + \eta_t$$

where z_t is observed through the observation equation

$$s_t = B_t z_t + \varepsilon_t.$$

Here s_t is directly observable; u_t is a vector of control variables; and η_t and ε_t are independently distributed random vectors. An exposition of this application can be found in Chow (1975, p. 186 ff).

In the statistics literature, a common application of the Kalman filter is to the estimation of a changing coefficient vector β_t in a linear regression model

$$y_t = x_t \beta_t + \varepsilon_t \qquad (t = 1, \ldots, T) \tag{1.1}$$

where β_t is assumed to have evolved according to the relation

$$\beta_t = M \beta_{t-1} + \eta_t \qquad (t = 1, \ldots, T) \tag{1.2}$$

The dependent variable y_t is directly observable; x_t is a row vector of k fixed explanatory variables, ε_t is normally and independently distributed with mean zero and variance s^2, and η_t is k-variate normal and independent with mean zero and covariance matrix $s^2 P \equiv V$. When $V = 0$ and $M = I$, this model is reduced to the standard normal regression model. We will be concerned with the estimation of this regression model and related econometric models by Kalman filtering techniques.

Assuming tentatively that s^2, V, and M are known, one may consider the problem of estimating β_t using information I_s up to time s. Denote by $E(\beta_t | I_s) \equiv \beta_{t|s}$ the conditional expectation of β_t given I_s. The evaluation of $\beta_{t|t}$ is known as filtering. The evaluation of $\beta_{t|s}$ ($s > t$) is called smoothing, and the evaluation of $\beta_{t|s}$ ($s < t$) is a prediction problem. In Section 2, we will derive the filtered and smoothed estimates of β_t recursively for $t = 1, 2, \ldots$, by the use of a regression of $\beta_1, \ldots, \beta_t$ on $y_1, \ldots, y_s$. The basic results are due to Kalman (1960). Section 3 contains an alternative derivation of the same results using the method of Aitken's generalized least squares applied to a regression of $y_1, \ldots, y_s$ on $x_1, \ldots, x_s$ with β_t as the regression coefficient. This exposition is due to Sant (1977). We will then study the problem of estimating s^2, V, and M by the method of maximum likelihood in Section 4. In Sections 5 and 6 respectively, we treat a system of linear and nonlinear simultaneous stochastic equations with changing parameters. In Section 7, we modify (1.2) by introducing a mean vector $\bar{\beta}$, thus replacing β_t and β_{t-1} in (1.2) by $\beta_t - \bar{\beta}$ and $\beta_{t-1} - \bar{\beta}$ respectively and assuming the characteristic roots of M to be smaller than one in absolute value. When $M = 0$, a random-coefficient regression model results. In Section 8, we consider the use of Kalman filtering in estimating seasonal components of economic time series which satisfy a system of simultaneous stochastic equations.

6.2   DERIVATION OF $\beta_{t|s}$ BY RECURSIVE REGRESSION OF β_t ON $y_1, \ldots, y_s$

Consider the regression of β_t on y_t, conditioned on $y_1, \ldots, y_{t-1}$. Denote $(y_1, \ldots, y_t)$ by Y_t. The regression of interest is by definition

$$E(\beta_t | y_t, Y_{t-1}) = E(\beta_t | Y_{t-1}) + K_t [y_t - E(y_t | Y_{t-1})]. \qquad (2.1)$$

This regression is linear because β_t and Y_t are jointly normal as a consequence of the normality of ε_t and η_t in the model (1.1)–(1.2). Taking expectation of y_t from (1.1) conditioned on Y_{t-1}, we have $y_{t|t-1} \equiv$

$E(y_t|Y_{t-1}) = x_t\beta_{t|t-1}$. Equation 2.1 can be written as

$$\beta_{t|t} = \beta_{t|t-1} + K_t(y_t - x_t\beta_{t|t-1}). \tag{2.2}$$

K_t is a column vector of regression coefficients, originally derived by Kalman (1960). If this vector is known, we can use (2.2) to update our estimate $\beta_{t|t-1}$ to form $\beta_{t|t}$.

To derive K_t we apply the well-known formula for a vector of regression coefficients

$$K_t = \left[E(\beta_t - \beta_{t|t-1})(y_t - y_{t|t-1}) \right] \left[\mathrm{Cov}(y_t|Y_{t-1}) \right]^{-1}. \tag{2.3}$$

Denoting the covariance matrix $\mathrm{Cov}(\beta_t|Y_{t-1})$ by $\Sigma_{t|t-1}$ and using

$$y_t - y_{t|t-1} = x_t(\beta_t - \beta_{t|t-1}) + \varepsilon_t,$$

we can write (2.3) as

$$K_t = \Sigma_{t|t-1} x_t' \left[x_t \Sigma_{t|t-1} x_t' + s^2 \right]^{-1}. \tag{2.4}$$

$\Sigma_{t|t-1}$ can be computed recursively as follows. First, by evaluating the covariance matrix of each side of (1.2) conditioned on Y_{t-1}, we obtain

$$\Sigma_{t|t-1} = M\Sigma_{t-1|t-1}M' + V. \tag{2.5}$$

Second, using (2.2) and (1.1) we write

$$\beta_t - \beta_{t|t} = \beta_t - \beta_{t|t-1} - K_t\left[x_t(\beta_t - \beta_{t|t-1}) + \varepsilon_t \right]. \tag{2.6}$$

Taking the expectation of the product of (2.6) and its transpose and using (2.4), we obtain

$$\Sigma_{t|t} = \Sigma_{t|t-1} - K_t\left(x_t\Sigma_{t|t-1}x_t' + s^2 \right)K_t'$$

$$= \Sigma_{t|t-1} - \Sigma_{t|t-1}x_t'\left(x_t\Sigma_{t|t-1}x_t' + s^2 \right)^{-1}x_t\Sigma_{t|t-1}. \tag{2.7}$$

(2.5) and (2.7) can be used to compute $\Sigma_{t|t}$ ($t = 1, 2, \ldots$) successively given $\Sigma_{0|0}$, without using the observations y_t ($t = 1, 2, \ldots$). Having computed $\Sigma_{t|t-1}$, we can use (2.4) to compute K_t and (2.2) to compute $\beta_{t|t}$ where, on account of (1.2),

$$\beta_{t|t-1} = M\beta_{t-1|t-1}. \tag{2.8}$$

Thus $\beta_{t|t}$ can be computed from $\beta_{t-1|t-1}$ using (2.8) and (2.2). The estimates $\beta_{t|t}$ so obtained are known as estimates by the Kalman filter.

In order to utilize future observations $y_{t+1}, y_{t+2}, \ldots, y_{t+n}$ for the estimation of β_t, we first consider the regression of β_t on y_{t+1}, conditioned on Y_t. Analogous to (2.2) and (2.3) are

$$\beta_{t|t+1} = \beta_{t|t} + D_{t|t+1}(y_{t+1} - y_{t+1|t}) \tag{2.9}$$

and

$$D_{t|t+1} = \left[E(\beta_t - \beta_{t|t})(y_{t+1} - y_{t+1|t})' \right] \left[\mathrm{Cov}(y_{t+1}|Y_t) \right]^{-1}. \tag{2.10}$$

Using (1.1) and (1.2), we write

$$y_{t+1} - y_{t+1|t} = x_{t+1}\beta_{t+1} + \varepsilon_{t+1} - x_{t+1}\beta_{t+1|t}$$

$$= x_{t+1}M\beta_t + x_{t+1}\eta_{t+1} + \varepsilon_{t+1} - x_{t+1}M\beta_{t|t},$$

which, in conjunction with (2.10), implies

$$D_{t|t+1} = \Sigma_{t|t}M'x'_{t+1}\left(x_{t+1}\Sigma_{t+1|t}x'_{t+1} + s^2 \right)^{-1}$$

$$= \Sigma_{t|t}M'\Sigma_{t+1|t}^{-1}K_{t+1}. \tag{2.11}$$

Equations 2.9 and 2.11 can be used to evaluate $\beta_{t|t+1}$. With the aid of (2.11) and (2.2), (2.9) can be rewritten as

$$\beta_{t|t+1} = \beta_{t|t} + \Sigma_{t|t}M'\Sigma_{t+1|t}^{-1}(\beta_{t+1|t+1} - \beta_{t+1|t}). \tag{2.12}$$

The smoothing formula (2.12) will be generalized to

$$\beta_{t|t+n} = \beta_{t|t+n-1} + H_t(\beta_{t+1|t+n} - \beta_{t+1|t+n-1}), \tag{2.13}$$

where $H_t \equiv \Sigma_{t|t}M'\Sigma_{t+1|t}^{-1}$. We will prove (2.13) by induction. Equation 2.13 was proved for $n = 1$. We next assume (2.13) to hold for $n - 1$, implying

$$\beta_{t|t+n-1} = \beta_{t|t+n-2} + H_t(\beta_{t+1|t+n-1} - \beta_{t+1|t+n-2})$$

$$= \beta_{t|t+n-2} + H_t H_{t+1}(\beta_{t+2|t+n-1} - \beta_{t+2|t+n-2})$$

$$= \beta_{t|t+n-2} + H_t H_{t+1} \ldots H_{t+n-2}(\beta_{t+n-1|t+n-1} - \beta_{t+n-1|t+n-2})$$

$$= \beta_{t|t+n-2} + H_t H_{t+1} \ldots H_{t+n-2}K_{t+n-1}(y_{t+n-1} - y_{t+n-1|t+n-2}).$$

$$\tag{2.14}$$

Consider the regression of β_t on y_{t+n-1}, conditioned on Y_{t+n-2}. Analogous to (2.9) and (2.10) are

$$\beta_{t|t+n-1} = \beta_{t|t+n-2} + D_{t|t+n-1}(y_{t+n-1} - y_{t+n-1|t+n-2}) \qquad (2.15)$$

and

$$D_{t|t+n-1} = \left[E(\beta_t - \beta_{t|t+n-2})(y_{t+n-1} - y_{t+n-1|t+n-2})' \right]$$

$$\times \left[\text{Cov}(y_{t+n-1}|Y_{t+n-2}) \right]^{-1}$$

$$= H_t H_{t+1} \ldots H_{t+n-2} K_{t+n-1}, \qquad (2.16)$$

where the last equality sign results from comparing (2.14) and (2.15). Equation 2.16 implies

$$E(\beta_t - \beta_{t|t+n-2})(y_{t+n-1} - y_{t+n-1|t+n-2})'$$

$$= E(\beta_t - \beta_{t|t+n-2})(\beta_{t+n-1} - \beta_{t+n-1|t+n-2})' x'_{t+n-1}$$

$$= H_t H_{t+1} \ldots H_{t+n-2} K_{t+n-1} \left(x_{t+n-1} \Sigma_{t+n-1|t+n-2} x'_{t+n-1} + s^2 \right)$$

$$= H_t H_{t+1} \ldots H_{t+n-2} \Sigma_{t+n-1|t+n-2} x'_{t+n-1}, \qquad (2.17)$$

where (2.4) has been used.

To proceed with our proof, we find the regression of β_t on y_{t+n}, conditioned on Y_{t+n-1},

$$\beta_{t|t+n} = \beta_{t|t+n-1} + D_{t|t+n}(y_{t+n} - y_{t+n|t+n-1}). \qquad (2.18)$$

To evaluate the vector of regression coefficients $D_{t|t+n}$ we write, using (2.15),

$$\beta_t - \beta_{t|t+n-1} = \beta_t - \beta_{t|t+n-2} - D_{t|t+n-1}(y_{t+n-1} - y_{t+n-1|t+n-2})$$

$$= \beta_t - \beta_{t|t+n-2} - D_{t|t+n-1}\left[x_{t+n-1}(\beta_{t+n-1} - \beta_{t+n-1|t+n-2}) + \varepsilon_{t+n-1} \right],$$

$$(2.19)$$

and using (2.2),

$$y_{t+n} - y_{t+n|t+n-1} = x_{t+n} M(\beta_{t+n-1} - \beta_{t+n-1|t+n-1}) + x_{t+n}\eta_{t+n} + \varepsilon_{t+n}$$

$$= x_{t+n} M \left[\beta_{t+n-1} - \beta_{t+n-1|t+n-2} - K_{t+n-1}(y_{t+n-1} - y_{t+n-1|t+n-2}) \right]$$

$$+ x_{t+n}\eta_{t+n} + \varepsilon_{t+n}$$

$$= x_{t+n} M \left[(I - K_{t+n-1} x_{t+n-1})(\beta_{t+n-1} - \beta_{t+n-1|t+n-2}) - K_{t+n-1}\varepsilon_{t+n-1} \right]$$

$$+ x_{t+n}\eta_{t+n} + \varepsilon_{t+n}. \tag{2.20}$$

Equations 2.19 and 2.20 imply

$$E(\beta_t - \beta_{t|t+n-1})(y_{t+n} - y_{t+n|t+n-1})'$$

$$= E(\beta_t - \beta_{t|t+n-2})(\beta_{t+n-1} - \beta_{t+n-1|t+n-2})'(I - x'_{t+n-1} K'_{t+n-1}) M' x'_{t+n}$$

$$- D_{t|t+n-1} \left[x_{t+n-1}\Sigma_{t+n-1|t+n-2}(I - x'_{t+n-1} K'_{t+n-1}) - s^2 K'_{t+n-1} \right] M' x'_{t+1}$$

$$= H_t H_{t+1} \dots H_{t+n-2}\Sigma_{t+n-1|t+n-1} M' x'_{t+n}$$

$$= H_t H_{t+1} \dots H_{t+n-1} K_{t+n}\left(x_{t+n}\Sigma_{t+n|t+n-1} x'_{t+n} + s^2 \right), \tag{2.21}$$

where the second equality sign results from using (2.16), (2.17), and (2.7), and the third equality sign is due to (2.4). Hence, the regression coefficient is

$$D_{t|t+n} = \left[E(\beta_t - \beta_{t|t+n-1})(y_{t+n} - y_{t+n|t+n-1})' \right] \text{Cov}(y_{t+n}|Y_{t+n-1})]^{-1}$$

$$= H_t H_{t+1} \dots H_{t+n-1} K_{t+n}, \tag{2.22}$$

which generalizes the coefficient given by (2.16). Substituting (2.22) into (2.18) yields

$$\beta_{t|t+n} = \beta_{t|t+n-1} + H_t H_{t+1} \dots H_{t+n-1}(\beta_{t+n|t+n} - \beta_{t+n|t+n-1})$$

$$= \beta_{t|t+n-1} + H_t(\beta_{t+1|t+n} - \beta_{t+1|t+n-1}), \tag{2.23}$$

where the last step is due to the third equality sign of (2.14) with t replaced by $t + 1$. Equation 2.23 completes the proof. (2.18) and (2.23) together provide three alternative formulas to evaluate $\beta_{t|t+n}$.

To derive the covariance matrix $\Sigma_{t|t+n}$, we use (2.18) and (2.21),

$$\Sigma_{t|t+n} = E(\beta_t - \beta_{t|t+n})(\beta_t - \beta_{t|t+n})'$$

$$= E\big[\beta_t - \beta_{t|t+n-1} - D_{t|t+n}(y_{t+n} - y_{t+n|t+n-1})\big]$$

$$\times \big[\beta_t - \beta_{t|t+n-1} - D_{t|t+n}(y_{t+n} - y_{t+n|t+n-1})\big]$$

$$= \Sigma_{t|t+n-1} - D_{t|t+n}\big(x_{t+n}\Sigma_{t+n|t+n-1}x'_{t+n} + s^2\big)D'_{t|t+n}. \quad (2.24)$$

By (2.22), (2.4), and (2.7), the formula (2.24) can be written alternatively

$$\Sigma_{t|t+n} = \Sigma_{t|t+n-1} - H_t \ldots H_{t+n-1}K_{t+n}$$

$$\times \big(x_{t+n}\Sigma_{t+n|t+n-1}x'_{t+n} + s^2\big)K'_{t+n}H'_{t+n-1}\ldots H'_t$$

$$= \Sigma_{t|t+n-1} - H_t \ldots H_{t+n-1}\Sigma_{t+n|t+n-1}x'_{t+n}\big(x_{t+n}\Sigma_{t+n|t+n-1}x'_{t+n} + s^2\big)^{-1}x_{t+n}$$

$$\times \Sigma_{t+n|t+n-1}H'_{t+n-1}\ldots H'_t$$

$$= \Sigma_{t|t+n-1} + H_t \ldots H_{t+n-1}\big(\Sigma_{t+n|t+n} - \Sigma_{t+n|t+n-1}\big)H'_{t+n-1}\ldots H'_t. \quad (2.25)$$

Equations 2.24 and 2.25 provide the covariance matrix of the smoothed estimate $\beta_{t|t+n}$ of β_t given the data up to $t + n$. The estimates $\beta_{t|s}$ and $\Sigma_{t|s}$ of this section require knowledge not only of the parameters s^2, V, and M, but also of the initial values $\beta_{0|0}$ and $\Sigma_{0|0}$ at time 0.

6.3   DERIVATIONS OF $\beta_{t|s}$ BY REGRESSION OF $y_1,\ldots,y_s$ ON $x_1,\ldots,x_s$

Econometricians might find it more appealing to view $\beta_{t|s}$ as a coefficient vector in the regression of $y_1,\ldots,y_s$ on $x_1,\ldots,x_s$. This interpretation was given by Sant (1977) as follows. Applying (1.2) repeatedly, we have

$$\beta_t = M\beta_{t-1} + \eta_t = M^2\beta_{t-2} + \eta_t + M\eta_{t-1}$$

$$= M^{t-1}\beta_1 + M^{t-2}\eta_2 + \cdots + M\eta_{t-1} + \eta_t,$$

which can be used to express $\beta_1,\ldots,\beta_{t-1}$ as functions of β_t, provided M^{-1}

exists. The observations $y_1, \ldots, y_t$ from (1.1) thus become

$$
\begin{bmatrix} y_1 \\ y_2 \\ \vdots \\ y_{t-1} \\ y_t \end{bmatrix} = \begin{bmatrix} x_1 M^{-t+1} \\ x_2 M^{-t+2} \\ \vdots \\ x_{t-1} M^{-1} \\ x_t \end{bmatrix} \beta_t + \begin{bmatrix} \varepsilon_1 \\ \varepsilon_2 \\ \vdots \\ \varepsilon_{t-1} \\ \varepsilon_t \end{bmatrix}
$$

$$
- \begin{bmatrix} x_1 M^{-1} & x_1 M^{-2} & \cdots & x_1 M^{-t+1} \\ 0 & x_2 M^{-1} & \cdots & x_2 M^{-t+2} \\ \vdots & \vdots & \ddots & \\ 0 & 0 & \cdots & x_{t-1} M^{-1} \\ 0 & 0 & \cdots & 0 \end{bmatrix} \begin{bmatrix} \eta_2 \\ \eta_3 \\ \vdots \\ \eta_{t-1} \\ \eta_t \end{bmatrix}. \quad (3.1)
$$

The filtered estimate $\beta_{t|t}$ is equivalent to the estimate of β_t in the regression model (3.1) by Aitken's generalized least squares. The covariance matrix of the residuals in this regression is $s^2[I_t + A_t(I_{t-1} \otimes P)A'_t]$, where $s^2 P = \mathrm{Cov}\,\eta_i$ and A_t is the coefficient of $(\eta'_2 \quad \eta'_3 \quad \cdots \quad \eta'_t)'$ in (3.1).

Similarly, $\beta_{t+s} = M^s \beta_t + M^{s-1} \eta_{t+1} + \cdots + M \eta_{t+s-1} + \eta_{t+s}$ is a function of β_t and observations on y_{t+s} $(s = 1, \ldots, n)$ can be used to form a regression model with β_t as the coefficient.

$$
\begin{bmatrix} y_{t+1} \\ y_{t+2} \\ \vdots \\ y_{t+n} \end{bmatrix} = \begin{bmatrix} x_{t+1} M \\ x_{t+2} M^2 \\ \vdots \\ x_{t+n} M^n \end{bmatrix} \beta_t
$$

$$
+ \begin{bmatrix} \varepsilon_{t+1} \\ \varepsilon_{t+2} \\ \vdots \\ \varepsilon_{t+n} \end{bmatrix} - \begin{bmatrix} x_{t+1} & 0 & \cdots & 0 \\ x_{t+2} M & x_{t+2} & \cdots & 0 \\ \vdots & & \ddots & \\ x_{t+n} M^{n-1} & x_{t+n} M^{n-2} & \cdots & x_{t+n} \end{bmatrix} \begin{bmatrix} \eta_{t+1} \\ \eta_{t+2} \\ \vdots \\ \eta_{t+n} \end{bmatrix}.
$$

$$
(3.2)
$$

The smoothed estimate $\beta_{t|t+n}$ is equivalent to the estimate of β_t in a regression model combining (3.1) and (3.2) by Aitken's generalized least squares.

A by-product of this interpretation should be noted. Whereas the recursive method of Section 2 requires the initial values $\beta_{0|0}$ and $\Sigma_{0|0}$, the GLS method of this section provides estimates of $\beta_{k|k}$ and $\Sigma_{k|k}$ by using the first k observations, β_t being a vector of k elements. Applying GLS to (3.1) for $t = k$, one obtains

$$\Sigma_{k|k} = s^2 \left\{ \left[M'^{-k+1}x_1' \quad M'^{-k+2}x_2' \quad \cdots \quad x_k' \right] \right.$$

$$\times \left[I_k + A_k(I_{k-1} \otimes P)A_k' \right]^{-1} \left. \begin{bmatrix} x_1 M^{-k+1} \\ x_2 M^{-k+2} \\ \vdots \\ x_k \end{bmatrix} \right\}^{-1} \tag{3.3}$$

and

$$\beta_{k|k} = s^{-2}\Sigma_{k|k} \left[M'^{-k+1}x_1' \quad M'^{-k+2}x_2' \quad \cdots \quad x_k' \right]$$

$$\times \left[I_k + A_k(I_{k+1} \otimes P)A_k' \right]^{-1} \begin{bmatrix} y_1 \\ \vdots \\ y_k \end{bmatrix}. \tag{3.4}$$

These estimates are functions of s^2, $P = s^{-2}V$, and M.

6.4 MAXIMUM LIKELIHOOD ESTIMATION OF s^2, V, AND M

To form the likelihood function, we note that

$$y_t - y_{t|t-1} = x_t(\beta_t - \beta_{t|t-1}) + \varepsilon_t = y_t - x_t\beta_{t|t-1}$$

is normal and serially uncorrelated. $\beta_t - \beta_{t|t-1}$ is the residual in the regression of β_t on $y_{t-1}, y_{t-2}, \ldots,$ and is therefore uncorrelated with $y_{t-1} - y_{t-1|t-2}$. The log-likelihood function based on observations $(y_1, \ldots, y_T)$ is

$$\log L = \text{const} - \frac{1}{2} \sum_{t=k+1}^{T} \log\left(x_t \Sigma_{t|t-1} x_t' + s^2\right)$$

$$- \frac{1}{2} \sum_{t=k+1}^{T} \frac{(y_t - x_t \beta_{t|t-1})^2}{(x_t \Sigma_{t|t-1} x_t' + s^2)}.$$

The first k observations are used to compute $\beta_{k|k}$ and $\Sigma_{k|k}$ by (3.3) and (3.4) as functions of s^2, V, and M. Hence the data $\beta_{t|t-1}$ and $\Sigma_{t|t-1}$ $(t = k + 1, \ldots, T)$ required to evaluate $\log L$ are functions of s^2, V, and M, as given by the Kalman filtering equations (2.5), (2.7), (2.8), (2.2), and (2.4).

To maximize $\log L$ with respect to s^2, we define $P \equiv s^{-2}V$, $R_t \equiv s^{-2}\Sigma_{t|t-1}$, and $u_t \equiv (y_t - x_t \beta_{t|t-1})/(x_t R_t x_t' + 1)^{1/2}$. The log-likelihood function can be rewritten as

$$\log L = \text{const} - \tfrac{1}{2}(T - k)\log s^2 - \frac{1}{2} \sum_{t=k+1}^{T} \log(x_t R_t x_t' + 1) - \frac{1}{2s^2} \sum_{t=1}^{T} u_t^2.$$

$$(4.1)$$

On maximizing (4.1) with respect to s^2, we obtain

$$\hat{s}^2 = \frac{1}{T - k} \sum_{t=k+1}^{T} u_t^2. \tag{4.2}$$

The concentrated likelihood function, after the elimination of s^2, is

$$\log L^* = \text{const} - \tfrac{1}{2}(T - k)\log\left[\sum_{t=k+1}^{T} \frac{(y_t - x_t \beta_{t|t-1})^2}{x_t R_t x_t' + 1} \right]$$

$$- \frac{1}{2} \sum_{t=k+1}^{T} \log(x_t R_t x_t' + 1), \tag{4.3}$$

where, by (2.5) and (2.7),

$$R_t = MR_{t-1}\left[I - x_{t-1}'(x_{t-1}R_{t-1}x_{t-1}' + 1)^{-1}x_{t-1}R_{t-1} \right]M' + P$$

$$(t = k + 2, \ldots, T), \quad (4.4)$$

and, by (2.8), (2.2), and (2.4),

$$\beta_{t|t-1} = M\left[\beta_{t-1|t-2} + R_{t-1}x'_{t-1}(x_{t-1}R_{t-1}x'_{t-1} + 1)^{-1}\right.$$

$$\left.(y_{t-1} - x_{t-1}\beta_{t-1|t-2})\right] \qquad (t = k+2, \ldots, T). \quad (4.5)$$

The initial conditions are

$$R_{k+1} = s^{-2}M\Sigma_{k|k}M' + P \qquad (4.6)$$

and

$$\beta_{k+1|k} = M\beta_{k|k} \qquad (4.7)$$

with $\Sigma_{k|k}$ and $\beta_{k|k}$ given by (3.3) and (3.4). One would have to rely on a numerical method to maximize (4.3) with respect to the unknown parameters in P and M, P being symmetric, positive semidefinite. Garbade (1977) gives an example.

An alternative approach to maximum likelihood estimation is to employ the normal regression model (3.1) for $t = T$, that is

$$y = Z\beta + \varepsilon - A\eta \qquad (4.8)$$

where

$$y = \begin{bmatrix} y_1 \\ y_2 \\ \vdots \\ y_T \end{bmatrix} \qquad Z = \begin{bmatrix} x_1 M^{-T+1} \\ x_2 M^{T+2} \\ \vdots \\ x_T \end{bmatrix} \qquad \varepsilon = \begin{bmatrix} \varepsilon_1 \\ \varepsilon_2 \\ \vdots \\ \varepsilon_T \end{bmatrix} \qquad \eta = \begin{bmatrix} \eta_2 \\ \eta_3 \\ \vdots \\ \eta_T \end{bmatrix},$$

$\beta = \beta_T$ and $A = A_T$ as defined by the last coefficient matrix of (3.1) for $t = T$. The log-likelihood function of this model is

$$\log L = \text{const} - \tfrac{1}{2}\log|s^2 I_T| - \tfrac{1}{2}\log|Q| - \tfrac{1}{2}(y - Z\beta)'Q^{-1}(y - Z\beta)/s^2$$

$$(4.9)$$

where

$$Q = I_T + A(I_{T-1} \otimes P)A'. \qquad (4.10)$$

Maximization of (4.9) with respect to s^2 yields

$$\hat{s}^2 = \frac{1}{T}(y - Z\beta)'Q^{-1}(y - Z\beta). \qquad (4.11)$$

Maximization of (4.9) with respect to β yields

$$\hat{\beta} = (Z'Q^{-1}Z)^{-1}Z'Q^{-1}y. \qquad (4.12)$$

Differentiating (4.9) with respect to the unknown elements $p_{ij} = p_{ji}$ of P, one obtains

$$\frac{\partial \log L}{\partial p_{ij}} = -\text{tr}\left(Q^{-1}\frac{\partial Q}{\partial p_{ij}}\right) - s^2(y - Z\beta)'\frac{\partial Q^{-1}}{\partial p_{ij}}(y - Z\beta) \quad (4.13)$$

To evaluate $\partial Q^{-1}/\partial p_{ij}$, we differentiate both sides of $QQ^{-1} = I$ with respect to p_{ij} to get

$$\frac{\partial Q^{-1}}{\partial p_{ij}} = -Q^{-1}\frac{\partial Q}{\partial p_{ij}}Q^{-1}. \qquad (4.14)$$

Using the definition (4.10) for Q, we have

$$\frac{\partial Q}{\partial p_{ij}} = A(I_{T-1} \otimes E_{ij})A' \qquad (4.15)$$

where E_{ij} is an elementary $k \times k$ matrix with all zero elements except the $i - j$ and $j - i$ elements which equal unity. Substituting (4.11), (4.12), (4.14), and (4.15) into (4.13) gives

$$\frac{\partial \log L}{\partial p_{ij}} = -\text{tr}\left[Q^{-1}A(I_{T-1} \otimes E_{ij})A'\right]$$

$$+ \left(\frac{1}{T}y'N'Q^{-1}y\right)^{-1} y'N'Q^{-1}A(I_{T-1} \otimes E_{ij})A'Q^{-1}Ny,$$

$$(4.16)$$

where N denotes $I - Z(Z'Q^{-1}Z)^{-1}Z'Q^{-1}$. Equation 4.16 is useful for the maximization of (4.9) when a numerical method requiring analytical first derivatives is applied. Furthermore, in econometric applications M is frequently assumed to be an identity matrix and P to be diagonal. In this important special case, the only unknown parameters in (4.9) are $p_{11} \ldots p_{kk}$.

One can start with zero as the initial value for each p_{ii} and increase its value if $\partial \log L / \partial p_{ii}$ as evaluated by (4.16) is positive.

For the general case, numerical methods can be applied to maximize (4.9) after the elimination of s^2 and β by (4.11) and (4.12), that is, $-\frac{1}{2} \log|(y'N'Q^{-1}y)Q|$, with respect to the unknown parameters in P and M.

6.5   SYSTEM OF LINEAR SIMULTANEOUS EQUATIONS

Let the tth observation of a system of m linear simultaneous equations with time-varying coefficients be written as

$$y_{\cdot t}\Gamma_t + x_{\cdot t}B_t = -\varepsilon'_{\cdot t}, \qquad (t = 1, \ldots, T), \tag{5.1}$$

where $y_{\cdot t} = (y_{1t} \cdots y_{mt})$ is a row vector of m endogenous variables; $x_{\cdot t}$ is a row vector of K exogenous variables; and the diagonal elements $\gamma_{ii,t}$ of Γ_t are normalized to be -1. The reduced form of (5.1) is

$$y_{\cdot t} = -x_{\cdot t}B_t\Gamma_t^{-1} - \varepsilon'_{\cdot t}\Gamma_t^{-1} \equiv x_{\cdot t}\Pi_t + u'_{\cdot t} \qquad (t = 1, \ldots, T), \tag{5.2}$$

where we have defined Π_t as $-B_t\Gamma_t^{-1}$ and $u'_{\cdot t}$ as $-\varepsilon'_{\cdot t}\Gamma_t^{-1}$. The jth structural equation can be written as

$$y_{jt} = y_{jt}^* \gamma_{jt} + x_{jt}^* \beta_{jt} + \varepsilon_{jt} \equiv z_{jt}^* \delta_{jt} + \varepsilon_{jt} \tag{5.3}$$

where y_{jt}^* is a row vector of endogenous variables appearing in equation j, other than y_{jt}; γ_{jt} is a column vector of unknown coefficients in equation j which is composed of selected elements from the jth column $\gamma_{\cdot jt}$ of Γ_{jt}, and similarly for x_{jt}^* and β_{jt}. We have also defined z_{jt}^* as $(y_{jt}^* \quad x_{jt}^*)$ and δ_{jt}' as $(\gamma_{jt}' \quad \beta_{jt}')$.

Corresponding to (1.1) and (1.2) are

$$\begin{bmatrix} y_{1t} \\ \vdots \\ y_{mt} \end{bmatrix} = \begin{bmatrix} z^*_{1t} & & 0 \\ & \ddots & \\ 0 & & z^*_{mt} \end{bmatrix} \begin{bmatrix} \delta_{1t} \\ \vdots \\ \delta_{mt} \end{bmatrix} + \begin{bmatrix} \varepsilon_{1t} \\ \vdots \\ \varepsilon_{mt} \end{bmatrix} \qquad (t = 1, \ldots, T) \tag{5.4}$$

$$\begin{bmatrix} \delta_{1t} \\ \vdots \\ \delta_{mt} \end{bmatrix} = \begin{bmatrix} M_1 & & 0 \\ & \ddots & \\ 0 & & M_m \end{bmatrix} \begin{bmatrix} \delta_{1,t-1} \\ \vdots \\ \delta_{m,t-1} \end{bmatrix} + \begin{bmatrix} \eta_{1t} \\ \vdots \\ \eta_{mt} \end{bmatrix} \qquad (t = 1, \ldots, T). \tag{5.5}$$

However, the techniques presented so far for the model (1.1) and (1.2) cannot be applied directly to (5.4) and (5.5) because (5.4), in contrast with (1.1), is a nonlinear function of the random coefficient vector $\delta_t' = (\delta_{1t}' \ldots \delta_{mt}')$. The y_{jt}^* component of z_{jt}^* is itself a nonlinear function of $(\gamma_{1t}' \ldots \gamma_{mt}')$ as seen from the reduced-form (5.2). In order to apply the techniques of Kalman filtering, it is proposed to approximate the right-hand side of (5.2) by a linear function of δ_t and $\varepsilon_{.t}$. This approach amounts to treating a regression problem involving a nonlinear model $y = f(x, \beta, \varepsilon)$ by approximating f by a linear function of β and ε. In the control engineering literature, the resulting estimation method is known as an extended Kalman filter.

We will linearize the right-hand side of (5.2) about $\delta_t^\circ = \delta_{t|t-1}$. Hence we will linearize Π_t about δ_t° and define

$$\Pi_t^\circ = -(B_{t|t-1})(\Gamma_{t|t-1})^{-1} = (\pi_{1t}^\circ \cdots \pi_{mt}^\circ). \tag{5.6}$$

The jth column of Π_t is $\pi_{jt} = -B_t \gamma_t^{\cdot j}$, with $\gamma_t^{\cdot j}$ denoting the jth column of Γ_t^{-1}. The linear approximation of π_{jt} is

$$\pi_{jt} \simeq \pi_{jt}^\circ + \left(\frac{\partial \pi_{jt}}{\partial \delta_t'}\right)_\circ (\delta_t - \delta_{t|t-1}), \tag{5.7}$$

where the subscript "o" indicates that the matrix $\partial \pi_{jt}/\partial \delta_t'$ is evaluated at $\delta_t^\circ = \delta_{t|t-1}$. Because

$$\frac{\partial \pi_{jt}}{\partial \gamma_{ik,t}} = -B_t \frac{\partial \gamma_t^{\cdot j}}{\partial \gamma_{ik,t}} = B_t \gamma_t^{\cdot j} \gamma_t^{kj}$$

or, with $\gamma_{\cdot k,t}$ denoting the kth column of Γ_t,

$$\frac{\partial \pi_{jt}}{\partial \gamma_{\cdot k,t}'} = B_t \Gamma_t^{-1} \gamma_t^{kj} = -\Pi_t \gamma_t^{kj} \tag{5.8}$$

and

$$\frac{\partial \pi_{jt}}{\partial \beta_{ik,t}} = -\frac{\partial B_t}{\partial \beta_{ik,t}} \gamma_t^{\cdot j} = -\begin{bmatrix} 0 \\ \vdots \\ \gamma_t^{kj} \\ \vdots \\ 0 \end{bmatrix} \quad (\gamma_t^{kj} \text{ in } i\text{th row})$$

or, with $\beta_{\cdot k, t}$ denoting the kth column of B_t,

$$\frac{\partial \pi_{jt}}{\partial \beta_{\cdot k, t}} = -I_K \gamma_t^{kj}, \tag{5.9}$$

the coefficient matrix $(\partial \pi_{jt}/\partial \delta_t')_o$ of (5.7) can be evaluated by (5.8) and (5.9) with Π_t replaced by Π_t^o and Γ_t^{-1} replaced by $\Gamma_t^{o^{-1}} = \Gamma_{t|t-1}^{-1}$. Similarly, approximating $-\varepsilon_{\cdot t}' \Gamma_t^{-1}$ by a linear function of $\varepsilon_{\cdot t}$ and $(\gamma_{1t} \ldots \gamma_{mt})$ about $\varepsilon_{\cdot t} = 0$ and $(\gamma_{1t} \ldots \gamma_{mt}) = (\gamma_{1t|t-1} \ldots \gamma_{mt|t-1})$ yields $-\varepsilon_{\cdot t}' \Gamma_{t|t-1}^{-1}$. Combining this result with (5.7) and denoting $x_{\cdot t} \pi_{jt}^o$ by y_{jt}^o, we can write the linearized version of (the transpose of) (5.2) as

$$\begin{bmatrix} y_{1t} \\ \vdots \\ y_{mt} \end{bmatrix} = \begin{bmatrix} y_{1t}^o \\ \vdots \\ y_{mt}^o \end{bmatrix} + \begin{bmatrix} x_{\cdot t}(\partial \pi_{1t}/\partial \delta_t')_o \\ \vdots \\ x_{\cdot t}(\partial \pi_{mt}/\partial \delta_t')_o \end{bmatrix} (\delta_t - \delta_{t|t-1}) - \Gamma_{t|t-1}'^{-1} \varepsilon_{\cdot t}, \tag{5.10}$$

or more compactly as

$$y_{\cdot t}' = y_{\cdot t}^o + W_t^o(\delta_t - \delta_{t|t-1}) - \Gamma_{t|t-1}'^{-1} \varepsilon_{\cdot t} \tag{5.11}$$

where the jth row of W_t^o is, by (5.8) and (5.9),

$$x_{\cdot t}\left(\frac{\partial \pi_{jt}}{\partial \delta_t'}\right) = -\left[(y_{1t}^{*o} \quad x_{1t}^*)\gamma_{t|t-1}^{1j} \ldots (y_{mt}^{*o} \quad x_{mt}^*)\gamma_{t|t-1}^{mj}\right]$$

$$= -\left[z_{1t}^{*o}\gamma_{t|t-1}^{1j} \ldots z_{mt}^{*o}\gamma_{t|t-1}^{mj}\right] \tag{5.12}$$

with y_{it}^{*o} denoting a row vector composed of those elements of $y_{\cdot t}^o = x_{\cdot t}\Pi_t^o$ which correspond to γ_{it}.

The linearized model (5.11) will replace (1.1) for the purpose of deriving filtering equations. For the model (5.11)–(5.5), the derivations are exactly the same as in Section 2, with $S = E\varepsilon_{\cdot t}\varepsilon_{\cdot t}'$, $V_i = E\eta_{it}\eta_{it}'$ $(i = 1, \ldots, m)$, and M_i $(i = 1, \ldots, m)$ treated as given. From the linear model (5.11), one finds the conditional expectation $y_{\cdot t|t-1}'$ to be $y_{\cdot t}^o$. Repeating the derivations from (2.2) to (2.8) one finds

$$\delta_{t|t} = \delta_{t|t-1} + K_t\left[y_{\cdot t}' - y_{\cdot t|t-1}'\right] \tag{5.13}$$

and, denoting $E(\delta_t - \delta_{t|t-1})(\delta_t - \delta_{t|t-1})'$ by $\Sigma_{t|t-1}$, and so forth,

$$K_t = \Sigma_{t|t-1}W_t^{o'}\left[W_t^o\Sigma_{t|t-1}W_t^{o'} + \Gamma_{t|t-1}'^{-1}S\Gamma_{t|t-1}^{-1}\right]. \tag{5.14}$$

Corresponding to (2.5), (2.7) and (2.8) are respectively

$$\Sigma_{t|t-1} = M\Sigma_{t-1|t-1}M' + V \qquad (5.15)$$

M being the coefficient matrix of (5.5) and V being the covariance matrix of its residual $\eta'_t = (\eta'_{1t} \ldots \eta'_{mt})$,

$$\Sigma_{t|t} = \Sigma_{t|t-1} - K_t\left[W_t^\circ\Sigma_{t|t-1}W_t^{\circ\prime} + \Gamma_{t|t-1}^{\prime-1}S\Gamma_{t|t-1}^{-1}\right]K_t \qquad (5.16)$$

and

$$\delta_{t|t-1} = M\delta_{t|t-1}. \qquad (5.17)$$

An alternate way of estimating $\delta_{T|T}$, given S, V_i, and M_i, is to form a regression model analogous to (3.1) using (5.11) for $y'_{\cdot t}$ ($t = 1, \ldots, T$) and denoting $y'_{\cdot t} - y_{\cdot t}^\circ{}' + W_t^\circ\delta_{t|t-1}$ by $\tilde{y}'_{\cdot t}$:

$$
\begin{bmatrix} \tilde{y}'_{\cdot 1} \\ \tilde{y}'_{\cdot 2} \\ \vdots \\ \tilde{y}'_{\cdot T-1} \\ \tilde{y}'_{\cdot T} \end{bmatrix}
=
\begin{bmatrix} W_1^\circ M^{-T+1} \\ W_2^\circ M^{-T+2} \\ \vdots \\ W_{T-1}^\circ M^{-1} \\ M_T^\circ \end{bmatrix}\delta_T
-
\begin{bmatrix} \Gamma_1^{\circ\prime-1}\varepsilon_{\cdot 1} \\ \Gamma_2^{\circ\prime-1}\varepsilon_{\cdot 2} \\ \vdots \\ \Gamma_{T-1}^{\circ}{}'^{-1}\varepsilon_{\cdot T-1} \\ \Gamma_T^{\circ\prime-1}\varepsilon_{\cdot T} \end{bmatrix}
$$

$$
-
\begin{bmatrix}
W_1^\circ(M^{-1} & M^{-2} & \cdots & M^{-T+1}) \\
0 & W_2^\circ(M^{-1} & \cdots & M^{-T+2}) \\
\vdots & \vdots & \ddots & \\
0 & 0 & \cdots & W_{T-1}^\circ M^{-1} \\
0 & 0 & \cdots & 0
\end{bmatrix}
\begin{bmatrix} \eta_2 \\ \eta_3 \\ \vdots \\ \eta_{T-1} \\ \eta_T \end{bmatrix}
$$

$$(5.18)$$

The covariance matrix of the residual vector of (5.18) has an i–j block

$$\delta_{ij}\Gamma_i^{\circ\prime-1}S\Gamma_i^{\circ-1} + W_i^\circ \sum_{t=\max(i,j)}^{T-1} M^{-(t-i+1)}VM'^{-(t-j+1)}W_j^{\circ\prime} \qquad (5.19)$$

where δ_{ij} is the Kronecker delta. Aitken's generalized least squares can be applied to estimate δ_T once the coefficients W_t° and Γ_t° of the linearized model (5.11) are evaluated. One can choose an initial guess δ_T^o for $\delta_{T|T}$, and the associated $\delta_t^o = M^{-(T-t)}\delta_T^o$ $(t = 1, \ldots, T)$. These initial values permit the evaluation of W_t^o, Γ_t^o, $y_{\cdot t}^o = -x_{\cdot t}B_t^o\Gamma_t^{o^{-1}}$ and $\delta_{t|t-1} = \delta_t^o$. Equation 5.18 will be treated as a linear regression model to estimate $\delta_{T|T}$. The resulting estimate will be used to form a new initial guess δ_T^o and the process continues iteratively.

In order to estimate the unknown parameters in S, V_i $(i = 1, \ldots, m)$, and M_i $(i = 1, \ldots, m)$, (5.18) can be used to form a likelihood function. However, unlike the situation with truly constant coefficients W_t^o and Γ_t^o, the evaluation of the likelihood function requires iterative solution of $\delta_{T|T}$ as described in the last paragraph. The computational problem involved in maximizing the likelihood function is hence more burdensome than in the case of a truly linear (in contrast with a linearized) model. This problem deserves further study.

6.6　SYSTEM OF NONLINEAR SIMULTANEOUS EQUATIONS

Let the tth observation of a system of m nonlinear simultaneous equations with time-varying parameters be written as

$$y_{\cdot t}' = \Phi(y_{\cdot t}, x_{\cdot t}, \delta_t) + \varepsilon_{\cdot t}, \qquad (t = 1, \ldots, T), \qquad (6.1)$$

where Φ is a vector function of m components and

$$\delta_t = M\delta_{t-1} + \eta_t \qquad (t = 1, \ldots, T), \qquad (6.2)$$

which is identical with (5.5). Like the reduced-form (5.2) for a system of linear structural equations, (6.1) is a nonlinear function of the parameter vector δ_t. The approach to be adopted is similar to the one used in Section 5. It amounts to linearizing the nonlinear observation equation (6.1) about some δ_t^o and the associated $y_{\cdot t}^o$ defined by

$$y_{\cdot t}^{o'} = \Phi(y_{\cdot t}^o, x_{\cdot t}, \delta_t^o).$$

Given δ_t^o and $x_{\cdot t}$, $y_{\cdot t}^o$ can be computed by the Gauss-Siedel method, for example.

Linearizing Φ in (6.1) about δ_t^o and $y_{\cdot t}^o$, we have

$$y_{\cdot t}' = y_{\cdot t}^{o'} + \left(\frac{\partial \Phi}{\partial y_{\cdot t}}\right)_o (y_{\cdot t}' - y_{\cdot t}^{o'}) + \left(\frac{\partial \Phi}{\partial \delta_t}\right)_o (\delta_t - \delta_t^o) + \varepsilon_{\cdot t},$$

where, as in Section 5, the subscript "o" indicates that the matrix of partial derivatives of Φ is evaluated at $y^\circ_{\cdot t}$ and δ°_t. Solving for $y'_{\cdot t}$, we get

$$
y'_{\cdot t} = y^{\circ\prime}_{\cdot t} + \left[I - \left(\frac{\partial \Phi}{\partial y_{\cdot t}} \right)_0 \right]^{-1} \frac{\partial \Phi}{\partial \delta_t} (\delta_t - \delta^\circ_t) + \left[I - \left(\frac{\partial \Phi}{\partial y_{\cdot t}} \right)_0 \right]^{-1} \varepsilon_{\cdot t}
$$

$$
\equiv y^\circ_{\cdot t} + W^\circ_t (\delta_t - \delta^\circ_t) + R_t \varepsilon_{\cdot t}, \tag{6.3}
$$

which replaces the linearized observation equation (5.11) of Section 5. The treatment of the model (6.3)–(6.2) is the same as in Section 5. The computational problem is only slightly more difficult because the linearization to achieve (6.3) requires the evaluation of the partial derivatives $(\partial \Phi / \partial y_{\cdot t})_0$ and $(\partial \Phi / \partial \delta_t)_0$ whereas the linearization to obtain (5.11) requires matrix inversion only. These partial derivatives can be evaluated numerically, and their evaluation is computationally much simpler than the maximization of the likelihood function for the linearized model with respect to the parameters S, V_i $(i = 1, \ldots, m)$, and M_i $(i = 1, \ldots, m)$ as discussed at the end of Section 5.

6.7 MODEL WITH STATIONARY COEFFICIENTS

An alternative specification to (1.1) and (1.2) is

$$
y_t = x_t \beta_t + \varepsilon_t \tag{7.1}
$$

$$
\beta_t - \bar{\beta} = M(\beta_{t-1} - \bar{\beta}) + \eta_t, \tag{7.2}
$$

where all characteristic roots of M are assumed to be smaller than one in absolute value. In stochastic equilibrium β_t will have mean $\bar{\beta}$ and a covariance matrix Γ satisfying

$$
\Gamma = M \Gamma M' + V,
$$

where, as before, V is the covariance matrix of η_t. In the special case with $M = 0$, the model (7.1)–(7.2) becomes a linear regression model with random coefficients.

The model (7.1)–(7.2) differs from (1.1)–(1.2) mainly by the introduction of the parameter vector $\bar{\beta}$. However, it can be rewritten in the same form as (1.1)–(1.2), so that our results in Section 2 are applicable here as well. Defining $\beta_t^* = \beta_t - \bar{\beta}$ and $\bar{\beta}_t = \bar{\beta}$ for all t, we write (7.1)–(7.2) as

$$y_t = (x_t \quad x_t) \begin{bmatrix} \bar{\beta}_t \\ \beta_t^* \end{bmatrix} + \varepsilon_t \qquad (7.3)$$

$$\begin{bmatrix} \bar{\beta}_t \\ \beta_t^* \end{bmatrix} = \begin{bmatrix} I & 0 \\ 0 & M \end{bmatrix} \begin{bmatrix} \bar{\beta}_{t-1} \\ \beta_{t-1}^* \end{bmatrix} \begin{bmatrix} 0 \\ \eta_t \end{bmatrix}, \qquad (7.4)$$

which is a special case of (1.1)-(1.2). In most applications, not all components of β_t in (7.2) are random. If only a subvector $\tilde{\beta}_t$ of β_t consisting of k_1 elements, say, is random, (7.3) and (7.4) will become

$$y_t = (x_t \quad \tilde{x}_t) \begin{bmatrix} \bar{\beta}_t \\ \tilde{\beta}_t^* \end{bmatrix} + \varepsilon_t \qquad (7.5)$$

$$\begin{bmatrix} \bar{\beta}_t \\ \tilde{\beta}_t^* \end{bmatrix} = \begin{bmatrix} I & 0 \\ 0 & M \end{bmatrix} \begin{bmatrix} \bar{\beta}_{t-1} \\ \tilde{\beta}_{t-1}^* \end{bmatrix} + \begin{bmatrix} 0 \\ \eta_t \end{bmatrix}. \qquad (7.6)$$

Because the model (7.5)–(7.6) is a special case of the model (1.1)–(1.2), all the filtering and smoothing equations of Section 2 and the log-likelihood functions (4.1) and (4.3) are applicable to this model. However, the estimation problem for this model deserves a special treatment. Because the roots of M are smaller than one in absolute value and the process generating $\tilde{\beta}_t^*$ is covariance-stationary, one may choose to estimate this model by assuming that the $\tilde{\beta}_t^*$ process starts in a stochastic equilibrium, rather than assuming a fixed, but unknown, initial value $\tilde{\beta}_1^*$ in period 1. The latter assumption was made in (3.1), where we used the relation

$$\tilde{\beta}_t^* = M\tilde{\beta}_{t-1}^* + \eta_t = M^{t-1}\tilde{\beta}_1^* + \eta_t + M\eta_{t-1} + \cdots + M^{t-2}\eta_2$$

and treated $\tilde{\beta}_1^*$ as fixed. In estimating the model (7.5)–(7.6), one may treat $\tilde{\beta}_1^*$ as random, with mean zero and covariance matrix Γ_0 satisfying

$$\Gamma_0 = M\Gamma_0 M' + V. \qquad (7.7)$$

The autocovariance matrix for the $\tilde{\beta}_t^*$ process is

$$\Gamma_s = E\tilde{\beta}_t^*\tilde{\beta}_{t-s}^{*\prime} = M^s\Gamma_0 = \Gamma'_{-s} \qquad (s \geq 0; t \geq 1). \qquad (7.8)$$

If $\tilde{\beta}_1^*$ is regarded as fixed, instead of (7.7) and (7.8), the covariance matrix of $\tilde{\beta}_t^*$ and $\tilde{\beta}_{t-s}^{*\prime}$ is

$$E\left(\tilde{\beta}_t^* - M^{t-1}\tilde{\beta}_1^*\right)\left(\tilde{\beta}_{t-s}^* - M^{t-s-1}\tilde{\beta}_1^*\right)'$$

$$= E\left(\eta_t + M\eta_{t-1} + \cdots + M^{t-2}\eta_2\right)\left(\eta_{t-s} + M\eta_{t-s-1} + \cdots + M^{t-s-2}\eta_2\right)$$

$$= \sum_{i=0}^{t-s-2} M^{s+i}VM'^{i} \qquad (s \geq 0; t \geq 1). \tag{7.9}$$

The difference in the treatment of $\tilde{\beta}_1^*$ has implications for estimation. When $\tilde{\beta}_1^*$ is regarded as fixed, all inferences are conditional on this assumption. When $\hat{\beta}_1^*$ is regarded as a random drawing from a distribution with mean zero and covariance matrix Γ_0 as specified by (7.7), the inferences are no longer conditional. Furthermore, to provide the initial estimates $\beta_{k|k}$ and $\Sigma_{k|k}$ to start up Kalman filtering equations for the evaluation of the log-likelihood functions (4.1) and (4.3), the two assumptions lead to different procedures. In the case of fixed $\tilde{\beta}_t^*$, we regard (7.5) as a special case of (1.1). Therefore, the number of initial observations required to perform a generalized least squares regression equals the number of elements in $\bar{\beta}_t$ and $\tilde{\beta}_t^*$, or $k + k_1$, say. Equations 3.3 and 3.4 are applied to these $k + k_1$ observations, and the analysis proceeds as before.

In the case of random $\tilde{\beta}_1^*$, (7.5) can be written as

$$y_t = x_t\bar{\beta} + \left(\tilde{x}_t\tilde{\beta}^* + \varepsilon_t\right) = x_t\bar{\beta} + u_t. \tag{7.10}$$

The term in parentheses, or u_t, is treated as a serially correlated residual satisfying

$$Eu_t u_{t-s}' = \tilde{x}_t\Gamma_s\tilde{x}_{t-s}' + \delta_{t,t-s}s^2 \tag{7.11}$$

where Γ_s is defined by (7.8) and $\delta_{t,t-s}$ is the Kronecker delta. Therefore, given (7.11) only k initial observations are required to obtain a GLS estimate $\bar{\beta}_{k|k}$ of $\bar{\beta}$ and its covariance matrix. Writing the first k observations of (7.10) as

$$y = X\bar{\beta} + u \tag{7.12}$$

where X is assumed to be a nonsingular $k \times k$ matrix and $Euu' = W$ is given by (7.11), we have

$$\bar{\beta}_{k|k} = (X'W^{-1}X)^{-1}X'W^{-1}y = X^{-1}y \qquad (7.13)$$

$$\text{Cov}\left(\bar{\beta}_{k|k} - \bar{\beta}\right) = (X'W^{-1}X)^{-1} = X^{-1}WX'^{-1}. \qquad (7.14)$$

For $\tilde{\beta}_k^*$ in equilibrium, we set its mean equal to zero and its covariance matrix to Γ_0, that is,

$$\tilde{\beta}_{k|k}^* = 0; \qquad \text{Cov}\left(\tilde{\beta}_k^* - \tilde{\beta}_{k|k}^*\right) = \Gamma_0 \qquad (7.15)$$

The covariance of $\bar{\beta}_{k|k} - \bar{\beta}$ and $\tilde{\beta}_k^* - \tilde{\beta}_{k|k}^*$ is

$$E\left(\bar{\beta}_{k|k} - \bar{\beta}\right)\tilde{\beta}_k^{*\prime} = EX^{-1}u\tilde{\beta}_k^{*\prime} = X^{-1}\begin{bmatrix} \tilde{x}_1\Gamma_{k-1}' \\ \vdots \\ \tilde{x}_k\Gamma_0' \end{bmatrix} \qquad (7.16)$$

Equations 7.13–7.16 provide the components of $\beta_{k|k}$ and $\Sigma_{k|k}$ to be used for the evaluation of the log-likelihood functions (4.1) and (4.3). They are to be contrasted with (3.3) and (3.4) for fixed β_1^* which would require $k + k_1$ initial observations.

Once the likelihood function (4.3) can be evaluated, a numerical method can be applied to maximize it with respect to the unknown parameters in $V = s^2P$ and M. The computations will be simplified when P and M are diagonal, being diag$\{p_i\}$ and diag$\{m_i\}$ respectively. Equations 7.7 and 7.8 would become

$$\gamma_{ii,0} = E\beta_{it}^{*2} = \frac{s^2p_i}{1 - m_i} \qquad (i = 1,\ldots,k_1) \qquad (7.17)$$

$$\gamma_{ii,s} = E\beta_{it}^*\beta_{i,t-s}^* = m_i^s\gamma_{ii,0} \qquad (i = 1,\ldots,k_1) \qquad (7.18)$$

and $E\beta_{it}^*\beta_{j,t-s}^* = 0$ for $i \neq j$ and for all s. Accordingly the matrix Γ_s used in (7.11) is a diagonal matrix with elements given by (7.17) and (7.18). As an alternative to using the likelihood function (4.3), one can form a likelihood function using the regression model (7.12) for all T observations, as it was done by using the model (4.8) in Section 4.

For further discussion of the stationary-coefficient regression model, the reader is referred to Rosenberg (1973), Cooley and Prescott (1976), Harvey and Phillips (1978), and Pagan (1980). The exposition of this section owes a great deal to Harvey and Phillips (1978). For a survey of the random-coefficient model, the reader is referred to Swamy (1971, 1974).

6.8 THE ESTIMATION OF SEASONAL COMPONENTS IN ECONOMIC TIME SERIES

Seasonal adjustment of economic time series is a topic that has been studied extensively in the literature. This section contains a modest suggestion to combine seasonal analysis with the estimation of an econometric model for cyclical fluctuations. Pagan (1975) has pointed out the possibility of applying the filtering and estimation methods for state-space models to the estimation of seasonal and cyclical components in economic time series. The following suggestion is essentially a combination of an econometric model for the cyclical components with the filtering and estimation of the seasonal components formulated in a state-space form.

Assume, first, that the vector y_t of endogenous variables is the sum of cyclical, seasonal, and irregular components, as given by

$$y_t = y_t^c + y_t^s + v_t \tag{8.1}$$

and, second, that the cyclical component y_t^c is governed by the following model:

$$y_t^c = A y_{t-1}^c + C x_t + b + u_t, \tag{8.2}$$

where x_t is a vector of exogenous variables and u_t is a vector of random disturbances. The exogenous variables might or might not be seasonally adjusted, but this issue does not affect our analysis, because the vector x_t, seasonally adjusted or not, is treated as predetermined. Third, an autoregressive seasonal model is assumed for the seasonal component, as illustrated by, but not confined to, the simple scheme

$$y_t^s = B y_{t-12}^s + w_t, \tag{8.3}$$

where w_t consists of random residuals. Combining (8.2) and (8.3), we can write the vector z_t of unobserved components in the form

$$z_t = M z_{t-1} + N x_t + \varepsilon_t, \tag{8.4}$$

where z_t includes both y_t^c and y_t^s as its first two subvectors as well as the necessary lagged y_{t-k}^c and y_{t-k}^s to transform the original model (8.2) of possibly higher order and (8.3) of order 12 into first order, the matrix M will depend on the matrices A and B, the matrix N will depend on C and b, the vector x_t will include dummy variables to absorb the intercept b of (8.2), and ε_t will depend on u_t and w_t. Equation 8.1 can be rewritten as

$$y_t = [\, I \quad I \quad 0 \,] z_t + v_t. \tag{8.5}$$

Thus, (8.4) and (8.5) are in the standard state-space form, the first explaining the unobserved state variables z_t and the second relating the observed y_t to z_t. Given observations on y_t and x_t, the conditional expectations of the unobserved components of z_t can be estimated by the well-known techniques of Kalman filtering and smoothing, provided that the parameters A, C, b, and thus M and N are known.

In practice, the parameters A, C, and b of the econometric model (8.2) are unknown. One can employ seasonally adjusted data for y_t^c, obtained by a standard seasonal adjustment procedure, and the standard statistical estimation techniques to obtain estimates of A, C, and b. Using these estimates, one can then compute estimates of the seasonal and cyclical components in z_t by Kalman filtering and smoothing. The new estimates of y_t^c will serve as new data for the reestimation of the econometric model (8.2). New estimates of the seasonal components y_t^s will result from this process. I believe that this approach deserves to be further studied and pursued.

Part 2
Economic Applications of Control Methods

CHAPTER 7

An Econometric Definition of the Inflation-Unemployment Trade-Off

Is it possible to achieve a 5 percent unemployment rate and keep annual inflation down to 4 percent? To raise this question in terms of a particular econometric model, we ask whether there exist values of the policy instruments that will give rise to solutions of 5 and 4 percent, respectively, for unemployment and inflation. What is the most favorable trade-off relationship between inflation and unemployment implicit in an econometric model of a national economy? In this chapter, we wish to point out that for many econometric models actually in use, the trade-off relationship is not rigid, but can be shifted toward the origin (but usually not all the way to the origin!) but suitable government policies. Accordingly, we suggest that the trade-off relationship implicit in an econometric model be defined as the set of points in the unemployment-inflation diagram that cannot be dominated. We will explain the circumstances under which there exists such a southwestern boundary for the points depicting the unemployment-inflation combinations that are achievable according to a given model. We will propose a systematic way to locate points on this boundary and demonstrate that our algorithm works.

Stimulated by and based upon A. W. Phillips' (1958) original paper on the relation between unemployment and the rate of change of money wage rates, numerous studies have appeared to refine, respecify, and estimate structural equations explaining the rates of change in the wage rates, the price level, unemployment, and related variables. It soon became apparent

---

This chapter was coauthored by Sharon Bernstein Megdal.

that these studies, though useful, may not be sufficient for ascertaining the trade-off relationship between unemployment and inflation. If unemployment and inflation are viewed as two of the many endogenous variables which are jointly determined by a system of simultaneous econometric equations, their relationship has to be derived by solving a whole system using alternative values for the policy variables subject to government control. The approach of deriving the unemployment-inflation trade-off by varying the policy variables and solving for these two endogenous variables in an econometric model has been adopted by Leonall Andersen and Keith Carlson (1970), Albert Hirsch (1972), George de Menil and Jared Enzler (1972), Saul Hymans (1972), and Ronald Bodkin (1972), among others.

Because, as we shall explain, the relationship between unemployment and inflation implicit in an econometric model is usually not rigid, an arbitrary choice of policy instruments in the above simulation approach will ordinarily produce combinations of these two variables that can be improved upon. We therefore suggest that the policy variables be chosen optimally, rather than arbitrarily, in order to derive the most favorable trade-off relationship. By choosing two alternative paths for the policy variables arbitrarily, one more expansionary than the other, one would expect to obtain two solutions for unemployment and inflation from an econometric model. However, by a more judicious choice of the policy variables, it may be possible to improve on both of these results. In general, the unemployment-inflation combinations resulting from varying the values of the policy variables in an econometric model would be a scatter and would not all fall on one rigid curve. Thus a unique trade-off relationship may not be attainable simply by trying out different values for the policy variables. Some form of optimization is required to derive the best possible trade-off relationship.

In Section 1 of this chapter, we will first point out the various possibilities for unemployment and inflation implicit in a static econometric model consisting of a set of simultaneous equations and propose a method to derive from the model the best tradeoff curve. Section 2 generalizes the discussion to the dynamic case. Section 3 applies our approach to derive the best inflation-unemployment trade-off from the St. Louis model, and Section 4 applies the same for the Michigan Quarterly Econometric Model. Section 5 contains some concluding remarks.[1]

---

[1]In this chapter, our main purpose is to propose a definition of the best inflation-unemployment trade-off and a method for deriving the relationship from an econometric model. We are not concerned with the actual shape of the price Phillips curve, and therefore, would avoid discussion of whether the long-run Phillips curve is nearly vertical.

7.1   INFLATION-UNEMPLOYMENT POSSIBILITIES IN A STATIC MODEL

Given a set of simultaneous equations determining a vector $y' = (y_1, y_2, \ldots, y_p)$ of endogenous variables by a vector $x' = (x_1, \ldots, x_q)$ of policy instruments, and given a set of exogenous variables not subject to government control which will be treated as fixed, we ask what combinations of unemployment y_1 and inflation y_2 are possible and how one can trace out the best possible combinations.

For our purpose, the set of possible solutions for y_1 and y_2 can conveniently be classified into three categories. The first is a rigid relation, the points all falling on one curve in the y_1-y_2 diagram. The second is a semirigid relation, the set of possible points forming an area in the y_1-y_2 plane which has a southwestern boundary. The second case is considered most important and it is the southwestern boundary which we would like to ascertain as the best possible trade-off relationship. The third is the least rigid, the set of possible points not being bounded by a southwestern boundary. As a special case of the third category, we may have the set of possible points covering the entire y_1-y_2 plane. This is a mathematical possibility, but the model involved would not be economically meaningful because y_1 cannot be negative.

The first possibility, namely a rigid trade-off curve, occurs when there is a structural equation explaining y_2 by y_1 and some exogenous variables, for example, $y_2 = -1.2 y_1 + z$. The variable z in this equation may incorporate exogenous variables and other variables as long as these variables cannot be influenced, directly or indirectly, by the policy instruments. Otherwise the relation between y_2 and y_1 can be shifted. The set z of variables in this structural equation may consist entirely of exogenous variables not subject to government control, or of some endogenous variables which are determined completely by uncontrollable exogenous variables. The equation relating y_2, y_1, and the other variables so specified might not itself be a structural equation, but the result of combining several structural equations. To illustrate, let y_3 be the rate of change in the wage rate. Assume a wage Phillips curve relating y_3 to y_1, y_2, and possibly some exogenous variables not subject to government control. Assume also a price Phillips curve relating y_2 to y_1, y_3, and possibly some exogenous variables. Eliminating y_3 from these two structural equations would yield a rigid trade-off relationship between y_1 and y_2. In terms of the reduced-form equations determining y_1 and y_2 by $x_1, \ldots, x_q$, the $2 \times q$ matrix of partial derivatives of y_1 and y_2 with respect to the q x's would be of rank 1, so that starting from a given point, when a small change in y_2 results from whatever changes in the x's, y_1 will be changed proportionally in the opposite direction.

If any of the other variables in an equation relating y_1 and y_2 (which may be itself a structural equation or, more likely, the result of combining several structural equations) can be influenced directly or indirectly by the policy variables, the relation between y_1 and y_2 will no longer be rigid. The possible combinations of y_1 and y_2 obtained by varying the x's will form an area in the y_1-y_2 plane. The $2 \times q$ matrix of partial derivatives of y_1 and y_2 with respect to the q x's via the reduced form will have rank 2 for many values of y and x. This gives rise to the second or the third category of possible solutions for y_1 and y_2. In general however, the possible combinations do not take up the entire y_1-y_2 plane as they would in the special case of the third category of our classification. If the equation relating y_2 to y_1 is linear, such as $y_2 = -1.2y_1 + z$, and z is a linear function of policy instruments which can take any positive or negative values, the trade-off curve can then be shifted at will. On the other hand, a nonlinear structural equation explaining the rate of unemployment y_1 may rule out negative values for y_1. For example, if $\log y_1$ but not y_1 appears in the model, y_1 cannot be negative. Furthermore, a southwestern boundary may exist for the possible combinations of y_1 and y_2. This can occur when the values of the x's are bounded (such as the tax rates, money supply, and government expenditures taking only nonnegative values). It can also occur because, in the equation relating y_1 and y_2, the other endogenous variables that can be influenced by government policies are bounded by their own nonlinearities or by the boundedness of the government instruments themselves. Econometric models belonging to our second category, those with a southwestern boundary for the possible y_1-y_2 combinations, appear to be economically reasonable. The first category would rule out the possibility of any bad policies which can make both inflation and unemployment worse. The third category would imply that one can achieve any desired inflation-employment combination as one pleases.[2]

If a southwestern boundary exists for the possible y_1-y_2 combinations, one can obtain points on this boundary by systematically varying the parameters k_1, k_2, a_1, and a_2 in a quadratic loss function

$$w(y_1, y_2) = k_1(y_1 - a_1)^2 + k_2(y_2 - a_2)^2 \tag{1}$$

and minimizing this function subject to the constraint of the econometric model. To see that one point in the boundary will result from such a

---

[2] In Chapter 2, it was found that by manipulating the policy instruments, one can reach any desired combination of the level of employment and the general price index according to the Klein-Goldberger model of the U.S. economy.

minimization, let $k_1 = k_2 = 1$ and $a_1 = a_2 = 0$. The points of equal loss will form a circle with center in the origin, and circles closer to the origin will have smaller losses. The minimum occurs when the smallest circle is tangential to the boundary of the possible y_1-y_2 points constrained by the econometric model. Assume that, in the first quadrant of the y_1-y_2 plane, a southwestern boundary exists, which means that the slope of the boundary is negative (or at least nonpositive). Since the slope of the circle in the first quadrant is also nonpositive, obtaining the smallest circle satisfying the constraint will mean that the y_1-y_2 point is on the boundary—if it were not, one could use a smaller circle satisfying the constraint and reducing the loss. To obtain another point on the boundary, one could change the ratio of k_1 to k_2, letting $k_1 = 100$ and $k_2 = 1$, say. The points of equal loss would be an ellipse that is elongated vertically. In sacrificing one unit of unemployment, one requires a greater reduction in inflation than before; the slope of the ellipse in the first quadrant of the y_1-y_2 plane is steeper than before. The new minimum will yield a smaller unemployment and a higher inflation rate. We can drop the above assumption that the southwestern boundary lies in the first quadrant. If it were in the fourth quadrant, this analysis would apply by placing the center (a_1, a_2) of the ellipse below and to the left of the boundary.

Although minimization of (1) with $k_1 = k_2 = 1$ and $a_1 = a_2 = 0$ will yield a point on the best trade-off curve in the first quadrant if it exists, one cannot anticipate the resulting value for either y_1 or y_2. To answer the question, what is the lowest inflation rate y_2 for a given unemployment rate $y_1 = 5$ (percent), one may set $k_1 = 1000$, $k_2 = 1$, $a_1 = 5$, and $a_2 = 0$. The points of equal loss form a highly vertically elongated ellipse with $(5, 0)$ as center. Minimization yields an unemployment rate close to 5 percent and the corresponding lowest inflation rate, because it chooses the smallest vertical ellipse centering in $(5, 0)$ that still satisfies the constraint of the econometric model. By the same argument, replacing $a_2 = 0$ by $a_2 = 2$ in the minimization would also work provided that the lowest inflation rate for 5 percent unemployment is above 2 percent.

In this section, we have classified the possible solutions for unemployment and inflation from a static econometric model, defined the best trade-off relationship implicit in the model, and suggested a method for tracing out this relationship.

7.2 UNEMPLOYMENT-INFLATION TRADE-OFF POSSIBILITIES IN THE DYNAMIC CASE

It is important to generalize our discussion to the dynamic case because econometric models are dynamic, and economists are interested in the best trade-off relationships between unemployment and inflation through time. In the dynamic setting, we have to consider the three-dimensional space with unemployment y_1, inflation y_2, and time t as the axes. The three categories of trade-off possibilities implicit in an econometric model will be discussed for the very short run, the intermediate run, and the very long run.

By the very short run, we mean one quarter if the econometric model is a quarterly model. The dynamic model consists of y_t, y_{t-1}, and x_t as variables, the uncontrollable exogenous variables being considered given as before. Endogenous variables lagged more than one period and lagged policy instruments can be eliminated from any dynamic model by introducing suitable identities, as explained in Chapter 1. For the one quarter immediately ahead, all lagged variables y_{t-1} are given, and the analysis reduces to the static case. The discussion of Section 1 applies entirely to the trade-off possibilities between y_{1t} and y_{2t}, given all lagged variables.

The intermediate run requires some discussion. When the time interval of interest is from period 1 to period T (where T is not very large), we are concerned with the possible points on the y_2-y_2-t diagram. The most rigid category 1 would be a surface on this diagram. This means that, for any given t, the possible combinations of y_{1t} and y_{2t} will lie on a curve on the y_1-y_2 plane. As an example, there may be a structural equation, or an equation resulting from eliminating other endogenous variables from several structural equations, which relates y_{1t}, y_{2t}, and other variables not subject to government control, either directly or indirectly. Again, category 1 is a very special case. By varying the time paths of the policy instruments, one may obtain combinations of y_{1t}, y_{2t}, and t that are not confined to a surface. However, not all points in the y_1, y_2, and t space are reachable by manipulation of government policies. There may be a set of surfaces serving as the lower boundaries of the possible time paths for y_1 and y_2 in the following sense. For any t, one cannot reduce y_{2t} without increasing y_{1t} or y_{2s} or y_{1s} for $s \neq t$. Thus it may be possible to reduce both y_{1t} and y_{2t}, but some y_{1s} or y_{2s} in another period s will have to increase—otherwise, the surface is not a lowest boundary possible. Category 2, where such surfaces exist, is considered more likely than both category 1 and category 3 where such boundary surfaces do not exist.

To obtain a path for y_1 and y_2 on such boundary surface, we minimize the loss function

$$\sum_{t=1}^{T} \left[k_{1t}(y_{1t} - a_{1t})^2 + k_{2t}(y_{2t} - a_{2t})^2 \right] \tag{2}$$

subject to the constraint of the dynamic econometric model. Consider the

$2T$-dimensional space with y_{1t}, y_{2t} $(t = 1, 2, \ldots, T)$ measured along its coordinates. The points in this space having the same loss are ellipsoids. Contracting one such ellipsoid while keeping the y_1 and y_2 paths attainable by the dynamic econometric model guarantees that the attainable point with minimum loss lies on the boundary surface. To keep the unemployment path close to 5 percent, say, and to find a best inflation path consistent with the econometric model, one may choose $a_{1t} = 5$, $a_{2t} = 0$ (or a small number), $k_{1t} = 1000$, and $k_{2t} = 1$ for $t = 1, 2, \ldots, T$. A numerical method for minimizing a quadratic loss function subject to the constraint of a nonlinear econometric model can be found in Chow (1975, Section 12.1), or in Chapter 2 of this book. It will be used for the calculations reported in Sections 3 and 4.

Once several optimal paths are obtained, with y_{1t} aimed at 4, 5, 6, and 7 percent, respectively, for instance, one may wish to summarize these paths along the best trade-off boundary in a two-dimensional diagram. One way to do so is to plot the mean inflation rate $(\Sigma_t y_{2t}/T)$ against the mean unemployment rate $(\Sigma_t y_{1t}/T)$ over the T periods. This would imply a constant rate of substitution between y_{1t} and y_{1s}, and between y_{2t} and y_{2s}. Such an implication would violate the specification of a quadratic loss function which measures the loss by the sums of squared deviations of the economic variables from their targets and not by their sums or their arithmetic means. A second way is to plot $[\Sigma_t(y_{2t} - a_{2t})^2/T]^{1/2}$ against $[\Sigma_t(y_{1t} - a_{1t})^2/T]^{1/2}$ which would penalize the increase of each variable by the square of its deviation from target. Note that when a two-dimensional diagram is used in the multiperiod case, the index number problem cannot be avoided.

For the very long run, if any one ever cares for such an analysis, we can define the equilibrium y_1 and y_2 combination as the constant values toward which these two variables approach as T increases in the multiperiod minimization problem specified above, if such constant values exist. Of course, y_{1t} and y_{2t} might not approach constant values as t increases. Because we treat the very long-run problem in the same way as the above intermediate-run problem by simply increasing the planning horizon T, we can still use such indices as $(\Sigma_t y_{it}/T)$ and $[\Sigma_t(y_{it} - a_i)^2/T]^{1/2}$ for $i = 1, 2$ even if y_{it} itself might not approach a limit as t increases. It is important to note that, as in the case of the intermediate-run problem, optimization is required to obtain the most favorable long-run trade-off. As long as there exist bad policies which would create more inflation in the long run without improving the unemployment situation, the time paths for y_{1t} and y_{2t} do not all fall on a rigid surface, and one needs to minimize in order to obtain a path on the lower boundary of all feasible paths.

7.3   ANALYSIS OF THE ST. LOUIS MODEL

The St. Louis model of Andersen and Carlson (1970) is well known. It has an equation explaining money GNP by the current and lagged values of money supply M and high-employment federal expenditures E. Demand pressure and expected price change will help determine the change in the price level. Because both policy instruments M and E affect the economy through the same money GNP variable, in effect the two instruments are only a single policy variable. Mathematically the 2×2 matrix of partial derivatives of the unemployment rate y_1 and the rate of price change y_2 with respect to these two instruments has rank 1. If the analysis is limited to one quarter, the St. Louis model therefore implies a rigid trade-off relation between y_1 and y_2.

However, in a multiperiod setting, in so far as inflation is affected by expected price change which is determined by past price changes and by the demand pressure which is influenced by the course of real output, alternative paths for the money supply can affect both the expected price change and the demand pressure, thus influencing the paths of inflation and unemployment. There is no reason to expect that arbitrary paths for M (or E) will yield paths for y_1 and y_2 on the lowest boundary for the unemployment-inflation trade-off through time. Using the 20 quarters from 1971.1–1975.4, and the loss function

$$\sum_{t=1}^{20} k_1(y_{1t} - a_1)^2 + \sum_{t=1}^{20} k_2(y_{2t} - a_2)^2 \tag{3}$$

with $k_1 = 10000$, $k_2 = 0.01$, $a_2 = 2$, and $a_1 = 3.5$, 4.5, 5.5, 6.5, 7.0, and 8.0, respectively, and letting E_t follow its historical path, we have obtained six optimal paths by minimizing (3) with respect to M_t. $(\Sigma_t y_{2t})/T$ is plotted against $(\Sigma_t y_{1t})/T$ in Figure 1, and $(\Sigma_t y_{2t}^2/T)^{1/2}$ against $(\Sigma_t y_{1t}^2/T)^{1/2}$ in Figure 2. The six optimal points are joined by a solid line. The corresponding points summarizing the paths for y_1 and y_2 resulting from the historical path for M_t are marked by a cross. The points resulting from using a constant percentage growth for M_t of 2, 4, and 6 percent are marked by small circles.

Note that the optimal points dominate the points resulting from the historical path and the smooth growth paths for M. Figure 1 shows that a mean unemployment rate of 4 percent is associated with about 12 percent inflation, and that a 7 percent unemployment corresponds to about 3.6

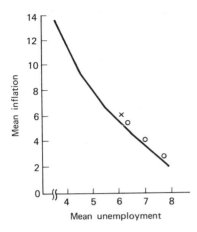

Figure 1.   Tradeoff from the St. Louis model.

percent inflation. It would be of interest to examine the dynamic characteristics of the optimizating paths for M, but space limitation prevents an
adequate discussion. Suffice it to say that the optimizing paths for M
exhibit sizeable fluctuations. To inhibit large fluctuations, we can add a
term $\Sigma_{t=1}^{20} k_3(M_t - a_{3t})^2$ in the loss function. Minimization of such a
function, again using $a_1 = 3.5, 4.5, 5.5, 6.5, 7.0$, and 8.0, respectively, will
yield a curve above the solid curves in Figures 1 and 2. This curve can also
be used to define the best trade-off relationship between y_1 and y_2, under
the assumption that fluctuations in the instrument are also penalized.

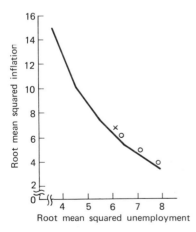

Figure 2.   Tradeoff from the St. Louis model.

7.4 ANALYSIS OF THE MICHIGAN QUARTERLY ECONOMETRIC MODEL

Our brief discussion using the Michigan Quarterly Econometric Model by Hymans and Shapiro (1973) follows closely the analysis for the St. Louis model, except that two instruments are used. The instruments are unborrowed reserves UR and nondefense federal expenditures GFO. With more than one instrument, an optimal path along the lowest boundary for the dynamic unemployment-inflation trade-off is obtained not simply by a suitable dynamic pattern for the one and only control variable (as in the case of the St. Louis model), but by an optimal combination of the time paths for the instruments. However, variations of the first instrument UR are inhibited by the inclusion of UR in the loss function, its target values being assumed to follow the historical path. The loss function is

$$\sum_{t=1}^{17} k_1(y_{1t} - a_1)^2 + \sum_{t=1}^{17} k_2(y_{2t} - a_2)^2 + \sum_{t=1}^{17} k_3(\mathrm{UR}_t - a_{3t})^2 \qquad (4)$$

with $k_1 = 10{,}000$, $k_2 = 1.0$, $k_3 = 0.1$, $a_2 = 2.0$, and $a_1 = 3.5$, 4.5, 5.5, and 6.0, respectively. The period covered is from 1971.1–1975.1, with $T = 17$ quarters. In the calculations, the residuals of the structural equations were given their estimated values so the application of the historical values of the instruments would reproduce the historical paths of the endogenous variables. This is the approach adopted by the NSF-NBER Seminar on Comparison of Econometric Models chaired by Lawrence Klein in its optimal control experiments. Figures 3 and 4 have been obtained in the same way as Figures 1 and 2. The four optimal points are joined by a solid line. The corresponding points summarizing the paths for y_1 and y_2

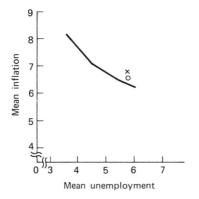

Figure 3. Tradeoff from the Michigan model.

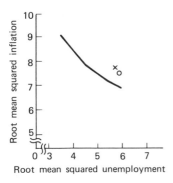

Figure 4. Tradeoff from the Michigan model.

resulting from using the historical values of UR_t and GFO_t are marked by a cross. The points indicated by a circle result from letting UR_t and GFO_t grow at an annual rate of approximately 4.5 and 16.5 percent, respectively. These are the average historical growth rates.

The optimal points clearly dominate the points resulting from the actual as well as the smoothed historical paths for the instruments. The optimal path for GFO exhibits some fluctuations. In contrast with the results of Figure 1 for the St. Louis model, Figure 3 shows that a mean unemployment rate of 4 percent is associated with only 7.6 percent inflation rather than 12 percent. The Michigan trade-off curve is much flatter than the St. Louis trade-off curve. The two curves cross at an unemployment rate of about 5.5 percent, with the corresponding inflation rate being 6.5. When the unemployment rate reaches 6.0 percent, the associated inflation rate according to the Michigan model is 6.3 percent, higher than the 5.6 percent according to the St. Louis model.

7.5 CONCLUDING REMARKS

We have proposed a definition of the best unemployment-inflation trade-off and a method of deriving it numerically from an econometric model. The notion is explained in both a static and a dynamic setting. The St. Louis model and the Michigan Quarterly Econometric Model have been used to derive the proposed trade-off relationships. In both cases, it has been shown that the outcomes of inflation and unemployment resulting from other than optimum values of the policy instruments are dominated by the results obtained by optimization. The examples illustrate clearly the need for optimization in order to ascertain the best possible trade-off. If the optimizing paths of the instruments according to a given econometric model fluctuate too violently for actual implementation, it may be reasonable to define and derive the best trade-off relationships by penalizing and inhibiting the instability in the instruments. The method proposed could also be employed to compare different econometric models in terms of the most favorable trade-off relationships that they imply and of the characteristics of the required time paths of the instruments.

At the present time, this use is probably more important than the use of the method proposed in the actual formulation of economic policy because of the possible weaknesses of the current generation of econometric models. For example, the trade-off relationship shown in Figures 1–4 for the St. Louis and the Michigan models are distinctly different. Policy makers, who have difficulties in reconciling these differences, however, may wish to consult Chapters 11 and 12 on the use of imperfect econometric models for economic policy decisions.

CHAPTER 8

Evaluation of Macroeconomic Policies by Stochastic Control Techniques

8.1 INTRODUCTION

The purpose of this chapter is to provide a method, based on the theory of optimal control for stochastic systems, which can be used to evaluate the macroeconomic policy prevailing during any historical period.

A reasonable evaluation of economic performance requires the following four elements. First, some objective or loss function of the relevant economic variables has to be agreed upon. Second, some model governing the economy has to be postulated. Such a model is necessary for the assertion that an alternative course of action could have led, with a reasonable degree of confidence, to a different and better result. Third, in a world of uncertainty, an action should be judged not by the actual outcome which is partly the result of chance (or luck!), but by the probability distribution (often summarized by its mathematical expectation) of the utility or loss resulting from the action. Fourth, if it is recognized that the consequences of decisions are extended to many periods, the action of one period has to be judged not only by the probability distribution of the outcome for that period resulting from it as compared with the probability distribution resulting from an alternative action, but by the distributions of all relevant outcomes in future periods. These four essential elements for policy evaluation will be explicitly taken into account in the proposed method.

123

Not all of these four elements are generally recognized and incorporated by economists attempting to evaluate government policies. For example, in the interesting paper by Kmenta and Smith (1973) historical fiscal and monetary policies in the quarters from 1954.2 to 1963.4 were evaluated using a (very simple) loss function and a quarterly macroeconometric model, thus incorporating the first two elements listed above. Uncertainty was partly accounted for by evaluating the change in the only target variable, real GNP, due to the changes in the policy variables, net of the random disturbances in the model. However, the multiperiod nature of the decision process was not adequately taken into account because a policy was judged by its effect only on current real GNP without considering its effect on real GNP in the future.

A recent study by Fair (1978a) on the use of optimal control techniques to measure economic performance does incorporate the above four elements. The main source of differences between the approach proposed here and Fair's approach is that ours is grounded on a theory of optimal control for stochastic systems whereas Fair's is based mainly on open-loop control for deterministic systems. As a consequence, our theory is more comprehensive and the computations required are much simpler. The contrast with Fair's approach will be briefly discussed in Section 3, after we have set out our theory in Section 2. Section 4 sets forth the limitations of our approach and the directions for improvement and refinement. Section 5 provides an illustrative evaluation.

8.2   A THEORY FOR POLICY EVALUATION

The theoretical framework on which we base our proposal for policy evaluation is the theory of optimal control for stochastic systems (see Chow, 1975, Chapters 8 and 12). Our proposed method follows directly from the stochastic control theory based on the method of dynamic programming. We will restate the main feature of this theory very briefly under simplifying assumptions, develop the method of policy evaluation from it, and discuss limitations and extensions of the method later on.

Initially we make two simplifying assumptions. First, a quadratic loss function for T periods

$$W = \sum_{t=1}^{T} (y_t - a_t)' K_t (y_t - a_t) = \sum_{t=1}^{T} (y_t' K_t y_t - 2 y_t' k_t + a_t' K_t a_t)$$

$$(2.1)$$

is assumed to measure the performance of a vector of economic variables y_t. Second, the econometric model used is linear, time-dependent, having known coefficients, A_t, b_t, and C_t, and a serially independent additive random disturbance u_t:

$$y_t = A_t y_{t-1} + C_t x_t + b_t + u_t, \tag{2.2}$$

where x_t is a vector of control variables which may be incorporated in y_t as a subvector if necessary.

Recall that, using the method of dynamic programming to find the optimal strategy (Chow, 1975, Section 8.1), we first minimize the expected loss for only the last period T with respect to x_T and obtain a linear feedback control equation $\hat{x}_T = G_T y_{T-1} + g_T$. We then minimize the sum of the expected losses for the last two periods with respect to x_{T-1}, assuming that the last period policy x_T shall be optimal, that is, substituting the minimum expected loss for period T into the minimand. Continuing the process backward in time, we finally minimize the sum of the expected losses for all T periods with respect to x_1 of the first period, assuming that $x_2, \ldots, x_T$ shall be optimal. This sum, after all the future minimum expected losses from period 2 onward have been duly inserted, is the expectation of a quadratic function of the economic variables y_1 for the first period only:

$$V_1 = E(y_1' H_1 y_1 - 2_1' h_1 + c_1), \tag{2.3}$$

where the coefficients H_1, h_1, and c_1 can be calculated by standard formulas (Chow, 1975, p. 179). Using (2.2) to substitute for y_1 in (2.3) and taking expectations, we have

$$V_1 = x_1' C_1' H_1 C_1 x_1 + 2 x_1' C_1' (H_1 A_1 y_0 + H_1 b_1 - h_1)$$

$$+ (A_1 y_0 + b_1)' H_1 (A_1 y_0 + b_1) + E u_1' H_1 u_1$$

$$- 2(A_1 y_0 + b_1)' h_1 + c_1. \tag{2.4}$$

Thus, assuming that the policies from period 2 onward shall be optimal, the expected multiperiod loss is a quadratic function of x_1, as given by (2.4). The optimal first-period policy $\hat{x}_1$ is obtained by minimizing (2.4) with respect to x_1, yielding the associated minimum expected multiperiod loss $\hat{V}_1 = V_1(\hat{x}_1)$.

To evaluate any policy x_1 adopted in the first period, we propose to use the difference $V_1(x_1) - V_1(\hat{x}_1)$. To evaluate a sequence of policies

$x_1, x_2, \ldots, x_N$ ($N < T$), we propose to use the sum of the differences

$$\sum_{t=1}^{N} \left[V_t(x_t) - V_t(\hat{x}_t) \right]. \tag{2.5}$$

Note that the function $V_2(x_2)$ measures the total expected loss from period 2 to period T if x_2 is adopted for period 2 and optimal policies shall be followed from period 3 onward.

The rationale of the proposed measure is as follows. At the beginning of period 1, if the optimal feedback policies $\hat{x}_t = G_t y_t + g_t$ are followed sequentially for $t = 1, 2, \ldots, T$, the minimum expected loss for all T periods is $V_1(\hat{x}_1)$. However, if a nonoptimal policy x_1 is chosen for the first period, but optimal policies are chosen from period 2 on, the total expected loss will be $V_1(x_1)$. The difference $V_1(x_1) - V_1(\hat{x}_1)$ measures the extra expected loss that is attributable to the nonoptimal policy x_1. At the beginning of period 2, again if the optimal feedback policies are followed until period T, the minimum expected loss is $V_2(\hat{x}_2)$. Because $V_2(x_2)$ is given by (2.4) with all subscripts increased by 1, it is a function of y_1. Whatever policy x_1 was chosen for the first period, it has affected the initial condition y_1 which in turn influences the total expected loss from period 2 on. But bygone is bygone. The best that one can do now is to choose $\hat{x}_2 = G_2 y_1 + g_2$. If x_2 is chosen instead, the extra expected loss due to the nonoptimal policy in period 2 is $V_2(x_2) - V_2(\hat{x}_2)$. This argument applies to many future periods, provided that the number of periods N chosen for policy evaluation is smaller than the planning horizon T used in the optimal control calculations.

The proposed measure can be applied to a nonlinear econometric model. Since a truly optimal solution to control a nonlinear model with random disturbances is not available, we employ the approximately optimal solution of Chow (1975, Chapter 12; 1976a). This amounts to finding the optimal path for the nonstochastic control problem formulated by setting the random disturbances equal to their expected values, and then linearizing the model around this path to yield a linear model with time-dependent coefficients as given in (2.2). We then follow the procedure recommended previously.

8.3 COMPARISON WITH FAIR'S APPROACH

We basically agree with the logic of Fair (1978a) in measuring the economic performance of several political administrations in the United States. However, there are several differences to be explained.

Fair's measure for one four-year administration equals (1) the expected loss during the four-year interval using the policy actually adopted, minus (2) the expected loss during the four-year interval using an optimal policy, plus (3) the expected loss in the next four-year period if the next administration behaved optimally given that the present administration did not, minus (4) the expected loss in the next four-year period if both administrations had behaved optimally. The difference between the components (3) and (4) is intended to measure the damage done by the administration being evaluated to the next administration.

To see the similarity between Fair's measure and ours, consider the case where $T = 32$ quarters and $N = 1$. That is, the performance of only the first quarter is to be evaluated, or, in Fair's terms, the administration lasted only for the first quarter. The sum of his terms (1) and (3) would measure the expected loss for all T periods if the actual x_1 is used for period 1 and optimal policies will be followed from period 2 on. Our $V_1(x_1)$ is intended to measure the same. The sum of Fair's terms (2) and (4) would measure the expected loss for all T periods if optimal policies were followed throughout. So does our $V_1(\hat{x}_1)$.

From the viewpoint of theory in the general case of policy evaluation for many quarters, there are three differences between our approaches. First, when Fair measures the expected loss for many periods resulting from the actual historical policy, he uses the open-loop approach. In other words, the decision maker is assumed to have decided on all future values of the policy instruments at the beginning of the first quarter of his administration. This is the assumption on which Fair's first term is evaluated. According to our theory, the policy maker was free at the beginning of each quarter to choose his policy. When the policy for quarter 2 was chosen, for example, the actual economic data y_1 were known to the decision maker and were used to compute $V_2(x_2; y_1)$ in our measure $V_2(x_2; y_1) - V_2(\hat{x}_2; y_1)$ of economic performance for quarter 2, which is the first period in the optimal control problem involving $T - 1$ periods. We believe that it is more realistic to assume that actual decisions were made sequentially quarter by quarter and not made once for all four years at the beginning of each administration. This difference would disappear if we were to evaluate an administration lasting for only one quarter.

Second, when Fair measures the expected loss for many periods resulting from the optimal policy, his expectation is conditional on the particular realization of the random residuals in the equations as they occurred in history. By contrast, our $V_1(\hat{x}_1)$ is not conditional on the historical observations on the equation residuals. To evaluate the multiperiod expected loss resulting from an optimal policy by stochastic simulation, one would have to use repeated random drawings of the residuals through time, and, for each set of residuals, perform the same calculations that Fair applies to the set of historical residuals. The resulting losses would have to be averaged to obtain the required expectation.

Third, the theory of Section 2 provides a measure of economic performance for each quarter (if a quarterly model is used) without having to break up the evaluation into four-year or whatever time intervals. Fair's measure can be applied to any time interval as desired, but the computations would have to be redone when the time interval changes.

From the viewpoint of computations, the method of Section 2 is much simpler than Fair's. Once we have obtained the (approximately) optimal control solution for the T period problem in the form of feedback control equations, the functions $V_t(x_t; y_{t-1})$ are available. Our measure merely requires the evaluation of $V_t(x_t)$ and $V_t(\hat{x}_t)$. The computations are extremely trivial using a modern computer. On the other hand, the expected values defined in the four components of Fair's measure would be very costly to compute if averages over stochastic simulations were performed. The cost of these simulations was thought to be so high that Fair did not actually compute the measure as he first defined it, but rather chose an approximation of the expectations by solving the model once using the historical or expected values of the residuals as the case requires. The computer program described in Chapter 5 has been applied to Fair's nonlinear model of 92 simultaneous equations for a problem involving 30 quarters. The (approximately) optimal feedback solution based on linearization as described above costs about $195 on the IBM 360-91 computer at Princeton University; it takes three rounds of linearizations to converge, with each round costing approximately 7 minutes of CPU time and $65.[1] The cost varies slightly less than the square of the number of simultaneous equations, is proportional to the number of periods, and remains constant as the number of control variables increases. Thus, solving the control problem using the Michigan Quarterly Econometric Model of 61 simultaneous equations for 17 quarters costs about $54 on the IBM 360-91 computer at Princeton; it also takes three rounds of linearizations to converge, with each round costing about $18. An illustrative calculation using the Michigan model will be provided in Section 5.

The evaluation of mathematical expectations by stochastic simulations always involves sampling errors which our analytical method using $V_t(x_t)$ avoids. However, our method is not truly optimal. Our feedback control

---

[1] The IBM 360-91 computer at Princeton is an order of magnitude faster and cheaper than the IBM 370-158 computer at Yale. Therefore the CPU time in this paper is not equivalent to the times reported in footnote 8 of Fair (1978a).

equations $\hat{x}_t = G_t y_{t-1} + g_t$ are not truly optimal because they are based on linearization about the optimal path derived from the deterministic control problem and the actual path will most probably deviate from that path. A different point used to perform the linearization would yield different coefficients A_t, C_t, and b_t for the model, and thus G_t and g_t for the feedback control equation, but the differences will not be large if the model is not highly nonlinear or if the actual path is not very far away from the above optimal path. To obtain an (approximately) optimal policy for period t, Fair minimizes the expectation (calculated by stochastic simulations) of a multiperiod loss function resulting from open-loop, rather than feedback, policies. His solution, besides incurring sampling errors due to stochastic simulations, is not optimal either, because open-loop policies are not optimal when random disturbances are present in an econometric model.

8.4   LIMITATIONS AND EXTENSIONS

Although we believe that the method of Section 2 can fruitfully be applied to the operating nonlinear econometric models for the purpose of economic policy evaluation, we mention several obvious extensions of the method when some assumptions are relaxed. First, the loss function may not be quadratic and the control variables may be subject to inequality constraints. To deal with these problems partially, we propose to incorporate the previous assumptions in deriving the optimal path for the deterministic control problem formulated by setting the random disturbances equal to their expected values, and then linearize the model about this path to obtain approximately optimal linear feedback control equations. Methods to solve the deterministic control problem required are given in Friedman (1973), Chow (1975, p. 284), and Gordon and Jorgenson (1976). Second, to deal with uncertainty in the parameters of a nonlinear econometric model, we can use the method of Chapter 3 by deriving an approximate probability distribution for the coefficients A_t, b_t, and C_t in the linearized reduced form from the assumed distribution of the parameters in the original structural equations, and obtaining the expectation $V_t(x_t)$ from the former distribution.

A computationally more difficult problem is to deal with the possible revision of the estimates of the parameters of the econometric model through time. To anticipate future revision of the parameter estimates in deriving an optimal policy for the current period, that is, to allow for active learning, is too difficult, and probably not worth the trouble. To allow for passive revision of the parameter estimates as time passes, which Fair also mentions in his paper, we would have to use a new set of parameter estimates for each period t in computing $V_t(x_t)$. This means that, for each period t, a different multiperiod control problem from t to T has to be solved, each with a new set of coefficients A_s, b_s, and C_s $(s = t, \ldots, T)$ which result from the corresponding set of estimates for the structural parameters.[2] One may question the value of the extra computations involved, but to solve a multiperiod control problem (from t to T) for each period t to evaluate $V_t(x_t)$ may be worthwhile in order to allow for the possible lack of information available to the decision maker concerning the future values of the exogenous variables outside his control. Our method incorporates the combined effect of these exogenous variables in the intercept b_t of (2.2). Rather than using the actual values of these variables after they have occurred, which the policy maker at the time of decision did not know, one may use the official forecasts at the time, and the resulting b_t, to calculate $V_t(x_t)$. Uncertainty in b_t can be treated by using a probability distribution, as pointed out in the last paragraph. The forecasts of the exogenous variable may turn out to be very poor, but the proposed method of policy evaluation is valid if the policy makers are not to blame for utilizing their imperfect knowledge to behave optimally.

8.5 AN ILLUSTRATIVE EVALUATION

To illustrate the method of Section 2, the Michigan Quarterly Econometric Model (Hymans and Shapiro, 1973) has been used to calculate the function $V_1(x_1)$. Because the function $V_t(x_t)$ is also recommended for the purpose of comparison of econometric models, which is the subject of Chapter 14, an illustrative example can be found in Section 4 of that chapter.

---

[2]Because Fair proposes to solve a multiperiod stochastic control problem by solving many deterministic control problems with shifting initial periods, his method would incur extra cost in obtaining a new set of parameter estimates for each period t, but no extra cost in computing its approximately optimal control solution.

CHAPTER 9

Has Government
Policy Contributed to
Economic Instability?

9.1 INTRODUCTION

This chapter provides an analytical framework to answer the question, has
government fiscal and monetary policy contributed to economic instability? The approach is econometric in three respects. First, an econometric
model is chosen to explain fluctuations in the macroeconomy. Second,
economic stability or instability is measured by a weighted average of the
variances of the important economic time series generated by the chosen
econometric model. Third, government policy is described by empirical
reaction functions which form a part of the econometric model used. An
answer to our question can then be found by comparing the instability
measures obtained from the chosen econometric model under two policy
regimes. These are the empirical reaction functions estimated by historical
time series data and the hypothetical reaction functions prescribing a
constant value or constant rate of change for each of the policy variables
that the government controls. It is also interesting to compare the stability
performance of a third regime, namely, the policy rule obtained by solving
an optimal control problem to minimize the instability measure subject to
the constraint of the econometric model. The third regime may serve as a
benchmark for the best performance under ideal conditions.

This chapter was coauthored by Suzanne Heller. Excellent research assistance from Stephen
Marks is acknowledged with our thanks.

131

Although the evaluation of government policy by the use of an econometric model has been practiced for some time, past studies have been characterized mainly by the use of stochastic or nonstochastic simulations, and government policy has been described by a fixed time path for each policy variable rather than by reaction functions. There are four features in the present study which, when combined, distinguish it from previous studies in this area. First, government policy is described by a set of empirical reaction functions or feedback rules, and not by given time paths or open-loop policies. To the extent that government authorities react to current and recent economic circumstances in making their decisions, and do not commit themselves to prescribed paths for the policy instruments irrespective of economic conditions, the description by reaction functions is more meaningful. Second, the behavior of the exogenous variables in the model which are not subject to government control but which are also responsible for fluctuations in the economy is described by autoregressive processes and not by the historical values that they happened to assume. This feature permits us to draw conclusions about the degree of economic stability or instability intrinsic in the system rather than occurring only incidentally for a particular historical episode. Third, the degree of economic instability is derived by analytical means rather than by stochastic simulations. The latter are subject to sampling errors. Our measures are based on the first two moments of the time series derived analytically from the econometric model used. However, because linearization is used in the derivation, some inaccuracies also creep in. Fourth, for comparison we provide a measure of instability under ideal conditions which is derived by optimization.

Section 2 outlines the analytical framework to be employed. It will elaborate on the four characteristics set forth above. Section 3 describes the econometric model used for the analysis. The basic model is the Michigan Quarterly Econometric Model as of 1977, but we will explain how the exogenous variables are described by simple autoregressive processes and how the reaction functions for the policy variables are estimated. Section 4 proposes a measure of instability, or an objective function, and presents a comparison of the instability measures under the three policy regimes: historical reaction functions, simple passive rules, and optimal rules.

9.2 ANALYTICAL FRAMEWORK

The starting point of our analysis is an econometric model that ordinarily takes the form of a system of nonlinear simultaneous stochastic equations explaining a vector of endogenous variables by their own lagged values, by a vector x_t of policy variables, a vector z_t of exogenous variables not subject to control, and by a vector of random disturbances. Our approach to stability analysis of this system consists of the following six steps. First, autoregressive schemes up to the third order are fitted to the time series data for z_t, thus in effect enlarging the system to make z_t endogenous, although z_t is still exogenous with respect to the subsystem governing the original endogenous variables. Second, empirical reaction functions are estimated for the control variables x_t. These two steps yield a dynamic model for the explanation of the originally endogenous variables as well as x_t and z_t. Third, a measure of instability is defined that is based on the first two moments of the vector y_t of state variables which may include x_t as a subvector to penalize the instability of the policy instruments. Fourth, the first two moments of the time series generated by the enlarged model obtained after step 2 are derived analytically, and the measure or measures of instability for the system are computed. Fifth, the empirical reaction functions in step 2 are replaced by passive trends for the policy instruments, and the instability measures are similarly computed for comparison. Sixth, the empirical reaction functions in step 2 are replaced by optimal feedback control equations derived by solving an optimal control problem using the chosen measure of instability as the objective function, and the resulting instability measures are also obtained for comparison. These steps will now be elaborated.

The first step consists of fitting a low-order autoregressive scheme to each element of the vector z_t of exogenous variables separately. In most cases, first- or second-order will suffice. Box-Jenkins techniques can be employed for this purpose. In the empirical work actually implemented in this study, however, the method is cruder than the Box-Jenkins techniques. We simply increase the order of the autoregressive process for each series until the residuals no longer show strong evidence of serial correlation. Bearing in mind that the purpose of fitting these autoregressions is to measure only the variances of the endogenous variables generated by the resulting system, and not the dynamic lead-lag relationships of the endogenous variables or the time series z_t themselves, perhaps one would consider a crude model for each exogenous variable to be appropriate. In our second step, we fit reaction functions for the control variables x_t. Unlike the autoregressive equations for z_t, these reaction functions employ lagged endogenous variables as explanatory variables. Existing literature on reaction functions is drawn upon for the specification of these functions.

Third, the measure of instability for each chosen endogenous or policy variable consists of two components. First, we specify a target for the variable in question, such as a target rate for inflation or a target rate for unemployment. This target rate is ordinarily beyond the rate that can be achieved—a low rate for inflation and unemployment and a high rate for the growth of real GNP. Each variable, for each time period included in the measure, is penalized by the squared deviation of its mean value from this target value. Second, the variance of each variable (about its mean value) is used to measure instability. Ordinarily, the variance by itself can be a useful measure of instability. We have included the first component in our measure to penalize mean values that reflect deviations from the desirable goals of price stability, full employment, and a high rate of growth in real GNP. The two measures combined are simply the expected deviation of each variable from its target value in each period included in the welfare measure. If we care to weight these measures for the several variables chosen to reflect economic instability, we are in effect adopting a quadratic loss function

$$E \sum_{t=1}^{T} (y_t - a_t)' K_t (y_t - a_t)$$

$$= \sum_{t=1}^{T} E(y_t - \bar{y}_t)' K_t (y_t - \bar{y}_t) + \sum_{t=1}^{T} (\bar{y}_t - a_t)' K_t (\bar{y}_t - a_t)$$

$$= \sum_{t=1}^{T} \text{tr}(K_t \Gamma_t) + \sum_{t=1}^{T} (\bar{y}_t - a_t)' K_t (\bar{y}_t - a_t), \tag{1}$$

where y_t denotes a vector of state variables which may include lagged endogenous variables (to convert the system into a first-order system) and current and lagged control variables (to include components of x_t in the loss function and to rid the system of lagged x_t which are present); $\bar{y}_t$ denotes its mean; a_t is a vector of targets; K_t is a weighting matrix; and Γ_t is the covariance matrix of y_t. If rates of change rather than levels are used when appropriate one can make a_t constant over time in practical applications. K_t is often, but not necessarily, assumed to be diagonal and time invariant, with nonzero diagonal elements corresponding to the variables selected to measure economic instability. Both an overall measure based on the quadratic loss function, or its two components, and the measures for the individual variables can be exhibited for comparison.

Our fourth step consists of deriving the measures of instability for the econometric model where dynamic equations for the explanation of z_t and x_t have been estimated. Let y_t denote a vector of state variables which include the originally endogenous variables, lagged endogenous variables for conversion of the model into first order, current and lagged x_t to rid the system of x_t, x_{t-1}, x_{t-2}, and so on (x_t being included in y_t and lagged x_t in y_{t-1}), and current and lagged z_t to rid the system of z_t, z_{t-1}, z_{t-2}, and so on (z_t being included in y_t and lagged z_t in y_{t-1}). Thus the system can be written as

$$y_t = \Phi(y_t, y_{t-1}) + \varepsilon_t, \tag{2}$$

where ε_t is a vector of random disturbances that is assumed to be independent and identically distributed with a covariance matrix V.

To find the first two moments of y_t generated by this system, given an initial condition y_0, we linearize the model about a path y_t° which is defined by

$$y_t^\circ = \Phi(y_t^\circ, y_{t-1}^\circ) \qquad (t = 1, \ldots, T; y_0^\circ = y_0). \tag{3}$$

That is, y_t° is obtained by solving the deterministic version of the system (after ε_t is set equal to zero) forward in time with initial condition $y_0^\circ = y_0$; it is thus obtained by nonstochastic simulation of the model. Gauss-Siedel methods can be employed to solve the nonlinear simultaneous equations for y_t° in each period. Note that only the originally endogenous variables are simultaneous; the remaining elements of the vector y_t of state variables are recursive. Using a first-order Taylor expansion, we write the model as

$$y_t = y_t^\circ + \left(\frac{\partial \Phi}{\partial y_t}\right)_{\!\!o} (y_t - y_t^\circ) + \left(\frac{\partial \Phi}{\partial y_{t-1}}\right)_{\!\!o} (y_{t-1} - y_{t-1}^\circ) + \varepsilon_t$$

where the subscripts "o" of the matrices of partial derivatives indicate that they are evaluated at y_t° and y_{t-1}°. Solving the system for y_t, we have

$$y_t - y_t^\circ = \left[I - \left(\frac{\partial \Phi}{\partial y_t}\right)_{\!\!o}\right]^{-1} \left(\frac{\partial \Phi}{\partial y_{t-1}}\right)_{\!\!o} (y_{t-1} - y_{t-1}^\circ) + \left[I - \left(\frac{\partial \Phi}{\partial y_t}\right)_{\!\!o}\right]^{-1} \varepsilon_t$$

$$= A_t(y_{t-1} - y_{t-1}^\circ) + B_t \varepsilon_t, \tag{4}$$

where A_t and B_t have been defined by the matrices in the previous line.

If we approximate the mean $\bar{y}_t$ generated by the nonlinear stochastic model (2) by y_t° which is obtained by nonstochastic simulations, (4) can be used to derive an equation for the covariance matrix $\Gamma_t = E(y_t - \bar{y}_t)$

$(y_t - \bar{y}_t)'$, namely,

$$\Gamma_t = A_t \Gamma_{t-1} A_t' + B_t V B_t' \qquad (\Gamma_o = 0). \qquad (5)$$

Equation 5 will be used to compute variances of the state variables which will enter the loss function (1) for the purpose of measuring instability.

Fifth, for the second policy regime, components of x_t will be explained by x_{t-1} and a constant. The results will represent passive policy without using feedback. When these equations replace the stated reaction functions for the comparison of economic instability, one has the choice of including or excluding random disturbances in these equations in calculating the variances by (5). It is perhaps more realistic to include some random disturbances to reflect the fact that the government authorities would not be able to execute any fixed rules without errors. The appropriate random disturbances would be identical with the observed residuals in the corresponding reaction functions used in the first regime to insure comparability. We will also present measures of instability for regimes 1 and 2 excluding the disturbances. These results will be used for comparison with regime 3 which employs feedback control equations without random disturbances.

Sixth, the (approximately) optimal feedback control equations are obtained by the control algorithm based on linearizing the nonlinear model as explained in Chow (1975, Chapter 12), and Chow (1976b), or Chapter 2 of this book. The computer program used to perform the calculations of the optimal feedback control equations as well as the associated covariance matrices Γ_t and the measures of welfare loss is described in Chapter 5.

9.3 DESCRIPTION OF THE MICHIGAN MODEL AND ADDITIONAL EQUATIONS

The econometric model used in this study is the November 1977 version of the Michigan Quarterly Econometric Model, which was kindly made available to us by S. Hymans. This version of the Michigan model consists of 77 equations explaining 77 endogenous variables, among which 30 are identities. In addition, there are 35 exogenous variables. As described in Section 2, the analysis here requires endogenizing all exogenous variables not subject to government control. To explain each of the 33 variables falling into this category, an equation that is primarily autoregressive in form is estimated. In Table 1 is a list of these exogenous variables and the orders of the autoregressive equations estimated. The equations themselves are contained in the Appendix.

Table 1 List of Exogenous Variables and Equations

Symbol	Meaning	Order of Lag
BTRP$	Business transfer payments	2
CCA$	Total capital consumption allowances with capital consumption adjustments	1
CCAC$	Corporate capital consumption adjustment	2
EGOV	Government employment, including Armed Forces	2
GAID$	Grants-in-aid	2
GFD$	Federal defense purchases of goods and services	2
GINTF$	Net interest paid by federal government	2
GINTSL$	Net interest paid by state and local governments	1
GSL$	State and local government purchasees of goods and services	2
GTRF$	Federal government transfer payments to foreigners	3
GTROF$	Government transfer payments to persons, excluding unemployment benefits	1
GTRSL$	State and local government transfer payments	2
HINT$	Interest paid by consumers to business	2
HTRF$	Personal transfers to foreigners	3
ICS	Index of consumer sentiment	1
IVA$	Inventory valuation adjustment for corporate profits	3
NINT$	Net interest	3
PCARS	Consumer price index for new cars	3
PCRUD	Wholesale price index for crude materials, excluding raw foodstuffs and feedstocks	3
PFP	Gross domestic farm product implicit deflator	2
PGAS	Consumer price index for gasoline and motor oil	3
PIINV[a]	Inventory investment implicit deflator	—
PM	Import implicit deflator	3
PX[a]	Export implicit deflator	2
RDIS%[a]	Discount rate, Federal Reserve Bank of N.Y.	2
RENT$	Rental income of persons with capital consumption adjustment	3
SLCSF$	Subsidies less current surplus of federal government enterprises	1
SLCSSL$	Subsidies less current surplus of state and local government enterprises	2
TSISL$	Contributions for social insurance: state and local	2
WALD$	Wage accruals less disbursements, total	2
X$	Exports	1
YGWS$	Government wage and salary disbursements	2
YINT$	Personal interest income	2

[a]Including additional explanatory variable(s) other than lagged values of the dependent variable.

137

For the purpose of this experiment, two variables are assumed to be controlled by the government in its setting of fiscal and monetary policy. These variables are the treasury bill rate (RTB) and nondefense purchases of goods and services of the federal government (GFO$). In the first policy regime, the government's use of its tools is described by empirical reaction functions of the general forms partly suggested by Fair (1978b). The reaction function for the treasury bill rate estimated using quarterly data from 1954.3 to 1978.2 is

$$
\text{RTB} = \underset{(0.31)}{1.027} + \underset{(0.10)}{1.069}\,\text{RTB}_{-1} - \underset{(0.10)}{0.233}\,\text{RTB}_{-2}
$$

$$
\begin{array}{ll}
+ \underset{(0.12)}{0.354}\,\Delta\text{PGNP}_{-1} - \underset{(0.05)}{0.151}\,\text{UG} & \quad R^2 = 0.94 \\
& \quad \text{DW} = 1.90 \\
& \quad \text{SE} = 0.47
\end{array}
$$

$$
+ \underset{(0.005)}{0.013}\,\Delta\text{GNP} + \underset{(0.006)}{0.011}\,\Delta\text{GNP}_{-1}
$$

where

$$
\text{PGNP} = \text{implicit deflator for gross national product}
$$

$$
\text{UG} = \text{global unemployment rate}
$$

$$
\text{GNP} = \text{gross national product (constant dollars).}
$$

The reaction function for nondefense purchases of the federal government was obtained by first estimating the following regression equation using quarterly data from 1954.3 to 1978.2:

$$
\frac{\text{GFO\$}}{\text{PGNP}} = \underset{(0.52)}{-0.528} - \underset{(0.01)}{0.014}\,\Delta\text{GNP} - \underset{(0.15)}{0.228}\,\Delta\text{PGNP} \qquad
\begin{array}{l}
R^2 = 0.98 \\
\text{DW} = 2.05 \\
\text{SE} = 1.20
\end{array}
$$

$$
+ \underset{(0.11)}{0.203}\,\text{UG}_{-1} + \left(\frac{\text{GFO\$}}{\text{PGNP}}\right)_{-1}.
$$

The equation was fitted using $(\text{GFO\$}/\text{PGNP}) - (\text{GFO\$}/\text{PGNP})_{-1}$ as the dependent variable; this procedure is equivalent to using $(\text{GFO\$}/\text{PGNP})$ as the dependent variable and imposing the restriction that the coefficient of $(\text{GFO\$}/\text{PGNP})_{-1}$ equals one. The equation explaining GFO$ in regime

1 is then simply

$$GFO\$ = \left[-0.528 - 0.014\Delta GNP - 0.228\Delta PGNP \right.$$

$$\left. + 0.203 UG_{-1} + \left(\frac{GFO\$}{PGNP} \right)_{-1} \right] (PGNP).$$

As can be observed, both reaction functions indicate that government behavior is leaning against the wind. Monetary and fiscal policies are contracting when recent economic data show signs of economic expansion, and vice versa.

In the second policy regime, movements of the government control variables follow smooth trends as approximated by first-order autoregressive equations. These are

$$RTB = 0.221 + 0.962\ RTB_{-1} \qquad R^2 = 0.89$$
$$ (0.19) \quad (0.04) \qquad\qquad DW = 1.34$$
$$ SE = 0.59$$

$$GFO\$ = 0.144 + 1.018\ GFO\$_{-1} \qquad R^2 = 0.98$$
$$ (0.30) \quad (0.02) \qquad\qquad DW = 2.02$$
$$ SE = 0.96$$

Finally, in the third regime, the government behaves according to feedback control equations that are given by the solution to an optimal control problem. The objective function used in this problem will be given in the next section.

9.4 MEASUREMENT OF INSTABILITY AND EMPIRICAL RESULTS

The measure of instability in the economy is taken to be the expected value of the weighted sum of squared deviations of selected economic variables from their desired values. In this study, the instability in the economy during eight quarters is measured by

$$E \sum_{t=1}^{8} \left[0.75(UG_t - 4.0)^2 + 0.75(GNP\ gap_t - 0)2 + (TB_t - 0)^2 \right.$$

$$\left. + (\dot{p}_t - 2.0)^2 \right], \quad (6)$$

where

UG = global unemployment rate

GNP gap = deviation of GNP from potential GNP (constant dollars),
as a percentage of average potential GNP over the period

TB = trade balance as a percentage of GNP

$\dot{p}$ = annual rate of inflation measured by the GNP price deflator.

E denotes expected value and $t = 0$ represents the fourth quarter of 1964. This measure of instability can be written as

$$E \sum_{t=1}^{8} (y_t - a)'K(y_t - a),$$

where

y_t is a 4×1 vector of the selected economic variables

a is a 4×1 vector of the desired values of these variables

K is a 4×4 diagonal matrix of weights.

Denoting $\bar{y}_t$ as the mean path of y_t and y_t^* as the deviation of y_t from $\bar{y}_t$, one can rewrite the above expression as

$$\sum_{t=1}^{8} (\bar{y}_t - a)'K(\bar{y}_t - a) + \sum_{t=1}^{8} \mathrm{tr}\, K(Ey_t^* y_t^{*\prime})$$

which measures respectively, the deterministic and the stochastic components of instability.

Given the initial condition y_0 of the economy in 1964.6, the equations of the first regime are used to generate the mean paths and the covariance matrices according to (5) for eight quarters required by this calculation. The results of two versions of the first regime are reported. In one, the equations explaining the control variables are subject to stochastic disturbances; in the other, they are not. A listing of mean paths and contributions to total instability of each of the important economic variables for the two versions of the first policy regime is given in Table 2.

**Table 2 Measures of Economic Instability Under Regime 1:
Empirical Reaction Functions**

A. Mean Paths of Selected Variables

	UG	GNP Gap	TB	$\dot{p}$	GNP	RTB	GFO$
1965.1	4.83	− 3.10	1.28	3.61	900.	3.73	16.8
1965.2	4.73	− 3.18	1.11	2.95	908.	3.96	17.1
1965.3	4.75	− 3.20	1.23	2.80	917.	4.06	17.4
1965.4	4.80	− 3.15	1.24	3.20	926.	4.12	17.6
1966.1	4.80	− 3.30	1.24	3.04	934.	4.18	17.9
1966.2	4.86	− 3.66	1.26	3.77	940.	4.17	18.2
1966.3	4.92	− 3.79	1.28	3.73	948.	4.20	18.5
1966.4	5.01	− 4.15	1.24	4.14	954.	4.21	18.9

B. Contributions to Measures of Instability

	UG	GNP Gap	TB	$\dot{p}$	
Control subject to stochastic disturbance					
Deterministic	4.3	71.8	12.2	17.4	
Stochastic	6.2	42.8	5.6	37.1	
Total	10.5	114.7	17.8	54.5	TOTAL: 197.4
Control free of stochastic disturbance					
Deterministic	4.3	71.8	12.2	17.4	
Stochastic	5.7	37.8	5.6	37.2	
Total	10.0	109.7	17.8	54.6	TOTAL: 192.0

The second policy regime is analyzed in a similar fashion; Table 3 provides analogous results. The variances of the stochastic disturbances in the equations explaining the two policy variables are assumed to equal those estimated for the corresponding reaction functions in regime 1.

In the third policy regime, the control equations of the government are those which minimize the sum of the basic measure of instability (6) and

$$E \sum_{t=1}^{8} \left[0.4(\text{RTB}_t - \gamma_{1t})^2 + 0.1(\text{GFO\$}_t - \gamma_{2t})^2 \right]$$

subject to the constraints of the other equations of the model, where γ_1 and γ_2 represent smooth expansionary paths of RTB and GFO$, respectively. The inclusion of these terms in the objective function serves to prevent erratic behavior of the control variables. Analysis focuses on a single version of the third regime in which government control equations are not

Table 3 Measures of Economic Instability Under Regime 2: Smooth Trends for the Policy Variables

A. Mean Paths of Selected Variables

	UG	GNP Gap	TB	$\dot{p}$	GNP	RTB	GFO$
1965.1	4.82	− 3.06	1.27	3.61	901.	3.76	17.0
1965.2	4.72	− 3.12	1.11	2.96	909.	3.84	17.5
1965.3	4.72	− 3.09	1.22	2.81	918.	3.92	17.9
1965.4	4.75	− 2.97	1.23	3.22	928.	3.99	18.4
1966.1	4.72	− 3.04	1.22	3.06	936.	4.06	18.9
1966.2	4.75	− 3.32	1.23	3.79	943.	4.13	19.3
1966.3	4.79	− 3.39	1.25	3.74	952.	4.20	19.8
1966.4	4.86	− 3.72	1.21	4.16	959.	4.26	20.3

B. Contributions to Measures of Instability

	UG	GNP Gap	TB	$\dot{p}$	
Control subject to stochastic disturbance					
Deterministic	3.5	62.2	11.9	17.7	
Stochastic	7.8	57.5	5.3	37.3	
Total	11.4	119.7	17.2	55.0	TOTAL: 203.3
Control free of stochastic disturbance					
Deterministic	3.5	62.2	11.9	17.7	
Stochastic	7.1	50.4	5.3	37.4	
Total	10.7	112.6	17.2	55.1	TOTAL: 195.6

subject to stochastic disturbance. The mean paths and components of the instability in the resulting model during the eight quarters of interest appear in Table 4.

A comparison of Tables 2–4 yields some interesting conclusions. First of all, the effect of including stochastic disturbances in the equations for the control variables is similar in the first two regimes. The inclusion of stochastic disturbances increases the contributions of the UG and GNP gap variables to the instability measurement, does not affect materially the contribution of the TB variable, and only negligibly diminishes the contribution of the inflation variable. On the whole, as expected, the versions without stochastic disturbances affecting the control variables have lower measures of instability.

Secondly, the mean paths in the second regime (Table 3) are generally slightly closer to the desired levels than the mean paths in the first regime (Table 2). The single exception to this statement is the path of inflation. However, the variances of the economic variables about the mean paths

**Table 4 Measures of Economic Instability Under Regime 3:
Optimal Control Policies**

A. Mean Paths of Selected Variables

	UG	GNP Gap	TB	$\dot{p}$	GNP	RTB	GFO$
1965.1	4.73	− 2.58	1.24	3.68	905.	0.94	20.5
1965.2	4.48	− 2.23	1.05	3.10	917.	1.51	20.4
1965.4	4.29	− 1.64	1.12	2.95	932.	1.97	20.1
1965.4	4.13	− 0.95	1.08	3.37	947.	2.35	19.5
1966.1	3.94	− 0.60	1.04	3.19	960.	2.92	19.7
1966.2	3.89	− 0.71	1.03	3.92	968.	3.52	19.9
1966.3	3.93	− 0.88	1.04	3.89	976.	4.02	20.1
1966.4	4.13	− 1.65	1.02	4.32	978.	4.21	19.8

B. Contributions to Measures of Instability

	UG	GNP Gap	TB	$\dot{p}$	
Deterministic	0.7	14.7	9.4	20.8	
Stochastic	2.9	18.0	5.7	40.6	
Total	3.6	32.7	15.0	61.4	TOTAL: 112.7

are larger in the second regime than in the first. The net result is larger measures of instability in the second regime for three of the four selected economic variables, with the fourth (trade balance) being only slightly less. Total instability in the second regime exceeds that of the first. This conclusion is very significant, for it asserts that historical government policies performed better than passive policies without the use of feedback. It is a piece of evidence contradicting the view that government policies have intensified economic instability.

Finally, while the government's historical reaction functions imply a somewhat more stable economy than the regime of smooth trends, the improvement is slight compared to what could be achieved. Under the assumption of perfect government control (without disturbances in the policy equations), total instability is lower by 1.8 percent from 195.6 in the second regime to 192.0 in the first. By contrast, an optimal control policy achieves a reduction of 42.4 percent from 195.6 for the second regime to 112.7 for the third. Component by component, optimal control reduces the contributions to instability in three of four variables. Though the inflation rate actually becomes more unstable in the third regime than in the previous two, the measure of instability due to GNP gap alone is 71 percent below that of the second regime. By comparison, in the first regime the measure of instability due to GNP gap is only 2.6 percent below that of the second. Similarly, the instability due to unemployment in the third regime is 66.4 percent lower than in the second; the reduction of this component realized in the first regime is only 6.5 percent. Lastly, optimal control policy is able to reduce the instability measure of the TB variable from its value in the second regime, while government policy according to historical reaction functions actually increases it.

The comparison with the results from the optimal control solution is meant to convey how much reduction in instability would be possible under ideal, and unrealistic conditions. There are a number of reasons why the government could not have achieved the optimal feedback control policy which we use in our regime 3. The econometric model was estimated using data up to the late 1970s and it was not precisely known by the government decision makers as of the first quarter of 1965, the first period of our experiment. Also, the model that we have used might not represent the economic environment very accurately, though hopefully accurately enough to demonstrate the point that, for the kind of economy that it depicts, government policy has not been destabilizing. The government's objective function might be different from the one we have chosen. There may be technical difficulties in executing an optimal policy. More importantly, political pressures asserted directly to the executive branch or through Congress could have prevented the achievement of the goals of price stability and full employment.

This chapter has suggested an analytical framework to measure the contribution of government policy to economic instability and has provided empirical measures for the U.S. economy using equations from the Michigan Quarterly Econometric Model. Government policies under three regimes are compared, representing, respectively, historical policy, inactive policy and an optimal policy. The method can be applied to study the effects of any alternative scheme on economic stability as long as the scheme can be represented by an equation in the econometric model used. An income tax scheme, for example, may be represented by an equation, or a set of equations, explaining disposable personal income. The method is analytical in nature, in contrast with the use of stochastic simulations. A by-product of the computations is a linearized version of a nonlinear simultaneous-equation model which can be used to obtain various policy multipliers and to study the dynamic properties of the system analytically. A major substantive conclusion of this paper is that U.S. government policies in the 1960s were more stabilizing, though only slightly so, than a passive policy would have been.

An important assumption implicit in our analysis is that when the government chooses alternative decision rules, the economic agents in the private sector will maintain the same behavioral relations. We have used the same equations for the rest of the model while inserting three different sets of policy rules for the government. Lucas (1976) argues that insofar as government decision rules constitute a part of the economic environment facing the decision makers in the private sector (consumers, wage earners, investors, and firm managers), the latter's decisions will change when the rules of the government change if these decision makers are to maximize their objective functions subject to the constraint of the economic environment. How important this point is for our analysis is an open question. When the consequences of two different policy rules of the government are studied, one would have to go through the remaining equations in the Michigan model and ask why and how each of them may or may not be affected by the policy change, and how important the effect is quantitatively. For a discussion of the econometric methods required to deal with this problem, the reader is referred to Chapters 15 and 16.

APPENDIX: EQUATIONS FOR THE EXOGENOUS VARIABLES

$$BTRP\$ = -0.018 + 1.275\ BTRP\$_{-1} - 0.250\ BTRP\$_{-2}$$
$$(0.03)\quad (0.10)\qquad\qquad (0.10)$$
$$R^2 = 0.997\quad DW = 1.93\quad SE = 0.14$$

$$CCA\$ = -0.802 + 1.033\ CCA\$_{-1}$$
$$(0.23)\quad (0.002)$$
$$R^2 = 0.999\quad DW = 1.82\quad SE = 1.15$$

$$CCAC\$ = -0.060 + 1.611\ CCAC\$_{-1} - 0.608\ CCAC\$_{-2}$$
$$(0.07)\quad (0.08)\qquad\qquad (0.09)$$
$$R^2 = 0.989\quad DW = 2.12\quad SE = 0.62$$

$$EGOV = 0.042 + 1.636\ EGOV_{-1} - 0.637\ EGOV_{-2}$$
$$(0.04)\quad (0.08)\qquad\qquad (0.08)$$
$$R^2 = 0.999\quad DW = 2.01\quad SE = 0.07$$

$$GAID\$ = 0.116 + 0.534\ GAID\$_{-1} + 0.512\ GAID\$_{-2}$$
$$(0.25)\quad (0.09)\qquad\qquad (0.09)$$
$$R^2 = 0.994\quad DW = 2.06\quad SE = 1.63$$

$$GFD\$ = 0.129 + 1.438\ GFD\$_{-1} - 0.434\ GFD\$_{-2}$$
$$(0.51)\quad (0.09)\qquad\qquad (0.09)$$
$$R^2 = 0.995\quad DW = 2.07\quad SE = 1.31$$

$$\text{GINTF\$} = -0.117 + 1.414 \text{ GINTF\$}_{-1} - 0.388 \text{ GINTF\$}_{-2}$$
$$(0.07) \quad (0.10) \qquad\qquad (0.10)$$

$R^2 = 0.998$
$DW = 1.98$
$SE = 0.35$

$$\text{GINTSL\$} = -0.029 + 1.031 \text{ GINTSL\$}_{-1}$$
$$(0.03) \quad (0.01)$$

$R^2 = 0.990$
$DW = 1.80$
$SE = 0.22$

$$\text{GSL\$} = -0.115 + 1.493 \text{ GSL\$}_{-1} - 0.478 \text{ GSL\$}_{-2}$$
$$(0.22) \quad (0.10) \qquad (0.11)$$

$R^2 = 0.999$
$DW = 1.74$
$SE = 1.18$

$$\text{GTRF\$} = 0.133 + 0.425 \text{ GTRF\$}_{-1} + 0.215 \text{ GTRF\$}_{-2}$$
$$(0.15) \quad (0.10) \qquad (0.11)$$

$$+ 0.319 \text{ GTRF\$}_{-3}$$
$$(0.10)$$

$R^2 = 0.73$
$DW = 2.19$
$SE = 0.29$

$$\text{GTROF\$} = 0.173 + 1.029 \text{ GTROF\$}_{-1}$$
$$(0.28) \quad (0.004)$$

$R^2 = 0.998$
$DW = 2.15$
$SE = 1.84$

$$\text{GTRSL\$} = -0.026 + 1.223 \text{ GTRSL\$}_{-1} - 0.200 \text{ GTRSL\$}_{-2}$$
$$(0.05) \quad (0.10) \qquad\qquad (0.11)$$

$R^2 = 0.999$
$DW = 2.06$
$SE = 0.27$

$$\text{HINT\$} = -0.043 + 1.512 \text{ HINT\$}_{-1} - 0.496 \text{ HINT\$}_{-2}$$
$$(0.04) \quad (0.09) \qquad\qquad (0.10)$$

$R^2 = 0.999$
$DW = 2.07$
$SE = 0.19$

$$\text{HTRF\$} = 0.085 + 0.387 \text{ HTRF\$}_{-1} + 0.221 \text{ HTRF\$}_{-2}$$
$$(0.05) \quad (0.10) \qquad (0.10)$$

$$+ 0.288 \text{ HTRF\$}_{-3}$$
$$(0.10)$$

$R^2 = 0.66$
$DW = 2.14$
$SE = 0.17$

$$\text{ICS} = 8.715 + 0.902 \text{ ICS}_{-1}$$
$$(3.97) \quad (0.04)$$

$R^2 = 0.81$
$DW = 2.04$
$SE = 4.37$

$$\text{IVA\$} = -0.726 + 1.319 \text{ IVA\$}_{-1} - 0.692 \text{ IVA\$}_{-2}$$
$$(0.48) \quad (0.10) \qquad (0.16)$$

$$+ 0.287 \text{ IVA\$}_{-3}$$
$$(0.10)$$

$R^2 = 0.85$
$DW = 2.04$
$SE = 3.85$

$$\text{NINT\$} = 0.075 + 1.761 \text{ NINT\$}_{-1} - 1.008 \text{ NINT\$}_{-2}$$
$$(0.12) \quad (0.10) \qquad (0.18)$$

$$+ 0.262 \text{ NINT\$}_{-3}$$
$$(0.10)$$

$R^2 = 0.999$
$DW = 2.10$
$SE = 0.75$

$$\text{PCARS} = \underset{(1.34)}{-3.582} + \underset{(0.10)}{1.430\ \text{PCARS}_{-1}} - \underset{(0.16)}{0.504\ \text{PCARS}_{-2}}$$

$$+ \underset{(0.10)}{0.112\ \text{PCARS}_{-3}}$$

$R^2 = 0.992$
$\text{DW} = 2.00$
$\text{SE} = 1.31$

$$\text{PCRUD} = \underset{(0.90)}{-1.113} + \underset{(0.10)}{1.788\ \text{PCRUD}_{-1}} - \underset{(0.19)}{0.951\ \text{PCRUD}_{-2}}$$

$$+ \underset{(0.11)}{0.179\ \text{PCRUD}_{-3}}$$

$R^2 = 0.997$
$\text{DW} = 2.05$
$\text{SE} = 3.16$

$$\text{PFP} = \underset{(2.10)}{-0.141} + \underset{(0.11)}{1.153\ \text{PFP}_{-1}} - \underset{(0.11)}{0.140\ \text{PFP}_{-2}}$$

$R^2 = 0.96$
$\text{DW} = 1.96$
$\text{SE} = 6.93$

$$\text{PGAS} = \underset{(1.24)}{-0.960} + \underset{(0.11)}{1.626\ \text{PGAS}_{-1}} - \underset{(0.18)}{0.939\ \text{PGAS}_{-2}}$$

$$+ \underset{(0.11)}{0.329\ \text{PGAS}_{-3}}$$

$R^2 = 0.993$
$\text{DW} = 1.97$
$\text{SE} = 2.85$

$$\text{PIINV} = \underset{(5.97)}{-5.043} + \underset{(0.07)}{1.144\ \text{PPNF}_{-1}}$$

$R^2 = 0.76$
$\text{DW} = 1.93$
$\text{SE} = 14.53$

where PPNF is deflator for business nonfarm GNP

$$\text{PM} = \underset{(0.67)}{0.164} + \underset{(0.10)}{1.551\ \text{PM}_{-1}} - \underset{(0.19)}{0.316\ \text{PM}_{-2}}$$

$$- \underset{(0.11)}{0.233\ \text{PM}_{-3}}$$

$R^2 = 0.997$
$\text{DW} = 1.80$
$\text{SE} = 2.42$

$$\text{PX} = \underset{(0.38)}{-1.235} + \underset{(0.08)}{1.369\ \text{PX}_{-1}} - \underset{(0.08)}{0.419\ \text{PX}_{-2}}$$

$$+ \underset{(0.01)}{0.076\ \text{PFP}_{-1}}$$

$R^2 = 0.999$
$\text{DW} = 2.13$
$\text{SE} = 1.07$

$$\text{RDIS\%} = \underset{(0.17)}{0.520} + \underset{(0.10)}{1.341\ \text{RDIS\%}_{-1}} - \underset{(0.09)}{0.432\ \text{RDIS\%}_{-2}}$$

$$+ \underset{(0.07)}{0.189\ \Delta\text{PGNP}_{-1}} + \underset{(0.003)}{0.005\ \Delta\text{GNP}}$$

$$+ \underset{(0.003)}{0.009\ \Delta\text{GNP}_{-1}} - \underset{(0.03)}{0.069\ \text{UG}}$$

$R^2 = 0.98$
$\text{DW} = 1.91$
$\text{SE} = 0.26$

$$\text{RENT\$} = \underset{(0.29)}{0.465} + \underset{(0.10)}{0.377}\ \text{RENT\$}_{-1} + \underset{(0.10)}{0.410}\ \text{RENT\$}_{-2}$$
$$+ \underset{(0.10)}{0.199}\ \text{RENT\$}_{-3}$$

$R^2 = 0.98$
$DW = 2.03$
$SE = 0.61$

$$\text{SLCSF\$} = \underset{(0.17)}{0.279} + \underset{(0.03)}{0.961}\ \text{SLCSF\$}_{-1}$$

$R^2 = 0.90$
$DW = 1.83$
$SE = 0.70$

$$\text{SLCSSL\$} = \underset{(0.03)}{-0.014} + \underset{(0.10)}{0.584}\ \text{SLCSSL\$}_{-1}$$
$$+ \underset{(0.10)}{0.433}\ \text{SLCSSL\$}_{-2}$$

$R^2 = 0.991$
$DW = 1.91$
$SE = 0.11$

$$\text{TSISL\$} = \underset{(0.02)}{-0.066} + \underset{(0.10)}{1.225}\ \text{TSISL\$}_{-1} - \underset{(0.11)}{0.190}\ \text{TSISL\$}_{-2}$$

$R^2 = 0.999$
$DW = 1.98$
$SE = 0.10$

$$\text{WALD\$} = \underset{(0.05)}{-0.002} - \underset{(0.10)}{0.237}\ \text{WALD\$}_{-1} - \underset{(0.10)}{0.208}\ \text{WALD\$}_{-2}$$

$R^2 = 0.08$
$DW = 2.10$
$SE = 0.51$

$$\log \text{X\$} = \underset{(0.03)}{-0.002} + \underset{(0.007)}{1.007}\ \log \text{X\$}_{-1}$$

$R^2 = 0.996$
$DW = 2.01$
$SE = 0.05$

$$\text{YGWS\$} = \underset{(0.23)}{0.009} + \underset{(0.10)}{0.777}\ \text{YGWS\$}_{-1} + \underset{(0.10)}{0.247}\ \text{YGWS\$}_{-2}$$

$R^2 = 0.999$
$DW = 2.06$
$SE = 1.11$

$$\text{YINT\$} = \underset{(0.14)}{-0.053} + \underset{(0.09)}{1.541}\ \text{YINT\$}_{-1} - \underset{(0.09)}{0.526}\ \text{YINT\$}_{-2}$$

$R^2 = 0.999$
$DW = 1.81$
$SE = 0.79$

CHAPTER 10

The Estimation of Total
Investable Resources

10.1 INTRODUCTION

This chapter attempts to answer the question, "what is the total amount
that a central government can invest in order to satisfy the goal of full
utilization of the nation's resources?" This question was raised to me while
I was consultant to the Economic Planning Council of the Republic of
China in Taiwan, in July 1978, but the answer appears to be of more
general applicability. Before presenting the answer, I should emphasize
that there is a second, and perhaps more important question, that of the
most efficient allocation of the total economic resources among alternative
uses. This question was also raised by the government officials in Taiwan
and was answered in a report (in Chinese) entitled *Economic Planning and
the Efficient Utilization of Resources* coauthored by other consultants (whose
names are listed in the first footnote) and myself, but it is not treated here.

The author would like to thank S. C. Tsiang of Cornell University, Mohuan Hsing of the
Chinese University of Hong Kong, John Fei of Yale University, and Anthony Koo of
Michigan State University for helpful comments and discussions. Members of the Economic
Planning Council of the Republic of China in Taiwan, in particular Shirley W. Y. Kuo, Y. C.
Chiu, and Sheng-Yann Lii have stimulated my interest in this problem. This research was
partially supported by the National Science Foundation.

10.2 DEFINITION OF INVESTABLE RESOURCES

To obtain an estimate of total investable resources I, one may begin with the following definition:

$$I \equiv GDP^* - C_p - C_g + Im - Ex$$

$$= (GDP_{-1} - C_p - C_g) + (Im - Ex) + (GDP^* - GDP_{-1}), \quad (1)$$

where GDP^* denotes potential gross domestic product, C_p and C_g denote private and government consumption, and Im and Ex denote imports and exports, all in real terms. The three terms in parentheses on the second line of (1) measure respectively total private and government savings out of the total output from the last period, import surplus, and the potential growth of gross domestic product. These are the three sources of the total investable resources available in the economy for private and government investments. One might attempt to estimate the items on the right-hand side of (1) in order to estimate the total investable resources I. This would require an estimate of potential GDP, which can be obtained by using an aggregate production function relating potential output to total labor force, total capital and technological trend, for example. It would also require estimates of total consumptions by the private and government sectors (the latter being a policy variable subject to government control), import surplus, and private investment I_p. I_p will be subtracted from I to obtain the amount of investable resources I_g available to the government. These estimates can be obtained from a suitable econometric model of the economy which includes the above variables (excepting C_g) as endogenous variables.

In order to estimate these endogenous variables from an econometric model, the values of certain exogenous and policy variables including government consumption and money supply have to be given. Using the projected values of these exogenous and policy variables, one can solve the econometric model to obtain estimates of the endogenous variables required in our estimation of total investable resources.

10.3 THE MATCHING OF INSTRUMENTS AND TARGETS

When we attempt to use an econometric model to estimate the required endogenous variables, our solution is subject to the restriction that the value of one endogenous variable, namely real GDP, has to equal its potential value estimated in the last section. On the other hand, one of the policy variables, namely government investment expenditures, is yet to be determined. This situation should present no difficulty for solution. Following the well-known approach of J. Tinbergen to economic policy, we can fix the value of one target variable (GDP) and find the value of the instrument (government investment expenditures) that would achieve the target, given the values of the other exogenous variables in the model. In other words, we exchange the roles of one dependent variable (GDP) and one exogenous variable (government investment) and solve the system of simultaneous econometric equations for the latter variable, together with other dependent variables, given the target value of the former variable, together with the projected values of the other exogenous and policy variables.

From this solution, we obtain not only the total investable resources I but its decomposition into private investment I_p (a dependent variable in the model) and government investment I_g. We can rewrite (1) as

$$\text{GDP} = \text{GDP*} = I_p + I_g + C_p + C_g + Ex - Im. \qquad (2)$$

Equation 2 appears to be an *ex post* GDP identity. However, it should be interpreted as an *ex ante* relationship between the estimates of the included endogenous and exogenous variables. It shows how potential GDP shall be distributed among its various uses, and is not simply an *ex post* accounting identity.

At first glance, we might appear to have obtained a satisfactory solution to the problem of estimating the government's total investable resources. A moment's reflection shows that this is not the case, because our solution might entail a high rate of inflation. If one finds the rate of inflation obtained from solving the econometric model in the way described to be other than desired, one can try to fix the inflation rate as another target variable and solve for the value of the required money supply (a natural instrument to control inflation). Here one exchanges the roles of a second pair of dependent variable (inflation rate) and exogenous variable (money supply). In terms of Tinbergen's approach to economic policy, we are using government investment and money supply as two instruments for the two targets, real GDP and the inflation rate. Computationally, this problem could be, but need not be, solved by using an (approximately) optimal control algorithm of Chow (1975, pp. 280–285) which aims at minimizing the expected value of a quadratic loss function subject to the constraint of a nonlinear econometric model. In this problem, the loss function includes the terms $(\text{GDP} - \text{GDP*})^2$ and $(\text{inflation rate} - \text{target rate})^2$. The two instruments or control variable are as mentioned earlier, the values of other exogenous and control variables being treated as given.

10.4   THE NEED FOR OPTIMAL CONTROL

At this stage, one might be tempted to conclude that we have solved our problem of finding an aggregate level of government investment to achieve full utilization of resources without inflation. Again, there are problems with our solution. First, there may be other objectives not yet allowed for. For example, the solution may entail an undesirable amount of trade surplus or deficit. To prevent this and possibly other undesirable results from occurring in the solution, one can include other target variables in the objective function and apply the method of optimal control to find a satisfactory solution. Not the least is the problem of possible severe fluctuations in some instruments, which can also be treated under the framework of optimal control by including the fluctuating instruments in the loss function with assigned target paths for their levels and/or rates of change. The consideration of other objectives necessitates the use of optimal control in order to minimize the expected value of a loss function subject to the constraint of a nonlinear stochastic model.

Second, the dynamic nature of our problem should be emphasized. Government investment and other policy variables in period t will have delayed effects on future GDP, inflation rate, and balance of payment. These delayed effects have to be taken into account in the planning of current government investment. Therefore, a multiperiod optimization problem as it is formulated in the optimal control framework has to be solved in order to achieve a desirable time path for government investment expenditures.

There are at least four advantages in using the method of optimal control to determine the level of government investment, as compared with the simple method of finding the values of the instruments to match the target values of an equal number of target variables. First, the assumed target values for GDP and inflation rate might be too conservative. Using the optimal control approach, one can start with more ambitious target values and find a solution which will, through optimization, come as close to these target values as possible (close in the sense of minimizing a weighted sum of squared deviations of the variables from their target values). Second, as we have mentioned, more target variables can be incorporated in the objective function than the number of instruments. The target variables may include some instruments themselves. Third, the determination of government investment and other policy variables is achieved in a dynamic setting, with due allowance for the delayed effects of policy action on future economic welfare. Fourth, uncertainty in the econometric model can be incorporated in the solution, as described for example in Chow (1975, Chapter 10).

To recapitulate, this chapter began with an apparently straight-forward econometric problem of estimating total investable resources defined by (1). It then turned into a problem of finding the value of government investment to achieve potential GDP using an econometric model in a static, one-instrument, one-target context. As the solution was being worked out, one was soon confronted with the additional problem of controlling inflation by a suitable adjustment in the supply of money. This led naturally to the problem of multiple targets and instruments. When the former outnumbers the latter because of objectives other than full employment without inflation, and when dynamic considerations are taken into account, not to speak of the difficulties created by uncertainty in the econometric model, our problem becomes one of optimal control. From the viewpoint of optimal control, to estimate a government's total investable resources is to find an optimal path for this variable which, together with the optimal paths of other policy variables, will help achieve as much as possible the objectives of full resource utilization, price stability, balance of payments equilibrium, and reasonable behavior of the instruments themselves.

It is hoped that this chapter will contribute, in a modest way, to solving an important practical problem of economic planning and to clarifying the potential usefulness as well as the conceptual basis of the method of optimal control.

CHAPTER 11

Usefulness of Imperfect Models for the Formulation of Stabilization Policies

11.1 INTRODUCTION

Econometric models are widely used to forecast the national economy. Are they accurate enough to be used by the government authorities for the formulation of macroeconomic policies? What kind of accuracy is required for them to be useful as a guide to policy? This chapter provides a theoretical framework to answer this accuracy equation, and applies it to ascertain the usefulness of two simplified models in the determination of stabilization policies.

In a review article on the comparative forecasting abilities and the multiplier effects of the major U.S. econometric models currently in use, Carl Christ writes (1975, p. 54), "though the models forecast well over horizons of four to six quarters, they disagree so strongly about the effects of important monetary and fiscal policies that they cannot be considered reliable guides to such policy effects, until it can be determined which of them are wrong in this respect and which (if any) are right." The method of this chapter can be applied to decide whether two models disagree significantly in terms of their policy recommendations. The existing models which imply different multiplier effects do "forecast well over horizons of four to six quarters." They do contain useful information, however imperfect, which can be exploited to make forecasts. Because sound economic policy is based on good economic forecasts made under the assumption of alternative policy proposals, one cannot automatically assume that the

154

same information is useless for the formulation of economic policy. Furthermore, just as two structures having different multiplier effects may produce forecasts closer to each other than to a naive forecast, they may also produce policy recommendations that are closer to each other than to a passive policy.

To show that two different models may yield the same or similar policy recommendations, consider the univariate difference equation

$$y_t = ay_{t-1} + cx_t + u_t, \tag{1.1}$$

where y_t is a dependent variable, x_t is a policy instrument or control variable, and u_t is a serially independent random disturbance with mean zero and variance v. If the objective is to minimize the expectation Ey_t^2, then the optimal feedback policy is to set $ay_{t-1} + cx_t$ equal to zero, so that Ey_t^2 achieves its minimum $Eu_t^2 = v$. The policy is therefore

$$x_t = (-c^{-1}a)y_{t-1}. \tag{1.2}$$

Another model, which has coefficients $\tilde{a}$ and $\tilde{c}$ instead of a and c, will yield the same policy provided that the ratio $\tilde{a}/\tilde{c}$ is the same as a/c. The multipliers $a^k c$ of x_{t-k} in the final form of model (1.1) could certainly be very different from those of the alternative model, as illustrated by $a = 0.9$, $c = 1$, $\tilde{a} = 0.09$ and $\tilde{c} = 0.1$. Thus, an imperfect model with coefficients 0.09 and 0.1 may yield a policy close to being optimal, if the true coefficients are 0.9 and 1 respectively.

An interesting question concerning the usefulness of imperfect models is whether they will yield policies that are superior to an inactive policy allowing for no feedback. In the above example, an inactive policy is to set $x_t = 0$. Under this policy and assuming (1.1) to be the true model with $|a| < 1$, we can easily find the variance to approach $v/(1 - a^2)$ as t increases. If the government authority uses the inaccurate coefficients $\tilde{a}$ and $\tilde{c}$ and the resulting feedback policy, the system (1.1) will become

$$y_t = \left[a + c(-\tilde{c}^{-1}\tilde{a}) \right] y_{t-1} + u_t, \tag{1.3}$$

which has the steady-state variance $v/\{1 - [a + c(-\tilde{c}^{-1}\tilde{a})]^2\}$. This variance is smaller than the variance prevailing under the inactive policy provided merely that $[a + c(-\tilde{c}^{-1}\tilde{a})]^2$ is smaller than a^2. Given a and c, a wide range of values for $\tilde{a}$ and $\tilde{c}$ will produce this required result. Hence using imperfect models can still be better than using a passive policy without feedback for the determination of macroeconomic policy.

We will generalize this discussion in Section 2 to treat dynamic econometric systems involving many variables and higher-order lags. Section 3 provides two illustrative models to be used for stabilization policy. Section 4 applies the method of Section 2 to evaluate the usefulness of one of the models of Section 3, assuming that the other model is the correct one. It illustrates how an imperfect model performs for the determination of policy as compared with using no feedback at all. Section 5 contains some concluding remarks.

11.2   EVALUATION OF IMPERFECT MODELS FOR POLICY ANALYSIS

Let the economy be governed by a time-varying linear system

$$y_t = A_t y_{t-1} + C_t x_t + b_t + u_t \tag{2.1}$$

where y_t is a vector of p endogenous variables, x_t is a vector of q policy or control variables with $q < p$, and u_t is a random vector independently distributed through time, having mean zero and covariance matrix V. The true parameters A_t, C_t, b_t, and V are of course unknown to the policy maker. We will assume that the policy maker has available an imperfect model explaining a subset of the endogenous variables y_t. Written in the form (2.1), with appropriate zeros added, this imperfect model has coefficients $\tilde{A}_t$, $\tilde{C}_t$, and $\tilde{b}_t$. The question is how well a policy based on these inaccurate parameters would work, as compared with a policy of using no feedback, for certain hypothetical values of A_t, C_t, and b_t. High-order lags in both the endogenous and policy variables are subsumed under the notation of (2.1) by suitable definitions, as will be illustrated by (3.2) in Section 3. Nonlinear systems can be approximated by time-varying linear systems of the form (2.1) for our analysis as will be explained later in this section.

The performance of the economy is measured by the expectation of the loss function

$$\sum_{t=1}^{T} (y_t - a_t)' K_t (y_t - a_t), \tag{2.2}$$

where a_t are the targets and K_t are diagonal matrices giving the relative penalties of the squared deviations of the different variables from their targets. If the behavior of the policy variables also matters, they will be included in the vector y_t by appropriate definitions. We will be interested in comparing the performance of three policies. Policy I is the optimal policy assuming perfect knowledge of the true model (2.1). Policy II is obtained by minimizing the expectation of (2.2) under the assumption of an imperfect model, with coefficients $\tilde{A}_t$, $\tilde{C}_t$, and $\tilde{b}_t$. Policy III specifies a smooth time path for the policy variables which will not be altered by future observations of the economy.

As shown in Chow (1975, Chapter 7), the optimal policy I is given by a set of linear feedback control equations

$$x_t = G_t y_{t-1} + g_t. \tag{2.3}$$

The coefficients G_t and g_t can be calculated from the model parameters A_t, C_t, and b_t, and the parameters a_t and K_t of the loss function. The economy under policy I will follow (2.1) and (2.3) which combine to yield

$$y_t = R_t y_{t-1} + r_t + u_t, \tag{2.4}$$

where

$$R_t = (A_t + C_t G_t); \qquad r_t = b_t + C_t g_t. \tag{2.5}$$

The mean path of the economy as of the beginning of the planning horizon will follow

$$\bar{y}_t = R_t \bar{y}_{t-1} + r_t. \tag{2.6}$$

By subtracting (2.6) from (2.4) and defining the deviation from the mean path as $y_t^* = y_t - \bar{y}_t$, we have

$$y_t^* = R_t y_{t-1}^* + u_t. \tag{2.7}$$

The covariance matrix of the system will therefore be

$$E y_t^* y_t^{*\prime} = R_t (E y_{t-1}^* y_{t-1}^{*\prime}) R_t' + V \qquad (t = 1,2,\ldots,T) \tag{2.8}$$

with initial condition $E y_0^* y_0^* = 0$ because y_0 is constant and $y_0^* = 0$.

By considering the deviation $y_t - a_t$ as the sum of y_t^* and $\bar{y}_t - a_t$, we will decompose the expectation of the loss function (2.2) into two parts,

$$\operatorname{tr} \sum_{t=1}^{T} K_t E y_t^* y_t^{*\prime} + \sum_{t=1}^{T} (\bar{y}_t - a_t)' K_t (\bar{y}_t - a_t). \tag{2.9}$$

One part is a weighted sum of the variances of y_t, to be calculated by using the covariance matrix (2.8). The other is a weighted sum of the squared deviations of the means $\bar{y}_t$ from the targets a_t. This decomposition will be used to study the expected losses of policies II and III as well.

Policy II is obtained by minimizing the expectation of (2.2) subject to a model of the form (2.1) with coefficients $\tilde{A}_t$, $\tilde{C}_t$, and $\tilde{b}_t$. This policy is given by a feedback control equation of the form (2.3), with coefficient $\tilde{G}_t$ and $\tilde{g}_t$ which are computed by using the coefficients $\tilde{A}_t$, $\tilde{C}_t$, and $\tilde{b}_t$ instead. The economy under policy II will be governed by (2.1) and this feedback control equation, namely

$$y_t = \tilde{R}_t y_{t-1} + \tilde{r}_t + u_t, \tag{2.10}$$

where

$$\tilde{R}_t = (A_t + C_t \tilde{G}_t); \qquad \tilde{r}_t = b_t + C_t \tilde{g}_t. \tag{2.11}$$

The mean path and the covariance matrix of this system will be given respectively by (2.6) and (2.8) with $\tilde{R}_t$ and $\tilde{r}_t$ replacing R_t and r_t. The expected loss under this regime can be similarly decomposed as in (2.9).

Policy III allows for no feedback. If one refuses to use econometric models for the formulation of macroeconomic policy, what alternatives are available? One alternative is still to adjust the policy instruments according to the current state of the economy by some ad hoc rules which are not derived systematically from an econometric model. Such rules, once stated explicitly in the form of feedback control equations, can and should be evaluated by the method here proposed. Skeptics of the use of econometric models are under the obligation to show that their alternatives are no worse. The second alternative, which we will further examine, is not to use any feedback. It can always be written as $x_t = g_t^0$ for some fixed path g_t^0 to be specified without regard to the state of the economy. Under such a rule, which implies $G_t = 0$ in our notation, the mean and covariance matrix of the economic variables will be given by (2.6) and (2.8) respectively, with $R_t = A_t$ and $r_t = b_t + C_t g_t^0$. The two components of the expected loss can be computed by (2.9).

If the true model is nonlinear and consists of random disturbances, one cannot obtain analytically an optimal policy that would minimize the expectation of (2.2) under the assumption of perfect knowledge of the model parameters. However, for our analysis, policy I will be replaced by the following nearly optimal policy, which is described more fully in Chow (1975, Chapter 12; 1976b). First, ignoring the random disturbances in the model, one finds an optimal path to minimize (2.2) using the resulting deterministic model. One then linearizes the model about this path, producing a system of the form (2.1) with time-varying coefficients. The analysis suggested above can be carried out in exactly the same way. The feedback control coefficients $\tilde{G}_t$ and $\tilde{g}_t$ for policy II are obtained by employing an imperfect nonlinear model which is similarly linearized to yield the coefficients $\tilde{A}_t$, $\tilde{C}_t$, and $\tilde{b}_t$ needed to compute them. Policy III remains to be $x_t = g_t^0$. The two components of the expected loss resulting from each policy can be calculated as before. As a generalization of the discussion of Section 1, an imperfect model yielding the feedback coefficients $\tilde{G}_t$ can be used to stabilize the economy better than using no feedback, provided that $R_t = (A_t + C_t \tilde{G}_t)$ entering (2.8) will produce smaller variances than $R_t = A_t$.

In this section, we have suggested some analytical methods to evaluate policy recommendations derived from imperfect models. Without them, one would have to perform very expensive stochastic simulations to obtain sample paths of the economy under the assumptions of a hypothetically true model and alternative policy rules. The analytical methods can be used to deduce the means and covariance matrices of the sample paths without resort to the perhaps prohibitive computer simulations.

11.3 FITTING TWO ILLUSTRATIVE MODELS

To illustrate the method of Section 2, we will employ two hypothetical linear models. These models are derived from the multipliers reported in Christ (1975) for the Michigan quarterly model and the Wharton Mark III model. Given the multipliers of the final from of an econometric model, the following procedure is applied to construct an approximate reduced form for policy analysis.

The procedure is based on the well-known relation between the reduced form and the final form. Let the reduced form be

$$y_t = B_1 y_{t-1} + B_2 y_{t-2} + B_3 x_t + B_4 x_{t-1} + B_5 x_{t-2} + b_0 + v_t. \quad (3.1)$$

We will convert it to first order and eliminate the lagged control variables by writing

$$
\begin{bmatrix} y_t \\ y_{t-1} \\ x_t \\ x_{t-1} \end{bmatrix}
=
\begin{bmatrix} B_1 & B_2 & B_4 & B_5 \\ I & 0 & 0 & 0 \\ 0 & 0 & 0 & 0 \\ 0 & 0 & I & 0 \end{bmatrix}
\begin{bmatrix} y_{t-1} \\ y_{t-2} \\ x_{t-1} \\ x_{t-2} \end{bmatrix}
+
\begin{bmatrix} B_3 \\ 0 \\ I \\ 0 \end{bmatrix} x_t
+
\begin{bmatrix} b_0 \\ 0 \\ 0 \\ 0 \end{bmatrix}
+
\begin{bmatrix} v_t \\ 0 \\ 0 \\ 0 \end{bmatrix}
$$

$$(3.2)$$

which will be rewritten simply as

$$y_t = Ay_{t-1} + Cx_t + b + u_t. \tag{3.3}$$

Note that the new vector y_t of dependent variables includes the original dependent variables and control variables as subvectors. The matrices A and C and the vector b in (3.3) are defined by (3.2). By repeated elimination of lagged y's using (3.3), we obtain the final form

$$y_t = Cx_t + ACx_{t-1} + A^2Cx_{t-2} + \cdots + A^{t-1}Cx_1$$

$$+ A^t y_0 + b + Ab + A^2 b + \cdots + A^{t-1}b$$

$$+ u_t + Au_{t-1} + A^2 u_{t-2} + \cdots + A^{t-1}u_1. \tag{3.4}$$

To construct a reduced form from the given final-form multipliers, we first make a tentative decision on the number of lagged y's and the number of lagged x's required as the reduced form was originally written in the form of (3.1). The coefficients B_i in (3.1) are related to A and C in (3.3) by definitions similar to those given in (3.2). The matrix C of impact multipliers are known. Denote the delayed multipliers $AC, A^2C, \ldots, A^kC$, respectively by $M_1, M_2, \ldots, M_k$ which are also known. We will use the relations

$$AC = M_1; \quad AM_1 = M_2; \quad AM_2 = M_3; \ldots; \quad AM_{k-1} = M_k, \tag{3.5}$$

or

$$A[C \; M_1 M_2 \cdots M_{k-1}] = [M_1 M_2 M_3 \cdots M_k].$$

Each row a_i' of unknown elements in A will be chosen to minimize the sum of squares of the deviations of $a_i'[C \; M_1 \cdots M_{k-1}]$ from the ith row m_i' of $[M_1 M_2 \cdots M_k]$. By the method of least squares,

$$a_i = [(C \; M_1 \cdots M_{k-1})(C \; M_1 \cdots M_{k-1})']^{-1}(C \; M_1 \cdots M_{k-1})m_i. \tag{3.6}$$

If the fit is poor, as judged by the sizes of the given deviations, we will increase the numbers of lagged y's and/or lagged x's in the reduced form (3.1).

For illustrative purpose, we have chosen two dependent variables, nominal and real GNP, and two instruments, Federal government non-defense purchases and unborrowed reserves. The multiplier effects of a $1 billion increase in nominal government purchases on nominal and real GNP (in billions of 1958 dollars) are given in Table 3 of Christ (1975, pp. 66–67), lines 3 and 11 showing the effects of the Michigan model and lines 5 and 13 for the Warton model. Similarly, the effects of a $1 billion increase in unborrowed reserves (or a cut of 50 basis point in the Treasury bill rate) are given in Table 4 of Christ (1975, pp. 68–69), lines 2 and 10 for the Michigan model and lines 4 and 12 for the Wharton model. The multipliers from the Michigan model are based on simulations for the 40 quarters from 1958.1 to 1967.4. From the Wharton model, they are based on simulations for the 16 quarters from 1962.1 to 1965.4. The results reported are the cumulative effects of a sustained increase in the instruments. In the notation of (3.5), they are the partial sums $M_1 + M_2 + \cdots + M_i$ for the different i. The 2×2 matrices M_i have been obtained from these cumulative effects by differencing. Since the cumulative effects were given in Christ (1975) only for selected i, crude graphic interpolations have been employed to obtain the multipliers M_i for each quarter as given by the figures under the columns M_i in Table 1A and B.[1]

After some experimentation with different numbers of lagged dependent variables and lagged instruments, it was decided that a reduced form having dependent variables lagged three quarters and instruments lagged nine quarters would fit the interpolated multipliers from the Michigan model reasonably well; and that dependent variables lagged three quarters and instruments lagged six quarters would suffice to approximate the multipliers from the Wharton model. Because of our crude graphic interpolation of the multipliers, our linearization of the models, our assumption that the parameters in the linear models are time-invariant, and our somewhat arbitrary truncation of the number of lagged variables in the reduced forms, the resulting models, to be called M and W respectively, may behave quite differently from the original Michigan and Wharton models, but they serve to illustrate the possible value of the policy recommendations from imperfect models. Note the differences between the multipliers in Tables 1A and B. For model M, the effects of government purchases on GNP become negative from period 7 on and are fairly

---

[1] A referee has pointed out the inaccuracies of our graphic interpretation of Christ's tables, especially for the multipliers M_i in column 5 of Table 1B measuring the effects of government purchases on real GNP according to the Wharton model. Because a main point of our chapter is to show that models having different multipliers may imply similar optimal policy responses, the illustrative models constructed from the multipliers of Table 1A and B will serve our purpose well.

Table 1   Final-Form Multipliers

Lag of x_1	Nominal GNP A^iC	M_i	Real GNP A^iC	M_i	Lag of x_2	Nominal GNP A^iC	M_i	Real GNP A^iC	M_i
A. Model M									
0	0.700	0.700	0.800	0.800	0	0.100	0.100	0.100	0.100
1	0.556	0.556	0.528	0.528	1	0.300	0.300	0.300	0.300
2	0.425	0.425	0.302	0.302	2	0.500	0.500	0.500	0.500
4	0.217	0.217	0.115	0.115	4	1.552	1.552	1.326	1.326
6	0.045	0.045	− 0.029	− 0.029	6	1.716	1.716	1.630	1.630
8	− 0.059	− 0.059	− 0.137	− 0.137	8	1.437	1.437	1.050	1.050
12	− 0.096	− 0.137	− 0.144	− 0.185	12	− 0.264	− 0.250	− 0.584	− 0.573
16	− 0.053	− 0.081	− 0.075	− 0.130	16	− 0.314	− 0.352	− 0.554	− 0.621
20	− 0.018	0.067	− 0.024	0.075	20	− 0.146	− 0.168	− 0.274	− 0.278
24	− 0.002	0.112	− 0.002	0.081	24	− 0.014	0.069	− 0.075	− 0.020
28	0.003	0.059	0.004	0.034	28	− 0.044	0.101	0.012	0.030
32	0.003	0.021	0.004	0.009	32	0.057	0.068	0.033	0.001
36	0.002	0.004	0.002	0.002	36	0.051	0.024	0.028	0.000
B. Model W									
0	1.300	1.300	1.300	1.300	0	1.300	1.300	1.400	1.400
1	0.258	0.258	0.983	0.983	1	1.240	1.240	1.330	1.330
2	0.205	0.205	0.750	0.750	2	1.180	1.180	1.260	1.260
4	0.132	0.132	0.351	0.351	4	1.030	1.103	1.070	1.070
6	0.084	0.084	0.100	0.100	6	0.800	0.800	0.817	0.817
8	0.046	0.054	− 0.019	− 0.022	8	0.389	0.350	0.385	0.400
10	0.012	0.035	− 0.061	− 0.092	10	0.068	0.075	− 0.016	− 0.049
12	− 0.015	0.020	− 0.068	− 0.128	12	− 0.106	− 0.090	− 0.200	− 0.181
14	− 0.029	0.009	− 0.057	− 0.123	14	− 0.155	− 0.187	− 0.216	− 0.213
16	− 0.029	0.000	− 0.038	− 0.083	16	− 0.131	− 0.220	− 0.145	− 0.171
18	− 0.022	− 0.002	− 0.018	− 0.040	18	− 0.077	− 0.157	− 0.058	− 0.086
20	− 0.011	− 0.003	− 0.002	0.004	20	− 0.025	0.048	0.008	− 0.027
23	0.002	0.000	0.010	0.000	23	0.020	0.000	0.045	0.000

large in absolute value; not so for model W. The multipliers of the monetary instrument increase in the first six quarters for model M while they decrease for model W. The reduced-form coefficients obtained by our fitting procedure are given in Table 2; they are also fairly different for the two models. The final-form coefficients A^iC of x_{t-i} deduced from the reduced form are given in Table 1; they resemble the observed coefficients M_i.

The intercepts of the reduced forms for M and W are assumed to be linear functions of time t, which takes the value 1 for 1966.1. Using the

Table 2 Reduced-Form Coefficients for Models M and W

Model	$y_{1,t-1}$	$y_{2,t-1}$	$y_{1,t-2}$	$y_{2,t-2}$	$y_{1,t-3}$	$t_{2,t-3}$	x_{1t}	x_{2t}	$x_{1,t-1}$	$x_{2,t-1}$
M	0.777	0.592	− 0.023	− 0.354	0.207	− 0.224	0.700	0.100	− 0.462	0.163
	− 0.556	1.935	0.430	− 0.788	0.121	− 0.185	0.800	0.100	− 0.631	0.162
W	1.545	− 0.392	− 0.604	0.568	− 0.111	− 0.177	1.300	1.300	− 1.241	− 0.219
	0.801	1.468	− 1.259	− 0.556	0.493	− 0.011	1.300	1.400	− 1.967	− 1.767

Model	$x_{1,t-2}$	$x_{2,t-2}$	$x_{1,t-3}$	$x_{2,t-3}$	$x_{1,t-4}$	$x_{2,t-4}$	$x_{1,t-5}$	$x_{2,t-5}$	$x_{1,t-6}$	$x_{2,t-6}$
M	− 0.021	0.127	0.051	0.130	− 0.035	0.787	− 0.067	− 0.044	− 0.040	0.014
	− 0.081	0.122	0.093	0.124	− 0.005	0.559	− 0.045	0.128	− 0.039	− 0.014
W	0.238	− 0.224	0.110	0.176	− 0.009	0.132	− 0.007	0.118	− 0.010	0.090
	1.461	0.730	− 0.490	0.062	0.005	0.031	− 0.014	0.073	0.006	0.003

Model	$x_{1,t-7}$	$x_{2,t-7}$	$x_{1,t-8}$	$x_{2,t-8}$	$x_{1,t-9}$	$x_{2,t-9}$	t	1	Model	t	1
M	− 0.027	− 0.080	− 0.028	− 0.149	− 0.020	− 0.745	0.717	21.296	W	1.863	87.162
	− 0.032	− 0.095	− 0.019	− 0.392	− 0.012	− 0.508	0.282	29.176		− 0.472	22.373

163

historical data[2] from 1966.1 to 1969.4 and the coefficients of Table 2, we have estimated the trend terms by least squares, as given in the lower right corner of Table 2. The sample residuals of these reduced-form equations have covariance matrices given by

$$V_M = \begin{bmatrix} 16.605 & 13.170 \\ 13.170 & 11.569 \end{bmatrix}; \quad V_W = \begin{bmatrix} 22.012 & 16.914 \\ 16.914 & 40.524 \end{bmatrix}. \quad (3.7)$$

The GNP figures are in billions of current or 1958 dollars. The standard deviations of the residuals are between 3.4 and 6.4 billion. The covariance matrices (3.7) will be used as the population values when the corresponding models are regarded as the true models in future analysis.

11.4   ILLUSTRATIVE EVALUATION OF TWO IMPERFECT MODELS

Before applying any stabilization policy, be it derived from an imperfect econometric model or from some ad hoc reasoning, the government authorities should examine how it would perform under reasonable assumptions about the dynamic structure of the economy. Although the structure is unknown, it is necessary to assume hypothetical structures to test the performance of any policy being seriously considered for adoption. In this section, we use one of the models of Section 3 as the hypothetical structure and evaluate the policy recommendations derived from using the other model. The planning horizon T is 32 quarters, with initial conditions given by historical data up to the last quarter of 1965. The target growth rates for nominal and real GNP are assumed to be 0.018 and 0.008 per quarter respectively; these are their average historical rates from 1966.1 to 1969.4. The diagonal elements of the K matrix are 1 and 1 for these target variables, and 0.2 and 0.2 for the instruments which are assigned growth rates of 0.011 and 0.013, their average historical rates from 1966 to 1969. This assignment is to inhibit excessive variations in the instruments.

The inactive policy provides constant growth rates for the two instruments. The growth rates chosen in our experiment are respectively 0.011 and 0.013, the average historical growth rates. In practice, a nondiscretionary policy of maintaining constant growth rates for the instruments is hard to design partly because one does not know what growth rates are

---

[2] The time series used are quarterly data on nominal GNP, GNP in 1958 dollars, Federal government nondefense purchases of goods and services (all in billions of dollars at seasonally adjusted annual rates, from the *Survey of Current Business*), and nonborrowed member bank reserves in billions of dollars (seasonally adjusted, from the *Federal Reserve Bulletin*).

consistent with price stability and full employment. We have partly bypassed the problem by using the average historical growth rates of nominal and real GNP as our target rates, and the historical growth rates of the instruments to define the inactive policy. Since both models M and W fit the historical data fairly well, applying the average historical growth rates to the instruments insures that the dependent variables will also follow the historical or target rates, on the average. A more realistic evaluation of a nondiscretionary policy would utilize the growth rates proposed by its advocate. Our analysis tends to favor the inactive policy.

Table 3A and B give the main results of our illustrative calculations. For Table 3A, Model M is assumed to be true. Policy I is the optimal policy derived from using Model M. Policy II is the optimal policy for model W. Policy III uses the average historical rates of change for the two instruments. For each policy and each period, we show separately the loss due to the variances of the variables and to the deviations of their means from the targets, as indicated by (2.9). Table 3B gives analogous results, assuming W to be the true model, with policy II being the optimal policy derived from model M. Without the stochastic control theory of Section 2, one would have to solve an optimal control problem for 32 periods using the true model or the imperfect model as the case may be, and obtain the optimum values for the instruments in period 1; apply these values, together with a random drawing of the residuals u_1 in period 1 from the true model, to generate a set of dependent variables y_1 for period 1; using y_1 as the initial condition, solve a second optimal control problem for 31 periods, and obtain the optimum values of the instruments in period 2; apply these values to generate y_2 stochastically and so forth. This tedious process only provides one observation, covering 32 periods, of the stochastic time path for a hypothetically true model and a given strategy. The process has to be repeated many times in order to estimate the mean vector and the covariance matrix of the multivariate stochastic time series describing the economy under control. The analytical method of Section 2 was used to calculate the means and variances for Table 3 in lieu of such stochastic simulations and numerous optimal control calculations.

Because the end of the time horizon is fixed, the policy recommendations for the later periods are subject to the well-known limitations of being myopic, and should therefore not be taken seriously. Furthermore, to evaluate the policy recommendations from an imperfect model realistically, one ought to allow for possible revisions of model parameters through time. For these two reasons, we consider the dynamic behavior of the economy described by Table 3A and B only for the first 12 periods. The sum for each component of the loss function over the first 12 periods is given at the bottom of Table 3A and B.

Table 3   Components of Welfare Loss

Period	Sum of Variances of GNP$ and GNP58			Sum of Squared Deviations of Means from Targets		
	Policy I	Policy II	Policy III	Policy I	Policy II	Policy III
A.	*Assuming Model M to Be True*					
1	28.2	28.2	28.2	2.6	8.7	53.8
2	31.1	34.1	74.5	8.3	32.7	156.9
3	32.7	41.5	126.7	18.0	17.3	255.5
4	34.1	43.5	180.3	27.4	63.3	322.8
5	35.5	46.3	232.3	43.2	22.5	338.3
6	37.1	55.9	279.7	42.7	61.5	317.3
7	38.5	64.0	320.6	36.1	29.1	272.7
8	39.5	73.1	354.8	29.2	68.2	214.6
9	40.2	74.9	382.6	30.7	15.8	146.5
10	41.0	77.7	404.9	22.1	59.9	83.1
11	41.6	107.3	422.5	16.5	12.6	34.2
12	42.1	178.0	436.6	13.6	40.8	6.3
Sum	441.6	824.4	3,243.7	290.4	432.4	2,202.0
B.	*Assuming Model W to Be True*					
1	62.5	62.5	62.5	30.1	96.0	121.6
2	119.8	326.9	242.0	14.9	50.2	279.2
3	135.6	540.1	420.6	4.4	129.1	344.3
4	138.5	917.6	544.3	1.3	139.6	359.2
5	139.2	1,349.7	627.1	0.5	73.8	340.9
6	139.4	1,693.8	680.9	0.3	24.9	294.6
7	139.5	1,909.9	714.2	0.1	111.3	236.1
8	139.5	2,108.5	736.2	0.0	121.6	176.8
9	139.5	2,438.9	753.3	0.0	303.8	121.3
10	139.5	3,332.8	767.4	0.1	303.3	73.9
11	139.5	4,577.6	778.7	0.2	349.6	39.9
12	139.5	6,313.0	787.0	0.3	464.7	25.2
Sum	1,572.0	25,571.3	7,114.2	52.2	2,167.9	2,413.0

For each combination of the true world and the policy, the total expected loss due to both the variances and the squared deviations of means from targets is given in the following payoff matrix (negative sign omitted).

	True Model	
	M	*W*
Optimal policy derived from *M*	731.0	27,739.2
Optimal policy derived from *W*	1,256.8	1,624.2
Inactive policy	5,445.7	9,527.2

Thus, the policy based on model W would be much better than the inactive policy even if the true world were model M, and in spite of the apparent differences in the multipliers and the reduced-form equations for the two models. However, the policy derived from model M would be much worse than the inactive policy if the true world were model W. If the policy maker were to face only these two possible states of the world, he should formulate his policy according to model W rather than following an inactive policy, because the latter policy is dominated by the former according to the payoff matrix. Of course, if the true state of the world were very different from both models M and W, one may do very poorly by following the optimal policy based on model W.

The calculations of this section are merely illustrative of the method of Section 2. The results are *not* intended to apply to the original Michigan and Wharton models for obvious reasons. The method, however, applies to nonlinear models as pointed out in Section 2, by using the (nearly) optimal feedback control equations of Chow (1975, Chapter 12; 1976b) for nonlinear models.

11.5 CONCLUDING REMARKS

In this chapter, we have described a method to evaluate the performance of the optimal policy derived from an econometric model, and illustrate it with two simplified models. Although model W differs a great deal from model M in terms of the reduced forms and the multipliers, it can still be used effectively as a guide to policy even if the world is accurately described by model M. We propose to calculate the expected loss associated with an optimal policy derived from an imperfect model under different assumptions about the true state of the world. Certainly, from an imperfect econometric model, other rules can be derived than the optimal rule given by Section 2. For example, uncertainty in the parameters can be allowed for as indicated in Chow (1975, Chapter 10; 1976a, c). Such a policy may perform better under the assumption that a different model is true. One may also devise a rule by somehow combining the parameter values from two different models so that it will behave reasonably well under both worlds. These matters are subjects for further research. Hopefully, the method outlined in this chapter will facilitate the evaluations of alternative policy recommendations and econometric models.

CHAPTER 12

Effective Use of Econometric Models in Macroeconomic Policy Formulation

At the beginning of each year, the *Economic Report of the President* of the United States makes projections of GNP in nominal and real terms for the coming year, the unemployment rate and the inflation rate and states the major fiscal and monetary policies required to achieve these target rates. For example, the *Report* of January 1976 estimates real GNP to be 6 to 6.5 percent higher in 1976 than in 1975 (p. 19), the unemployment rate to fall by almost a full percentage point and the inflation rate measured by the rise in the GNP deflator to be about 6 percent (p. 24). The associated fiscal policies include proposed Federal outlays in fiscal 1977 of $394 billion, a cut in taxes beginning in July 1976 of about $28 billion relative to what they would be under the 1974 law (p. 22). The rate of growth in the money supply M_1, as announced by the Federal Reserve, ranges between $5\frac{1}{2}$ and $7\frac{1}{2}$ percent, but the *Report* asserts that maintaining a rate of money growth at the upper limit of this range would hinder the progress toward lower inflation rates (pp. 21–22). Assuming that econometric models are being used for policy analysis, this chapter presents a systematic approach to apply some recently developed techniques of stochastic control to improve the formulation of macroeconomic policies and the accompanying economic projections.

The analysis starts with the tentative paths for the policy variables[1] that result from the existing procedure without the benefits of stochastic control

[1] The determination of which variables are the policy variables subject to the control of government authorities is often a difficult problem in practice. We will not discuss this issue because any policy analysis using an econometric model has already faced this issue and the purpose of this chapter is to introduce stochastic control techniques to implement such policy analyses.

methods. Although we assume that an econometric model is used, its inaccuracies will be duly considered. The recommended procedure consists of twelve steps.

STEP 1   Insert the tentative paths of the policy variables and the best available estimates of the exogenous variables not subject to control into the econometric model to obtain projections of the key economic variables for eight quarters. This step is already being performed in Great Britain, because the Treasury is required to maintain an econometric model in the public domain and to make and publish projections from the model given the current policy proposals.

STEP 2   Modify the econometric model, the estimates of the uncontrollable exogenous variables, and/or the economic projections if the projections from step 1 differ from those obtained from whatever existing procedure used in the formulation of macroeconomic policies. When making forecasts, econometric forecasters in the United States adjust the constants in their model utilizing observations of the equation residuals in recent quarters and other information. Others might insist on forecasting without adjustment of the model, in which case only the estimates of the uncontrollable exogenous variables and the final economic projections can be changed. Whatever adjustments of model parameters and economic projections are made, the essence of step 2 is to arrive at a set of forecasts of the important endogenous variables y_t°, a set of estimates for the future uncontrollable variables z_t°, and an econometric model which are consistent with one another, given the tentative paths for the control variables x_t°. Thus these variables satisfy each of the p simultaneous structural equations in the model

$$y_{it}^\circ = \Phi_i(y_t^\circ, y_{t-1}^\circ, x_t^\circ, z_t^\circ) + \varepsilon_{it} \qquad (i = 1, \ldots, p) \qquad (1)$$

if the random residual ε_{it} is set equal to zero.

STEP 3   Set target values for the future unemployment rate, inflation rate, real GNP, measures of balance of payments and possibly other important economic variables which are somewhat more desirable than the values given by y_t° in step 2. The motivation here is to find out whether the tentative path x_t° for the policy variables can be improved upon by performing optimal control calculations. To do so, we choose a quadratic loss function and use the above target values as elements in the vector a_t:

$$W = \sum_{t=1}^{T} (y_t - a_t)' K_t (y_t - a_t), \qquad (2)$$

where K_t is a diagonal matrix giving weights according to the relative importance of the target variables, and the planning horizon T can be set equal to about 20 quarters.[2]

STEP 4   Linearize the equations (1) about the tentative paths y_t° and x_t°, given z_t°, obtaining a linear model of time-dependent coefficients, and compute the optimal feedback control equation

$$x_t = G_t y_{t-1} + g_t \tag{3}$$

which minimize the expectation of the loss function (2) subject to the constraint of the linear stochastic model. A computer program is available for this purpose, as described in Chapters 2, 4, and 5.

Briefly, the computer program applies the Gauss-Siedel iterative method to solve the possible nonlinear econometric model for y_t°, given z_t° and x_t°, as required in step 1. It automatically linearizes the nonlinear structural equations (1) which are input to the program in Fortran code, and solves the resulting linear structural equations to obtain a set of linear reduced-form equations

$$y_t = A_t y_{t-1} + C_t x_t + b_t + u_t, \tag{4}$$

where the intercepts b_t incorporate the effects of z_t and the vectors of random residuals u_t are related to the residuals ε_{it} of (1) in a well-known manner. Then the coefficients G_t and g_t of the optimal feedback control equations (3) are computed. In the previous notation, the vector y_t includes variables introduced to eliminate endogenous variables lagged more than one period and includes x_t as a subvector so that the loss function (2) has only y_t as argument.

By the use of this computer program after a set of optimal feedback control equations is obtained, a new set of y_t° will be calculated to correspond to the new policies, and the nonlinear model will be linearized around the new tentative paths for y_t° and x_t°, yielding a new set of linear reduced-form equations (4). Another set of optimal feedback control equations are obtained, and the computations are repeated until the process converges. Our experience with several U.S. models, including the Klein-Goldberger model, the St. Louis model, and the University of Michigan Quarterly Econometric Model, is that it takes about three rounds of linearizations to converge. The Michigan model contains 61 endogenous

---

[2] In using a planning horizon as long as 20 quarters, we are not assuming that the econometric model will be very accurate in making projections that far ahead, but we have to anticipate and incorporate the delayed effects of current policy in order to avoid recommending policies that will yield desirable results in the near future but undesirable consequences later on.

variables from the original simultaneous equations plus 71 more new endogenous variables to convert the system into first order, plus three variables $y_{133,t} = x_{1,t}, \ldots, y_{135,t} = x_{3,t}$ which are equal to the three control variables selected for our experiments, giving a vector of 135 elements for y_t in (1). To compute the optimal solution in one round of linearizations using the Michigan model for a 17-period control problem with three control variables, it costs about \$20 at the Princeton University Computer Center equipped with an IBM 360-91 Computer. The cost is expected to be about four times (or 2^2) if the size of the model doubles. If the number of planning periods changes, the cost will change linearly because the program takes advantage of the time structure of the problem and computes the feedback coefficients G_t and g_t period by period. Control algorithms which treat a minimization problem with respect to the total number of variables (equal to the number of control variables times the number of periods) without regard to the time structure of the optimization problem will become much more than twice as expensive when the number of variables doubles. Our program has the additional property that its cost will hardly increase at all when the number of control variables increases.

STEP 5 Change systematically the weighting matrix K_t and the targets a_t in the loss function (2) and reoptimize in order to trace out the best combinations of the future inflation rates and unemployment rates attainable given the econometric model. The procedure is described in detail in Chapter 7. Essentially, if the weight $k_{11,t}$ corresponding to the unemployment rate y_{1t} is very large as compared with the weight $k_{22,t}$ for the inflation rate y_{2t}, and if the target a_{1t} for y_{1t} is set at 5 percent and the target for the inflation rate is set low enough, the solution will give the lowest inflation rate attainable for a 5 percent unemployment. By varying a_{1t} from 4 to 8 percent, one can compute the optimum solutions to find out the best inflation rates corresponding to these various unemployment rates and the associated policies required to achieve them. Because we are dealing with T periods, it may be useful to plot the mean unemployment and inflation rates over these periods, or to plot the root mean squared deviations of these rates form their targets.

STEP 6 Present the results of step 5 to the policy makers who will then make a choice among the best feasible combinations of unemployment and inflation. It is quite likely that the unemployment and inflation rates from the tentative solution in step 1 are dominated by the solutions obtained in step 5. If the solution for the unemployment rate is around 6 percent in step 1, say, the solution in step 5 using $a_{1t} = 6$ percent guarantees that the resulting inflation rates are the lowest possible as a consequence of optimization. The choice made here and the corresponding optimal policy will constitute set of intermediate solutions paths for y_t and x_t for further analysis and improvement.

STEP 7   If the solution paths for the policy variables in step 6 drift very far away from the paths in step 1 or show severe fluctuations, impose penalties in the loss function for them and reoptimize. The weights in the K_t matrix may be assigned to the levels of the policy variables which are given certain reasonable target paths. Or the quarter-to-quarter changes in some policy variables can be dampened by introducing the first differences as new variables which are then given appropriate weights in the K_t matrix and steered toward the target zero. Perhaps trials and errors are required in this step to obtain reasonable solution paths for the control variables.

STEP 8   Examine the reasonableness of the new solutions for y_t and x_t in step 7 using any outside information available. Adjust the econometric model and reoptimize if necessary. The need to adjust the econometric model and/or the estimates of the uncontrollable exogenous variables may arise at this stage because the new solutions in step 7 may be quite far from the solutions in step 1, affecting the accuracy of the econometric model as an approximation of reality and even conceivably affecting the values of some variables which have been treated as exogenous but may indeed react to sizable changes in policies. Reoptimize after the model is adjusted.

STEP 9   If a second reasonable econometric model is available, it would be useful to apply the policy paths in step 8 to it and compare its projections of unemployment, inflation, and real GNP with those obtained from the first model in step 8. If the two sets of projections are similar, or if the second set is as satisfactory as the first set from the original model (so that there is no risk of very bad performance if the alternative model is true), conclude the search for optimal policies and go to step 11. Otherwise, go to step 10.

STEP 10   Examine the consequences of at least three policies, (a) the optimal policy based on the first model as obtained in step 9, (b) the optimal policy based on the second model using the same loss function to be similarly computed, and (c) the originally proposed policy used in step 1, under the alternative assumptions that one of the two models is correct. Here a 3×2 payoff matrix can be utilized, with three policies combined with two possible states of the world or models. By applying the three policies to the two models, we can compute the total expected losses for eight quarters, say, to be entered in the above payoff matrix. If policy (a) or (b) dominates policy (c), as shown by the first or second row of the matrix having smaller losses than the third row, we have found an improvement over the policy originally proposed. If neither policy (a) nor (b) dominates (c), the payoff matrix will still serve as a useful tool of analysis. If one takes the Bayesian approach, he assigns probabilities to the two models and chooses that policy which minimizes the expected loss obtained by weighing the losses from the policy by the probabilities. If one is conservative, he may choose the minimax strategy. An illustrative analysis using such a payoff matrix can be found in Chapter 11.

What if the two models disagree, as shown by large expected losses in the 1-2 and 2-1 entries in the matrix, and one is unwilling to take the Bayesian approach to resolve the conflict? A further analysis can be performed. It is based on the idea that policies are made sequentially period by period, and that the policy maker does not have to follow the policy recommendations computed from one model for many future periods after he decides to follow it for a quarter or two. The analysis described in the last paragraph ignores the possibility of shifting and revising models as it examines the expected total loss for many periods when the policy recommendations from one model are followed throughout. The disagreements between the policy recommendations from two different models would be reduced and the difficulties in choosing between conflicting policies would diminish if this possibility is taken into account. The first-period policies from the two models may not differ by very much even if following the recommendations from the two models for many periods would lead to very different consequences. Furthermore, assuming that the first-period policies based on the two models differ greatly, and that their multiperiod expected losses also differ, the policy maker would still not face a serious dilemma if he knows that following the policies from model 1 for one or two quarters and shifting to the policies from model 2 afterwards will be nearly as good as following the policies from model 2 for all periods when model 2 happens to be the true model.

In essence the *i-j* entry of payoff matrix in this analysis should show the total expected loss for many periods if the policy recommendation from model *i* is followed *only for period 1* but the policies from model *j* will be followed afterwards. This construction is based on the notion that the decision for the first quarter, even if it is mistaken, can be corrected in the following quarters. Therefore, the damage done in this quarter is measured by the difference between the multiperiod losses incurred when (1) following the wrong policy of model *i* for one quarter but the correct policies of the right model *j* afterwards, and (2) following the policies of the correct model *j* all through, the latter being given by the *j-j* entry of the payoff matrix. Such a matrix is quite easy to compute if the optimal stochastic control algorithm described in step 4 is used. This algorithm is derived from the method of dynamic programming (Chow, 1975, Chapter 8) by which one reduces successively the problem of minimizing the expected loss for T periods to the problem of minimizing the expected loss for one period, starting with the problem for period T, and then the problem for the last two periods, and so forth, until the problem for all T periods is solved. The final problem amounts to minimizing the expectation of a quadratic function $y_1'Hy_1 - 2y_1'h + c$ of only the variables y_1 in period one with respect to the first-period policy x_1, it being understood that, whatever the outcome y_1 for period 1 turns out to be, the future policies $x_2,\ldots,x_T$ shall be optimally chosen (See Chow, 1975, pp. 178–179). Using the right-hand side of (4) to substitute for y_1 in the given quadratic loss function and taking its expectation, we find the total expected loss for T periods to be a quadratic function of x_1, say $x_1'Q_jx_1 - 2x_1'q_j + d_j$, where the subscript j indicates that the optimal control calculations are performed using model j. This function gives the expected T-period loss if x_1 is applied in the first period *and* x_2 to x_T shall be optimally chosen according to model j, under the assumption that model j is true. If we minimize this function with respect to x_1, we obtain the optimal first-period policy according to model j. If we apply the three different first-period policies x_1 used in the construction of the 3×2 payoff matrix to evaluate this function, we will obtain the entries for the jth column of the required payoff matrix.

The purpose of step 10 is to arrive at a final policy recommendation for the current quarter. Even the payoff matrix constructed in the last paragraph may show seriously conflicting first-period recommendations from the two alternative models, but a decision has to be reached by the Bayesian, Minimax, or some other criterion. It is better to know the various risks involved under the alternative states of the world when making a decision than not to know them at all. When faced with conflicting recommendations, one may attempt to find a robust policy which would work reasonably well under the alternative models. This is a subject requiring further research. One approach is to modify the optimal policies by allowing for the uncertainty in the estimated parameters of the econometric models used, as described in Chapter 3.

STEP 11   Calculate the mean paths and the covariance matrix of the major economic variables using a reasonable model and the optimal feedback control policy chosen at the last step. The decision makers should be informed of the likely consequences in the future when the recommended policy is applied. Using (3) and (4) obtained in step 4, we obtain a linear approximation of the dynamic stochastic system under control

$$y_t = (A_t + C_t G_t)y_{t-1} + (b_t + C_t g_t) + u_t$$

$$= R_t y_{t-1} + r_t + u_t. \tag{5}$$

The mean path of this system is given by

$$\bar{y}_t = R_t \bar{y}_{t-1} + r_t. \tag{6}$$

Using $y_t^* = y_t - \bar{y}_t = R_t y_{t-1}^* + u_t$, we can compute the covariance matrix by

$$Ey_t^* y_t^{*\prime} = R_t(Ey_{t-1}^* y_{t-1}^{*\prime})R_t' + Eu_t u_t',$$

where the covariance matrix $Eu_t u_t'$ of the reduced form residuals are calculated from the estimated covariance matrix of the residual ε_t in the structural equations (1).

STEP 12   If the previous steps are followed each quarter, the econometric models used will be revised and improved, and more weights will eventually be given to the recommendations from the models that have shown a better tracking record.

Why should the procedure outlined be adopted? It will make explicit the underlying rationale in the making of macroeconomic policies. If such an approach is not used, one would wonder on what basis government macroeconomic decisions are reached, what dynamic relationships among the important economic variables are assumed in policy making, and what objectives the government is trying to achieve. Once these questions are answered explicitly and quantitatively, the logical approach is to write down the dynamic economic equations and the objective function, and to find the policies that would best achieve the objectives. This is precisely our recommendation. We have simply filled in the details in implementing such an approach by bringing the available econometric knowledge to bear and by designing a computationally efficient procedure to find optimal policies that are to be made sequentially and to ascertain the economic consequences of such policies.

The reader will have recognized that, although we suggest the use of stochastic control techniques for policy analysis, we are far from advocating the automatic use of these techniques without the intervention of human judgment and political considerations. Needless to say, poor policy recommendations are likely to follow from poor econometric models, no matter whether optimization techniques are used or not. In reality, technical economic advice may play only a limited role in the formulation of economic policies. Whatever its limited role, the current practice has already incorporated the use of econometric models to simulate the likely outcomes of alternative policy proposals. We merely suggest a computationally more efficient way to obtain good policy proposals and to deduce the likely consequences of the proposed policies as indicated in step 11. Furthermore, by subjecting the econometric models to more serious scrutiny through the optimal control solution in step 8 and to continuous reexamination in step 12, it is hoped that the quality of econometric models will be improved in the process.

CHAPTER 13

Econometric Analysis of Soviet Economic Planning by Optimal Control

13.1 THREE USES OF OPTIMAL CONTROL IN THE ANALYSIS OF PLANNING

Most applications of optimal control techniques to economics that have appeared in the literature, including those set forth in this book, are concerned with western economies rather than with the eastern, planned economies. This phenomenon is due more to the familiarity and interest on the part of the authors who are mostly residents of the western world, than to the appropriateness and applicability of the techniques themselves. Insofar as optimal control techniques are invented to find the optimal ways to maximize a given criterion function over time subject to the constraint of the economic environment, they are useful in solving the main problem of dynamic economics, namely the optimal allocation of limited resources over time to achieve a set of competing objectives. This economic problem is no less important for the centrally planned economies than for the essentially market and private-enterprise economies. In fact, the central planner faces a more formidable task than a government economics official in a market economy because the latter leaves to the forces of the market the solution of many economic problems. In an economy where the government is engaged in central economic planning,

This chapter was coauthored by Donald W. Green. We would like to thank SRI-International for supporting the initial phase in this project and Ozer Babakol, Everett Rutan, and Vladimir Kontorovitch for very able programming assistance, and to acknowledge financial support from the National Science Foundation.

177

the techniques of optimal control are very useful. This chapter illustrates the applications of control methods to the study of Soviet economic planning.

To understand the allocation problem over time facing the central planner, consider first an extremely simplified economy where only one good Y is produced with two inputs, labor L and capital K, and where the quantity of labor is assumed to be fixed. The only control variable is investment I_t, and the objective function has consumptions C_t ($t = 1, \ldots, T$) as arguments. The model consists of three equations: the production function $Y_t = f_1(L_t, K_{t-1})$, the output identity $Y_t = C_t + I_t$, and the investment identity $K_t = (1 - \delta)K_{t-1} + I_t$, where δ is the rate of depreciation. There is a trade-off between current consumption and future consumption. Future consumption can be augmented by increasing current investment which means curtailment of current consumption. The method of optimal control can be used to determine the optimal time path for I_t.

It is not difficult to generalize this simple model to allow for many commodities. Total output Y has many components Y_i ($i = 1, \ldots, m$). Final demand may include different consumption goods, investment goods, and defense expenditures. For example, in the model of the Soviet economy to be used in this study, gross domestic product includes total industrial output, construction output, transport-communication output, domestic trade, services, and total agricultural output. Total industrial output is further composed of outputs of (1) electric power, (2) coal products, (3) petroleum and gas, (4) industrial materials, (5) machine-building and metal-working, (6) industrial consumer goods, and (7) processed foods. These are components of Y_t and each component requires a production function with labor and capital used in its production as arguments. The end uses of Y_t are total consumption, total investment, total defense spending, investment in capital repair, and investment in total livestock. The control variables include investments in the 12 different output categories (seven industrial products, plus construction, transport, agriculture, housing, and livestock). Again, there is a trade-off between current consumption and future consumption which can be augmented by current investment. Investment in one product category takes away from current consumption because of the total output identity and helps to increase the capital stock for future production of that product. Furthermore, there are trade-offs between investments in different product categories. Different products contribute to total gross domestic product according to a set of fixed weights, but the marginal product of the services from the capital stock used in producing any product is diminishing. The method of optimal control can be used to determine the optimal time paths for the investments in different product categories.

Among the many uses of optimal control for the econometric study of central planning, our discussion will be confined to only three. First, we will show how optimal control is used to examine the validity of the constraints as specified by the econometric model. It has been pointed out in Chapter 2 that the Klein-Goldberger model does not impose a trade-off between inflation and unemployment. By choosing appropriate government policy, according to that model, any targets for real GNP (or total employment) and the price level can be achieved. This characteristic was uncovered by our optimal control experiments described in Chapter 2. On the other hand, both the Michigan model and the St. Louis model impose a trade-off relationship between unemployment and inflation, as we have discussed in Chapter 7. Similarly, optimal control can be used to find out whether an econometric model of a centrally planned economy imposes appropriate restrictions on total output and appropriate trade-offs between consumption expenditures and defense expenditures. In the optimal control problems to be reported below, the objective function includes the following six variables: meat production, gold stock, housing stock, real GDP, defense procurement expenditures, and household consumption. One way to find out whether the model constraints are appropriate is to specify the target values for these six variables to be 10 percent above their historical values and try to use optimal control to achieve these targets. If these targets can be achieved simultaneously, and the values of the control variables are feasible, the model would be considered inappropriate. This exercise is useful in checking the validity of an econometric model for central planning.

Second, having ascertained the existence of a set of appropriate constraints in the model of a planned economy, one can trace out the trade-off relationships between important variables such as consumption and defense in the same way that the relation between inflation and unemployment implicit in a model of the U.S. economy was traced in Chapter 7. This can be done by imposing a high weight for defense expenditures and a lower weight for consumption expenditures in the objective function. The targeted path for the former will be achieved and the values of consumption expenditures will be made as high as possible given the target path for defense expenditures. By specifying alternative target paths for defense, one can trace out the best achievable consumption paths associated with them, thus uncovering the trade-off relationship between the two.

Third, if we are willing to make the assumptions that the Soviet government maximizes the objective function having the same form as the one we have selected and that our model is a good description of the Soviet economy as conceived by the Soviet government, we can use optimal control methods to estimate the parameters of the preference function of the Soviet government. If one succeeds in estimating these parameters, one can use control techniques to find the optimal paths for the control variables (including investments in different production sectors, among others) and for the associated endogenous variables in the model for the future. Thus, for the purpose of forecasting the Soviet economy, one can dispense with the investment equations in the original econometric model which use as explanatory variables the announcements of the five-year plan targets, and replace them by the investment paths obtained by solving an optimal control problem on behalf of the Soviet government.

This chapter will illustrate only the first use of optimal control in the econometric analysis of Soviet planning. The third use is closely related to the problem of estimating rational expectations models as discussed in Chapter 16. The estimation of the parameters in the preference function of government authorities is still a topic of ongoing research. Although several statistical methods of estimation are set forth in Chapter 16, their empirical implementation remains to be further investigated.

In Section 2, we provide a description of the econometric model to be analyzed. Section 3 describes how our control experiments are set up. It specifies the target variables, the control variables, and the objective function to be used. Sections 4 and 5 report on our efforts to check the validity of the model constraints on total production and on the allocation of investments in different industries, respectively. Section 6 suggests some respecifications of the model to deal with certain weaknesses uncovered in Sections 4 and 5.

The model that we have analyzed was constructed for forecasting purposes. In certain respects, it did not impose sufficiently tight constraints on the production sectors for the analysis of economic planning. We will show how control techniques can be used to uncover weaknesses in the model, and how the model can be modified for the derivation of the production frontiers in a planned economy. Therefore, the detailed analysis to be reported will serve mainly to illustrate the first use of optimal control.

13.2   THE STRUCTURE OF SOVMOD V

To illustrate the first use of optimal control, we have employed SOVMOD V which is the latest version of SOVMOD, the SRI-WEFA Soviet Econometric Model. SOVMOD V has 127 endogenous variables and is of approximately the same size as the original model presented in Green and Higgins (1977). However, there have been significant changes in the level of disaggregation in various blocks of the model and some changes in the specification of certain relationships. Considerable detail has been added in agriculture, energy, industrial production, and foreign trade by using the experience gained in the development of larger versions of SOVMOD. On the other hand, the original detail provided in SOVMOD I in such areas as prices, wage rates, household incomes and the State Budget has been significantly reduced in the new model. Those features of the model that have been most important in forecasting and scenario analysis have been expanded and refined, whereas those elements that have been less important for those purposes have been compressed.

This econometric model is our best representation of the Soviet economy for the period 1960–1978, and corresponds in most respects to the conception of the Soviet economy held by Soviet economic decision makers. This latter description of the Soviet economy is, of course, much more complex than SOVMOD V and would differ in some respects:

1 Soviet planners view technology as more nearly linear in the medium term, but they give considerable attention to projecting future changes in "linear technologies."

2 Given more extensive information on potential investment projects, Soviet planners focus more on the consistency of the investment plan and would not be interested in SOVMOD's investment functions. This is precisely the component in SOVMOD that is suppressed under optimal control, where the model itself and other imposed constraints should help insure investment consistency along the growth path.

In SOVMOD V, the following features of the Soviet economy have been incorporated in the specification:

1 Technological regularities in production, the end-use composition of final output, and the lags in capital construction.

2 Behavioral responses to short-run circumstances outside of the planners' control such as weather and the world economy.

3 Institutional patterns with regularity in the medium term such as the five-year-plan cycle in construction, allocations of labor, household income and consumption, and foreign trade with socialist countries.

4 Purposive behavior in the accumulation of physical capital, livestock, and imported capital and technology to meet medium-term and long-run objectives.

The structure of equations in SOVMOD V is presented in Table 1 and the level of disaggregation in production is presented in Table 2. The remainder of this section discusses briefly the specification of the equations in the same order as they are listed in the Fortran code MODELS used in the optimal control program. Variable numbers are provided to facilitate reference to the code given in the Appendix. For a description of the method of coding, the reader is referred to Section 4.2 of Chapter 5.

Table 1 Structure of Equations in SOVMOD V: Optimal Control Version

Block	Behavioral		Identities	Total
	Stochastic	Control		
A Agricultural production	8		3	11
F Balance of payments	3	1	7	11
I Investment	2	12	4	18
K Capital formation	14		4	18
N Employment	15		1	16
X Nonagricultural production	12		4	16
Foreign Trade				
E Exports	8	1	4	13
M Imports	11	1	2	14
Z Incomes	5		0	5
C Consumption	4		1	5
Total	82	15	30	127

Table 2 Sector of Origin Disaggregation in SOVMOD V

Symbol	Sector or Branch
XCROP70	Total crops, in billions of 1970 rubles
XANIM70	Animal product output
AFEED70	Animal feed (minus)
XAGT70	Total agricultural production
XIEP	Electric power
XICP	Coal products
XIPP	Petroleum and gas
XIEN	Domestic energy production
XIMA	Industrial materials (ferrous and nonferrous metallurgy, chemicals, construction materials, wood products, paper and pulp)
XIMB	Machine-building and metal-working
XISG	Industrial consumer goods
XIPF	Processed foods
XIT	Total industrial output
XICN	Construction output
XITC	Transport and communication
XIDT	Domestic trade
XISV	Services
XIGDP	Gross domestic product

13.2.1 Agricultural Production

Normal output of total crops y_1 and total grain y_4 are determined by land w_1, labor y_{61}, capital y_{54}, and current inputs y_{11} (fertilizers, fuels, etc.). The production functions used are Cobb-Douglas, restricted to constant-returns-to-scale, and have imposed output elasticities for capital. The actual outputs of crops y_2 and grain y_5 are functions of normal output and three weather variables—spring and summer precipitation w_2, winter temperature w_3, and winter precipitation (snow cover) w_4.

The output of total animal products y_6 and meat y_7 are determined by the initial size of the herd y_{10} and the feed fed to livestock y_8. Meat production y_7 can also be augmented in the short term by a higher slaughtering rate. Feed fed to livestock y_8 is determined by normal crop output y_1, the current and lagged state of the harvest y_3, and imported grain from the West. Agricultural current purchases from other sectors y_{11} are determined by normal crop output (requirements) and lagged materials production y_{80} (availability).

In our experiments, the planners can influence agricultural output by new capital investment in agriculture $y_{36} = x_{11}$, investment in the livestock herd $y_{39} = x_{12}$, investment in the branch of industrial materials $y_{26} = x_4$, and grain imports from the West x_{15}. Land sown to crops is given exogenously and agricultural employment y_{61} can only be influenced slightly by housing investment x_{10}.

13.2.2 The Balance of Payments

The merchandise trade balance y_{12} is a function of the trade balances with the West y_{101} and with LDC's $y_{109} - y_{110}$. The determination of gold sales $y_{13} = x_{13}$ is driven by the exogenous discrete variable w_6 which indicates whether gold will be sold during the year. If gold is sold, the value of gold sales is determined by the price w_7 and the level of indebtedness y_{21} relative to the target level w_8. Interest payments y_{14} are a simple function of the level of indebtedness y_{16} with an estimated interest rate of 8 percent per annum.

Net indebtedness y_{16} shifts each year given the balance on current account y_{15}. Deposits abroad w_{11} and official credits w_{13} are treated as exogenous variables in this simple model. The residual debt category is commercial debt y_{18}. A debt service ratio y_{20} is computed in the model and used with the net debt ratio y_{21} to estimate behavioral response in foreign trade and gold sales. Gold reserves y_{22} are determined by a final identity given annual production w_{14} and current sales y_{13}.

Under simulation, Soviet gold sales becomes a control variable to defray deficits in merchandise trade with the West. Hopefully, we may establish the trade-offs among machinery imports, domestic energy, and gold reserves.

13.2.3   Investments

In the forecasting version of SOVMOD V, budgetary financing variables (*ex ante* in the annual plan) and defense expenditures (procurement and operating categories) influence the growth and composition of new capital investment in the economy. Dummy variables are introduced for certain patterns such as the five-year-plan cycle and centralized interventions. The state of the harvest y_3 and gross profits y_{122} also affect the growth of new capital investment in certain sectors and branches. However, those two endogenous variables are determined largely by exogenous variables so that there is only a very small degree of endogeneity in the investment block.

In SOVMOD V, an additional equation determines the supply of investment goods y_{38} as a function of machinery production y_{81}, defense procurement y_{90}, net imports of machinery, and total construction activity y_{85}. This equation is used to constrain total investment when the model is operated under optimal control. Most categories of investment become instruments for the optimization experiments. Capital repair expenditures y_{40}, the Soviet category closest to depreciation, is determined as a percentage of total capital stock y_{58}.

Net investment in livestock $y_{39} = x_{12}$ is a function of the current and lagged state of the harvest y_3, with certain interventions after the 1963 harvest and in the late 1960s. Under optimal control, the actual investment in livestock becomes a control variable.

13.2.4   Capital Stock

Gross increments to end-year capital stocks y_{41} to y_{54} for 14 sectors are determined by lag distributions over capital investment expenditures. The equations for these variables which translate flow expenditures into stocks (measured in different prices) also include the five-year-plan cycle w_{16} and various central interventions as explanatory variables. For stocks of imported machinery y_{55} to y_{57}, identities are used to cumulate nominal machinery imports into real stocks measured in domestic rubles.

13.2.5   Employment

Urban population y_{59} is explained by an exogenous total population, a lagged value of housing stock, and lagged ratio of industrial to agricultural wage rates. Rural population y_{60} is the residual. The levels of employment

y_{61} to y_{74} in 14 categories in any year are largely predetermined, they are functions of exogenous and lagged endogenous variables including their own lagged values. The current state of the harvest y_3 has a small impact on total nonagricultural employment y_{62} and a more significant impact on employment levels y_{73} and y_{74} in light industry. Poor harvests will reduce the growth of employment levels in many categories, because central planners seek to restrain the growth of nominal incomes and consumer demand when havests are poor. Higher growth in nonagricultural investment does not augment total employment growth but does increase the employment levels of the capital goods sectors, including y_{64} in the construction sector and y_{74} in the industrial materials branch of the industrial sector.

In our experiments under optimal control, the planners are not given authority to shift the allocation of employment. By raising investment in housing, they can accelerate the rate of urban migration and, by increasing the tempo of capital investment, shift the structure of nonagricultural employment.

13.2.6 Nonagricultural Production

The main explanatory variables in the production functions for nonagricultural outputs are labor and lagged capital stock. Except for the services sector, the variables in these production functions are expressed in growth rates $(y_{it}/y_{i,t-1}) - 1$. Elasticities for certain inputs and rate of technological progress are often imposed rather than estimated. Total domestic energy production (in physical units) y_{78} is determined by the electricity generation y_{75}, the output of coal y_{76}, and petroleum and gas y_{77}. The subtraction of net energy exports y_{116} provides a measure of domestic energy supply y_{79}. The growth of energy supply enters as a determinant of the growth of industrial materials y_{80} and transportation y_{86}. The growth of industrial materials output in turn affects the growth of machine-building y_{81}, construction y_{85}, and agricultural current purchases y_{11}. The state of the harvest y_3 has an impact on the growth rates in soft goods y_{82} and processed food y_{83}. Consequently, a rise in net energy exports will have a negative impact on most components of domestic output.

The other significant factors influencing domestic output are the stocks of imported machinery y_{55}, y_{56}, and y_{57}. Higher growth in imported machinery has a positive impact on the outputs in the branches of petroleum and gas, industrial materials (chemical machinery only), and machine-building.

Soviet gross domestic product y_{89} is a weighted sum of the output indices of the sectors listed in Table 2 using value-added weights in 1970 prices.

This measure constrains the total output to be distributed among the end-use categories, so that an increase in investment during a given year will reduce consumption or defense expenditures. The residual category w_{15} of end use, which includes inventories, governmental expenditures other than investment and public consumption, and statistical discrepancies, is fixed at historical values during simulation so that the GDP-constraint is binding. Net exports y_{117} and capital depreciation y_{40} are also identified categories of GNP end use.

13.2.7 Foreign Trade

The foreign-trade sector distinguishes four geographical areas: the Council for Mutual Economic Assistance (CMEA), Developed West, Other Socialist Economies, and Less-Developed Countries. Soviet exports y_{91} to the CMEA Six are deflated by exogenous CMEA prices and determined by aggregate economic activity w_{62} in Eastern Europe. An additional price w_{63} for the ratio of fuel to other materials prices is included in the equations for total exports and exports of fuel and materials y_{92}. Total imports y_{94} from the CMEA Six are a function of industrial output y_{84}, total investment y_{37}, and the state of the harvest y_3; imports from the CMEA are higher during poor harvest years in the USSR. The import equations for raw materials y_{95} and machinery y_{96} include the corresponding exports as explanatory variables because of bilateral balancing within the CMEA as an institutional arrangement.

Soviet exports to the Developed West $y_{100} = y_{97} + y_{98} + y_{99}$ are a function of world prices w_{68}, w_{40}, and w_{71}, Western demand w_{70}, and Soviet hard currency debt y_{16}. Exports of fuels y_{97} are determined in part by domestic energy production y_{78}. The impact of external debt on Soviet exports is measured by the relationship of the net debt ratio y_{21} to a target net debt ratio w_8. Soviet imports from the West $y_{106} = y_{102} + y_{103} + y_{104} + y_{106}$ are functions of world prices w_{71}, w_{52}, w_5, and w_{74}, Soviet domestic activity (industrial output, industrial investment, or total consumption), and the debt service ratio relative to its target.

Soviet trade with Other Socialist Economies and Less-Developed Countries is highly politicized. Soviet exports y_{107} and y_{109} to these groups are primarily related to the total volume of LDC imports w_{76}. Imports y_{108} from other socialist countries are determined by lagged Soviet exports. Several other trade equations have been included to provide linkages to the domestic economy—net exports of energy, net exports in domestic rubles, and imports of certain categories of machinery.

Very few options have been allowed for Soviet planners to alter the patterns of foreign trade. Exports of fuel to the West $y_{97} = x_{14}$ has been made a control variable which permits an evaluation of the trade-off between domestic energy consumption and imported Western machinery.

13.2.8 Wages and Incomes

An exogenous price index w_{84} is used in SOVMOD V to deflate nominal wage rates y_{118} and y_{119} in industry and state farms respectively, disposable household income y_{120}, and time deposits y_{121}. The increment in the real industrial wage is a function of the increment in industrial labor productivity. The nominal wage on state farms is determined by the nominal industrial wage with short-run variation due to the state of the harvest. These two wage rates are then used together with employment to determine nominal disposable income of households y_{120}.

Real household saving in time deposits is a function of initial assets and real disposable income. Short-run variation in the savings rate is explained by the availability of food. When food supplies on the retail market are low, household purchases from collective farmers increase and household savings are therefore reduced. Real gross profit y_{122} in the economy is a function of gross domestic product y_{89}, the state of the harvest y_3, and a dummy variable representing the price and budgetary reforms after 1967.

13.2.9 Consumption

Food consumption y_{123} and the index of services consumed y_{126} are strictly determined by supply factors in SOVMOD V. The consumption of soft goods (nondurables other than food) y_{124} is primarily a function of demand (real income and a substitution term for food consumption) and current production. The consumption of durables y_{125} is explained by a demand equation, with real time deposits and current real income as explanatory variables. The only supply constraint on durables consumption is represented by a ratio of defense expenditure to machinery production. Total consumption y_{127} is the sum of consumption in the four categories.

In control experiments, household consumption is raised primarily by increasing the output of agriculture and light industry without an effective option of using net imports to augment consumption (except through the impact of grain imports on animal production).

13.3 SETTING UP THE OPTIMAL CONTROL EXPERIMENTS

In order to test the validity of the production constraints of SOVMOD V and to trace out the trade-off relationship between consumption and defense spending implicit in this model, we have performed several optimal control experiments. In these experiments, the loss function is assumed to be quadratic:

$$W = \frac{1}{2} \sum_{t=1}^{T} (y_t - a_t)' K (y_t - a_t),$$ (3.1)

where y_t is a vector consisting of both endogenous variables and control variables (policy instruments) a_t is a vector of target values, and K is a diagonal matrix whose diagonal elements measure the penalties assigned to the squared deviations of y_t from their targets a_t. If the vector y_t consists of all endogenous and control variables in the model, most of the diagonal elements of K will usually be zero. We define as target variables those elements of y_t that are of concern to the Soviet government, that is, those associated with the positive diagonal elements of K. The choice of the quadratic function (3.1) is due mainly to mathematical convenience. A major criticism of it is that positive and negative deviations from a_t are penalized equally. To avoid this criticism, the user could set the values of a_t for variables like real GNP high enough, and for variables like the inflation rate low enough, so that the resulting y_t under optimal control will almost always fail to achieve the targets, or fall on the side which should be penalized.

The target variables, among the endogenous variables of the model, are:

1 Gross domestic product (XIGDP) = y_{89}
2 Defense procurement expenditures (BDP9) = y_{90}
3 Household consumption (CTOT) = y_{103}
4 Meat production (XMEAT70) = y_7
5 Housing stock (KHS) = y_{53}
6 Gold stock (FGOLD) = y_{22}

The control variables include twelve categories of investment:

1 Electric power generation (IIEP) = x_1
2 Coal industry (IICP) = x_2
3 Petroleum and gas (IIPP) = x_3
4 Basic materials (IIMA) = x_4
5 Machine-building (IIMB) = x_5
6 Industrial consumer goods (IISG) = x_6
7 Processed foods (IIPF) = x_7
8 Construction (ICRUB) = x_8
9 Transport and communications (ITRUB) = x_9
10 Agriculture (IA) = x_{10}
11 Housing (IHS) = x_{11}
12 Livestock (IALVR) = x_{12}

and three variables affecting foreign trade: gold sales (FGSALES) = x_{13}, exports of fuels to the West (EFUELDW\$) = x_{14}, and grain imports (MGRDW\$) = x_{15}. All these control variables will also be treated as target variables in our control experiments. Their target paths are the historical paths, and some positive weights are assigned to the corresponding diagonal elements of the K matrix to stabilize the optimal paths of these instruments. The time horizon is 12 years, beginning in 1966.

In the first experiment, we set the target paths for the six target variables to be 10 to 15 percent higher than their values which were obtained by simulating the model using the historical values for the 15 control variables. These simulation values are close to the historical values for these six variables because the model was estimated to fit the historical data. To assign penalty weights (diagonal elements in the K matrix) to these target variables, we followed the rule that if the squared percentage deviation of each variable from its target value $(y_{it} - a_{it})^2/a_{it}^2$ is equal, the weights should be inversely proportional to the squares of the target values. This rule helped guide us in assigning a weight of unity to GDP, household consumption, meat production, and housing stock, and a weight of 4 to defense procurement expenditure which has smaller target values. We assigned a large weight of 2 to gold stock in spite of its large target values (in different units) in order to freeze this variable; gold stock was selected as a target variable mainly to prevent the optimal policy from drawing down gold stock in order to meet the other targets. The control variables were assigned penalty weights in the range of 0.05 to 0.30 to insure some degree of instrument stability; these weights are quite small in view of the small target values for the control variables.

The reader will recall from Chapter 2 that the (nearly) optimal policies for a nonlinear econometric model such as SOVMOD V are obtained by repeated linearizations of the model and applying the optimal control algorithm to the linearized models iteratively. For the calculations of this study, only one linearization was performed for each run. Each solution could therefore be improved upon, but it was good enough for our purpose which is to test the constraints of the model and to trace the approximate trade-off relations between important target variables. To economize on computing cost, we recommend one linearization to readers engaged in similar studies in the future. If a higher degree of accuracy is desired, a second round of linearizations can always be performed.

13.4 TESTING THE CONSTRAINTS ON TOTAL OUTPUT

Before reporting on the results of the first control experiment, it will be useful to review the theoretical framework which would impose restrictions on total output. If total output fails to be restricted in our control experiments, the framework will guide us in looking for the leakages and in modifying the model and/or the specifications of future experiments.

To understand the essential features of the restrictions, assume for simplicity that the supply of labor in each industrial sector is fixed so that only the capital stock can be changed by investment decisions, that the production functions are Cobb-Douglas, and that output in year t is a function of the quantity of labor used in year t (which is fixed, and suppressed) and of the quantity of capital stock $K_{i,t-1}$ at the end of $t-1$. Total output Y_t in year t is therefore predetermined:

$$ Y_t = \sum_{i=1}^{m} w_i Y_{it} = \sum_{i=1}^{m} w_i \alpha_i K_{i,t-1}^{\beta_i} = \sum_{i=1}^{m} w_i \alpha_i (\gamma_i K_{i,t-2} + I_{i,t-1})^{\beta_i}. \quad (4.1) $$

Investments $I_{i,t}$ in year t, however, can influence the capital stocks in year t and hence productions in year $t+1$. They have to compete with the other end-uses for a fixed total output, according to the identity

$$ Y_t = C_t + \sum_{i=1}^{m} I_{i,t} + \text{defense} + \text{capital repair} + \text{net exports}. \quad (4.2) $$

If the constraints are appropriately specified, it should be impossible to increase appreciably the values of all target variables in the end-use categories.

It was exciting to wait for the computer output of the first optimal control run! The results showed that the values of all six target variables were increased significantly during the 12 years of the planning period as compared with their simulation values generated by the historical paths of the control variables. Not only were the target values of these six variables in the later periods practically reached by the "optimal" solution (after only one linearization), the values of these variables were increased appreciably from their historical simulation values right from the beginning. For example, the "optimal" values of GDP were 83.5 and 89.8 for periods 1 and 2 respectively, as compared with the historical simulation values of 80.4 and 84.3. The "optimal" values of defense procurement expenditures were 8.7 and 13.0 for periods 1 and 2, as compared with 9.3 and 10.6; for total consumption, they were 77.8 and 86.0 as compared with 78.8 and 82.9. The "optimal" solutions for defense and consumption showed small reductions in the first period, but total investment showed a very large increase from 62.6 to 74.5 in the first period, and GDP was increased from 80.4 to 83.5 as just reported.

In looking for leakages, we quickly discovered three possible sources. The first is net foreign debt y_{16} which increased by a great deal to finance the capital expansion. The second is investment in the services industry y_{33} which showed large fluctuations in the "optimal" solution because it was not used directly as a control variable but was calculated as a residual by subtracting all other investments from total investment y_{37}. The third is the total supply of investment $y_{38} = y_{37}$ which showed a large increase in the "optimal" solution from the historical simulation. This result indicates that the supply equation for total investment y_{38} fails to impose an appropriate constraint.

As we were still trying to detect sources of the leakages in the constraints, before suggesting respecifications of the model in Section 6, we decided to impose penalty weights of 3, 1, and 10 respectively to the variables net foreign debt y_{16}, investment in services y_{33}, and total investment y_{38} in the second control experiment, while setting the historical simulation paths of these variables as their target paths. In addition the penalty weights for some control variables were increased to reduce their fluctuations. As a result, the six target variables could no longer increase simultaneously as in the first experiment. While GDP was on the average about 2 percent above its historical simulation path and consumption and housing stock were also somewhat higher, defense spending and meat production were both lower. This means that the constraints on total output were now binding. Our next task is to examine the redistribution of investment expenditures and of productions in different industrial sectors.

13.5   EXAMINING THE ALLOCATION OF INVESTMENT AND PRODUCTION

There are two major sets of factors in SOVMOD V that determine the relative sizes of the optimal capital stocks in different industries and thus also the relative rates of investment in different industries, given the initial sizes of the capital stocks at the beginning of the planning period. The first is the set of weights w_i in the definition of total output given by (4.2), or by the equation for $y_{89} =$ GDP in MODELS listed in the Appendix. These are value-added weights in 1970 prices. They specify how important different component products are in the formation of real GDP which enters the objective function. The second is the set of elasticities β_i of the component outputs with respect to the capital stocks used in their production. For simplicity of reasoning, let total investment $\sum_{i=1}^{m} I_{i,t}$ in year t be fixed, although in the model only total output is limited by the capital stocks at the end of $t - 1$. A two-period optimization problem involving period t and $t + 1$ would essentially be to maximize, according to (4.1),

$$Y_{t+1} = \sum_{i=1}^{m} w_i \alpha_i K_{i,t}^{\beta_i} = \sum_{i=1}^{m} w_i \alpha_i (\gamma_i K_{i,t-1} + I_{i,t})^{\beta_i} \qquad (5.1)$$

with respect to $I_{i,t}$, subject to the constraint $\sum_{i=1}^{m} I_{i,t} =$ constant. The optimal values of $I_{i,t}$ and hence $K_{i,t}$ (because $K_{i,t-1}$ are treated as given) are determined by the equalization of their marginal contributions to total output Y_{t+1},

$$\frac{\partial Y_{t+1}}{\partial I_{it}} = w_i \beta_i \alpha_i K_{i,t}^{\beta_i - 1} = \lambda \qquad (i = 1,\dots,m), \qquad (5.2)$$

where λ is the Lagrangian multiplier in the above constrained maximization problem. In this formulation, we have abstracted from the choice between $I_t = \sum_{i=1}^{m} I_{i,t}$, C_t, and defense, while concentrating on the choice among the components $I_{i,t}$ of I_t.

Rewriting (5.2) as

$$K_{i,t} = \left(\lambda^{-1} w_i \beta_i \alpha_i\right)^{1/(1 - \beta_i)} \qquad (i = 1,\dots,m) \qquad (5.3)$$

we see how the optimal capital stocks are positively influenced by w_i, β_i, and α_i (the last being a scaling factor which depends on the units of measurement), under the assumption of Cobb-Douglas production functions. Our optimal control experiments did show that the rates of investments in different industries and thus the corresponding stocks of capital depended on the factors w_i and α_i as indicated in (5.3), and that investments in some industries became negative in certain periods so that the capital stocks and therefore outputs in these industries decreased accordingly. The question is whether this model for the allocation of investments and productions in different industries is an adequate description of the allocative mechanism in a centrally planned economy.

13.6 POSSIBLE RESPECIFICATIONS OF SOVMOD V

Having applied optimal control calculations and theoretical reasoning to examine the constraints on total outputs and the allocative mechanism for investments and production, we are in a position to suggest some possible respecifications of the model.

First, concerning the constraint on total investment y_{38}, we have discovered that the supply equation for y_{38} was insufficient to restrain total investment. This equation, as listed in MODELS of the Appendix, determines y_{38} by the production of machine-building and metal-working y_{81} (less its demand due to total defense procurement y_{90}), machinery imports from CMEA y_{96} (less machinery exports to CMEA y_{93}) deflated by appropriate price indices, machinery imports from the West y_{103} (less machinery exports to the West y_{98}) also properly deflated, and the output of construction y_{85}. Not only might there be leakages through possibly insufficient constraints on the net imports of machinery to augment total supply, which can be further examined; the domestic production of the machine-building and metal-working industry and the output of construction might be insufficiently constrained. If these two variables are determined by fixed labor supplies and past capital stocks, nothing can be done to raise their levels. However, an examination of the equations for these two variables y_{81} and y_{85} reveals that they are both positively affected by the output of industrial materials y_{80} *of the same year*, which is in turn positively influenced by total nonagricultural investment y_{35}. Because total nonagricultural investment is subject to control, y_{80} and hence y_{81} and y_{85} can be increased by manipulating the current levels of investments which are components of total nonagricultural investment y_{35}.

When SOVMOD V was constructed partly for forecasting purpose, it seemed reasonable to include y_{35} as an explanatory variable for the *demand* of output of industrial materials y_{80}. However, such an explanatory variable would not be suitable if the equation for y_{80} is intended to be a production function in an optimal control experiment to find the optimal investments in different industries. One way to tighten the constraint on total investment is to restrict the explanatory variables in the production functions to labor inputs and lagged capital inputs. Certainly other explanatory variables could be included provided that they cannot be easily increased by current investments.

Secondly, concerning the allocative mechanism for investments in different industries described in Section 5, there appear to be two possible weaknesses. First, it might be inappropriate to specify as a target variable the quantity of total output which is a weighted sum of outputs in different industries with fixed weights. These weights were the relative prices in 1970. As the output of one industry relative to other industries increases through cumulative investments, its relative weights should decrease, as would be the case in a market economy. In a planned economy, the planning authority would not, and should not, attach the same value to a product when its supply increases relative to other products. One possible solution to this problem is to include the final products themselves as arguments in the objective function for the optimal control experiments.

The second weakness has to do with the specification of the inputs in the production functions. According to the present specification, total output, irrespective of what kinds, can be used for investment in any industry. Thus, for example, one million 1970 rubles worth of electricity output could be used to form capital stock in the housing industry even if the latter were mainly construction materials. In other words, the actual production relationships between physical output and physical inputs have been ignored. Input-output tables are familiar ways to summarize such relationships. One could also use Cobb-Douglas production functions by specifying the inputs in physical terms. For example, the production function for housing may include as arguments labor input, electric power, industrial materials, and so forth, as well as capital stock in the housing industry. This would insure that sufficient electric power is produced for the purpose of housing construction. Needless to say, such specifications of production relationships in physical terms would be more complicated, but they are necessary for actual economic planning and therefore also for our description of central planning by the framework of optimal control.

In this chapter, we have pointed out three uses of optimal control for the econometric analysis of central planning. Detailed discussion, however, has been confined mainly to the first use, that is, to check the validity of the constraints in an econometric model and the possible specifications of the production constraints for the study of planning. Although the weaknesses of the model pointed out in Sections 4 and 5 now appear obvious, they could hardly have been discovered without the optimal control experiment. Once a good model is obtained, the second use to trace out the trade-off possibilities implicit in the model would not be difficult to implement, as the techniques are similar to those employed in Chapter 7. Again, the third topic of estimating the preference function of the planning authority and forecasting its behavior will receive a theoretical treatment in Chapter 16, but its empirical implementation will require further study.

APPENDIX A: LIST OF VARIABLES AND EQUATIONS IN SOVMOD V (ENDOGENOUS VARIABLES y_1–y_{127})

Agricultural Production (Block A)

1.	XCROPN	Normal crop output
2.	XCROP70	Actual crop output

3.	DXAC	Deviation of crop output from normal output
4.	XGRTN	Normal grain production
5.	XGRT	Actual grain production
6.	XANIM70	Animal products output
7.	XMEAT70	Meat production
8.	AFEED70	Feed fed to livestock
9.	XAGT70	Total net agricultural output
10.	ALVR	Value of livestock (end-year)
11.	AVCP70	Value of agricultural current purchases

Balance of Payments (Block F)

12.	FTBAL$	Hard currency trade balance
13.	FGSALE$	Value of gold sales
14.	FINT$	Interest payments
15.	FCURB$	Balance on current account
16.	FNDEBT$	Net debt to the West
17.	FGDEBT$	Gross debt to the West
18.	FDCOM$	Commercial debt
19.	FREP$	Debt repayments
20.	FDSRAT	Debt service ratio
21.	FNDRAT	Net debt ratio
22.	FGOLD	Gold reserves (end-year)

Capital Investment (Block I)

23.	IIEP	Investment: Electric power
24.	IICP	Investment: Coal products
25.	IIPP	Investment: Petroleum products
26.	IIMA	Investment: Industrial materials
27.	IIMB	Investment: Machine-building
28.	IISG	Investment: Soft goods
29.	IIPF	Investment: Processed foods
30.	IIN	Investment: Total industry
31.	ICRUB	Investment: Construction sector
32.	ITRUB	Investment: Transport and communications
33.	ISER	Investment: Services

34.	IHS	Investment: Housing
35.	INA	Investment: Nonagricultural
36.	IA	Investment: Agricultural
37.	ITOTAL	Investment: Total
38.	ITX	Total capital goods supplied
39.	IALVR	Net investment in livestock
40.	ICR	Capital repair investment

Capital Stock (Block K)

41.	KEP	Capital stock: Electric power (end-year)
42.	KCP	Capital stock: Coal products (end-year)
43.	KPP	Capital stock: Petroleum products (end-year)
44.	KMA	Capital stock: Industrial materials (end-year)
45.	KMB	Capital stock: Machine-building (end-year)
46.	KSG	Capital stock: Soft goods (end-year)
47.	KPF	Capital stock: Processed foods (end-year)
48.	KIN	Capital stock: Total industry (end-year)
49.	KCN	Capital stock: Construction sector (end-year)
50.	KTC	Capital stock: Transport and communications (end-year)
51.	KDT	Capital stock: Domestic trade (end-year)
52.	KSV	Capital stock: Services (end-year)
53.	KHS	Capital stock: Housing (end-year)
54.	KAIR	Capital stock: Agriculture (mid-year)
55.	KPPF	Imported machinery: Petroleum products (end-year)
56.	KMBF	Imported machinery: Machine-building (end-year)
57.	KCHW	Imported machinery: Chemicals (end-year)
58.	KTOT	Total capital stock (end-year)

Employment (Block N)

59.	NPOPU	Urban population (end-year)
60.	NPOPR	Rural population (end-year)
61.	NAT	Agricultural employment
62.	NMNA	Nonagricultural employment
63.	NMI	Employment: Total industry

64.	NMC	Employment: Construction
65.	NMTC	Employment: Transport and communications
66.	NMS	Employment: Domestic trade
67.	NMG	Employment: Government and services
68.	NMIEP	Employment: Electric power
69.	NMICP	Employment: Coal products
70.	NMIPP	Employment: Petroleum products
71.	NMIMA	Employment: Industrial materials
72.	NMIMB	Employment: Machine-building
73.	NMISG	Employment: Soft goods
74.	NMIPF	Employment: Processed foods

Nonagricultural Production (Block X)

75.	XIEP	Production: Electric power
76.	XICP	Production: Coal products
77.	XIPP	Production: Petroleum products
78.	XIEN	Production: Total energy
79.	XSEN	Domestic energy supply
80.	XIMA	Production: Industrial materials
81.	XIMB	Production: Machine-building
82.	XISG	Production: Soft goods
83.	XIPF	Production: Processed foods
84.	XIT	Production: Total industry
85.	XICN	Production: Construction
86.	XITC	Production: Transport and communications
87.	XIDT	Production: Domestic trade
88.	XISV	Production: Services
89.	XIGDP	Gross domestic product
90.	BDP9	Total defense procurement

Foreign Trade (Blocks E and M)

91.	ETCM$	Total exports to CMEA
92.	ERMCM$	Raw materials exports to CMEA
93.	EMACM$	Machinery exports to CMEA
94.	MTCM$	Total imports from CMEA
95.	MRMCM$	Raw material imports from CMEA
96.	MMACM$	Machinery imports from CMEA

97.	EFUELDW$	Fuel exports to West
98.	EMADW$	Machinery exports to West
99.	ERDW$	Other exports to West
100.	ETDW$	Total exports to West
101.	ENETDW$	Net exports to West
102.	MRMDW$	Raw material imports from West
103.	MMADW$	Machinery imports from West
104.	MGRDW$	Grain imports from West
105.	MRDW$	Other imports from West
106.	MTDW$	Total imports from West
107.	EOS$	Exports to other socialist countries
108.	MOS$	Imports from other socialist countries
109.	ETLDC$	Exports to developing countries
110.	MTLDC$	Imports from developing countries
111.	ETW$	Total exports to world
112.	MTW$	Total imports from world
113.	MTM100-5*	Machinery imports: Metal-working equipment
114.	MTM120-9*	Machinery imports: Petroleum equipment
115.	MIECH$	Machinery imports: Chemical equipment
116.	ENETEN	Net exports of energy
117.	EW	Net exports in domestic prices

Incomes (Block Z)

118.	WI*	Average wage, industry
119.	WAS*	Average wage, state farms
120.	ZD*	Disposable money income
121.	ZSAV*	Time deposits (end-year)
122.	ZPG	Real gross profits

Consumption (Block C)

123.	CF	Consumption: Food
124.	CSG	Consumption: Soft goods
125.	CD	Consumption: Durables
126.	CS	Consumption: Services
127.	CTOT	Consumption: Total

```
0001          SUBROUTINE MODELS(NY,NX,NW,D,Y,YL,XL,X,W,*)
0002          IMPLICIT REAL*8(A-H,O-Z)
0003          DIMENSION D(170),Y(170),YL(170),XL(20),X(20),W(105)
0004    C     AGRICULTURE
0004          D( 1)=DEXP(-.2038      +.1516*DLOG(W(   1))+.2*DLOG(Y(54))+.4892*DL
               $OG(Y(61))+.1592*DLOG(Y(11)))
0005          D( 2)=DEXP(DLOG(Y(   1)) - .0122       + .1447*W(   2)+.0061*W(   3)+
               $.0996*W(   4))
0006          D(3)=Y(2)/Y(1) - 1.
0007          D( 4)=DEXP(1.1069+.35*DLOG(W(   1))+.25*DLOG(Y(54))+.2413*DLOG(Y(6
               $1))+.1587*DLOG(Y(11)))
0008          D( 5)=DEXP(DLOG(Y(   4))-.053+.2043*W(   2)+.00683*W(   3)+.1477*W(
               $4))
0009          D(   6)=DEXP(.32732+.53601*DLOG(YL(10)+Y(10))+.45937*DLOG(Y(8)))
0010          D(   7)=DEXP(-.80843+.79406*DLOG(YL( 10))+.40177*DLOG(Y(8))-.34303
               $*(Y(39)/YL(10)   ))
0011          D(   8)=-7.27895+.50064*Y(   1)+.04424*(Y(104)/W(   5))+2.73*(Y(3)+YL(
               $3))
0012          D(   9)=Y(2)+Y(6)-Y(8)
0013          D(  10)=YL(10)+Y(39)
0014          D(  11)=-8.204 + .34625*Y(   1)+.05660*YL(80)
0015    C     BALANCE OF PAYMENTS
0015          D(12)=-306.5 +1.21200*(Y(100)-Y(106))+.44372*(Y(109)-Y(110)))
0016          D(13)=X(13)
0017          D( 14)=1.33+.016*YL(16)+.0648*Y(16)
0018          D( 15)=Y(12)+Y(13)-Y(14)+W(   9)+W( 10)+W( 11)
0019          D( 16)=YL(16)-Y(16)
```

199

```
0020      D( 17)=Y(16)+W( 12)
0021      D( 18)=Y(17)-W( 13)
0022      D(19)=123.3+.13784*YL(17)
0023      D (20)=(Y(19)+Y(14))/Y(100)
0024      D( 21)=Y(16)/Y(100)
0025      D( 22)=YL(22)+W(14)  -Y(13)/W(  7)
C   INVESTMENT
0026      D(23)=X(1)
0027      D(24)=X(2)
0028      D(25)=X(3)
0029      D(26)=X(4)
0030      D(27)=X(5)
0031      D(28)=X(6)
0032      D(29)=X(7)
0033      D(30)=Y(23)+Y(24)+Y(25)+Y(26)+Y(27)+Y(28)+Y(29)+W(105)
0034      D(31)=X(8)
0035      D(32)=X(9)
0036      D(34)=X(11)
0037      D(36)=X(10)
0038      D(38)=-.9089+.62485*(.41068*Y(81)-.75*Y(90)+2.2455*(Y(96)-Y(93))/
         $(10.*W(33)*W(39))+2.314*(Y(103)-Y(98))/(10.*W(38)*W(40))-11.7346+
         $.67865*Y(85)+1.8672*W(29)
0039      D(37)=Y(38)
0040      D(33)=Y(37)-Y(30)-Y(31)-Y(32)-Y(34)-Y(36)
0041      D(35)=Y(30)+Y(31)+Y(32)+Y(35)+Y(34)
0042      D(39)=X(12)
0043      D( 40)=YL(33)+(.15289-.001830*(#(35)-22.)*W(41)-.004886*W(45))
C   CAPITAL STOCK
0044      D( 41)=.9o*YL(41)+.49663*(Y(23)+.2*YL(23)+.2*YL(129)+.5*YL(130)+.5
```

```
0045        $*YL(161)+.2863*W(16)
            D( 42)=.97*YL(42)+.2041*(Y(24)+YL(24)+YL(131))+.14455*(W(16)-.474)

0046        $-.31632*W(45)
            D(43)=.975*YL(43)+.16242*(Y(25)+YL(25)+YL(132))-.228929*(W(29)-.1
            $6/85)

0047        D(44)=YL(44)*.955+.49389*Y(26)+.39011*YL(26)+.22549*YL(133)+.818*(
            $W(16)-.474)

0048        D(45)=YL(45)*.95+.53057*(Y(27)+YL(27)+.30465*(W(16)-.474)+.87508*
            $(W(26)-.6526)

0049        D(46)=.95*YL(46)+1.04975*Y(28)+.27712*(W(47)-W(46))

0050        D(47)=YL(47)*.95+.44428*Y(29)+.36917*YL(29)+.22107*YL(134)+.93094*
            $(W(47)-W(48))

0051        D(48)=.95*YL(48)+.11553*Y(30)+.33421*YL(30)+.38785*YL(135)+.27644*
            $YL(136)+1.5/50*(W(10)-.474)

0052        D(49)=.94*YL(49)+1.04155*Y(31)+.22482*(W(49)-.5263)

0053        D(50)=.575*YL(50)+.6329*(Y(32)+YL(32)+2.40433*(W(50)-.0526)+2.264
            $05*W(33)

0054        D(51)=.96*YL(51)+.69439*(YL(33)+YL(137))+3.65854*W(50)+2.06112*(W(
            $46)-W(87))

0055        D(52)=.96*YL(52)+.4533*(YL(136)+YL(139))+5.69696*W( 42)-3.07542*(W
            $(24)-W(86))

0056        D(53)=.96*YL(53)+.48439*(Y(34)+YL(34))+/.5234*W(46)

0057        D(54)=.95*YL(54)+.80708*YL(36)-1.2744*(W(26)+W(51)+W(17))

0058        D(55)=YL(55)*.95+.6712*(Y(114)/(.75*W(52)+.25*W(39)/1.013))

0059        D(56)=.95*YL(56)+.0712*(Y(113)/(.5*W(52)+.5*W(39)/1.013))

0060        $5(57)=.95*YL(57)+.0712*(Y(115)/(W(52)*W(36))

0061        D(56)=Y( 46)+Y(49)+Y(50)+Y(51)+Y(52)+Y(53)+Y(54)
```

201

```
C  EMPLOYMENT
0062      D(59)=(W(53)/100.)*(-35.3853+22.113*W(54)+.036518*YL(140)+2.52469
         $*(YL(141)/YL(142)))
0063      D(60)=W(53)-Y(59)
0064      D(61)=(Y(60)+YL(60))/200.*(-20.7620-1.30183*W(55)+14.7269*W(54)-24
         $.0519* W(91) *(W(54)-3.8907)+2.8217*YL(3))
0065      D(62)=(Y(59)+YL(59))/.2*(-41.2965+26.7222*   W(54)*(1.-W(50))+100.2
         $64*W(58)+12.2161*((   W(57)+W(90))/(  W(53)+W(89))-.5439)+1.11499*
         $(Y(3)+YL(3)))
0066      D(63)=YL(63)-182.3+.46886*(Y(62)-YL(62))-294.6 *W(58)-1433.8*(Y(35
         $)/YL(35)-1.)-537.78*YL(3)
0067      D(64)=YL(64)-508.9+.34917*(Y(62)-YL(62))-232.3*(1.-W(56))+2180.*(Y
         $(35)/YL(35)-1.)
0068      D(65)=YL(65)+76.08+.065676*(Y(62)-YL(62))-73.*W(92)+49.5*W(50)
0069      D(66)=YL(66)-60.14+.14331*(Y(62)-YL(62))-135.3*W(50)+138.05*YL(3)
0070      D(67)=YL(67)+228.9+.27144*(Y(62)-YL(62))-1529.7*(Y(35)/YL(35)-1.)+
         $332.0*Y(3)+201.5*YL(3)
0071      D(68)=YL(68)-4.83+.02711*(Y(63)-YL(63))+11.16*W( 59)
0072      D(69)=YL(69)-95.81+.00632*(Y(63)-YL(63))+63.014*(YL(42)-YL(143))+8
         $.844*W(59)
0073      D(70)=YL(70)+2.335+9.417*(W(43)+W(29))
0074      D(71)=YL(71)-40.92+.15068*(Y(63)-YL(63))+601.07*(Y(35)/YL(35)-1.)+
         $70.2*W(59)
0075      D(72)=YL(72)+274.7+.1272*(Y(63)-YL(63))+244.11*YL(3)+165.84*W(59)
0076      D(73)=YL(73)-56.59+.16373*(Y(63)-YL(63))+38.53* W(41)+283.79*Y(3)
0077      D(74)=YL(74)+48.93+.04983*(Y(63)-YL(63))-62.42*W(56)+165.16*(Y(3)+
         $YL(3))/2.
C  PRODUCTION
0078      D(75)=YL(75)*(1.+(2.5+1.2965+.5773*(Y(68)/YL(68)-1.)*100.+.2451*(
```

```
0079        $YL(41)/YL(144)-1.)*100.-3.6179*W(26))/100.)

0080         D(76)=YL(76)*(1.+(.1*(Y(69)/YL(69)-1.)*100.+.39124*(YL(42)/YL(143)
            $-1.)*100.-1.7804*(W(47)+W(93)-2.*W(94)))/100.)
             D(77)=YL(77)*(1.+(.5*(Y(70)/YL(70)-1.)*100.+2.+.24888*(YL(43)/YL(1
            $45)-1.)*100.+.14426*(YL(55)/YL(146)-1.)*100.)/100.)

0081         D(78)=.50729*Y( 75)+2.9553*Y(76)+8.91306*Y(77)
0082         D(79)=Y(78)-Y(116)
0083         D(80)=YL(80)*(1.+.4*(Y(71)/YL(71)-1.)*100.+12*(Y(79)/YL(79)-1.)*
            $100.+.5+.05804*((YL(44)-YL(57))/(YL(147)-YL(148))-1.)*100.+.037*(Y
            $L(37)/YL(148)-1.)*100.+.3869*(Y(35)/YL(35)-1.)*100.-1.2855*(W(30)+
            $W(28)))/100.)

0084         D(81)=YL(81)*(1.+(.2*(Y(80)/YL(80)-1.)*100.+.4*(Y(72)/YL(72)-1.)*1
            $00.+2.+.22208*((YL(45)-YL(56))/(YL(149)-YL(150))-1.)*100.+.08097*(
            $YL(56)/YL(150)-1.)*100.-2.9794*W(60))/100.)

0085         D(82)=YL(82)*(1.+.15*(YL(46)/YL(151)-1.)*100.+1.5+.79625*(Y(73)/Y
            $L(73)-1.)*100.+11.4254*Y(3))/100.)

0086         D(83)=YL(83)*(1.+(  1.201*(Y(74)/YL(74)-1.)*100.+.1080*(YL( 47)/Y
            $L(152)-1.)*100.+20.449 *YL(3)+5.111 *(W(50)-W(43))+5.913*W(24))/10
            $0.)

0087         D(64)=1.66792*(.046254*Y(5)+.032119*Y(6)+.058852*Y(77)+.231556*Y
            $(80)+.25855*Y(81)+.165178*Y(82)+.165754*Y(83))-2.02855*W(31)

0088         D(85)=YL(85)*(1.+.3*(Y(80)/YL(80)-1.)*100.+1.+.3149*(Y(64)/YL(64)
            $-1.)*100.+.1139*(YL(49)/YL(153)-1.)*100.)/100.)

0089         D(86)=YL(86)*(1.+(-.1*(Y(65)/YL(65)-1.)*100.+.3*(Y(79)/YL(79)-1.)*1
            $00.+1.+.54263*(YL(50)/YL(128)-1.)*100.+3.7418*Y(3)+2.2161*W(33))/1
            $00.)
```

203

```
0090  D(87)=YL(87)*(1.+(-1.+.05*(YL(51)/YL(154)-1.)*100.+1.+.5112*(YL(66)/YL
      &(155)-1.)*100.+8.4138*Y(3)+.3655*(.555*Y(83)+.445*Y(32))/(.555*YL
      $(83)+.445*YL(82))-1.)*100.)/100.)

0091  D(88)=DEXP(-4.90683+1.02392*(.83*DLOG(Y(67))+.17*DLOG(YL(53)+YL(52
      $))))

0092  D(89)=1.09022*(.4104*Y(84)+.06657*Y(85)+.08345*Y(86)+.04374*Y(87)+
      $.10792*Y(88)+.18600*(Y(9)-Y(11))/.74301))+1.3426*W(31)

0093  D(90)=3.31450+Y(89)-2.19645*Y(127)-Y(37)-.18011*Y(40)-Y(39)-W(19)-
      &Y(117)-W(15)

      FOREIGN TRADE

0094  D(91)=(W(61)*W(38))*(-18.155+.4514*W(62)+7.763*W(63)+2.993*W(95)
      $)

0095  D(92)=(W(36)*W(64))*(-10.280+.2343d+W(62)+7.0036*W(63)+3.054*W(95
      $))

0096  D(93)=(W(38)*W(65))*(-10.366+.15717*W(62)+.5752*W(16)-1.794*W(95))
0097  D(94)=(W(38)*W(66))*(-24.905+.63289*Y(84)+.38293*Y(37)-37.598*(Y(3
      $)+YL(3))/2.)

0098  D(95)=(W(36)*W(67))*(0.996+.15001*Y(92)/(W(65)*W(38))-4.0392*W(63)
      $)

0099  D(96)=(W(36)*W(39))*(.9551+.13165*Y(37)+1.2146*Y(93)/(W(38)*W(65))
      $)

0100  D(97)=X(14)
0101  D(98)=195.7-348.5*W(69)+1.563*(W(38)*W(40))+83.89*(YL(21)-W(96))
0102  D(99)=-1448.+20.614*W(70)+11.924*(W(38)*W(71))
0103  D(100)=Y(97)+Y(98)+Y(99)
0104  D(101)=Y(100)-Y(106)
0105  D(102)=(W(38)*W(71))*(-4.2909+.12705*Y(84)-30.548*(YL(20)-W(97)))
0106  D(103)=(W(98)*Y(30))*(.704-.2982*W(69)-1.07145*(YL(20)-W(97)))
0107  D(104)=X(15)
0108  D(105)=-2440.+14.61*(W(33)*W(74))+11.993*Y(127)-595.7*W(59)
```

```
0109        D(106)=Y(102)+Y(103)+Y(104)+Y(105)
0110        D(107)=-3079.5+.1595*W(76)+40.7807*(W(38)*W(66))-412.2*W(77)
0111        D(108)=-666.4+1.26701*YL(107)+593.*W(77)
0112        D(109)=W(40)*(.48424+.002091*W(76)-1.63123*W(75))
0113        D(110)=-2862.6+1317*W(76)+30.024*W(78)+880.9*W(25)
0114        D(111)=Y(91)+Y(100)+Y(107)+Y(109)+W(79)
0115        D(112)=Y(94)+Y(106)+Y(108)+Y(110)
0116        D(113)=(W(96)*Y(27))*(.5/73-.1390*W(29)+.15135*(W(20)+W(24))-.56
           $276*(YL(20)-W(97)))
0117        D(114)=(W(95)*Y(25))*(.72293+.2101*W(100)-.28478*W(80))
0118        D(115)=(2.3395-1.3305*W(101)-.3942*W(16)-8.1958*(YL(20)-W(97))) *(
           $W(98)*W(31))
0119        D(116)=39.529+3.1638*((Y(92)-Y(95))/(W(38)*W(64)))+ 2.3451*Y(97)/W
           $(66)
0120        D(117)=.1*(1.5*Y(111)/W(82)-2.*Y(112)/W(63))/W(38)
      C     WAGES
0121        D(118)=W(84)*(YL(118)/ W(102)+23.43+101.38 *1000.*(Y(64)/Y(63)-Y
           $L(84)/YL(63))+56.88 *W(85))
0122        D(119)=-280.95+.95935*Y(118)+121.33*Y(3)+53.76*YL(3)
0123        D(120)=-9.09/+.91615*Y(62)*Y(119)*.000001+1.24056*Y(61)*Y(119)*.00
           $1
0124        D(121)=W(84)*(YL(121)/W(102)-5.76+.0591 *YL(121)/W(102)+.0542 *(Y
           $(120)/W(84))+.3952*(Y(123)-YL(123))
0125        D(122)=-42.52+1.2141*Y(89)+12.601*Y(3)+20.56*(.5*W(46)+W(20)+W(24)
           $)
      C     CONSUMPTION
0126        D(123)=16.65/+.73582*Y(53)+.2113>*Y(2)-9.//34*YL(3)+4.159*W(20)
0127        D(124)=14.198+.54599*Y(82)+.62778*(YL(120)/W(84)-.73535*Y (123)
0128        D(125)=37.623+1.5781*(YL(121)/W(102))+.15322*(Y(120)/W(84)-67.176
           $*((W(19)+Y(90)/Y(81)))
0129        D(126)=-5.092+1.67484*Y(86)
0130        D(127)=.502*Y(123)+.22548*Y(124)+.06162*Y(125)+.2111*Y(126)
0131        RETURN
0132        END
```

205

```
0001            SUBROUTINE MODEL1(NY,NX,NW,D,Y,YL,XL,X,W,*)
0002            IMPLICIT REAL*8(A-H,O-Z)
0003            DIMENSION D(170),Y(170),YL(170),XL(20),X(20),W(105)
0004            D(128)=YL(56)
0005            D(129)=YL(23)
0006            D(130)=YL(129)
0007            D(131)=YL(24)
0008            D(132)=YL(25)
0009            D(133)=YL(26)
0010            D(134)=YL(29)
0011            D(135)=YL(30)
0012            D(136)=YL(135)
0013            D(137)=YL(33)
0014            D(138)=YL(137)
0015            D(139)=YL(133)
0016            D(140)=YL(53)
0017            D(141)=YL(118)
0018            D(142)=YL(119)
0019            D(143)=YL(42)
0020            D(144)=YL(41)
0021            D(145)=YL(43)
0022            D(146)=YL(55)
0023            D(147)=YL(44)
0024            D(148)=YL(57)
0025            D(149)=YL(45)
0026            D(150)=YL(58)
0027            D(151)=YL(46)
0028            D(152)=YL(47)
0029            D(153)=YL(49)
0030            D(154)=YL(51)
0031            D(155)=YL(66)
0032            D(156)=YL(5)
0033            D(157)=YL(4)
0034            D(158)=YL(156)
0035            D(159)=YL(157)
0036            D(160)=YL(27)
0037            D(161)=YL(130)
0038            RETURN
0039            END
```

CHAPTER 14

Comparison of Econometric Models by Optimal Control Techniques

An econometric model is ordinarily a system of simultaneous, stochastic difference equations involving endogenous variables, exogenous variables, policy variables, and parameters. It has many numerical characteristics. To characterize an econometric model or to compare two econometric models is a complicated task because of the many dimensions involved. Which characteristics are important depend on the particular use of the model. The purpose may be the estimation of certain structural parameters, the explanation of various aspects of business cycles, long-term or short-term forecasting, or policy analysis. In this chapter, we will first summarize the existing, well-known characterizations of an econometric model (Section 1). We will then discuss two sets of techniques to describe the properties of a model. One is based on the theory of optimal control for deterministic systems (Section 2) and the other on the theory of optimal control for stochastic systems (Section 3). An illustration of the techniques of Section 3 using the Michigan Quarterly Econometric Model is given in Section 4. It should be pointed out at the outset that the word "comparison" in the title of this chapter means "bringing out the important characteristics of" and does not mean comparative evaluation or deciding which model is better. The latter subject is discussed in Chow (1981).

14.1 EXISTING CHARACTERIZATIONS OF AN ECONOMETRIC MODEL

It will be convenient for our discussion to start with a static system of simultaneous equations and then treat a dynamic system of simultaneous difference equations, leaving the problem of characterizing a dynamic stochastic system as the last topic.

14.1.1 Static Model

Both general and partial equilibrium models are systems of simultaneous equations. Two types of characteristics are of interest for such systems. First are the characteristics of individual equations, as summarized by their parameters, such as the elasticity of demand or the marginal propensity to consume. Second are the properties of the solution to the system. These are the properties of the reduced-form equations of an econometric model. Rather than characterizing the relationships among endogenous variables, such as the elasticity of demand and the marginal propensity to consume, they describe the responses of the solution values of the endogenous variables to changes in the exogenous variables and/or the parameters in the system. They describe the "comparative statics" induced by the system, and they contain the "multipliers" of an econometric model.

14.1.2 Dynamic Deterministic Model

Once the model becomes dynamic, being a system of difference or differential equations, its characteristics will be more complicated but can still be divided into two types. The characteristics of individual equations include short-run, intermediate-run, and long-run relationships among the variables in an equation, such as the short-run and long-run elasticities of demand and the short-run and long-run marginal propensities to consume. The long-run characteristics are the characteristics of the solution paths of the system, and they represent the effects of the exogenous variables on the solution paths. The solution paths may be damped or explosive; they may oscillate in various ways. The effects of the exogenous variables on the solutions are the subject of comparative dynamics. These effects are partly described by the various dynamic multipliers, including the impact multipliers, delayed multipliers (measuring the effects of a change in an exogenous variable in one period on the endogenous variables in a later period), and intermediate-run and long-run multipliers (measuring the cumulative effects of persistent changes in an exogenous variable for several or many periods on the current endogenous variables). The number of different dynamic multipliers is large because the time dimension is added into the picture. These multipliers are the coefficients of the "final form" of an econometric model that expresses the endogenous variables as functions of the exogenous variables after the lagged endogenous variables have been eliminated.

14.1.3 Dynamic Stochastic Model

After incorporating stochastic disturbances into an econometric model, we need further tools to characterize the stochastic solution paths of an econometric model. The first two moments of the solution path are of particular interest. The mean solution paths can be treated in the same way as in Section 1.2; all the dynamic multipliers and the comparative dynamic analyses are applicable to the mean paths. The variances and covariances of the endogenous variables may not be constant through time. If the time series generated by a system of stochastic difference equations are covariance-stationary or nearly so, one can use the autocovariance matrix or the spectral density matrix to summarize many of the cyclical properties, as described, for example, in Chow (1975). Dynamic relationships between several variables can be summarized by cross-spectral densities and by observing the leads and lags between their turning points, in the same way that cycles of individual endogenous variables can be described by the spectral density functions and by the time intervals between turning points.

In this brief discussion of the existing tools to characterize econometric models, we have mentioned the use of structural parameters, reduced-form parameters and final-form parameters, and the tools to study cyclical properties of an econometric model. For any econometric model we can also derive the variances and covariances of the errors of its forecasts of the future values of the endogenous variables, given projected values of the exogenous variables. Thus models can be characterized and compared by the variances and covariances of the disturbances in the structural equations, in the reduced-form equations (measuring errors of forecasts one period ahead), and in the final-form equations (measuring errors of forecasts many periods ahead). For example, for an autoregressive model

$$y_t = a y_{t-1} + u_t = a^2 y_{t-2} + u_t + a u_{t-1}$$

the error of a two-period-ahead forecast has a variance equal to $\mathrm{var}(u_t + a u_{t-1})$. One can also measure forecasting errors of an econometric model by comparing its various forecasts with actual historical observations. The remainder of this chapter will be concerned with the characterization of an econometric model for the purpose of formulating an optimal economic policy.

14.2. CHARACTERIZATION OF AN ECONOMETRIC MODEL BY DETERMINISTIC CONTROL

In the optimal control of a deterministic econometric model (with its random disturbances set equal to their expected values), a multiperiod loss function is postulated, and its value is minimized with respect to the time paths of the policy or control variables (a subset of exogenous variables), subject to the constraint of the dynamic model. If the econometrician is willing to choose a loss function, then models can be characterized and compared by the solution paths of the key endogenous and policy variables. Such comparisons have recently been made by the U.S. econometric model builders who were participants in an NSF-NBER Seminar on Econometric Model Comparison under the chairmanship of Lawrence Klein. Some of the results are described in Hirsch, Hymans, and Shapiro (1978) and in Chow and Megdal (1978a). Optimal deterministic control paths were obtained from several models of the U.S. economy for the 17 quarters from 1971.1 to 1975.1 using the same loss function which penalizes the squared deviations of the inflation rate, unemployment rates, real GNP, and balance of trade from their preassigned targets. To illustrate the results, the optimal solutions for the inflation rate show whether the two-digit inflation in 1974 could have been avoided by suitable economic policy beginning in 1971.1 according to the participating models. The answer is mostly negative. The solutions for the unemployment rate by and large show that significant reductions could have been achieved during quarters of high unemployment without seriously aggravating the inflation situation. Note that this solution does not take into account the possible delayed effects of an expansionary policy on inflation after 1975.1, which was the terminal quarter of the multiperiod optimization problem.

Similarly, the optimal solution paths for the policy variables can also be compared to show similarities and differences among models. In the experiments conducted by the participants of the Econometric Model Comparison Seminar, the policy variables are federal government nondefense expenditures and unborrowed reserves. The optimal solutions for government expenditures according to several models require fairly sizable increases, in the order of 50 to 60 billion (at an annual rate) in the later quarters over the actual expenditures. One can further compare the relative roles played by the fiscal and monetary instruments across different models. Not only the average deviations of the optimal settings of these instruments from some norms (such as historical trends) but also their relative fluctuations through time can be compared. In short, different characteristics of the optimal solution paths for the important endogenous and policy variables in a deterministic control problem can be compared among different econometric models.

A natural extension of the above comparison is to vary the parameters in the loss function and to observe the resulting changes in the optimal solution paths. This is an application of the method of comparative dynamics to deterministic models. In fact, it has been suggested by Chow and Megdal (1978b) that the parameters in a quadratic loss function should be varied in a systematic way in order to trace out the best available trade-off possibilities for unemployment and inflation implicit in an econometric model. Econometricians have attempted to derive the trade-off relationships between unemployment and inflation from an econometric model by recording the behavior of these two variables in simulations using more or less expansionary, but still fairly arbitrary, paths for the policy instruments. Simulations of this type have been performed by Anderson and Carlson (1972), de Menil and Enzler (1972), Hirsch (1972), Bodkin (1972), and Hymans (1972), among others. This method is defective because the unemployment and inflation rates so obtained without optimization could usually be improved upon, as demonstrated by the calculations using the St. Louis model and the Michigan Quarterly Econometric Model reported in Chow and Megdal (1978b).

In order to determine the lowest inflation rate corresponding to a 6 percent unemployment rate, we solve an optimal control problem using a quadratic loss function with 1 and 6 percent as the targets for the inflation and unemployment rates, respectively (assuming a 1 percent annual inflation rate to be lower than achievable), and 1 and 100, respectively, as the weights penalizing the squared deviations of inflation and unemployment from their targets. Optimization will ensure that the unemployment rate is close to 6 percent and the inflation rate will be made as low as possible. Here we are dealing with a multiperiod optimization problem. The inflation rates obtained from the optimal solution will change from quarter to quarter, but the entire set of inflation rates could not be improved upon in the sense that, given a 6 percent unemployment rate, the sum of squared deviations of the inflation rates in all periods from 1 percent is the minimum. If one wishes to depict in a two-dimensional diagram the trade-off possibilities between inflation and unemployment for many periods, then the mean rates of these variables over time or their root mean squared deviations over time could be plotted. The points in the diagram are obtained by solving several optimal deterministic control problems as we just formulated, with the target for the unemployment rate varying from 4 to 9 percent or over whatever range of values required. Thus each econometric model is characterized by one optimal unemployment-inflation trade-off curve. This curve permits us to answer the important question concerning the model: Can a 4 percent inflation rate be achieved while maintaining an unemployment rate of 5 percent during a particular time period?

Before closing this section, we would like to describe briefly some of the available algorithms to calculate the solutions to deterministic control problems using an econometric model. The algorithms can be divided into two categories. The first treats the problem strictly as a deterministic control problem, ignoring all the random elements in the econometric model. Because the time paths of the endogenous variables are determined by the time paths of the control variables through the econometric model, and the multiperiod loss is a function of the endogenous (and possibly also the control) variables, one can regard the loss function as a function of the control variables. Various gradient-type algorithms have been applied to minimize the loss function with respect to the time paths of the control variables, including the works of Fair (1974), Holbrook (1974), Craine, Havenner, and Tinsley (1976), Kalchbrenner and Tinsley (1976), Ando and Palash (1976), and Norman, Norman and Palash (1975). The second category is a by-product of a solution to an optimal stochastic control problem that allows for random disturbances in an econometric model. The mathematical expectation of a multiperiod loss function is minimized subject to the constraint of a stochastic econometric model, as will be illustrated by (3.2) and (3.3) of Section 3. The optimal solution will take the form of feedback control equations, that is, $x_t = G_t y_{t-1} + g_t$, where x_t and y_t are respectively vectors of control and endogenous variables, and G_t and g_t are respectively a matrix and a vector of constants to be determined by the optimal control algorithm. To obtain a solution to a deterministic control problem, however, we can apply these optimal feedback control equations to a deterministic econometric model and calculate the time paths of both the endogenous and the control variables when the model is subject to optimal control.

One method to obtain a set of optimal feedback control equations to minimize a quadratic loss function subject to a system of nonlinear structural equations as described in Chow (1975, p. 285; 1976b) is the following. First, tentative paths x_t^0 of the control variables are chosen. The Gauss-Siedel method is applied to solve the nonlinear equations to obtain the paths y_t^0 of the endogenous variables corresponding to the chosen paths of the control variables. The econometric model is linearized about these paths:

$$y_t = \phi(y_t, y_{t-1}, x_t) \simeq \phi(y_t^0, y_{t-1}^0, x_t^0) + \Phi_{1t}(y_t - y_t^0)$$

$$+ \Phi_{2t}(y_{t-1} - y_{t-1}^0) + \Phi_{3t}(x_t - x_t^0),$$

where Φ_{it} denotes the matrix of the derivatives of the vector function ϕ with respect to its ith argument evaluated at y_t^0, y_{t-1}^0, and x_t^0. A set of time-varying linear structural equations is thus obtained. These equations are solved to produce a set of time-varying, linear reduced-form equations. Given these reduced-form equations the the quadratic loss function, the solution to the deterministic optimal control problem is computed in the form of optimal feedback control equations. These equations, together with the original nonlinear structural equations, determine the time paths of the endogenous and control variables when the system is governed by the new set of control rules. The model is again linearized about these paths as before. The process continues until the solution paths from successive linearization converge.

14.3 CHARACTERIZATION OF AN ECONOMETRIC MODEL BY STOCHASTIC CONTROL

The feedback control algorithm described at the end of Section 2 provides a nearly optimal solution to the original stochastic control problem when the random disturbances in the econometric model are retained. It can therefore be used to characterize a stochastic econometric model from the viewpoint of optimal economic policy. When the random disturbances of an econometric model are taken into account in the formulation of economic policy, two important consequences should be noted. First, as we have pointed out, the solution will take the form of feedback control equations. Second, the solution paths for both endogenous and control variables become stochastic. In order to characterize them, we need at least the expected paths and the autocovariance matrices of the variables in the system under feedback control. The expected paths can be approximated by the solution to the deterministic control problem obtained by replacing the random disturbances by their expected values. The autocovariance matrix of the system can be easily computed by using the time-varying, linear feedback control equations and the linearized reduced-form equations obtained from the last iteration (or linearization) using the preceding algorithm. See Chow (1975, Chapter 3), for example, on the methods of computing the autocovariance matrix. Hence the dynamic properties of the optimal control paths of the endogenous and control variables can be used to characterize and compare stochastic econometric models as well as deterministic models.

When dealing with stochastic models, we can supplement the unemployment-inflation trade-off curves proposed in Section 2. These curves are constructed from the deterministic time paths of these variables in the optimal deterministic control solution or from the expected time paths, denoted by $\bar{y}_t$, of the (approximately) optimal stochastic control solution. Let y_{1t} and y_{2t} stand for the unemployment and inflation rates respectively. We could vary the weights in the loss function, as suggested in Section 2, and plot the resulting combinations of $\Sigma_{t=1}^{T} \bar{y}_{1t}/T$ and $\Sigma_{t=1}^{T} \bar{y}_{2t}/T$. We could also plot the square roots of $\Sigma_{t=1}^{T}(\bar{y}_{1t} - a_{1t})^2/T$ and $\Sigma_{t=1}^{T}(\bar{y}_{2t} - a_{2t})^2/T$, where a_{1t} and a_{2t} are some target paths for unemployment and inflation and may be set equal to zero. The contribution of the ith variable to the multiperiod expected loss is given by

$$\sum_{t=1}^{T} E(y_{it} - a_{it})^2 = \sum_{t=1}^{T} (\bar{y}_{it} - a_{it})^2 + \sum_{t=1}^{T} E(y_{it} - \bar{y}_{it})^2. \qquad (3.1)$$

Hence the sums $\Sigma_{t=1}^{T} E(y_{it} - \bar{y}_{it})^2$ of the variances over T periods for the unemployment rate and the inflation rate can be plotted. Or the total contributions, consisting of $\Sigma_{t=1}^{T}(\bar{y}_{it} - a_{it})^2$ and $\Sigma_{t=1}^{T} E(y_{it} - \bar{y}_{it})^2$, from the unemployment and inflation rates can be plotted on a two-dimensional diagram. A curve can be traced out by varying the parameters of the loss function as the unemployment-inflation trade-off curve was traced out in Section 2.

The main purpose of this section, however, is to propose some summary measures to characterize an econometric model for policy purpose, rather than simply exhibiting the mean paths and the covariance matrix of the major economic variables prevailing when the model is subject to optimal feedback control. The basic idea is a generalization of the reduced-form equations of a static model relating the endogenous variables to the control variables. The multipliers are the derivatives of these reduced-form equations. Our problem is complicated because we are studying the effects of the policy variables in the context of a nonlinear, dynamic, stochastic econometric model, which is being controlled to minimize the expectation of a multiperiod objective function. Rather than measuring the effects on many individual endogenous variables, we propose to measure the effects of the current control variables on the total expected loss for all future periods until the end of the planning horizon. We will choose a scalar function relating the multiperiod expected loss to the control variables of the first period. This function is derived directly from the well-known stochastic control theory based on the method of dynamic programming as follows.

First, assume a quadratic loss function for T periods with $k_t = K_t a_t$

$$W = \sum_{t=1}^{T} (y_t - a_t)' K_t (y_t - a_t) = \sum_{t=1}^{T} (y_t' K_t y_t - 2y_t' k_t + a_t' K_t a_t). \quad (3.2)$$

Second, the nonlinear econometric model is linearized about the solution paths of the optimal deterministic control problem as described at the end of the last section, yielding the following reduced-form equations

$$y_t = A_t y_{t-1} + C_t x_t + b_t + u_t, \quad (3.3)$$

where x_t is a vector of control variables which may be incorporated as a subvector of the endogenous variables y_t if necessary and u_t is a vector of serially uncorrelated random disturbances. Using the method of dynamic programming (Chow, 1975, Section 8.1), we find the optimal strategy by first minimizing the expected loss $E(y_T - a_T)' K_T (y_T - a_T)$ for only the last period T with respect to x_T. Substituting (3.3) for y_T in this expectation and differentiating the result with respect to x_T, we obtain a linear feedback control equation $x_T = G_T y_{T-1} + g_T$. We then minimize the sum of the expected losses for the last two periods with respect to x_{T-1}, assuming that the last period policy x_T shall be optimal, that is, substituting the minimum expected loss for period T into the minimand. Continuing the process backward in time, we finally minimize the sum of the expected losses for all T periods with respect to x_1 of the first period, assuming that $x_2, \ldots, x_T$ will be optimal. This sum, after all the future minimum expected losses from period 2 onward have been duly inserted, is the expectation of a quadratic function of the economic variables y_1 for the first period only:

$$V_1 = E(y_1' H_1 y_1 - 2y_1' h_1 + c_1), \quad (3.4)$$

where the coefficients H_1, h_1, and c_1 can be calculated by standard formulas (Chow, 1975, p. 179). Using (3.3) to substitute for y_t in (3.4) and taking expectations, we have

$$V_1 = x_1'C_1'H_1C_1x_1 + 2x_1'C_1'(H_1A_1y_0 + H_1b_1 - h_1)$$

$$+ (A_1y_0 + b_1)'H_1(A_1y_0 + b_1) + E(u_1'H_1u_1) - 2(A_1y_0 + b_1)'h_1 + c_1$$

$$= x_1'Qx_1 + 2x_1'q + d \tag{3.5}$$

Thus, assuming that the policies from period 2 onward will be optimal, the expected multiperiod loss is a quadratic function of x_1 as given by (3.5). The optimal first-period policy $\hat{x}_1$ is obtained by minimizing (3.5) with respect to x_1, yielding the associated minimum expected multiperiod loss $\hat{V}_1 = V_1(\hat{x}_1)$. Note that the subscript of V denotes the fact that this cumulated expected loss is computed from period 1 onward.

Our proposal is to use the quadratic function $V_1(x_1)$, as given by (3.5), to characterize and compare econometric models. This function gives the total expected loss from period 1 to period T in terms of the control variables x_1 in the first period, assuming that future policies from period 2 to period T will be chosen optimally. It appears to capture the essential information contained in an econometric model concerning the effects of the current policy variables on economic welfare as measured by the loss function. It is applicable to deterministic models as a special case where the vectors u_t of random disturbances for all periods are set equal to zero. The constant term d in the quadratic function (3.5) will be affected since $E(u_1'H_1u_1)$ is zero and its component c_1 is dependent on future $E(u_t'H_tu_t)$.

To compare two econometric models A and B, we use the functions $V_{1A}(x_1)$ and $V_{1B}(x_1)$ obtained by the dynamic programming algorithm applied to these models respectively, given the same multiperiod loss function. Let $\hat{x}_{1A}$ and $\hat{x}_{1B}$ respectively minimize V_{1A} and V_{1B}. One can certainly compare the two models by their first-period optimal policies $\hat{x}_{1A}$ and $\hat{x}_{1B}$. In fact, in Section 2 we have pointed out that the entire optimal solution paths $\hat{x}_{tA}$ and $\hat{x}_{tB}(t = 1, \ldots, T)$ obtained from two deterministic models can be compared. However, by simply inspecting the values of $\hat{x}_{1A}$ and $\hat{x}_{1B}$ we cannot tell how different the policy recommendations from the two models are. Perhaps the function $V_{1A}(x_1)$ is fairly flat around $\hat{x}_{1A}$, and $V_{1A}(\hat{x}_{1B})$ is not much larger than $V_{1A}(\hat{x}_{1A})$. This means that, as far as model A is concerned, $\hat{x}_{1B}$ is about as good a policy as x_{1A}. On the other hand, $V_{1B}(\hat{x}_{1A})$ may be much larger than $V_{1B}(\hat{x}_{1B})$; that is, as far as model B is concerned, its optimal policy $\hat{x}_{1B}$ is much superior to the optimal policy $\hat{x}_{1A}$ derived from model A.

To depict the differences between two models A and B for the purpose of obtaining a reasonable first-period policy x_1, the following payoff matrix can be used as an example:

	States of the World	
	A	B
Optimal strategy from A	$V_{1A}(\hat{x}_{1A})$ 100	$V_{1B}(\hat{x}_{1A})$ 95
Optimal strategy from B	$V_{1A}(\hat{x}_{1B})$ 300	$V_{1B}(\hat{x}_{1B})$ 90

When we consider the welfare consequence of using the optimal policy $\hat{x}_{1A}$ from model A if model B happens to be true, we do not assume that the policy recommendations from model A will be followed period after period. Rather, we assume that the (mistaken) policy from model A will be followed only in the current period and the (correct) policies from the hypothetically true model B might be followed from period 2 on. The rationale for this payoff matrix is that the decision maker is not committed to follow the mistaken policies from an incorrect model in the future. To measure the welfare loss in adopting $\hat{x}_{1A}$ for only the first period while allowing for the possibility to behave optimally later on assuming model B to be true, we compare $V_{1B}(\hat{x}_{1A})$ with $V_{1B}(\hat{x}_{1B})$ in the matrix. If $V_{1B}(\hat{x}_{1A})$ $- V_{1B}(\hat{x}_{1B})$ is small while $V_{1A}(\hat{x}_{1B}) - V_{1A}(\hat{x}_{1A})$ is large, as illustrated by the numbers given for the payoff matrix, one would adopt $\hat{x}_{1A}$ by a minimax criterion. A Bayesian would assign probabilities $P(A)$ and $P(B)$ to the two models and adopt the policy to minimize expected loss. In this numerical illustration, unless $P(A)$ is very small as compared with $P(B)$, $\hat{x}_{1A}$ will yield a smaller expected loss than $\hat{x}_{1B}$.

If a model A is assumed to be fairly accurate, we can evaluate a historically adopted policy x_1 by the difference $V_{1A}(x_1) - V_{1A}(\hat{x}_{1A})$, where the function $V_{1A}(\cdot)$ is obtained by using the historical period in question as period 1. This difference measures the welfare cost of adopting the historical policy x_1, rather than the optimal policy $\hat{x}_{1A}$. The logic is identical with that of comparing $V_{1A}(\hat{x}_{1B})$ and $V_{1A}(\hat{x}_{1A})$ as suggested in the previous paragraph. This approach to the evaluation of historical policies is discussed in Chapter 8.

14.4   AN ILLUSTRATION USING THE MICHIGAN MODEL

To illustrate the method of Section 3, the Michigan Quarterly Econometric Model (Hymans and Shapiro, 1973) has been used to calculate the function $V_1(x_1)$. The optimal control problem solved is the one posted by the participants of the NSF-NBER Econometric Model Comparison Seminar referred to in Section 2. That is, the number of periods is 17, covering the quarters from 1971.1 to 1975.1. The objective is to minimize the loss function

$$\sum_{t=1}^{17} \left[(\dot{p}_t - \alpha_t)^2 + 0.75(u_t - 4.0)^2 + 0.75(\text{GNP gap}_t - 0)^2 \right.$$

$$\left. + (TB_t - 0)^2 + 0.1(\text{UR\$}_t - \gamma_t)^2 \right], \tag{4.1}$$

where $\dot{p}$ is the annual rate of inflation measured by the GNP deflator, $\alpha_t = 3.0$ for $t = 1, \ldots, 12$, $\alpha_t = 7.0$ for $t = 13, \ldots, 17$, u is the unemployment rate, GNP gap is the percentage deviation of GNP in 1958 dollars (GNP58) from capacity output, TB is trade balance as a percentage of GNP in current dollars, UR\$ is unborrowed reserves in billions of current dollars, and γ_t represents a smooth expansionary path for UR\$. The policy variables set up for our computations are government transfer payments GTRP\$, unborrowed reserves UR\$, and nondefense government purchases of goods and services GFO\$, all in billions of current dollars. However, the first control variable GTRP\$ was not treated as such by the participants of the Econometric Model Comparison Seminar. Therefore, we simply fixed it as its historical path by using the historical path as the target path and assigning a large penalty weight of 100 to the square of its deviation from target [this part of the loss function not being shown in function (4.1)]. The UR\$ term in the loss function serves to prevent erratic behavior of the monetary instrument. The estimated residuals in the structural equations were added back to the intercepts, at the suggestion of the seminar participants, resulting in a deterministic control problem although our method can handle the stochastic case as well. The optimal control solution paths for the major endogenous and control variables have been discussed elsewhere (Chow and Megdal, 1978a). We will study the function $V_1(x_1)$ below.

The quadratic function $V_1(x_1) = x_1'Qx_1 + 2x_1'q + d$ is given by the following matrix Q and vector q

$$Q = \begin{bmatrix} 100.00097 & 0.00003 & 0.00237 \\ 0.00003 & 0.10301 & 0.00100 \\ 0.00237 & 0.00100 & 0.00861 \end{bmatrix} \quad q = \begin{bmatrix} -8270.316 \\ -2.798 \\ -0.897 \end{bmatrix}. \tag{4.2}$$

The vector of control variables in period 1 which minimizes V_1 is

$$\hat{x}_1' = [82.7005 \quad 26.3770 \quad 78.3233]. \tag{4.3}$$

The derivatives of V_1 with respect to the three control variables are $2Qx_1 + 2q$. They are of course zero at $x_1 = \hat{x}_1$. If the first control variable x_{11} deviates slightly from its minimizing value 82.70, say $x_{11} = 83.70$ billion, and the other two control variables retain their optimum values, the derivative of V_1 with respect to the first is very large, being equal to 100.0, which is the leading diagonal element of Q. On the other hand, when the second and third control variables are increased by 1 billion from their optimum values, the derivatives will only be 0.1030 and 0.0086, respectively. The function V_1 increases very sharply as x_{11} deviates from its optimum value because we have put a heavy penalty on the deviation of this variable from its historical or target value 82.70; we are in fact not treating this variable as a genuine control variable. V_1 increases more rapidly when the second control variable (unborrowed reserves) deviates from its optimum than when the third control variable (nondefense government purchases) deviates from its optimum, partly because the former variable enters explicitly in the loss function (4.1).

Because the first control variable is really fixed, we simplify our analysis by reducing V_1 to a function of only the second and third control variables. When x_{11} is fixed at its historical value 82.70, the quadratic function V_1 is given by

$$Q = \begin{bmatrix} 0.103013 & 0.000999 \\ 0.000999 & 0.008614 \end{bmatrix} \qquad q = \begin{bmatrix} -2.7954 \\ -0.7011 \end{bmatrix}. \qquad (4.4)$$

If we had computed the function V_1 for another econometric model, we would use its optimum values for the two control variables to evaluate the function (4.4) and compare the result with the minimum value of (4.4). We would also use the optimum values of (4.4) to evaluate the function V_1 derived from the other model and compare the result with the minimum of the latter function. We could also plot the contour maps of these two functions on the same diagram and compare them. Without the second V_1 at our disposal, we will evaluate (4.4) at the historical values of the control variables, which are 29.5 and 24.1 respectively. Note that the second figure differs a great deal from the optimum value 78.3 given in (4.3). At these historical values, the multiperiod loss V_1 given by (4.4) is 26.00 higher than its minimum.

To examine the figure 26.00 more closely, we will compute the difference between the first-period losses of the two policies. The figure 26.00 is composed of this difference and the remainder which measures the extra loss from period 2 to T attributable to the historical (nonoptimal) policy as it affects the initial economic condition at the end of period 1. The optimum solution values and the historical solution values of the variables entering the loss function (4.1) for period 1 (1971.1) are given in the accompanying tabulation.

Solution	$\dot{p}_1$	u_1	GNP Gap$_1$	TB$_1$	UR$\$_1$
Optimum	6.07	5.08	0.48	− 0.182	26.4
Historical	4.69	5.95	5.01	0.278	29.5

The first-period losses resulting from these two solutions are 11.47 and 24.61 respectively, the difference being 13.14. [Note that the target value for UR$\$_1$ was set at its historical value 29.5, accounting for a contribution of $0.1(26.4 - 29.5)^2 = 0.961$ to the first-period loss of the optimum policy.] The main contribution to the first-period loss of the historical policy is from the GNP gap, equal to $0.75(5.01)^2 = 18.83$. Although the loss function (4.1) weighs the inflation term by 1 and the unemployment term by only 0.75, it penalizes low output quite heavily through the GNP gap. In short, 13.14 or about half of the extra multiperiod loss 26.00 is allotted to the difference between the first-period losses. The assumption is that, no matter whether the first-period policy is optimal or not, the policies from period 2 on will be optimally chosen. The nonoptimal policy in period 1 adds 13.14 to the loss in period 1 itself, as computed from the two sets of solution values of the variables included in the loss function shown. It adds an almost equal amount to the total loss from period 2 to period 17, assuming the policies in these periods to be optimal. The 26.00 figure can also be compared with the total loss of 248.03 for all 17 periods if optimal policies had been followed throughout.

The fairly sizable difference between the outcomes of the two policies is not surprising because the historical value of federal government nondefense purchases in 1971.1 is 24.1 billion and its optimal value from solving the optimal control problem using the loss function (4.1) is 78.3 billion. We have not considered the political feasibility of such a large increase in government expenditures. To do so would require putting an extra term for this control variables in the loss function. Several questions are of interest when optimal control techniques are applied to analyze and compare econometric models. When the optimal solution deviates so much from the historical trend, would the model remain valid? If not, how should the model be changed? Or should we keep the model and pull the solution closer to the trend by adding extra terms in the loss function? In fact, an important use of optimal control is to reveal the properties of an econometric model under systematic variations of the control variables. If we adopt a policy closer to the historical trend, such as 40.0 billion for federal nondefense purchases as compared with the optimal value of 78.3 billion, how much would we lose if the model remained valid at the optimum solution? (The answer is that the multiperiod loss would increase from the minimum 248.03 by only 12.65, instead of 26.00, when the two control variables equal 26.377 and 40.0, respectively.)

In this chapter we have reviewed briefly some existing tools for characterizing and comparing econometric models and described several techniques based on the theories of optimal control of deterministic and stochastic econometric models. In particular, a curve depicting the best inflation-unemployment trade-off can be used to characterize an econometric model. Furthermore, we propose the use of a quadratic function $V_{1A}(x_1)$ that measures the T-period expected loss based on a model A if x_1 is the policy for period 1 while the policies for the remaining periods from 2 to T will be optimal. This function is simple; it has nine parameters as illustrated by (4.2) when there are three control variables, and five parameters as illustrated by (4.4) when there are two control variables no matter how complicated model A is. It captures the essential information concerning the response of the model to the policy variables and can be used to characterize a model from the viewpoint of policy analysis and formulation.

Part 3

Stochastic Control Under Rational Expectations

CHAPTER 15

Econometric Policy Evaluation and Optimization Under Rational Expectations

15.1 INTRODUCTION

This chapter is concerned with methods for evaluating given economic policies and for finding optimal policies using an econometric model under the assumption of rational expectations. For the purpose of this discussion, the assumption of rational expectations will be granted without implying that the author will necessarily subscribe to it for most macroeconomic applications. This work, as well as several of the papers to be cited later, has been stimulated by the critical comments of Lucas (1976) on econometric policy evaluation that takes inadequate account of the effects of government policy on the expectations formed by the economic agents. One answer to this critique which Lucas himself advocates is the use of rational expectations. These are conditional expectations of the endogenous variables generated by the econometric model itself given the available information inclusive of the government policy. Such an approach to policy evaluation raises theoretical and computational problems which are to be addressed in this chapter. Similar problems will also arise when one wishes to formulate optimal policy under the assumption of rational expectations. Some authors, including Kydland and Prescott (1977) in particular, feel strongly that these problems are insoluble and therefore optimal control theory should not be applied to economic planning. We will attempt to solve these problems and to show that optimal control is applicable in an environment of rational expectations.

There appears to be a consensus among several authors, including Shiller (1977), Wallis (1980), Anderson (1979), and Taylor (1977, 1979), that policy evaluation using an econometric model under rational expectations is fairly straightforward, provided that (1) the model is linear and (2) expectations of future endogenous variables do not appear in the model. We will therefore use this simple setup as the starting point of our discussion of econometric policy evaluation in Section 2. The complications due to the presence of expectations of future endogenous variables and of nonlinear relationships in the model will be introduced in turn. In Section 3, we consider the formulation of optimal control policies. Section 4 includes some concluding remarks.

15.2 ECONOMETRIC POLICY EVALUATION

15.2.1 Linear Model Without Expectations of Future Variables

In the simple situation where the model is linear and expectations of future endogenous variables are absent, we can write the model in its reduced form as

$$y_t = B y_{t|t-1}^* + A y_{t-1} + C x_t + b_t + v_t. \tag{1}$$

Here y_t denotes a vector of endogenous variables, x_t denotes a vector of policy instruments or control variables, b_t is a vector summarizing the combined effects of the exogenous variables not subject to control, and v_t is a vector of serially uncorrelated, identically distributed disturbances. $y_{t|s}^*$ is the conditional expectation $E(y_t | I_s)$ of y_t given the information I_s as of the end of period s. As is well known, one can eliminate the variables y_{t-k} for $k \geq$ and x_{t-k} for $k \geq 1$ if they exist in the original model and rewrite it as (1) by suitable definitions of new variables. Because the expectations of only a small fraction of the endogenous variables may appear in the model, many columns of the matrix B will be zero.

One well-known method to eliminate the expectations $y_{t|t-1}^*$ from the model (1) and to derive a model for only the directly observables is to take conditional expectations of both sides of (1) given I_{t-1} and solve for $y_{t|t-1}^*$,

$$y_{t|t-1}^* = (I - B)^{-1}(A y_{t-1} + C x_{t|t-1}^* + b_{t|t-1}^*). \tag{2}$$

Substituting the right-hand side of (2) for $y_{t|t-1}^*$ in (1) and simplifying gives

$$y_t = (I - B)^{-1}(Ay_{t-1} + Cx_{t|t-1}^* + b_{t|t-1}^*) + C(x_t - x_{t|t-1}^*)$$

$$+ b_t - b_{t|t-1}^* + v_t. \tag{3}$$

The model (3) can be used for policy evaluation as rational expectations are already incorporated by using (2) to represent the expectations $y_{t|t-1}^*$ in the model (1). To specify completely the time path for y_t from model (3), it is sufficient to assume that both the public and the government policy maker share the same expectations $x_{t|t-1}^*$ and $b_{t|t-1}^*$ for the control variables and the combined effects of the other exogenous variables, and, secondly, that the deviations $(x_t - x_{t|t-1}^*)$ and $(b_t - b_{t|t-1}^*)$ are serially uncorrelated and have zero mean. The terms $C(x_t - x_{t|t-1}^*) + (b_t - b_{t|t-1}^*)$ can be combined with v_t in (3) to form a new residual.

15.2.2 Linear Model with Expectations of Future Variables

A complication arises if $y_{t+1|t-1}^*$ appears in the model, that is,

$$y_t = By_{t|t-1}^* + B_1 y_{t+1|t-1}^* + Ay_{t-1} + Cx_t + b_t + v_t. \tag{4}$$

Taking conditional expectations of both sides of (4) given I_{t-1}, solving for $y_{t|t-1}^*$, and substituting the resulting expression for $y_{t|t-1}^*$ back into (4), one obtains a generalization of (3),

$$y_t = (I - B)^{-1}(B_1 y_{t+1|t-1}^* + Ay_{t-1} + Cx_{t|t-1}^* + b_{t|t-1}^*) + \eta_t$$

$$= \tilde{B}_1 y_{t+1|t-1}^* + \tilde{A}y_{t-1} + \tilde{C}x_{t|t-1}^* + \tilde{b}_{t|t-1}^* + \eta_t. \tag{5}$$

where we have let η_t denote $C(x_t - x_{t|t-1}^*) + (b_t - b_{t|t-1}^*) + v_t$, and have defined $\tilde{B}_1$ as $(I - B)^{-1}B_1$, and so on. Unlike (3), the model (5) retains an expectation vector $y_{t+1|t-1}^*$ that is not directly observable. [If $B_2 y_{t+2|t-1}^*$ appears in (4), $\tilde{B}_2 y_{t+2|t-1}^*$ will appear in (5), and the algebra of our proposed solution later will be affected, but not its basic logic.]

We shall distinguish between two types of policy, an open-loop policy where a vector $(x_1, \ldots, x_T)$ of values for the policy instruments is announced for T periods, T being the planning horizon, and a linear feedback policy which takes the form $x_t = G_t y_{t-1} + g_t$. In either case, the policy is announced at the beginning of the planning period and the economic agents are assumed to form their expectations according to the announcements. In other words, $x^*_{t|t-1}$ is known; it equals the announced policy in the case of an open-loop policy and equals $G_t y_{t-1} + g_t$ in the case of a feedback policy, G_t and g_t being given constants. Furthermore, it will be assumed that both the policy maker and the public share identical expectations $b^*_{t|t-1}$ for the combined effects of the exogenous variables; otherwise policy evaluation would be impossible under rational expectations.

For the purpose of policy evaluation, consider (4) for period T. It explains y_T using $y^*_{T+1|T-1}$. To obtain a unique (stochastic) model for y_T, and in fact for all $y_t (t = 1, \ldots, T)$, we will assume that $y^*_{T+1|T-1}$ is a given linear function of $y^*_{T|T-1}$ (and of y_{T-1} if necessary). Each linear function assumed will yield a model for y_T and thus for $y_t (t = 1, \ldots, T)$. This is not to provide a general answer to the multiple-solution problem arising from models under rational expectations as discussed in Taylor (1977) and Shiller (1977), for example. We are merely suggesting that in order to arrive at a unique sequence of predictions, an advocate of rational expectations needs to supply an additional condition, and that (4) for the terminal period T is a convenient place to state and examine such a condition. When T is sufficiently large, it is reasonable to assume that selected elements of $y^*_{T+1|T-1}$ are equal or proportional to the corresponding elements of $y^*_{T|T-1}$ for making a policy evaluation in period 1. This assumption can be replaced by the assumption of equality or proportionality between $y^*_{T+1|0}$ and $y^*_{T|0}$. Since the expectations of $y_t (t = 1, \ldots, T)$ to be evaluated are all conditioned on information at time zero, variables in the following procedure can be replaced by their expectations given I_0 without affecting the calculations. Having made an assumption for $y^*_{T+1|T-1}$, we can eliminate it from (4), take expectations given I_{T-1}, and solve out $y^*_{T|T-1}$ to obtain

$$y_T = \tilde{A}_T y_{T-1} + \tilde{C}_T x^*_{T|T-1} + \tilde{b}_{T|T-1} + \eta_T. \tag{6}$$

Given the terminal condition (6), and given an open-loop policy, the set of difference equations (4) can be solved backward in time. Taking expectations of both sides of (6) given I_{T-2} and substituting the result for $y^*_{T|T-2}$ in the equation for y_{T-1}, we have

$$y_{T-1} = B y^*_{T-1|T-2} + B_1 \left(\tilde{A}_T y^*_{T-1|T-2} + \tilde{C}_T x^*_{T|T-2} + \tilde{b}^*_{T|T-2} \right)$$

$$+ A y_{T-2} + C x_{T-1} + b_{T-1} + v_{T-1}. \tag{7}$$

Because (7) no longer contains the expectation $y^*_{T|T-2}$ of future endogenous variables, we can take conditional expectations given I_{T-2} to obtain an equation for $y^*_{T-1|T-2}$ and substitute the result back into (7) to yield an equation analogous to (3),

$$y_{T-1} = \left(I - B - B_1\tilde{A}_T\right)^{-1}\left(Ay_{T-2} + B_1\tilde{C}_T x^*_{T|T-2}\right.$$

$$+ B_1\tilde{b}^*_{T|T-2} + Cx^*_{T-1|T-2} + b^*_{T-1|T-2}\bigg)$$

$$+ C\left(x_{T-1} - x^*_{T-1|T-2}\right) + b_{T-1} - b^*_{T-1|T-2} + v_{T-1}$$

$$\equiv \tilde{A}_{T-1}y_{T-2} + \tilde{C}_{T-1,T}x^*_{T|T-2} + \tilde{C}_{T-1,T-1}x^*_{T-1|T-2}$$

$$+ D_{T-1,T}\tilde{b}^*_{T|T-2} + \bar{b}^*_{T-1|T-2} + \eta_{T-1}. \tag{8}$$

The process continues by taking expectations of both sides of (8) given I_{T-3} and substituting the result for $y^*_{T-1|T-3}$ in the equation for y_{T-2}, yielding an equation for y_{T-2} corresponding to (7). This equation no longer contains the expectation $y^*_{T-1|T-3}$ of future endogenous variables, and can be converted into an equation like (8). In general, the resulting equation for y_t is

$$y_t = \tilde{A}_t y_{t-1} + \sum_{i=t}^{T} \tilde{C}_{t,i}x^*_{i|t-1} + \sum_{i=t}^{T} D_{t,i}\tilde{b}^*_{i|t-1} + \eta_t, \tag{9}$$

where $D_{t,t} = I$. Given an open-loop policy that specifies the expectations of all future x_t and given the initial condition y_0, (9) can be used to generate predictions for $y_t (t = 1, \ldots, T)$ for the purpose of policy evaluation.

If a linear feedback policy $x_t = G_t y_{t-1} + g_t$ is to be evaluated, we can substitute this rule for x_t in (4) to obtain

$$y_t = By^*_{t|t-1} + B_1 y^*_{t+1|t-1} + R_t y_{t-1} + \bar{b}_t + v_t, \tag{10}$$

where $R_t = A + CG_t$ and $\bar{b}_t = b_t + Cg_t$. (10) can be solved backward in time once a terminal condition for $y^*_{T+1|T-1}$ is specified. Using the feedback rule, we can replace $x^*_{T|T-1}$ in (6) by $G_T y_{T-1} + g_T$ to yield the terminal condition

$$y_T = \tilde{R}_T y_{T-1} + \bar{b}^*_{T|T-1} + \eta_T, \tag{11}$$

where $\tilde{R}_T = \tilde{A}_T + \tilde{C}_T G_T$ and $\bar{b}^*_{T|T-1} = \bar{b}^*_{T|T-1} + \tilde{C}_T g_T$. One can follow the derivation from (6) to (9) and obtain an equation analogous to (9),

$$y_t = \tilde{R}_t y_{t-1} + \sum_{i=t}^{T} D_{t|i} \bar{b}^*_{i|t-1} + \eta_t, \tag{12}$$

where the expectations of the policy variables have disappeared as they are incorporated in $\tilde{R}_t$, $D_{t|i}$ and $\bar{b}^*_{i|t-1}$. In obtaining the matrix coefficients in (9) and (12), one should be aware of the problems of computational errors due to repeated matrix-multiplications in the backward solutions. However, the author's experience with the similar problem in solving matrix Riccati equations backward in time for systems of about 100 equations for 20 periods indicates that the problem can usually be solved using double-precision arithmetics with a modern computer.

15.2.3 Nonlinear Model with Expectations of Future Variables

If the model is nonlinear, but expectations of future endogenous variables are absent and the random disturbances are ignored, then the expectations of the endogenous variables generated by the model under rational expectations are equal to the values of the endogenous variables themselves. Therefore, to find the solutions for the endogenous variables (or equivalently their expectations) one can replace all expectations $y^*_{t|t-1}$ by the variables y_t themselves in the model and proceed to perform nonstochastic simulations given any policy to be evaluated. This approach was taken by Anderson (1979) for the St. Louis model and the FRB-MIT-Penn model. Anderson's main finding is that the short-run Phillips curve is much more nearly vertical according to both models under rational expectations than under the distributed lag formulations of expectations with the lag structure assumed to be constant over alternative policies.

If the model is nonlinear and stochastic, and the expectation $y^*_{t+1|t-1}$ appears, we suggest linearizing the model about a tentative solution path, applying the methods of Section 2.2 to obtain the solution for the linearized model, relinearizing about the expectation of the new solution path, and iterating till convergence. Specifically, let the nonlinear model be

$$F(y_t, y^*_{t|t-1}, y^*_{t+1|t-1}, y_{t-1}, x_t) = u_t, \tag{13}$$

where F is a vector function and u_t is a vector of random disturbances. Using some distributed lag or any reasonable estimates for the expectations $y^*_{t|t-1}$ and $y^*_{t+1|t-1}$, simulate the model (13) for $t = 1, \ldots, T$ with

$u_t = 0$, given either an open-loop policy $x = (x_1^0, \ldots, x_T^0)$ or a feedback policy $x_t = G_t y_{t-1} + g_t$ which is to be evaluated. Let the result of this simulation be $y_1^0, \ldots, y_T^0$.

We next linearize the model about y_t^0, $y_{t|t-1}^0 = y_t^0$, $y_{t+1|t-1}^0 = y_{t+1}^0$ and y_{t-1}^0. Denoting by F_{jt} the partial derivative of F with respect to its jth argument evaluated at the above point, we write

$$F_{1t}\left(y_t - y_t^0\right) + F_{2t}\left(y_{t|t-1}^* - y_t^0\right) + F_{3t}\left(y_{t+1|t-1}^* - y_{t+1}^0\right)$$

$$+ F_{4t}\left(y_{t-1} - y_{t-1}^0\right) = u_t. \quad (14)$$

In evaluating F_{jt} in (14), we let $x_t = x_t^0$ if an open-loop policy is to be evaluated. For a feedback policy, we let $x_t = G_t y_{t-1} + g_t$ and combine in F_{4t} the derivates of F with respect to both its fourth and fifth arguments, the latter being replaced by $G_t y_{t-1} + g_t$. Multiplying (14) by F_{1t}^{-1} which is assumed to exist if the simultaneous equations model (13) provides a unique solution, we obtain a linear model,

$$y_t = B_t y_{t|t-1}^* + B_{1t} y_{t+1|t-1}^* + A_t y_{t-1} + b_t + v_t, \quad (15)$$

where $v_t = F_{1t}^{-1} u_t$. Equation 15 corresponds to (4), except that the coefficients are now time-dependent and that the given policy has already been incorporated, with no need for the term Cx_t in (4). We can therefore apply the methods of Section 2.2 to solve for y_t from the linear model (15). The result, with the residuals η_t set equal to zero, will provide a new set of initial values $y_1^0, \ldots, y_T^0$ about which the model (13) can be relinearized. One can continue to iterate until convergence.

As in the case of policy evaluation for linear models in which expectations of future endogenous variables appear, some terminal condition on $y_{T+1|T-1}^*$ would have to be imposed to obtain a unique solution. Given such a condition, one could start with some initial guess for the expectations, simulate the model given these expectations, use the results of the simulation to provide a new set of expectations, and continue iteratively. Such an iterative procedure was used by Fair (1978c). It differs from the method recommended above as it involves no linearizations of the model and does not solve the equations recursively backward in time. Once a condition on $y_{T+1|T-1}$ is imposed, and with $u_t = 0$, the set of equations (13) for $t = 1, \ldots, T$ becomes a set of nonlinear algebraic equations in $(y_1, \ldots, y_T) = (y_1^*, \ldots, y_T^*)$. The method suggested in the last paragraph amounts to the Gauss-Newton method for solving a nonlinear system of equations by repeated linearizations, except that the solution in each linearization is obtained recursively backward in time. For many practical problems, the Gauss-Newton method has been found to have reasonably good convergence properties.

15.3 ECONOMETRIC POLICY OPTIMIZATION

15.3.1 Linear Model Without Expectations of Future Variables

For a linear model without expectations of future variables as treated in Section 2.1, the standard techniques of optimal control apply because the expectation $y_{t|t-1}^{*}$ can be eliminated from model (1) to yield model (3), the parameters of which are invariant with respect to government policy under rational expectations. An interesting application of this case has been provided by Taylor (1977, 1979). There appears to be general agreement that policy optimization using an econometric model under rational expectations is possible and useful at least when the expectations of future variables are absent from the model.

At one time, there might have been some misunderstanding of the conclusion reached by Sargent and Wallace (1975) to the effect that "rational expectations" would rule out any effect of monetary policy on the real economy. These authors stated clearly in their paper (1975, p. 254) that their conclusion depends, in addition, on the aggregate supply hypothesis of Lucas which embodies the natural rate hypothesis. According to this hypothesis, real output can deviate from the natural rate only when there is a deviation of the actual price level from the expected price level. As is well known and is easily seen from (3) under the assumption of rational expectations, the deviation of any endogenous variable (including the price level) from its expectation in a linear model is determined by the deviations of the policy instruments from their expectations and is thus unaffected by announced policy changes. Hence, announced monetary policy has no effect on real output. Note that the assumption of rational expectations alone does not rule out the effectiveness of monetary policy. Also, the effects of fiscal policy on the real economy and the effect of monetary policy on the price level are interesting questions to pursue even when some form of the natural rate hypothesis is accepted in addition. Therefore, one cannot escape the conclusion that the tools of optimal control remain useful under rational expectations at least for models having no expectations of future endogenous variables.

15.3.2 Linear Model with Expectations of Future Variables

The situation is more complicated when expectations of future endogenous variables appear in the model, as we will discuss in this subsection. However, for readers of Section 2.2, the applicability of optimal control techniques to such a model seems obvious. If the consequences of a given policy, be it open-loop or feedback, can be evaluated, then one can always search for an optimal policy once a welfare or loss function is given. Let us pursue this viewpoint. We assume that a loss function is given and that the proposed policy is to be announced at the beginning of period 1 and it will be used, together with the econometric model, by the economic agents to form their expectations. The policy maker wishes to find an optimal policy in this setting which will minimize total expected loss for T periods. We will consider in turn open-loop policy and feedback control policy.

Optimal open-loop policy can be obtained by first stacking up the difference equations (6) and (9) as a system, with x_t replacing $x_{t|s}^*$, as the policy is announced and accepted, and assuming $\tilde{b}_{t|s}^* = \tilde{b}_{t|0}^* \equiv \tilde{b}_t^*$,

$$
\begin{bmatrix}
I & -\tilde{A}_T & 0 & \cdots & 0 \\
0 & I & -\tilde{A}_{T-1} & \cdots & 0 \\
& & \ddots & & \\
0 & & \cdots & 0 & I
\end{bmatrix}
\begin{bmatrix}
y_T \\
y_{T-1} \\
\vdots \\
y_1
\end{bmatrix}
$$

$$
=
\begin{bmatrix}
\tilde{C}_T & 0 & & 0 \\
C_{T-1,T} & \tilde{C}_{T-1,T-1} & \cdots & 0 \\
& \cdots & & \\
\tilde{C}_{1,T} & \tilde{C}_{1,T-1} & \cdots & \tilde{C}_{1,1}
\end{bmatrix}
\begin{bmatrix}
x_T \\
x_{T-1} \\
\vdots \\
x_1
\end{bmatrix}
$$

$$
+
\begin{bmatrix}
I & 0 & \cdots & 0 \\
D_{T-1,T} & I & \cdots & 0 \\
& \cdots & & \\
D_{1,T} & D_{1,T-1} & \cdots & I
\end{bmatrix}
\begin{bmatrix}
\tilde{b}_T^* \\
\tilde{b}_{T-1}^* \\
\vdots \\
\tilde{b}_1^* + \tilde{A}_1 y_0
\end{bmatrix}
+
\begin{bmatrix}
\eta_T \\
\eta_{T-1} \\
\vdots \\
\eta_1
\end{bmatrix},
$$

$$(16)$$

or, written more compactly,

$$Ay = Cx + Db + \eta. \tag{17}$$

If the loss function is quadratic in y, one can easily solve (17) for y, substitute the result in the loss function, evaluate expected loss given I_0, and minimize with respect to x. Note, however, that a vector of control variables $(x_1, \ldots, x_T)$ determined at the beginning of period 1 and not to be altered as more observations become available cannot be optimal. In the model (4), the first three terms on the right-hand side are all functions of y_{t-1}, implying that knowledge of y_{t-1} will be useful in controlling y_t. Hence a feedback policy may be better than a deterministic open-loop policy.

To find an optimal feedback policy, one might be tempted to apply the familiar method of dynamic programming using (6) and (9). By this method, one would first minimize with respect to x_T the expected loss attributable to y_T of the last period, given I_{T-1}, and obtain an optimal feedback control equation for x_T. Having obtained the optimal rule for x_T, one would go back in time to find an optimal rule for x_{T-1}, and so on. As pointed out by Kydland and Prescott (1977), this method would not be optimal because, by considering (6) alone for determining x_T, one ignores the effects of expected x_T on previous $y_t (t < T)$ as given by (9). Kydland and Prescott (1977, p. 474) write, "current decisions of economic agents depend in part upon their expectations of future policy actions ... only if these expectations were invariant to the future policy plan selected would optimal control theory be appropriate." They claim (pp. 473–474) that optimal control theory "is not the appropriate tool for economic planning even when there is a well-defined and agreed-upon fixed social objection function ... Rather, by relying on some policy rules, economic performance can be improved." I agree with these authors that, if expectations of future endogenous variables enter an econometric model, the method of dynamic programming cannot be applied without allowing for the expectational effects of future policy on current actions. However, I cannot concur that optimal control theory is useless and that "by relying on some policy rules, economic performance can be improved." What rules should the policy maker follow? If one considers linear, time-invariant feedback rule of the form $y_t = Gy_{t-1} + g$, one can use (11) and (12) for a description of the dynamics of the system under any given rule. The expectations of welfare loss associated with any given parameters G and g can be evaluated. One can then minimize expected loss with respect to G and g by some gradient method.

Furthermore, dynamic programming can be applied to (5) to find an optimal feedback rule. Treating $y^*_{t+1|t-1}$ in (5) as given and minimizing the expectation of a quadratic loss function for T periods, we can apply dynamic programming as in Chow (1975, Chapter 8) to find an optimal feedback control equation,

$$\hat{x}_t = G_{1t} y^*_{t+1|t-1} + G_{2t} y_{t-1} + g_t. \tag{18}$$

Under certain conditions concerning the system parameters as discussed in Chow (1975, pp. 170–172), the coefficients G_{1t}, G_{2t}, and g_t may become time-invariant as T increases. It may also happen that G_{1t} and G_{2t} are time-invariant and g_t changes through time to reflect changes in $\tilde{b}^*_{t|t-1}$, but the system under optimal control will remain covariance-stationary. Let us assume that the system (4) or (5) can be made covariance-stationary by using such a rule, that is, when (18) is substituted for $x^*_{t|t-1}$ in (5), we will obtain a covariance-stationary system,

$$y_t = R_1 y^*_{t+1|t-1} + R_2 y_{t-1} + r + \eta_t, \tag{19}$$

where $R_1 = \tilde{B}_1 + \tilde{C} G_1$, $R_2 = \tilde{A} + \tilde{C} G_2$ and $r = \tilde{b}^*_{t|t-1} + \tilde{C} g_t$. If (19) is co-variance-stationary under rational expectations, there must exist an observationally equivalent system

$$y_t = Q y_{t-1} + q + \eta_t, \tag{20}$$

where the roots of the matrix Q are all smaller than one in absolute value. To find the matrix Q, we use (20) to derive the expectation

$$y^*_{t+1|t-1} = Q^2 y_{t-1} + (Q + I) q, \tag{21}$$

and substitute the result into (19),

$$y_t = (R_1 Q^2 + R_2) y_{t-1} + R_1 (Q + I) q + r + \eta_t. \tag{22}$$

Equating coefficients in (20) and (22) yields

$$Q = (I - R_1 Q)^{-1} R_2, \quad q = [I - R_1 (Q + I)]^{-1} r. \tag{23}$$

Having solved for Q and q, we can substitute (21) into (18) to get an optimal feedback rule as a function of y_{t-1} only. This rule is optimal because it is a time-invariant feedback on $y^*_{t+1|t-1}$ formed by rational expectations, thus allowing for the effect of future policy on current actions. If the matrices G_{1t} and G_{2t} computed from the optimal control algorithm turn out to change appreciably for $t = 1, 2, \ldots$, then the system cannot be made stationary and the method of dynamic programming breaks down. Yet, one can still fall back on the gradient method mentioned in the preceding paragraph.

Therefore, contrary to the claim of Kydland and Prescott (1977), optimal control theory is still applicable when "current decisions of economic agents depend in part upon their expectations of future policy actions." Kydland and Prescott have correctly pointed out that optimal control theory cannot be applied to models such as (4) where expectations of future variables enter without appropriately taking these expectations into account. However, if the effects of future expectations are properly incorporated, as in the procedure described above, optimal control theory is applicable. This discussion is parallel to the discussion following the original critique of Lucas (1976) on existing econometric policy evaluation. The consensus, shared by Lucas (1976), Shiller (1977), Wallis (1980), Anderson (1979), and Taylor (1977, 1979), appears to be that although one should not apply policy analysis directly to model (1) without adequately allowing for the effects of policy on the expectation $y_{t|t-1}^*$, one can apply policy analysis and optimal control to model (3) because the effects of policy on $y_{t|t-1}^*$ are properly incorporated. The comment of Kydland and Prescott appears to be that one should not apply optimal control to model (4) without due allowance for the effects of future policy on $y_{t+1|t-1}^*$. Our response is that, if the model can be made stationary, one can incorporate the effects of future policy on $y_{t+1|t-1}^*$ by using rational expectations to derive optimal control policies. Even if the model cannot be made stationary, one can apply some gradient method to minimize expected loss for T periods once the consequences of any policy rule can be properly evaluated under rational expectations.

A few words should be said concerning the usefulness of the assumption that the model can be made stationary through time. My view is that this assumption is likely to be appropriate if one formulates the econometric model correctly as one should. Variables such as the rate of inflation and the rate of unemployment as generated by an econometric model should eventually approach a covariance-stationary state. For growth variables such as real GNP, if we formulate the model and specify the loss function in terms of the rates of change, the system under control can be covariance-stationary. The level of GNP will not be stationary, but it is determined, through an identity, from a stationary system under control. Even when one fails to obtain a covariance-stationary system from the optimum control calculations, one uncovers important dynamic properties of the model through these calculations. One would learn that no control rules with constant coefficients can make the economic system covariance-stationary under rational expectations.

The methods of this chapter assume that the policy makers will follow the policy that they announce and that the public in forming its expectations believes the policy makers to be honest. We have not studied the possibility of government deception by announcing a future policy to influence the public's expectations and then revising it when the time comes. As Lucas (1976, p. 42) remarks, "policy makers, if they wish to forecast the response of citizens, must take the latter into their confidence."

15.3.3 Nonlinear Model with Expectations of Future Variables

As in Section 2.3 dealing with policy evaluations, we propose to linearize a nonlinear model and apply the methods of Section 3.2 iteratively to obtain an approximately optimal policy under rational expectations when expectations of future endogenous variables are present. Given any tentative policy, be it open-loop or feedback, one can linearize the nonlinear model as described in Section 2.3. The only modification is that, when policy optimization is considered, one needs to treat the policy variables x_t explicitly by adding the term $F_{5t}(x_t - x_t^0)$ in (14) and accordingly the term $C_t x_t$ in (15). The modified (15) takes the place of (4). It can be converted to (5) or (9) as needed, with the subscript t added to the coefficient matrices. To obtain an optimal open-loop policy, we use (9) which can be rewritten as (16) for the purpose of optimization. The tentatively optimal policy will provide a new initial path for relinearizing the model. To obtain an approximately optimal linear feedback rule, we use (5) to obtain the feedback control equations (18). We then apply the control equation for period one as a stationary rule and use the method of (19)–(23) to obtain a new feedback rule for the purpose of relinearization. If this iterative process fails to produce a nearly time-invariant feedback rule, we will use (11) and (12) to evaluate the expected loss for a given time-invariant feedback rule, and apply a gradient method to minimize the expected loss with respect to the parameters of the rule.

15.4 CONCLUDING REMARKS

In this chapter, I have shown that policy evaluation and optimal policy formulation can be carried out under the assumption of rational expectations. The methods proposed amount to modest modifications of the existing methods of policy evaluation and optimal control.

We have assumed throughout that the econometric model to be employed has been properly estimated, and have not treated the problem of estimating an econometric model under rational expectations. The estimation problem has been treated by Wallis (1980) under the assumption that the model is linear and that the control variables themselves follow an autoregressive-moving-average process. If either assumption is relaxed, the latter being replaced by the assumption that the government acts as if it attempts to maximize the expectation of an objective function with unknown parameters, there appear to be interesting theoretical and applied econometric problems for further research. Some of these problems are discussed in Chapters 16 and 17.

CHAPTER 16

Estimation
of Rational
Expectations Models

This chapter considers the estimation of linear rational expectations models when the objective function of the decision maker is quadratic. It presents methods for maximum likelihood estimation in the general case and in a special case when the decision maker's action is assumed to have no effect on the environment (as under perfect competition). It proposes a family of consistent estimators for the general case. It also comments on the assumptions of rational expectations models, and extends the above methods to estimating nonlinear models.

16.1 INTRODUCTION

An outstanding problem in the optimal control literature is the statistical estimation of the parameters of the objective function. Given a linear model

$$y_t = Ay_{t-1} + Cx_t + b + u_t \tag{1}$$

where y_t is a vector of state variables, x_t is a vector of control variables, and u_t is a vector of random disturbances, and given a quadratic objective function

$$-\sum_{t=1}^{T} (y_t - a_t)'K_t(y_t - a_t) \tag{2}$$

having K_t and a_t as parameters, the optimal control problem is to maximize the expectation of (2), resulting in a set of optimal feedback control rules

$$x_t = G_t y_{t-1} + g_t. \tag{3}$$

As in Chapter 1, (1) may represent a higher-order system including the lagged variables $y_{t-2}, y_{t-3}, \ldots, x_{t-1}, x_{t-2}$, and so on, but has been converted to state-space form with the vector y_t incorporating x_t as a subvector by definition. The present chapter is concerned with an inverse problem: Having observed the evolution of y_t as generated by the model (1), and the optimal behavior of the decision makers as described by (3), estimate the parameters of (1) and (2).

This problem has important applications in economics. For example, (1) may represent a macroeconometric model of a national economy, and (2) the preference function of the government authorities which controls x_t. Equation 3 is then the optimal decision rule for the government. Having observed the macroeconomy and the optimal behavior of the government, the econometrician's problem is to estimate the parameters of the econometric model and of the government's preference function. Alternatively, (1) may represent the economic environment facing some economic decision makers in the private sectors (business firms or consumers), and (2) their objective function. Equation 3 would be the optimal investment function, demand function for inputs, or consumption function. In this chapter, we assume $K_t = \beta^t K$ and $a_t = \phi^t a$, β being a discount factor and ϕ being a diagonal matrix, with some diagonal elements known to be unity if the targets in a_t are time-invariant. We will be concerned with the estimation of the parameters β, K, ϕ, and a in the objective function and the parameters A, C, and b of the model, using data on (y_t, x_t).

In the literature of macroeconomic policy analysis following the tradition of Theil (1958) and Friedlaender (1973), this chapter would be entitled "the estimation of government preference functions in policy optimization problems." Its present title is motivated by the more recent literature on macroeconomic modeling and analysis which has been stimulated by the works of Muth (1961) and Lucas (1976), and further extended by Sargent (1978, 1979), Hansen and Sargent (1980), and Taylor (1979), among others. Consider economic agents (firms, households) facing a stochastic environment described by (1) and having an objective function (2). They are assumed to derive their behavioral equations (the demand equations for inputs, the consumption functions, etc.) given by (3) through the maximization of (2) subject to the constraint (1). Under the assumption of rational expectations, the econometrician shares the same functions (1) and (2) with the economic agents. The econometrician's problem is to estimate (1) and (2) by observing the data on x_t and y_t. It is important to estimate the parameters of (2) because, as Lucas (1976) has pointed out, when the government's policy rule changes, the environment (1) facing the private economic agents will change. In order to predict the latter's behavior as given by their new optimal feedback control equation (3), knowledge of the parameters of (2) is required; (3) will be rederived by the maximization of (2) given the new environment (1).

This chapter presents methods for the maximum likelihood estimation of linear rational expectations models just described, covering the general case and the special case when the agent's action x_t does not affect the economic environment as in the model of perfect competition. The special case is exemplified by the models used by Sargent (1978, 1979) and by Hansen and Sargent (1980). We obtain explicit expressions for the coefficients in the agent's behavioral equation (3) in terms of the parameters of (1) and (2) using the known results on stochastic control theory in Chow (1975). To ease the computations in the general case, we propose a family of consistent estimators that are analogous to the methods of limited-information maximum likelihood and two-stage least squares for the estimation of linear simultaneous equations. In this chapter, we will frequently be interested in estimating the parameters when the coefficient matrix G_t in (3) reaches a steady state G. The results will be extended to estimating nonlinear models.

16.2   MAXIMUM LIKELIHOOD ESTIMATION IN THE GENERAL CASE

Our problem is to estimate the parameters of (1) and (2) using observations on y_t and x_t. A system involving high-order autoregressive and moving average processes can be written in the form (1) where u_t are serially uncorrelated and identically distributed, as is done in Chow (1975). If one is willing to add a residual to (3) due to error in controlling x_t, and assume a multivariate normal distribution for this residual and u_t, the likelihood function based on (1) and (3) is well known. It has A, C, b, G_t, g_t, and the covariance matrix of the residuals as arguments. If (1) is a set of reduced-form equations derived from a system of linear simultaneous structural equations, the parameters A, C, b, and the covariance matrix of u_t will be replaced by the corresponding structural parameters as arguments in the likelihood function.

What makes our problem different from the standard problem of estimating the parameters of a system of linear structural equations is that we need to maximize the likelihood function with respect to the parameters β, K, ϕ, and a of the objective function (with $K_t = \beta^t K$ and $a_t = \phi^t a$) instead of the coefficients G_t and g_t in the behavioral equation (3). To apply any gradient or conjugate gradient method for maximization (see Goldfeld and Quandt, 1972), it is first required to evaluate the likelihood function in terms of the parameters A, C, b, β, K, ϕ, and a (after the covariance matrix of the residuals has been concentrated out), where A, C, and b will further be written as functions of the coefficients of the structural equations if necessary. The problem then boils down to the convenient expression of G_t and g_t as functions of A, C, b, β, K, ϕ, and a.

The coefficients of (3) as solution to the optimal control problem (1)–(2) are given in Chow (1975, pp. 178–179):

$$G_t = -(C'H_tC)^{-1}C'H_tA \tag{4}$$

$$H_t = K_t + (A + CG_{t+1})'H_{t+1}(A + CG_{t+1}) \tag{5}$$

$$g_t = -(C'H_tC)^{-1}C'(H_tb_t - h_t) \tag{6}$$

$$h_t = K_ta_t + (A + CG_{t+1})'(h_{t+1} - H_{t+1}b_{t+1}) \tag{7}$$

with conditions $H_{t+N} = K_{t+N} = \beta^N K_t$ for (5) and $h_{t+N} = K_{t+N}a_{t+N} = K_{t+N}\phi^N a_t$ for (7) if the planning horizon is N. To compute G_t, we evaluate the right-hand sides of (4) and (5) backward in time starting from $t + N$, using the initial condition $H_{t+N} = \beta^N K_t$. Having completed these calculations, we compute g_t by evaluating the right-hand sides of (6) and (7) backward in time starting from $t + N$, using the initial condition $h_{t+N} = K_{t+N}\phi^N a_t$.

Even for fairly large N, these computations are inexpensive provided that the (symmetric) matrix H_t is not too large, say with order less than 100. Some computational experience is recorded in Chow and Megdal (1978a). The computations consist mainly of matrix multiplications. The matrix $C'H_tC$ to be inverted is of the same order as the number of control variables, which is very small as judged by the cost of matrix inversion using a modern computer. Furthermore, even if N is very large, experience shows that a steady-state solution for G_t and H_t from (4) and (5) is often reached after four or five time periods backward from $t + N$, as illustrated in Chow (1975, pp. 208, 270). Thus only several evaluations of (4) and (5) are required. If (4) and (5) do converge slowly, the model of rational expectations adopted to derive a steady-state G in (3) should itself be questioned. The failure of (4) and (5) to converge would mean that a constant-coefficient reaction function does not exist for the behavior of the economic agent. A slow convergence means that the economic agent needs to plan many periods ahead under the questionable assumption of a constant economic structure for all future periods (the same matrices A and C being used in the calculations of (4) and (5) for all future periods). We thus argue that in practice the coefficients G and g_t in (3) can frequently be computed inexpensively from the parameters A, C, b, β, K, ϕ, and a.

Because the computation of G and g_t is only a first step (the step of evaluating the likelihood function) in the method of maximum likelihood, the second step being to maximize numerically, it would be very desirable if G could be expressed explicitly as a function of the parameters without resorting to repeated calculations of (4) and (5). In the next section, we treat a special case where this can be done. In the remainder of this section, we provide a method to maximize the likelihood function under the assumptions $K_t = \beta^t K$ and $a_t = a$. Under these assumptions, the steady-state G and g from (4)–(7) are found by solving the following pairs of algebraic equations.

$$(C'HC)G + C'HA = 0 \qquad (8)$$

$$H - K - \beta(A + CG)'H(A + CG) = 0; \qquad (9)$$

$$(C'HC)g + C'(Hb - h) = 0 \qquad (10)$$

$$[I - \beta(A + CG)']h - Ka + \beta(A + CG)'Hb = 0. \qquad (11)$$

Assume that u_t in (1) is independent and normal, having a covariance matrix Σ, that, due to errors in the execution of the optimal policy, a residual exists in (3) that is also independent and normal, having a covariance matrix V, and that the residuals in (1) and (3) are uncorrelated. The last assumption can easily be relaxed without affecting the major steps used to obtain the maximum likelihood estimates to be stated below. We also assume that the discount factor β is given, as the maximization of the likelihood function with respect to this scalar should present no great difficulty once the remaining parameters can be estimated. Our problem is the estimation of the parameters A, C, b, and Σ of (1), K and a of (2), and G, g, and V of (3), subject to the constraints (8), (9), (10), and (11).

We form a Lagrangian expression which combines the log-likelihood with these constraints

$$L = \text{constant} - \frac{n}{2} \log|\Sigma| - \frac{n}{2} \log|V|$$

$$- \tfrac{1}{2} \text{tr} \left[\Sigma^{-1} (Y' - AY'_{-1} - CX' - bz')(Y - Y_{-1}A' - XC' - zb') \right]$$

$$- \tfrac{1}{2} \text{tr} \left[V^{-1} (X' - GY'_{-1} - gz')(X - Y_{-1}G' - zg') \right] - \text{tr} \left[\Omega(8) \right]$$

$$- \tfrac{1}{2} \text{tr} \left[\Phi(9) \right] - \omega' \left[(10) \right] - \phi' \left[(11) \right] - \tfrac{1}{2} \theta \left[\text{tr}(KK) - r \right]$$

where Y is an $n \times p$ matrix of observations on the endogenous variables; Y_{-1} is an $n \times p$ matrix of observations on the lagged endogenous variables; X is an $n \times q$ matrix of observations on the control variables; z represents a dummy variable being a vector consisting of n ones; Ω $(p \times q)$ and $\Phi = \Phi'$ $(p \times p)$ are matrices of Lagrangian multipliers; ω $(q \times 1)$ and ϕ $(p \times 1)$ are vectors of Lagrangian multipliers; the numbers 8–11 in parentheses denote the corresponding constraints; and the last constraint $\text{tr}(KK) = r$ serves to normalize the matrix K, r being the number of target variables, or the number of nonzero diagonal elements in K. The unknowns in this problem consist of Σ, V, A, C, b, G, H, g, h, K, and a.

Using the differentiation rules $\partial \log|A|/\partial A = A^{-1'}$ and $\partial \text{tr}(AB)/\partial A = B'$, we differentiate L to obtain

$$\frac{\partial L}{\partial \Sigma^{-1}} = n\Sigma - (Y' - AY'_{-1} - CX' - bz')$$

$$\times (Y - Y_{-1}A' - XC' - zb') = 0 \qquad\qquad (12)$$

$$\frac{\partial L}{\partial V^{-1}} = nV - (X' - GY'_{-1} - gz')(X - Y_{-1}G' - zg') = 0 \qquad (13)$$

$$\frac{\partial L}{\partial A'} = Y'_{-1}(Y - Y_{-1}A' - XC' - zb')\Sigma^{-1}$$

$$- \Omega C'H + \beta\Phi(A + CG)'H - \beta\phi(Hb - h)' = 0 \qquad (14)$$

$$\frac{\partial L}{\partial C'} = X'(Y - Y_{-1}A' - XC' - zb')\Sigma^{-1} - \Omega'(A + CG)'H - G\Omega C'H$$

$$+ \beta G\Phi(A + CG)'H - g\omega'C'H - \omega g'C'H - \omega(Hb - h)'$$

$$- \beta G\phi(Hb - h)' = 0 \qquad\qquad (15)$$

$$\frac{\partial L}{\partial b'} = z'(Y - Y_{-1}A' - XC' - zb')\Sigma^{-1}$$

$$- \omega'C'H + \beta\phi'(A + CG)'H = 0 \tag{16}$$

$$\frac{\partial L}{\partial G'} = Y'_{-1}(X - Y_{-1}G' - zg')V^{-1} - \Omega C'HC + \beta\Phi(A + CG)'HC$$

$$- \beta\phi(Hb - h)'C = 0 \tag{17}$$

$$\frac{\partial L}{\partial H} = -(A + CG)\Omega C' - C\Omega'(A + CG)'$$

$$- \Phi + \beta(A + CG)\Phi(A + CG)' - Cg\omega'C' - C\omega g'C'$$

$$- b\omega'C' - C\omega b' - \beta b\phi'(A + CG)' - \beta(A + CG)\phi b' = 0 \tag{18}$$

$$\frac{\partial L}{\partial K} \overset{*}{=} \Phi + a\phi' + \phi a' - \theta K \overset{*}{=} 0 \tag{19}$$

$$\frac{\partial L}{\partial g'} = z'(X - Y_{-1}G' - zg')V^{-1} - \omega'C'HC = 0 \tag{20}$$

$$\frac{\partial L}{\partial h} = C\omega - [I - \beta(A + CG)]\phi = 0 \tag{21}$$

$$\frac{\partial L}{\partial a} \overset{*}{=} K\phi \overset{*}{=} 0. \tag{22}$$

Although K is a symmetric $p \times p$ matrix and a is a column vector of p elements many of the elements in K and a are known to be zero. If there are r target variables, only an $r \times r$ submatrix of K and r elements in a are nonzero. The symbol $\overset{*}{=}$ in (19) and (22) indicates that only the derivatives of L with respect to the unknown elements of K and a are set equal to zero. Equations 8–22 will be solved for the unknown parameters.

First, consider (21) and (22). They are $p + r$ linear equations in the $p + q$ unknowns in ϕ and ω. If the number r of target variables equals or exceeds the number q of instruments [as we will so assume to make (3) a unique solution of the economic agent's optimization problem], both Lagrangian multipliers ϕ and ω will be zero provided that the $(p + r) \times (p + q)$ matrix, with K^* composed of the r rows of K corresponding to the nonzero elements of a,

$$\begin{bmatrix} C & -[I - \beta(A + CG)] \\ 0 & K^* \end{bmatrix}$$

is of rank $p + q$. The solution $\phi = 0$ and $\omega = 0$ from (21) and (22) simplifies many of the remaining equations.

Second, observe that as usual consistent estimates of the covariance matrices Σ and V can be obtained from (12) and (13) respectively, where the coefficients $(A \ C \ b)$ and $(G \ g)$ are replaced by the least squares estimates. We therefore will treat Σ and V as given for the solution of the remaining equations. A firm believer in the method of maximum likelihood could always revise these estimates of Σ and V after the remaining equations are solved, and iterate until convergence.

Third, given any estimates of $(A \ C \ b)$, $(G \ g)$, and K, we will revise them for the next iteration by solving the following equations. [The initial estimates of $(A \ C \ b)$ and $(G \ g)$ are obtained by least squares; the initial K may be a diagonal matrix with r nonzero elements.] Equations 8 and 9 are used to solve for G and H. On account of (8) and $\phi = 0$, the last two terms of (17) vanish, and (17) can be used to solve for Ω. Equation 18 is used to obtain Φ by iteration.

$$\Phi = \beta(A + CG)\Phi(A + CG)' - (A + CG)\Omega C' - C\Omega'(A + CG)'.$$

Equation 19 gives $K \overset{*}{=} \theta^{-1}\Phi$ for the unknown elements of K, where the Lagrangian multiplier θ is found by taking the trace of both sides of $\Phi^*\Phi^* = \theta^2 KK$ to yield $\theta^2 = \mathrm{tr}(\Phi^*\Phi^*)/r$ where, by (19), Φ^* is composed of nonzero elements from Φ and zero elements corresponding to the zero elements of K. Equations 14 and 15 are solved for A and C; they are modified "normal equations" for these coefficients. Equations 16 and 20 then give respectively

$$b = n^{-1}(Y' - AY'_{-1} - CX')z$$

$$g = n^{-1}(X' - GY'_{-1})z.$$

Now $(A \ C \ b)$, $(G \ g)$, and K are revised, and the iterations continue until convergence.

Fourth, there are only two remaining equations (10) and (11) to be solved for h and a. Solving (11) for h and substituting the result in (10), we obtain, denoting $A + CG$ by R,

$$C'[I - \beta R']Ka = C'HCg + C'[I - \beta(I - \beta R')^{-1}R']Hb. \quad (23)$$

Because C' is $q \times p$, this is a system of q linear equations for the r unknowns in a. If the number r of target variables equals the number q of control variables, the solution for a is unique. If $r > q$, the solution for a is not unique. This result is reasonable because the observable behavior of the economic agents that is relevant for the estimation of a consists of a $q \times 1$ vector g in the optimal feedback control equation. If a has more elements than g, it cannot be estimated uniquely. We have thus provided a solution to the maximum likelihood estimation of the parameters of (1) and (2) under the assumption that $K_t = \beta'K$ and $a_t = a$. For alternative approaches to the estimation problem in some special cases, the reader is referred to Sargent (1979) and Hanson and Sargent (1980).

16.3 ESTIMATION WHEN ENVIRONMENT IS UNAFFECTED BY AGENT'S ACTION

Let the environment be described by

$$\tilde{y}_t = A_1 \tilde{y}_{t-1} + \tilde{u}_t \tag{24}$$

which is not affected by the agent's action x_t. This special case includes the examples given by Sargent (1978, 1979) and Hansen and Sargent (1980). These references use an example of a firm trying to determine its optimal employment of an input while facing a set of stochastic difference equations (24) which explain the price of the input and a technological coefficient. To allow for the costs of the control variables and their changes, we introduce x_t and Δx_t as state variables in the objective function and write the model as

$$\begin{bmatrix} \tilde{y}_t \\ x_t \\ \Delta x_t \end{bmatrix} = \begin{bmatrix} A_1 & 0 & 0 \\ 0 & 0 & 0 \\ 0 & -I & 0 \end{bmatrix} \begin{bmatrix} \tilde{y}_{t-1} \\ x_{t-1} \\ \Delta x_{t-1} \end{bmatrix} + \begin{bmatrix} 0 \\ I \\ I \end{bmatrix} x_t + \begin{bmatrix} \tilde{u}_t \\ 0 \\ 0 \end{bmatrix}. \tag{25}$$

which is a special case of (1) with

$$A = \begin{bmatrix} A_1 & 0 & 0 \\ 0 & 0 & 0 \\ 0 & -I & 0 \end{bmatrix}; \quad C = \begin{bmatrix} 0 \\ I \\ I \end{bmatrix}.$$

Note the special feature of the matrix C allowing for no effect of x_t on $\tilde{y}_t$.
The objective function is given by (2) with

$$K_t = \beta'K = \beta' \begin{bmatrix} K_{11} & K_{12} & 0 \\ K'_{12} & K_{22} & 0 \\ 0 & 0 & K_{33} \end{bmatrix},$$

where K_{22} and K_{33} are assumed to be diagonal, the former capturing increasing marginal costs of using the inputs x_t in the example on the demand for inputs, and the latter measuring the adjustment costs of changes in the inputs. We are concerned with the steady-state solution of (4) and (5), namely

$$G = -(C'HC)^{-1}C'HA \tag{26}$$

$$H = K + \beta(A + CG)'H(A + CG)$$

$$= K + \beta A'H(A + CG) \tag{27}$$

where the second equality sign of (27) is due to (26).

Using (26) and the definitions for A and C, with (symmetric) H partitioned into 3×3 blocks corresponding to K, we have

$$G = -[H_{22} + H_{23} + H'_{23} + H_{33}]^{-1}$$
$$[(H'_{12} + H'_{13})A_1 \quad -(H_{23} + H_{33}) \quad 0]. \tag{28}$$

Because A' has all zeros in its last row, so does $\beta A'H(A + CG)$. By (27) the last row of H equals the last row of K, that is,

$$H'_{13} = K'_{13} = 0; \qquad H'_{23} = K'_{23} = 0; \qquad H_{33} = K_{33}. \tag{29}$$

Using (29), we write (28) as

$$G = -[H_{22} + K_{33}]^{-1}[H'_{12}A_1 \quad -K_{33} \quad 0]. \tag{30}$$

We need to find only H_{22} and H_{12} to evaluate G. Using (30) and letting $\theta = [H_{22} + K_{33}]^{-1}$, we have

$$A'H(A + CG) = \begin{bmatrix} A'_1(H_{11} - H_{12}\theta H'_{12})A_1 & A'_1 H_{12}\theta K_{33} & 0 \\ K_{33}\theta H'_{12}A_1 & K_{33} - K_{33}\theta K_{33} & 0 \\ 0 & 0 & 0 \end{bmatrix}. \tag{31}$$

Equations 31 and 27 imply

$$H_{22} = K_{22} + \beta K_{33} - \beta K_{33}[H_{22} + K_{33}]^{-1}K_{33} \tag{32}$$

$$H_{12} = K_{12} + \beta A'_1 H_{12}[H_{22} + K_{33}]^{-1}K_{33}. \tag{33}$$

Because K_{22} and K_{33} are diagonal by assumption, a diagonal H_{22} is a solution of (32), with its ith diagonal element satisfying

$$h_{22,i} = k_{22,i} + \beta k_{33,i} - \beta \frac{k_{33,i}^2}{h_{22,i} + k_{33,i}}$$

or

$$h_{22,i}^2 - (k_{22,i} + k_{33,i}\beta - k_{33,i})h_{22,i} - k_{22,i}k_{33,i} = 0 \qquad (34)$$

which can be solved for $h_{22,i}$. We take the smaller root of the quadratic equation (34) since we wish to make $h_{22,i}$ as small as possible. The dynamic programming solution to the linear-quadratic control problem (see Chow, 1975) transforms a multiperiod maximization problem into many one-period problems. For each period t, one minimizes the expectation of a quadratic function in y_t involving $y_t' H_t y_t$, $H_t \geq 0$. Hence H_{22} should be diagonal with small elements. Having obtained H_{22}, we use (33) to compute $H_{12} = (h_{12,ij})$. Denoting the diagonal matrix $[H_{22} + K_{33}]^{-1}K_{33}$ by $D = \text{Diag}\{d_i\}$, and the elements of A_1 by a_{ij}, we have

$$h_{12,ij} = k_{12,ij} + \beta \sum_l a_{li} d_l h_{12,lj}. \qquad (35)$$

The elements $h_{12,ij}$ in the jth column of H_{12} satisfy a set of linear equations (35). We have thus provided an explicit expression for G as a function of A_1, β, and K by using formulas (30), (34), and (35).

As an illustration for a scalar x_t consider the example of Sargent (1979, p. 335) and Hansen and Sargent (1980) where x_t (our notation) denotes the demand for an input labor; y_{1t} is technology which satisfies a qth order univariate autoregression

$$y_{1t} = a_{11}y_{1,t-1} + \cdots + a_{1q}y_{1,t-q} + u_{1t};$$

$y_{2t} = y_{1,t-1}, \ldots, y_{q,t} = y_{q-1,t-1}$ are introduced to make the model first-order; and $y_{q+1,t}$ is the wage rate that satisfies an rth-order multivariate autoregression. This model can certainly be written as our equation 1.

The objective function is, for the current period 0,

$$E_0 \sum_{t=1}^T \beta^t \left[(\gamma_0 + y_{1,t} - y_{q+1,t})x_t - \frac{\gamma_1}{2}x_t^2 - \frac{\delta}{2}(\Delta x_t)^2 \right],$$

where $\gamma_1 = K_{22}$ and $\delta = K_{33}$ in our notation, both being scalars. Equations

(32) and (34) are identical for a scalar x_t. They become

$$h_{22}^2 - (\gamma_1 + \delta\beta - \delta)h_{22} - \gamma_1\delta = 0,$$

implying

$$h_{22} = \tfrac{1}{2}\left[(\gamma_1 + \delta\beta - \delta) - \sqrt{(\gamma_1 + \delta\beta - \delta)^2 + 4\gamma_1\delta}\,\right].$$

The matrix K_{12} becomes a column vector consisting of the coefficients of the products of x_t and y_{it} in the objective function. Because $H_{22} + K_{33}$ in (33) is the scalar $h_{22} + \delta$, we can write the solution of (33) as

$$H_{12} = \left[I - \beta\delta(h_{22} + \delta)^{-1}A_1'\right]^{-1}K_{12}.$$

The coefficient of x_{t-1} in the optimal feedback control equation (or a demand for labor equation) is $[H_{22} + K_{33}]^{-1}K_{33}$ according to (30), or $\delta/(h_{22} + \delta)$. This result agrees with the coefficient obtained by Sargent (1979, p. 336) and Hansen and Sargent (1980) using classic (pre-1970) control techniques. Their coefficient ρ_1 is the inverse of the (smaller) root of the quadratic equation

$$\delta\beta - (\gamma_1 + \delta + \delta\beta)z + \delta z^2 = 0.$$

The explicit solution of this section breaks down when the matrix C does not have a submatrix of zeros, for then $(C'HC)^{-1}$ can no longer be written as $[H_{22} + K_{33}]^{-1}$ as in (30) and one cannot solve an equation corresponding to (32) explicitly for the elements of H_{22} even if K_{22} is diagonal.

16.4 A FAMILY OF CONSISTENT ESTIMATORS FOR THE GENERAL CASE

A family of consistent estimators is proposed for the general case. It is based on the observations that the least-squares estimator $\hat{G}$ of the coefficients G in the regression of x_t on y_{t-1} (which includes x_{t-1} as a subvector) is consistent, and that, if the rational expectations model is correct, G should satisfy (26) and (27). The situation is analogous to the estimation of structural parameters $(B\,\Gamma)$ in linear simultaneous equations by the use of the least-squares estimates $\hat{\Pi}$ of the reduced-form coefficients Π. The latter are consistent, and, if the model is correct, Π satisfies $B\Pi = \Gamma$ which corresponds to (26) and (27) in the present problem. Therefore, if we solve

(26) and (27) for H, K, and β (the structural parameters) using the least-squares estimate $\hat{G}$ for G and consistent estimates $\hat{A}$ and $\hat{C}$ for A and C, we will obtain consistent estimates of the former, as we will obtain consistent estimates of B and Γ by solving $B\hat{\Pi} = \Gamma$.

As the first step of this method, we obtain least-squares estimates $\hat{G}$ of the coefficients in the multivariate regression of x_t on y_{t-1}. If the target vector a_t and the intercept b_t in the model are constant through time, h_t is also a constant satisfying (7) with the subscript $t + 1$ replaced by t. We have $g_t = g$. Otherwise, the coefficients $\hat{G}$ will be estimated by adding some smooth trends in the regression equations.

Having obtained $\hat{G}$, we will find H, K, and β to satisfy (26) and (27), but as in the case of overidentified structural equations, there may be more equations than unknowns. Defining $R = (r_{ij}) = \hat{A} + \hat{C}\hat{G}$, we write these equations as

$$C'HR = 0 \tag{36}$$

$$K = H - \beta R'HR. \tag{37}$$

Let H be a symmetric $p \times p$ matrix with elements h_{ij}, and let C be a $p \times q$ matrix with elements c_{ij}. These two equations imply respectively

$$\sum_{i,j}^{p} c_{im}r_{jl}h_{ij} = 0 \quad (m = 1,\ldots,q; \, l = 1,\ldots,p) \tag{38}$$

$$h_{ml} - \beta\sum_{i,j}^{p} r_{im}r_{jl}h_{ij} = 0 \quad \text{if } k_{ml} = 0. \tag{39}$$

Equations 38 and 39 are linear equations in $h_{ij} = h_{ji}$. Let h be the column vector consisting of the $p(p + 1)/2$ elements h_{ij} ($i = 1,\ldots,p; \, j \geq i$). Write (38) and (39) as

$$Qh = 0. \tag{40}$$

Exact, over, or under identification occurs according as the rank of Q is equal to, larger than, or smaller than $p(p + 1)/2$ minus one. In the overidentified case, there will be more equations than unknowns in (40); the elements on its right-hand side cannot all vanish. Corresponding to the method of indirect least squares, one can suggest discarding extra equations in (40) and solving the remaining $p(p + 1)/2$ homogeneous linear equations which are made nonhomogeneous by a normalization $h_{pp} = 1$.

This method is still consistent but it discards useful information. Corresponding to the method of two-stage least squares, according to the interpretation of Chow (1964), we normalize by setting $h_{pp} = 1$ (or any $h_{ii} = 1$), partition Q and h' respectively as $(Q_1 \; q_2)$ and $(h'_1 \; 1)$ to write (24) as

$$Q_1 h_1 + q_2 = 0 \tag{41}$$

and estimate h_1 by $\hat{h}_1 = -(Q'_1 Q_1)^{-1} Q'_1 q_2$ using the method of least squares.

Corresponding to the method of limited-information maximum likelihood, according to the interpretations of Chow (1964), we normalize symmetrically by setting $h'h = $ constant and find h to minimize $h'Q'Qh$ subject to this normalization constraint. The minimizing h is the characteristic vector associated with the smallest characteristic root of $Q'Q$. Unlike the method of two-stage least squares, this method yields a vector estimate of h that is invariant with respect to the choice of the variable for normalization. However, if the order of Q is very large, the symmetric normalization is not recommended as it is computationally expensive. If β is unknown, one has to find a scalar to minimize the appropriate sum of squares, be it $h'_1 Q'_1 Q_1 h_1$ or $h'Q'Qh$, but this is an easy problem. Having obtained h and β, we use the remaining equations of (37), other than (39), to compute the nonzero elements of K. Having estimated G, g, A, C, b, and H consistently, we can use (23) to estimate a. Given H, $\hat{A}$, and $\hat{C}$, we can obtain a new estimate $\hat{G}_{(2)}$ of G by using (10).

If the estimates of H, β, and K by the method of this section are not accepted as final, they can serve as initial estimates to be used in the (more expensive) maximization of the likelihood function by the method of Section 2. The consistent estimates of this section can be recommended if the numerical maximization of the likelihood function is too expensive.

16.5   THE ASSUMPTIONS OF RATIONAL EXPECTATIONS MODELS

Besides providing practical methods, the above discussion has pinpointed the problems involved in the estimation of linear rational expectations models. It should be pointed out that even when the problems are overcome, the estimates by the method of Section 2 will still not satisfy the assumptions of rational expectations.

If the economic agents and the econometrician share the same model (1) and (1) indeed is the true model of the economic environment (two strong assumptions), the optimal policy for maximizing the expectation of the objective function (2), correctly specified by the econometrician (another assumption), is *not* (3) with coefficients given by (4)–(7) because the economic agents do not know (and are not assumed to know) the numerical values of the parameters A, C, and b exactly. Given uncertainty concerning A, C, and b, (4)–(7) no longer specify the parameters of the optimal behavioral equation for the agents to maximize the expectation of (2). If fact, no one knows how to compute the truly optimal behavioral equation. Some perhaps nearly optimal solutions are given in Chapters 10 and 11 of Chow (1975), for example. Equations (4)–(7) only specify the certainty-equivalent solution which is not optimal when A, C, and b are uncertain. Strictly speaking, a true believer in rational expectations models should use the optimal behavioral equation which no one knows, or at least the more complicated, but more nearly optimal behavioral equation as referenced earlier. Economists who build models other than rational expectations models have been criticized for their failure to take optimizing behavior into account. The question is how far one should push optimizing behavior in building economic models for multiperiod decisions under uncertainty and where one should stop.

As has been recognized, current practitioners of rational expectations models often ignore, or fail to model explicitly, the process of learning by the economic agents about the economic environment (1) and assume, as in the method of Section 3, that a steady state is always observed for the optimal behavioral equation (3). The modeling of learning will automatically be incorporated if one uses a behavioral equation which is more nearly optimal than the certainty-equivalent strategy by taking into account the uncertainty in the model parameters. Such a behavioral equation incorporates the process of learning, is strictly speaking nonlinear in y_{t-1} and is time dependent. The estimation of such models is much more difficult. Again, how far should one push the assumption of optimal behavior? How useful are the models based on approximate solutions (how approximate?) to optimal behavior as exemplified by the methods of this chapter?

16.6   ESTIMATING NONLINEAR RATIONAL EXPECTATIONS MODELS

It is well recognized that the assumption of rational expectations makes the construction of nonlinear models difficult (because the expectation of a nonlinear function is not the nonlinear function of the expectation). Insofar as the world is nonlinear, it becomes an unattractive assumption to use. Since this assumption is not strictly followed by its practitioners even for linear models with uncertain coefficients, one may boldly apply the certainty-equivalent strategy to nonlinear stochastic models by first linearizing the models as suggested in Chow (1975, Chapter 12). The methods of this chapter will then be applicable to the estimation of nonlinear models by introducing the following modifications.

For the methods of Sections 2 and 3:

(a) Starting with some estimates of the parameter vector θ of a nonlinear model (1) and the parameters β, K, ϕ, and a of the objective function (2), linearize the model (1) to yield

$$y_t = \hat{A}_t y_{t-1} + \hat{C}_t x_t + \hat{b}_t + \hat{u}_t.$$

(b) Compute the coefficients G_t and g_t of the optimal linear feedback control equation (3) using the linear model and the parameters of (2). Note that (4)–(7) will have time subscripts for A and C.

(c) Evaluate the likelihood function for models (1) and (3).

(d) Take one step in a numerical maximization algorithm and return to (a).

For the method of Section 4:

(a') Using a consistent estimate $\hat{\theta}$ of the parameter vector of a nonlinear model (1), linearize the model as in (a).

(b') Compute least-squares estimates $\hat{G}$ and $\hat{g}_t$ of the coefficients in a regression of x_t on y_{t-1} and appropriate trends.

(c') Define $R_t = (\hat{A}_t + \hat{C}_t \hat{G})$. For each t, follow the methods of Section 4 to form $Q_t h_t = 0$ as in (40). Combine these equations by using

$$\left(\frac{1}{n}\sum_t^n Q_t\right)h = Qh = 0$$

for (40) and proceed as before.

CHAPTER 17

Estimation and Optimal Control of Dynamic Game Models Under Rational Expectations

This chapter extends the results of Chapter 16 on the estimation of rational expectations models in two directions. First, two players are introduced instead of only one, and the estimation of a model of dynamic games is studied under the assumption of a dominant player or a noncooperative Nash equilibrium. Second, with the second player (government) treated as the dominant player, we consider policy evaluation and optimization by the government under the assumption of rational expectations.

This chapter is concerned with further developments of Chapter 16, where I have proposed two methods for the estimation of the parameters of a linear model

$$y_t = Ay_{t-1} + Cx_t + b_t + u_t \tag{1}$$

which describes the environment of a set of economic decision makers, and the parameters of a quadratic objective function

$$- E_0 \sum_{t=1}^{T} (y_t - a_t)' K_t (y_t - a_t) \tag{2}$$

which the decision makers are assumed to maximize. Resulting from this maximization is a linear behavioral equation (feedback control equation)

255

for the decision makers who control x_t, written as

$$x_t = G_t y_{t-1} + g_t. \tag{3}$$

The parameters G_t and g_t in (3) are derived from the parameters of (1) and (2). The econometrician observes the data on x_t and y_t, and wishes to estimate the parameters of (1) and (2). The two methods proposed in Chapter 16 are maximum likelihood and a consistent method corresponding to two-stage least squares.

The present chapter is concerned with two extensions of the above estimation problem. First, there are two sets of economic decision makers, so that the model becomes

$$y_t = A y_{t-1} + C_1 x_{1t} + C_2 x_{2t} + b_t + u_t. \tag{4}$$

Each set i of decision makers chooses its control variables x_{it} to maximize an objective function

$$- E_0 \sum_{t=1}^{T} (y_t - a_{it})' K_{it} (y_t - a_{it}) \qquad (i = 1, 2) \tag{5}$$

and derives its optimal behavioral equation

$$x_{it} = G_{it} y_{t-1} + g_{it} \qquad (i = 1, 2). \tag{6}$$

The econometric problem is to estimate the parameters of (4) and (5). Second, when one decision maker is the government, we are concerned with the evaluation of the effects of government policy changes and the choice of an optimum policy for the government.

To illustrate the application of this model, let x_{1t} be the variables subject to the control of some group of decision makers of the private sector and x_{2t} be the variables subject to the control of the government. If the government adheres to a policy rule, that is, if G_2 and g_{2t} are given, the environment facing the private decision makers is

$$y_t = (A + C_2 G_2) y_{t-1} + C_1 x_{1t} + (b_t + C_2 g_{2t}) + u_t$$

$$\equiv A_{12} y_{t-1} + C_1 x_{1t} + b_{12, t} + u_t. \tag{7}$$

They would maximize their objective function to derive their behavioral equation. As Lucas (1976) has stressed, if the policy rule of the government changes, the behavioral equation of the private decision makers will also change. Therefore, an econometrician should not rely on a stable relation (3) to evaluate the effects of government policy. A correct procedure is to estimate (1) and (2), rather than (1) and (3), and then derive the changes in (3) due to changes in (1). Lucas (1976, p. 20) reminded the reader that this point had been made by the proponents of structural estimation for simultaneous-equation models, and cited Marschak (1953) for having pointed out the change in the reduced-form equations due to a policy change. Another manifestation of this problem occurs when the behavioral equations of the private sector contain expectations variables which are explained by some distributed lag relationships. As government policy changes, the model (1) or (7) will change, and these expectations will also change under rational expectations, thus making the historical distributed lag relationships unstable. The solution again is to rederive the expectations using the new structure (1) or (7), but this topic will not be treated in the present paper as the estimation and control problems associated with it are discussed in Taylor (1979), Wallis (1980), and Chow (1980a).

The first extension of this chapter is to allow for two sets of decision makers whose actions affect the environment of each other. In the previous example, although the government policy rule $x_{2t} = G_2 y_{t-1} + g_{2t}$ affects the optimal policy of the private sector, the latter's optimal behavioral relation $x_{1t} = G_1 y_{t-1} + g_{1t}$ will also affect the policy rule of the government if it is also assumed to maximize its objective function. We will study this dynamic game model in this chapter. Section 2 deals with the estimation of the parameters of this model under the assumption that Player 2 (the government) is the dominant player. Section 3 treats the estimation problem when the two players are assumed to be in a noncooperative Nash equilibrium. Section 1 sets the stage by treating the topic of government policy evaluation and optimization under the assumption that the government is the dominant player. In this chapter, we assume that the optimal reaction coefficient G_{it} in (6) for both players will reach a steady state G_i, that is, the rational expectations equilibrium. Otherwise, no stable relationships can be estimated.

17.1 POLICY EVALUATION AND OPTIMIZATION UNDER RATIONAL EXPECTATIONS

The critique by Lucas (1976) of econometric policy evaluation is essentially that when the policy of Player 2 (the government) is being evaluated, the econometrician should not take the behavioral equation $x_{1t} = G_1 y_{t-1} + g_{1t}$ for the private sector as given. To evaluate the consequences of any government policy rule (G_2, g_{2t}), proper account has to be taken of the optimizing reaction of the private sector because its environment consists of (4) and $x_{2t} = G_2 y_{t-1} + g_{2t}$. The private sector derives its optimum behavioral equation $x_{1t} = G_1 y_{t-1} + g_{1t}$ by maximizing its objective function subject to this environment. Linear-quadratic optimal control theory as found in Chow (1975) can be used to find this optimal feedback control equation. The problem of policy evaluation is thus solved.

Turning to policy optimization by the government, we observe that its optimal policy is the strategy of the dominant player in a two-person dynamic game. We will derive a pair of optimal steady-state strategies (G_1, g_1) and (G_2, g_2) for the two players when the system is in a covariance-stationary equilibrium, assuming that b_t, a_{1t}, K_{1t}, a_{2t}, and K_{2t} are all time-invariant, the time subscript t for these variables being omitted in the remainder of this section.

If the dominant player adheres to a feedback control policy $x_{2t} = G_2 y_{t-1} + g_2$, Player 1 will face (7) as its environment and adopt the optimal equilibrium strategy $x_{1t} = G_1 y_{t-1} + g_1$ where (see Chow, 1975, pp. 170–171):

$$C_1' H_1 C_1 G_1 + C_1' H_1 (A + C_2 G_2) = 0 \qquad (8)$$

$$H_1 - K_1 - (A + C_2 G_2 + C_1 G_1)' H_1 (A + C_2 G_2 + C_1 G_1) = 0 \qquad (9)$$

$$C_1' H_1 C_1 g_1 + C_1' \left[H_1 (b + C_2 g_2) - h_1 \right] = 0 \qquad (10)$$

$$\left[I - (A + C_2 G_2 + C_1 G_1)' \right] h_1 - K_1 a_1$$

$$- (A + C_2 G_2 + C_1 G_1)' H_1 (b + C_2 g_2) = 0. \qquad (11)$$

Given G_2, (8) and (9) can be solved to obtain G_1 and H_1. Given g_2 in addition, (10) and (11) can be solved to obtain g_1 and h_1. In a covariance-stationary equilibrium, the system will have a mean vector $\bar{y}$ and a covariance matrix $\Gamma = E(y_t - \bar{y})(y_t - \bar{y})'$ that satisfy (see Chow, 1975, pp. 51–52):

$$(I - A - C_1 G_1 - C_2 G_2)\bar{y} - b - C_1 g_1 - C_2 g_2 = 0 \qquad (12)$$

$$\Gamma - (A + C_1 G_1 + C_2 G_2)\Gamma(A + C_1 G_1 + C_2 G_2)' - E u_t u_t' = 0. \qquad (13)$$

Player 2's problem is to minimize

$$\tfrac{1}{2} E(y_t - a_2)' K_2 (y_t - a_2) = \tfrac{1}{2} \operatorname{tr}(K_2 \Gamma) + \tfrac{1}{2}(\bar{y} - a_2)' K_2 (\bar{y} - a_2)$$

with respect to G_2 and g_2 in its feedback control equation, subject to the constraints (8)–(13). This problem can be solved by forming the Lagrangian expression

$$L = \tfrac{1}{2}\operatorname{tr}(K_2\Gamma) + \tfrac{1}{2}(\bar{y} - a_2)'K_2(\bar{y} - a_2) - \omega'(10) - \phi'(11) - \lambda'(12)$$

$$- \operatorname{tr}\{\Omega(8)\} - \tfrac{1}{2}\operatorname{tr}\{\Phi(9)\} - \tfrac{1}{2}\operatorname{tr}\{\psi(13)\},$$

where ω, ϕ, λ, Ω, $\Phi = \Phi'$ and $\Psi = \Psi'$ are vectors and matrices of Lagrangian multipliers and, for brevity, the equation number in parentheses denotes the corresponding constraint.

Using the differentiation rule $\partial \operatorname{tr}(AB)/\partial A = B'$, we obtain the following equations, with R denoting $A + C_1G_1 + C_2G_2$,

$$\frac{\partial L}{\partial g_1} = -C_1'H_1C_1\omega + C_1'\lambda = 0 \tag{14}$$

$$\frac{\partial L}{\partial h_1} = C_1\omega - (I - R)\phi = 0 \tag{15}$$

$$\frac{\partial L}{\partial g_2} = -C_2'H_1C_1\omega + C_2'H_1R\phi + C_2'\lambda = 0 \tag{16}$$

$$\frac{\partial L}{\partial \bar{y}} = K_2(\bar{y} - a_2) - (I - R')\lambda = 0 \tag{17}$$

$$\frac{\partial L}{\partial G_1} = C_1'\big[H_1C_1\Omega' + H_1R\Phi + \Psi R\Gamma + h_1\phi' + H_1(b + C_2g_2)\phi' + \lambda\bar{y}'\big]$$

$$= 0 \tag{18}$$

$$\frac{\partial L}{\partial G_2} = C_2'\big[H_1C_1\Omega' + H_1R\Phi + \Psi R\Gamma + h_1\phi' + H_1(b + C_2g_2)\phi' + \lambda\bar{y}'\big]$$

$$= 0 \tag{19}$$

$$\frac{\partial L}{\partial H_1} = -\Phi + R\Phi R' - C_1g_1\omega'C_1' - C_1\omega g_1'C_1' - (b + C_2g_2)\omega'C_1'$$

$$- C_1\omega(b + C_2g_2)' + (b + C_2g_2)\phi'R + R'\phi(b + C_2g_2)'$$

$$= 0 \tag{20}$$

$$\frac{\partial L}{\partial \Gamma} = K_2 - \Psi + R'\Psi R = 0. \tag{21}$$

To solve these equations, we first consider an approximate solution for G_2, G_1, and H_1 in a simpler problem. The problem is the minimization of $\text{tr}(K_2\Gamma)$ when $b = 0$, $a_1 = 0$, and $a_2 = 0$. The optimal strategies are $x_{1t} = G_1 y_{t-1}$ and $x_{2t} = G_2 y_{t-1}$; the constraints (10), (11), and (12) are no longer relevant. One only needs to solve (18)–(21), with $\omega = 0$, $\phi = 0$, $\lambda = 0$, $\bar{y} = 0$, and $g_2 = 0$. Equation 20 would become $\Phi = R\Phi R'$, which has a solution $\Phi = 0$. Equation 18 would imply

$$\Omega' = -(C_1'H_1C_1)^{-1}(\Psi R\Gamma),$$

which, when substituted into (19), would yield

$$C_2'\left[I - H_1C_1(C_1'H_1C_1)^{-1}\right]\Psi(A + C_1G_1 + C_2G_2)\Gamma = 0. \qquad (22)$$

Starting with an initial guess for G_2, we solve (8) and (9) for G_1 and H_1. Given G_1, we solve (21) for Ψ. Equation 22, postmultiplied by Γ^{-1}, can be used to compute a new G_2.

$$G_2 = \left\{C_2'\left[I - H_1C_1(C_1'H_1C_1)^{-1}\right]\Psi C_2\right\}^{-1}$$

$$\times C_2'\left[I - H_1C_1(C_1'H_1C_1)^{-1}\right]\Psi(A + C_1G_1).$$

This iterative process can be continued to find G_2, G_1, and H_1 for the simpler problem.

To solve the original problem, we start with the preceding approximate solution for G_2, G_1, and H_1. Equations 14, 15, 16, and 17 imply respectively, with $P_1 = C_1(C_1'H_1C_1)^{-1}C_1'$,

$$\omega = (C_1'H_1C_1)^{-1}C_1'\lambda \qquad (14a)$$

$$\phi = (I - R)^{-1}P_1\lambda \qquad (15a)$$

$$C_2'\left\{I - H_1\left[I - R(I - R)^{-1}\right]P_1\right\}\lambda = 0 \qquad (16a)$$

$$\lambda = (I - R')^{-1}K_2(\bar{y} - a_2). \qquad (17a)$$

Equations 17a and 12 give

$$\lambda = (I - R')^{-1}K_2\left[(I - R)^{-1}(b + C_1g_1 + C_2g_2) - a_2\right]. \qquad (23)$$

Combining (23) with (16a), we get

$$C_2'\{I - H_1[I - R(I - R)^{-1}]P_1\}(I - R')^{-1}$$

$$\times K_2[(I - R)^{-1}(b + C_1g_1 + C_2g_2) - a_2] = 0. \qquad (24)$$

With G_2, G_1, and H_1 given, (24), (10), and (11) can be solved for g_2, g_1, and h_1. Equation 24 is used to express g_2 as a linear function of g_1; (10) and (11) become two linear equations in g_1 and h_1. Equations 23, 14a, and 15a are then used to find λ, ω, and ϕ, and (12) is used to compute $\bar{y}$.

We now follow the steps of the simpler problem to solve (18)–(21). Equation 20 is used to solve for Φ iteratively, that is $\Phi^{(i+1)} = R\Phi^{(i)}R' +$ known matrix. Equations 18 and 19 imply

$$\Omega' = - (C_1'H_1C_1)^{-1}C_1'[H_1R\Phi + \Psi R\Gamma + \cdots] \qquad (18a)$$

$$C_2'[I - H_1P_1][H_1R\Phi + \Psi R\Gamma + h_1\phi' + H_1(b + C_2g_2)\phi' + \lambda\bar{y}'] = 0. \qquad (19a)$$

Because (13) and (21) can be used to compute Γ and Ψ respectively, (19a) after being postmultiplied by Γ^{-1} can be solved for G_2 iteratively, that is

$$C_2'[I - H_1P_1]\Psi C_2G_2 = C_2'[I - H_1P_1]$$

$$\times [H_1R\Phi\Gamma^{-1} + \Psi(A + C_1G_1) + \cdots], \qquad (22a)$$

where we have recalled $R = (A + C_1G_1 + C_2G_2)$. Having thus obtained a new matrix G_2, we can continue with the iterative process by returning to the beginning of the preceding paragraph.

Mathematically, the solution to the two-person dynamic game formulated earlier in this section but under a Nash (or Cournot) equilibrium is simpler, for each player would treat the other's strategy as given, without being affected by his own strategy. Given (G_2, g_2), Player 1 would find (G_1, g_1) by (8)–(10) as before. Symmetrically, given (G_1, g_1), Player 2 would find (G_2, g_2) by solving an identical set of equations with subscripts 1 and 2 interchanged. A Nash equilibrium is found by solving these two sets of equations.

17.2 ESTIMATION OF DYNAMIC GAME MODEL WITH A DOMINANT PLAYER

When x_{2t} in (4) represents the policy instruments of the government and the government is treated as the dominant player, we will study the estimation problem in two stages. First, assuming that the government adheres to a policy rule $x_{2t} = G_2 y_{t-1} + g_{2t}$, which is decided upon by whatever means, we will consider the estimation of the parameters of (4) and (5) for $i = 1$ under the assumption that the private sector behaves optimally. Second, from the above framework we take the next step by assuming that the government is also trying to maximize (5) for $i = 2$ and consider the estimation of the parameters of its objective function as well.

For the first problem, the stochastic environment facing the private sector consists of two equations, (4) and

$$x_{2t} = G_2 y_{t-1} + g_{2t} \qquad (6b)$$

These two equations comprise the model (1) in the framework of Chapter 16. In that chapter, two methods were provided to estimate the parameters of (1), now consisting of (4) and (6b), and of (2), now represented by (5) with $i = 1$. The methods are maximum likelihood and a consistent method analogous to two-stage least squares. The latter method requires consistent estimates of the parameters of (1) and (3), and, using them, solves for the parameters of (2) in the second stage of two-stage least squares.

We now incorporate the assumption that the government also maximizes to obtain its behavioral equation (6b). If we are not interested in estimating the objective function of the government, and are willing to assume that the parameters of (4) and (5) remained unchanged for the sample observations, then (6b) is a stable equation and the methods of Chapter 16 would suffice, as pointed out in the last paragraph. The new problem is to estimate the objective function of the government as well. From the viewpoint of the maximizing government, the stochastic environment consists of (4) and (5) with $i = 1$, which, together with its own policy (G_2, g_{2t}), determine G_1 and g_{1t} in (6) as a result of the private sector's maximizing behavior.

Maximum-likelihood estimation of the parameters of (4) and (5) under the assumption that Player 2 (the government) is the dominant player can proceed as follows. Adding a residual v_{it} to (6) and assuming a joint normal distribution of u_t, v_{1t}, and v_{2t}, one can easily write down the likelihood function which has the parameters of (4) and (6) as arguments. As a first step, we postpone the estimation of K_{2t} and a_{2t}, and assume some given values for G_2 and g_{2t} (which could be the coefficients of a least-squares regression of x_{2t} on y_{t-1} and appropriate trend terms). Given

G_2 and g_{2t}, we can express G_1 and g_{1t} as functions of the parameters of (4) and K_{1t} and a_{1t} in (5) through the maximization of the private sector. K_{1t} and a_{1t} thus replace G_1 and g_{1t} as arguments in the likelihood function. To reduce the number of parameters, we assume here as in Chapter 16 that $K_{1t} = \beta_1^t K_{10}$ and $a_{1t} = \phi_1^t a_{10}$, β_1 being the discount factor for the private sector and ϕ_1 being a diagonal matrix with some elements known to be one if the targets in a_t are constant through time. Given G_2 and g_{2t} then, we can maximize the likelihood function with respect to the parameters of (1) and K_{10}, β_1, a_{10}, and ϕ_1. This problem was solved in Chapter 16.

In order to solve the more difficult problem of estimating K_{2t} and a_{2t}, we treat a more restrictive case by introducing the assumption of Section 1 that b_t, K_{1t}, a_{1t}, K_{2t}, and a_{2t} are all time-invariant. Given K_1, a_1, K_2, a_2, and the parameters of (4) we can apply the method of Section 1 to find (G_1, g_1) and (G_2, g_2); thus the likelihood function can be evaluated. A gradient method can in principle be applied to maximize the likelihood with respect to these parameters, but this numerical maximization problem requires further investigation.

17.3 ESTIMATION OF DYNAMIC GAME MODEL UNDER NASH EQUILIBRIUM

The estimation problem for a dynamic game model under a Nash equilibrium is simpler. We can apply iterative techniques by considering this estimation problem in two stages. First, assuming tentatively that the government adheres to a policy rule (G_2, g_{2t}), we will consider the estimation of the parameters of (4) and $K_{1t} = \beta_1^t K_{10}$ and $a_{1t} = \phi_1^t a_{10}$ under the assumption that the private sector behaves optimally. Our estimation procedure assumes optimal behavior (G_1, g_{1t}) of the private sector, with (G_2, g_{2t}) taken as given. Second, assuming that the private sector adheres to the policy (G_1, g_{1t}) as determined previously, we consider the estimation of the parameters of (4) and $K_{2t} = \beta_2^t K_{20}$ and $a_{2t} = \phi_2^t a_{20}$ under the assumption that the government behaves optimally. Similarly, the estimation procedure assumes optimal behavior (G_2, g_{2t}) of the government, with (G_1, g_{1t}) taken as given. We now go back to step one, and iterate back and forth until convergence.

As pointed out previously, given (G_2, g_{2t}), the methods of Chapter 16 can be used to estimate the parameters of (4), K_{10}, β_1, a_{10}, ϕ_1, and, accordingly, G_1 and g_{1t}. Similarly, given (G_1, g_{1t}), the same methods can be used to estimate the parameters of (4), K_{20}, β_2, a_{20}, ϕ_2, and, accordingly, G_2 and g_{2t}. If the method of maximum likelihood is used, we start with some consistent estimates of G_2 and g_{2t} (as obtained by regressing x_{2t} on y_{t-1} and appropriate trends), and maximize the likelihood function with respect to the parameters of (4), K_{10}, β_1, a_{10}, and ϕ_1, yielding maximum likelihood estimates of G_1 and g_{1t} as well. Using these estimates of G_1 and g_{1t}, we again maximize the likelihood function with respect to the parameters of (4), K_{20}, β_2, a_{20}, and ϕ_2, and so forth until convergence. This procedure amounts to maximizing the likelihood function with respect to two sets of parameters iteratively, that is, to one set while holding the other set fixed and alternatively.

If we are willing to assume time-invariant K_i and a_i ($i = 1, 2$), we can maximize the likelihood subject to two sets of constraints. One set of constraints consists of the four equations (8)–(11), and the second set is identical except with the subscripts 1 and 2 interchanged. A Lagrangian expression is formed which is to be maximized. Given the parameters of the objective function and the optimal decision rule for Player 1, the method of Section 2 of Chapter 16 can be used to find the remaining parameters of the model. Given the estimates of the parameters pertaining to Player 2 so obtained, one can maximize the likelihood function with respect to the parameters for Player 1, and the process proceeds iteratively until convergence.

To propose a simpler and yet consistent method, we start with consistent estimates of the parameters of (4), and of (G_2, g_{2t}) and (G_1, g_{1t}), by the method of least squares, for instance. The parameters of (4) and (G_i, g_{it}) can be employed to solve for K_{i0}, β_i, a_{i0}, and ϕ_i for $i = 1, 2$ by the method analogous to two-stage least squares as given in Section 4 of Chapter 16. Given the parameters of (4) and K_{i0}, β_i, a_{i0}, and ϕ_i ($i = 1, 2$), one can then find the Nash equilibrium solution for (G_1, g_{1t}) and (G_2, g_{2t}) iteratively, to improve upon the initial, consistent estimates of these parameters.[1] The situation is exactly analogous to the estimation of the reduced-form parameters Π in linear simultaneous stochastic equations. Consistent estimate $\hat{\Pi}$ of Π by least squares can be used to estimate the parameters $(B\ \Gamma)$ of the structure using the method of two-stage least squares. Given these estimates of $(B\ \Gamma)$, denotes by $(\hat{B}\ \hat{\Gamma})$, we can obtain a new estimate of Π as $\hat{B}^{-1}\hat{\Gamma}$, to improve upon the initial estimate $\hat{\Pi}$.

This section has treated the estimation of rational expectations models under the assumption of Nash equilibrium. If Player 2 represents the government, the solution concept of having a dominant player as expounded in Section 2 may be more appropriate. Given their likelihoods, these two solution concepts can be tested statistically, but this topic is not pursued here.

---

[1]An algebraic expression for the Nash equilibrium can be found in Kydland (1975, pp. 323–326) for instance, but here we need only a numerical solution by iterations, that is, by solving a standard optimal control problem to get G_1 and g_{1t} for the first player, given G_2 and g_{2t}, and then solving a standard optimal control problem to find G_2 and g_{2t}, given the above G_1 and g_{1t}, and so forth. For more references on dynamic games, see Cruz (1975).

Part 4
Optimal Control Methods for Stochastic Models in Continuous Time

CHAPTER 18

Optimum Control of Stochastic Differential Equation Systems

18.1 INTRODUCTION

This chapter is a tutorial exposition of the basic techniques of optimal control for stochastic systems in continuous time and of several important applications in economics. Its main purpose is to introduce these techniques to readers who already have some familiarity with the techniques and applications of stochastic control in discrete time, as can be found in Chow (1975) for example, but wish to avoid a heavy investment in the highly mathematical treatments of the subject currently available. The basic idea is to construct a stochastic model in discrete time and let the time intervals between successive measurements become very small. For readers already familiar with the analysis and control of stochastic models in discrete time, we will study continuous-time models using similar tools.

  To begin with, we will introduce a system of linear stochastic differential equations and study its dynamic properties, applying the notions developed for a system of linear stochastic difference equations. We then describe the method of dynamic programming in continuous time, formulate a system of nonlinear stochastic differential equations and derive Ito's differentiation rule for a scalar function of stochastic processes that satisfy a system of stochastic differential equations. The major areas of application of continuous time models are in economic theory rather than econometric analysis. We will use for illustration the problem of optimal consumption and portfolio selection over time studied by Robert Merton (1969, 1971). Dynamic programming will be applied to solve this optimal stochastic control problem in continuous time. An extension of the basic

267

model due to Merton (1973) to explain the prices of capital assets will be discussed. The next application will be the pricing of stock options originally studied by Black and Scholes (1973). We will then return to the control problem of minimizing the expected value of a quadratic loss function subject to the constraint of a system of linear stochastic differential equations. At the last application, we will study in Chapter 19 the problem of optimal exploitation of a limited natural resource when the probability distribution of its reserves is unknown.

18.2   LINEAR STOCHASTIC DIFFERENTIAL EQUATIONS

As in the formulation of a system of linear stochastic difference equations, consider the evolution of a vector time series $y(t)$ from time t to time $t + h$, where h need no longer be an integer and, in fact, will be assumed to take as small a value as we please. A reasonable extension of the discrete-time model is

$$y(t + h) - y(t) = A(t)y(t)h + v(t + h) - v(t), \qquad (1)$$

where the random residual $v(t + h) - v(t)$, as in the discrete-time formulation, is assumed to have mean zero and to be statistically independent through time whatever the choice of h. If the residual were absent, we could divide both sides of (1) by $h = dt$, let dt approach zero and obtain a system of linear differential equations in the limit. We now have the random term in (1) and need to specify it further.

For $h = 1$, let the covariance matrix of the vector of residuals be Σ. For smaller h, we divide the time interval between t and $t + 1$ into n segments of equal length, that is, let $h = 1/n$ time units. Because the n successive increments $v(t + h) - v(t), v(t + 2h) - v(t + h), \ldots,$ are assumed to be statistically independent and identically distributed, the covariance matrix Σ of their sum equals n times the covariance matrix of each increment, implying

$$\text{cov}\left[v(t + h) - v(t) \right] = \frac{1}{n}\Sigma = h\Sigma, \qquad (2)$$

Σ being the covariance matrix of $v(t + 1) - v(t)$. A vector time series $v(t)$ whose successive differences, however divided up, are statistically independent is called a *stochastic process with independent increments*. If, in addition, the successive differences are normally distributed it is called a *Wiener process* or *Brownian motion*. It has been shown in (2) that the covariance matrix of the increment $v(t + h) - v(t)$ is proportional to the time h. This means that the standard deviation of each component of the vector $v(t + h) - v(t)$ is proportional to $\sqrt{h}$. This property is important because terms involving the squares of the elements of $v(t + h) - v(t)$ are of order h and not of order h^2; they do not vanish as h becomes very small. As h becomes small, we write h as dt and rewrite (1) as

$$dy = A(t)y\,dt + dv, \tag{3}$$

where $E(dv) = 0$ and $\text{cov}(dv) = \Sigma(t)\,dt$. Equation 3 is a system of *linear stochastic differential equations*. The covariance matrix Σ can be a function of t in the more general case, as we write $\Sigma(t)$ in (3). Since $\text{cov}(dv) = \Sigma\,dt$, the covariance matrix of dv/dt is $\Sigma(dt)^{-1}$ which increases without bound as dt approaches zero. Therefore, the derivative dv/dt does not exist and one cannot divide (3) by dt to obtain an equation explaining the derivative dy/dt by dv/dt.

To find the solution $y(t)$ of (3) given $y(t_0)$, we divide the time interval between t_0 and t into n equal segments at points $t_1 < t_2 < \cdots < t_n = t$ and let the length of each segment be h, which can be made as small as we please by increasing n. If we define $dy(t_i)$ as $y(t_i + h) - y(t_i)$ or $y(t_{i+1}) - y(t_i)$ and $dv(t_i)$ as $v(t_{i+1}) - v(t_i)$, (1) or (3) implies

$$y(t_n) = \left[I + A(t_{n-1})h \right] y(t_{n-1}) + dv(t_{n-1})$$

$$= \left[I + A(t_{n-1})h \right]\left[I + A(t_{n-2})h \right] y(t_{n-2})$$

$$+ \left[I + A(t_{n-1})h \right] dv(t_{n-2}) + dv(t_{n-1}). \tag{4}$$

By repeated substitutions of $y(t_{n-2})$ by $y(t_{n-3})$, and so forth, and by defining the *state transition matrix*

$$\Phi(t_i, t_j) = \prod_{k=j}^{i-1} \left[I + A(t_k)h \right], \qquad i \geq j + 1,$$

$$\Phi(t_i, t_i) = I, \tag{5}$$

we can rewrite (4) as

$$y(t_n) = \Phi(t_n, t_0)y(t_0) + \sum_{j=0}^{n-1} \Phi(t_n, t_{j+1})dv(t_j), \tag{6}$$

which is a solution to (1). Note that by the definition (5) the state transition matrix satisfies the difference equation

$$d\Phi(t_i, t_0) \equiv \Phi(t_{i+1}, t_0) - \Phi(t_i, t_0)$$

$$= A(t_i)\Phi(t_i, t_0)h. \tag{7}$$

The solution (6) provides a heuristic argument for the following solution to the linear stochastic differential equation (3) as $h \to 0$:

$$y(t) = \Phi(t, t_0)y(t_0) + \int_{t_0}^{t} \Phi(t, s)\,dv(s). \tag{8}$$

The integral in (8) involving the stochastic process $v(s)$ is a *stochastic integral*. Following Ito, a stochastic integral of a deterministic or stochastic function f is defined as the limit of the sum

$$\int_{t_0}^{t} f(s)\,dv(s) = \lim_{n \to \infty} \sum_{j=1}^{n} f(t_j)\big[v(t_{j+1}) - v(t_j) \big], \tag{9}$$

where the limit of a sequence of random variables g_n is defined by convergence in mean square, that is,

$$\lim_{n \to \infty} g_n = g \Leftrightarrow \lim_{n \to \infty} E\,|g_n - g|^2 = 0. \tag{10}$$

This integral has the property that the operations of taking mathematical expectation and integration can be interchanged. If $f(t_j)$ in (9) is stochastic, say being $f[v(t_j), t_j]$, it makes a difference in taking the limit whether $f(t_j)$ is weighted by the forward difference $v(t_{j+1}) - v(t_j)$ according to Ito or by the backward difference $v(t_j) - v(t_{j-1})$. When $f(t_j)$ is a deterministic function, defined as the limit of a sequence of piecewise constant functions that are constant over intervals (t_j, t_{j+1}), as $\Phi(t_n, t_j)$ in (6), the resulting integral is the same no matter whether a forward or backward difference is taken. An exposition of this point can be found in Åström (1970, Chapter 3, Section 5).

It follows from (7) that the state transition matrix $\Phi(t, t_0)$ satisfies the differential equation

$$\frac{d\Phi(t, t_0)}{dt} = A(t)\Phi(t, t_0). \tag{11}$$

In the special case $A(t) = A$, we will solve this differential equation by iteration. Let $t_0 = 0$, and let the successive iterations be $\Phi_0(t, 0), \Phi_1(t, 0), \ldots$.

We have

$$\Phi_0(t,0) = I,$$

$$\Phi_1(t,0) = I + \int_0^t A\Phi_0(s,0)ds$$

$$= I + At,$$

$$\Phi_2(t,0) = I + \int_0^t A\Phi_1(s,0)ds$$

$$= I + At + A^2\frac{t^2}{2},$$

$$\Phi_i(t,0) = I + \int_0^t A\Phi_{i-1}(s,0)ds$$

$$= I + At + A^2\frac{t^2}{2} + \ldots + A^i\frac{t^i}{i!}.$$

As i increases, $\Phi_i(t,0)$ converges to

$$\Phi(t,0) = I + At + A^2\frac{t^2}{2} + A^3\frac{t^3}{3!} + \ldots = e^{At}.$$

The solution to (11) is therefore

$$\Phi(t,t_0) = e^{A(t-t_0)}. \tag{12}$$

18.3 MEAN AND COVARIANCE OF SOLUTION TO LINEAR STOCHASTIC DIFFERENTIAL EQUATIONS

To find the mean path $Ey(t) \equiv \bar{y}(t)$ of the solution (8), we take expectations of both sides of (8). Interchanging expectation and integration on the right-hand side and using $E\,dv(s) = 0$, we obtain

$$\bar{y}(t) = \Phi(t,t_0)\bar{y}(t_0). \tag{13}$$

This result could also be obtained by taking expectations of both sides of (3) to yield

$$d\bar{y} = A(t)\bar{y}\,dt, \tag{14}$$

the solution of which is (13). Thus the mean satisfies the deterministic differential equation (14) after dropping the stochastic term in (3).

To find the autocovariance matrix, we subtract (13) from (8) and consider the deviation $y^*(t) = y(t) - \bar{y}(t)$. This deviation satisfies the same equation (8) as $y(t)$ does. Therefore we will simply use (8) for $y^*(t)$ without writing the superscript explicitly. The autocovariance matrix is, for $s < t$,

$$\Gamma(t,s) = Ey(t)y(s)'$$

$$= E\left[\Phi(t,s)y(s) + \int_s^t \Phi(t,\tau)dv(\tau)\right]y(s)'$$

$$= \Phi(t,s)Ey(s)y(s)'$$

$$= \Phi(t,s)\Gamma(s,s), \tag{15}$$

and, similarly, for $s > t$,

$$\Gamma(t,s) = \Gamma(t,t)\Phi(s,t)'. \tag{16}$$

The covariance matrix $\Gamma(t,t) = P(t)$ is

$$P(t) = E\left[\Phi(t,t_0)y(t_0) + \int_{t_0}^t \Phi(t,s)dv(s)\right]$$

$$\times \left[\Phi(t,t_0)y(t_0) + \int_{t_0}^t \Phi(t,s)dv(s)\right]'$$

$$= \Phi(t,t_0)P(t_0)\Phi(t,t_0)' + \int_{t_0}^t \Phi(t,s)\Sigma(s)\Phi(t,s)'ds, \tag{17}$$

where we have taken expectation on the right-hand side of the integral sign and utilized $E\,dv(s)dv(s)' = \Sigma(s)ds$.

One can derive a differential equation for the covariance matrix $P(t)$ by considering the differential dP and appealing directly to (3),

$$dP = P(t + dt) - P(t)$$

$$= Ey(t + dt)y(t + dt)' - Ey(t)y(t)'$$

$$= E[y(t) + dy][y(t) + dy]' - Ey(t)y(t)'$$

$$= Ey(t)[A(t)y(t)dt + dv]' + E[A(t)y(t)dt + dv]y(t)'$$

$$\quad + E[A(t)y(t)dt + dv][A(t)y(t)dt + dv]'$$

$$= P(t)A(t)'dt + A(t)P(t)dt + \Sigma(t)dt, \tag{18}$$

where we have recalled the statistical independence of $y(t)$ and dv. Dividing (18) by dt, we obtain

$$\frac{dP}{dt} = PA' + AP + \Sigma. \tag{19}$$

Equation 19 could also be derived by differentiating (17) with respect to t.

18.4 DYNAMIC PROGRAMMING FOR MODELS IN CONTINUOUS TIME

We will now state the method of dynamic programming for stochastic models in continuous time, assuming that the objective is to maximize the expectation

$$E_0\left\{ \int_{t_0}^{T} u(y,x,t)\,dt + B[\,y(T),T\,] \right\}, \tag{20}$$

where $y(t)$ satisfies a system of stochastic differential equations with the vector $x(t)$ as control variables. In the discrete time version, the integral would be replaced by an appropriate sum, and the vector y_t is assumed to satisfy a system of stochastic difference equations with the vector x_t as control variables.

In the discrete-time optimization problem, one would define $V(y_t, t)$ as the maximum expected utility, or minimum expected loss, from period t onward, assuming y_t to be the initial condition at time t and an optimal policy to be followed from t on. [In the notation of Chow (1975), this function was written as $\hat{V}$.] By the principle of optimality of dynamic programming, we have

$$V(y_t, t) = \max_{x_t} E_{t-1}\left[u(y_t, x_t, t) + V(y_{t+1}, t+1) \right]. \tag{21}$$

This maximization problem could be solved beginning from period T and proceeding backward in time to period t_0. The method for optimization in continuous time can be derived by letting the time interval h between successive decisions become as small as one pleases. The relation for small h is

$$V[\,y(t),t\,] = \max_{x_t} E_t\left\{ \int_{t}^{t+h} u(y,x,s)\,ds + V[\,y(t+h),t+h\,] \right\}$$

$$= \max_{x_t} \left\{ u[\,y(t),x(t),t\,]h + E_t V[\,y(t+h),t+h\,] \right\}. \tag{22}$$

If we let $dV(t)$ denote $V[y(t + h), t + h] - V[y(t), t]$, the above equation can be written as

$$V(y, t) = \max_{x_t} \{u(y, x, t)h + V(y, t) + E_t dV\}. \tag{23}$$

Dividing through by $h = dt$, we obtain

$$0 = \max_{x} \left\{ u(y, x, t) + E_t \frac{1}{dt} dV \right\}, \tag{24}$$

which is to be solved. To solve the optimization problem thus requires the evaluation of the stochastic differential dV where V is a function of y and t and y satisfies a given stochastic differential equation. To evaluate dV, a differentiation rule developed by Ito will be used. Furthermore, we would need to evaluate the expectation $E_t(1/dt)dV$. For this purpose, a differential generator related to Ito's differential for dV will be derived. These are the subjects of the next section.

18.5 ITO'S DIFFERENTIATION RULE

We will have occasions to consider nonlinear stochastic differential equations of the form

$$dy = f(y, t)dt + dv$$

$$= f(y, t)dt + S(y, t)dz, \tag{25}$$

where the vector function $f(y, t)$ replaces the linear function $A(t)y$ in (3) and the covariance matrix of dv may be a function of y and is written as $\Sigma(y, t)dt$. If we let z be a Wiener process with $R\,dt$ as the covariance matrix for its increment, we can write dv as $S(y, t)dz$ where $SRS' = \Sigma$. Formally, the solution of (2) is

$$y(t) = y(t_0) + \int_{t_0}^{t} f[y(s), s]ds + \int_{t_0}^{t} S[y(s), s]dz(s), \tag{26}$$

where the stochastic integral was defined by (9). Although we may not need to express the solution in explicit form, we would like to study the properties of a stochastic process that is a scalar function of y, as exemplified by the function V in the last section on the method of dynamic programming. Let $F = F(y, t)$ be such a function, assumed to be continuously differentiable in t and twice continuously differentiable in y. We wish to derive a stochastic differential equation for F.

We expand the function F in a Taylor series, with $h = dt$,

$$dF = F[y(t + h), t + h] - F[y(t), t]$$

$$= \frac{\partial F}{\partial t} dt + \left(\frac{\partial F}{\partial y}\right)' dy + \frac{1}{2}(dy)' \frac{\partial^2 F}{\partial y \partial y'} dy + o(dt), \qquad (27)$$

where $o(dt)$ denotes terms of order smaller than dt. Denoting the matrix of second partial derivatives of F with respect to y by F_{yy}, using (25) for dy and noting that dv is of order, $\sqrt{dt}$, we have

$$(dy)' F_{yy} dy = (dv)' F_{yy} dv + o(dt)$$

$$= \text{tr}(F_{yy} dv\, dv') + o(dt). \qquad (28)$$

Substituting (25) and (28) into (27) gives

$$dF = \left[\frac{\partial F}{\partial t} + \left(\frac{\partial F}{\partial y}\right)' f\right] dt + \frac{1}{2}\text{tr}(F_{yy} dv\, dv') + \left(\frac{\partial F}{\partial y}\right)' dv + o(dt), \quad (29)$$

implying, together with $E\, dv\, dv' = \Sigma dt$,

$$E(dF) = \left[\frac{\partial F}{\partial t} + \left(\frac{\partial F}{\partial y}\right)' f + \frac{1}{2}\text{tr}(F_{yy}\Sigma)\right] dt, \qquad (30)$$

and

$$\text{var}(dF) = E[dF - E(dF)]^2$$

$$= E\left[\frac{1}{2}\text{tr}(F_{yy} dv\, dv') - \frac{1}{2}\text{tr}(F_{yy}\Sigma) dt + \left(\frac{\partial F}{\partial y}\right)' dv + o(dt)\right]^2$$

$$= E\left[\left(\frac{\partial F}{\partial y}\right)' dv\right]^2 + o(dt)$$

$$= \left(\frac{\partial F}{\partial y}\right)' \Sigma \left(\frac{\partial F}{\partial y}\right) dt + o(dt). \qquad (31)$$

Equations 30 and 31 provide a justification for *Ito's differentiation rule*,

$$dF = \left[\left(\frac{\partial F}{\partial t} \right) + \left(\frac{\partial F}{\partial y} \right)' f + \frac{1}{2} \mathrm{tr}(F_{yy} \Sigma) \right] dt + \left(\frac{\partial F}{\partial y} \right)' dv, \qquad (32)$$

where $F = F(y, t)$ and dy is given by (25). Note that (32) remains valid if the functions f and Σ (or S) have a third argument x, that is, they become $f(y, x, t)$ and $\Sigma(y, x, t)$. Here x can be viewed as a vector of parameters of the functions f and Σ. It can be used as a vector of exogenous variables or control variables for the system of stochastic differential equations (25).

A related concept to Ito's differential dF is the operation

$$\lim_{h \to 0} E_t \left[\frac{dF}{h} \right] \equiv \mathcal{L}_y [F(y, t)], \qquad (33)$$

where dF is defined by the first line of (27) and E_t is the conditional expectation given $y(t)$. The result gives the expected rate of change through time of the function $F(y, t)$ as induced by the stochastic process y. The operator $\mathcal{L}_y$ so defined is the *differential generator* of the stochastic process $y(t)$. Formally, it can be obtained by $(1/dt)E_t(dF)$, using (32) for dF, that is, by taking the expectation of (32) and dividing the result by dt. This gives

$$\mathcal{L}_y [F] = \left\{ \frac{\partial}{\partial t} + f' \frac{\partial}{\partial y} + \frac{1}{2} \mathrm{tr} \left(\Sigma \frac{\partial^2}{\partial y \partial y'} \right) \right\} [F]. \qquad (34)$$

The stochastic differential (32) and the differential generator (34) will be applied to solve optimal control problems by the method of dynamic programming in the following sections.

18.6 OPTIMUM CONSUMPTION AND PORTFOLIO SELECTION OVER TIME

The problem of this and the following section was studied by Merton (1969, 1971), and its discrete version partly by Samuelson (1969). At time t, the individual chooses his rate of consumption $C(t)$ per unit time during period t (between t and $t + h$) and the number $N_i(t)$ of shares to be invested in asset i during period t, given his initial wealth $W(t) = \sum_i^n N_i(t - h) P_i(t)$ and the prices $P_i(t)$ per share of the assets. The prices are assumed to follow the stochastic differential equations,

$$\frac{dP_i}{P_i} = \alpha_i(P, t) dt + s_i(P, t) dz_i, \qquad (35)$$

where P is the vector of assest prices and z_i are components of a multivariate Wiener process, with $E(dz_i) = 0$, $\text{var}(dz_i) = 1$ and $E(dz_i dz_j) = \rho_{ij}$. If α_i and s_i are constants, (35) describes a "geometric Brownian motion" hypothesis for asset prices. If there is no wage income and all incomes are derived from capital gains (dividends being included in changes in asset prices), it can be shown that the change in wealth from t to $t + h$ satisfies the budget constraint

$$dW = \sum_{1}^{n} N_i(t)dP_i - C(t)dt. \tag{36}$$

Let $w_i(t) = N_i(t)P_i(t)/W(t)$ be the fraction of wealth invested in asset i, with $\Sigma_i w_i = 1$. We substitute (35) for dP_i in (36) to obtain

$$dW = \sum_{1}^{n} w_i W\alpha_i dt - C dt + \sum_{1}^{n} w_i W s_i dz_i. \tag{37}$$

If we assume the nth asset to be risk-free, that is, $s_n = 0$, and denote the instantaneous rate of return α_n of this asset by r, we can write (37) as, with $m = n - 1$,

$$dW = \sum_{1}^{m} w_i(\alpha_i - r)W dt + (rW - C)dt + \sum_{1}^{m} w_i W s_i dz_i. \tag{38}$$

The endogenous or state variables of this problem, corresponding to the vector y of the previous sections, are W and P. They are governed by the stochastic differential eqs. (37) and (35) which correspond to (25) when the vector of control variables x is added to the arguments of f and S. The control variables are C and $w = (w_1, \ldots, w_n)'$, with $\Sigma_1^n w_i = 1$. The problem is to maximize

$$E_0\left\{ \int_0^T U[C(t), t]dt + B[W(T), T] \right\},$$

where U is the utility function and B is the bequest function. This model assumes that assets are traded continuously in time and that there are no transaction costs in trading. The latter assumption is unrealistic, but we will consider in Section 8 a consequence of dropping this assumption.

We apply the method of dynamic programming to solve this problem. By the result of Section 4, this amounts to solving (24), which, using the differential generator $\mathcal{L}_y$ of Section 5, can be written as

$$\max_{C(t), w(t)} \{ U(C, t) + \mathcal{L}_y[V(y, t)] \} = 0. \tag{39}$$

Thus the optimum policy for $C(t)$ and $w(t)$ will be found by solving (39).

Using (37) and (35) as stochastic differential equations for $(W, P) = y$, and (34) for the operator $\mathcal{L}_y$, we find

$$\mathcal{L}_y[V(y,t)] = \frac{\partial V}{\partial t} + \left[\sum_1^n w_i\alpha_i W - C \right]\frac{\partial V}{\partial W} + \sum_1^n \alpha_i P_i \frac{\partial V}{\partial P_i}$$

$$+ \frac{1}{2}\sum_1^n \sum_1^n \sigma_{ij}w_iw_jW^2\frac{\partial^2 V}{\partial W^2} + \frac{1}{2}\sum_1^n \sum_1^n P_iP_j\sigma_{ij}\frac{\partial^2 V}{\partial P_i\partial P_j}$$

$$+ \sum_1^n \sum_1^n P_iw_jW\sigma_{ij}\frac{\partial^2 V}{\partial P_i\partial W}, \tag{40}$$

where $\sigma_{ij} = \rho_{ij}s_is_j$. We perform the maximization (39) by differentiating with respect to C and w the Lagrangian expression

$$L = U(C,t) + \mathcal{L}_y[V] + \lambda\left[1 - \sum_1^n w_i\right], \tag{41}$$

and obtain the first-order conditions, with subscripts denoting partial derivatives and $V_{jw} = \partial^2 V/\partial P_j \partial W$,

$$L_c(C,w) = U_c(C,t) - V_w = 0, \tag{42}$$

$$L_{w_k}(C,w) = W^2V_{ww}\sum_1^n \sigma_{kj}w_j - \lambda + WV_w\alpha_k$$

$$+ W\sum_1^n P_j\sigma_{kj}V_{jw} = 0, \qquad k = 1,\ldots,n, \tag{43}$$

$$L_\lambda(C,w) = 1 - \sum_1^n w_i = 0. \tag{44}$$

Equations 42–44 can be solved to obtain the optimal C and w as functions of the partial derivatives of V. These functions can be substituted for C and w in (40) and, by (39), we need to solve the resulting partial differential equation $U(C,t) + \mathcal{L}_y[V(y,t)] = 0$ for the function $V(y,t)$.

18.7   CONSUMPTION AND PORTFOLIO SELECTION WHEN ASSET PRICES ARE LOG-NORMAL

Interesting results can be obtained for the special case when the asset prices follow a geometric Brownian motion, that is, when α_i and s_i in (35) are constants. In this case, current prices P provide no information on the relative rates of change in the prices according to (35) and the maximum expected future utility V is a function of W and t only, and not of P. The terms involving P_i drop out in (40). Equations 42 and 43 become respectively

$$U_c(C,t) - V_w = 0, \tag{45}$$

$$W^2 V_{ww} \sum_1^n \sigma_{kj} w_j - \lambda + W V_w \alpha_k = 0. \tag{46}$$

Defining the inverse function $G = [U_c]^{-1}$, we solve (45) to obtain the optimum consumption

$$\hat{C} = G(V_w, t). \tag{47}$$

To obtain the optimal portfolio w, we solve (46) and (44) for w and λ, or solve

$$
\begin{bmatrix}
\sigma_{11} & \sigma_{12} & \cdots & \sigma_{1n} & 1 \\
 & \cdots & & & \vdots \\
 & & & & \vdots \\
 & & & & \vdots \\
\sigma_{n1} & \sigma_{n2} & \cdots & \sigma_{nn} & 1 \\
1 & 1 & \cdots & 1 & 0
\end{bmatrix}
\begin{bmatrix}
w_1 \\ w_2 \\ \vdots \\ \vdots \\ w_n \\ \mu
\end{bmatrix}
= -\frac{V_w}{W V_{ww}}
\begin{bmatrix}
\alpha_1 \\ \alpha_2 \\ \vdots \\ \vdots \\ \alpha_n \\ 1
\end{bmatrix},
\tag{48}
$$

where $\mu = -\lambda / W^2 V_{ww}$. By partitioning the bordered matrix in (48), we find the first n rows of its inverse to be

$$
\begin{bmatrix}
\sigma^{11} & \sigma^{12} & \cdots & \sigma^{1n} \\
\cdots & \cdots & \cdots & \cdots \\
\sigma^{n1} & \sigma^{n2} & \cdots & \sigma^{nn}
\end{bmatrix}
- \Gamma^{-1}
\begin{bmatrix}
(\Sigma \sigma^{1j})(\Sigma \sigma^{1j}) \\
\cdots \\
(\Sigma \sigma^{1j})(\Sigma \sigma^{nj})
\end{bmatrix}
$$

$$
\begin{matrix}
(\Sigma \sigma^{1j})(\Sigma \sigma^{2j}) & \cdots & (\Sigma \sigma^{1j})(\Sigma \sigma^{nj}) \\
\cdots & & \cdots \\
(\Sigma \sigma^{2j})(\Sigma \sigma^{nj}) & \cdots & (\Sigma \sigma^{nj})(\Sigma \sigma^{nj})
\end{matrix}
\Bigg],
\quad
\Gamma^{-1}
\begin{bmatrix}
\Sigma \sigma^{1j} \\ \vdots \\ \Sigma \sigma^{nj}
\end{bmatrix},
\tag{49}
$$

where $(\sigma_{ij})^{-1} = (\sigma^{ij})$ and $\Gamma = \Sigma_i \Sigma_j \sigma^{ij}$. Therefore the optimal portfolio rules are

$$\hat{w}_k = \sum_l \left[\sigma^{kl} - \Gamma^{-1} \left(\sum_j \sigma^{kj} \right) \left(\sum_i \sigma^{li} \right) \right] \left[\frac{-V_w}{W V_{ww}} \alpha_l \right] + \Gamma^{-1} \sum_j \sigma^{kj}$$

$$= \Gamma^{-1} \sum_j \sigma^{kj} - \frac{V_w}{W V_{ww}} \left[\sum_l \sigma^{kl} \alpha_l - \Gamma^{-1} \sum_j \alpha^{kj} \sum_l \sum_i \sigma^{li} \alpha_l \right]$$

$$= h_k + m(W,t) \cdot g_k, \qquad k = 1, \ldots, n, \tag{50}$$

where we have defined

$$h_k = \Gamma^{-1} \sum_j \sigma^{kj}, \tag{51}$$

$$m(W,t) = -\frac{V_w}{W V_{ww}}, \tag{52}$$

$$g_k = \sum_j \sigma^{kj} \left[\alpha_j - \Gamma^{-1} \sum_l \sum_i \sigma^{li} \alpha_l \right], \tag{53}$$

implying $\Sigma_1^n h_k = 1$ and $\Sigma_1^n g_k = 0$.

The first component h_k of the optimal fraction $\hat{w}_k$ invested in asset k is proportional to the elements σ^{kj} in the kth row of the inverse of the covariance matrix of the relative rates of returns dP_j / P_j stipulated by (35). The factor g_k in the second component of $\hat{w}_k$ is a weighted average, using σ^{kj} as weights, of the difference between the expected rate of return α_j for asset j and the average expected rate of return $\Gamma^{-1} \Sigma_l \Sigma_i \sigma^{li} \alpha_l$ for all assets. If the covariances σ_{ij} were zero for $i \neq j$, g_k would become $\sigma_{kk}^{-1} [\alpha_k - \Sigma_l \sigma_{ll}^{-1} \alpha_l]$, thus measuring the expected rate of return α_k for asset k as compared with the average expected rate $\Sigma_l \sigma_{ll}^{-1} \alpha_l$ for all assets. The first component h_k recommends investment proportional to the inverses of the variances and covariances. Since $V_w > 0$ and $V_{ww} < 0$ for maximum V, $m(W,t) > 0$ by (52). The second component $m(W,t)g_k$ recommends investment in asset k proportional to the expected rate of return α_k for k (and to the expected rates α_j for other assets correlated with it), as compared with the average expected rate for all assets. The factors h_k and g_k are determined entirely by the means, variances, and covariances of the relative rates of returns of the assets, and not by the utility function, the amount of wealth, and the time horizon. $m(W,t)$ certainly depends on the wealth and the utility function of individual i making the decision.

Because an individual's relative demand $\hat{w}_k$ for the kth asset has only one parameter $m(W,t)$ that is affected by his wealth and his utility function, *the demand can be satisfied by selection from shares of only two "mutual funds,"* the first holding a fraction δ_k of its value in asset k and the second a fraction λ_k, with

$$\delta_k = h_k + (a - b)g_k,$$

$$\lambda_k = h_k - bg_k, \qquad k = 1, \ldots, n, \tag{54}$$

where a and b are arbitrary constants. Any value of $m(W,t)$ for an individual can always be met by a suitable linear combination of δ_k and λ_k, that is, by

$$m = \theta(a - b) + (1 - \theta)(-b)$$

$$= \theta a - b,$$

or by investing a fraction $\theta = (m + b)/a$ in the first fund and the remainder $(1 - \theta)$ in the second fund. This is known as a *mutual fund theorem.*

If the nth asset is riskless, $s_n = 0$, $\alpha_n = r$, and (38) replaces (37). We need only to solve for $m = n - 1$ optimal control equations for $\hat{w}_k$, $k = 1, \ldots, m$, with $\hat{w}_n = 1 - \Sigma_1^m \hat{w}_k$. The Lagrangian multiplier in (41) and (46) disappears. In our derivations, m replaces n, $(\alpha_i - r)$ replaces α_i and (48) becomes

$$\begin{bmatrix} \sigma_{11} & \sigma_{12} & \cdots & \sigma_{1m} \\ \cdots & \cdots & \cdots & \cdots \\ \sigma_{m1} & \sigma_{m2} & \cdots & \sigma_{mm} \end{bmatrix} \begin{bmatrix} w_1 \\ w_2 \\ \vdots \\ w_m \end{bmatrix} = \frac{-V_w}{WV_{ww}} \begin{bmatrix} \alpha_1 - r \\ \alpha_2 - r \\ \vdots \\ \alpha_m - r \end{bmatrix}, \tag{55}$$

the solution of which is

$$\hat{w}_k = m(W, t)g_k, \qquad k = 1, \ldots, m, \tag{56}$$

where

$$g_k = \sum_{j=1}^{m} \sigma^{kj}[\alpha_j - r], \qquad k = 1, \ldots, m. \tag{57}$$

To satisfy the demands $\hat{w}_k$ for any individual, there need be only two mutual funds, the first holding a fraction $\delta_k = (a - b)g_k$ of its value in asset k $(k = 1, \ldots, m)$ and the second holding a fraction $\lambda_k = -bg_k$. To achieve any $m(W, t)g_k$ desired, the individual again invests a fraction $\theta = (m + b)/a$ of his wealth in the first fund. We can let $b = 0$, so that the second fund holds only the riskless assets n and no risky assets. Thus only one mutual fund holding the risky asset by proportions ag_k, with $\sum_{k=1}^{m} ag_k = 1$, and a second fund holding only the riskless asset will satisfy the demand of any individual.

Let the nth asset be money, with $r = 0$. The relative holdings of the risky fund are, by (57),

$$\delta_k = ag_k = a \sum_{j=1}^{m} \sigma^{kj} \alpha_j, \qquad k = 1, \ldots, m, \tag{58}$$

where, to insure $\sum_{k=1}^{m} ag_k = 1$, $a = (\sum_k \sum_j \sigma^{kj} \alpha_j)^{-1}$. The holdings (58) are in agreement with the traditional Tobin-Markowitz mean-variance analysis. We find the portfolio $\delta = (\delta_1, \ldots, \delta_m)'$ for the fund which minimizes the variance $\sigma^2 = \delta' \Sigma \delta$ of the rate of return for a given mean rate of return $m = \delta' \alpha$, with $\alpha = (\alpha_1, \ldots, \alpha_m)'$, yielding a function $\sigma(m)$. In the (m, σ) diagram, if we draw a line going through the origin and tangential to the curve $\sigma(m)$, we will find the portfolio δ given by (58).

This mutual fund theorem and generalization of the mean-variance portfolio analysis were obtained without using a specific form for the utility function and without deriving the function $V(y, t)$ explicitly. The reader is referred to Merton (1969) and (1971) for explicit solutions of $V(y, t)$ and for further discussions of the economics of this problem, and to Rosenberg and Ohlson (1976) for a critique of the assumption that the rates of return are stationary and serially independent.

18.8 CAPITAL ASSET PRICING WITH SHIFTS IN INVESTMENT OPPORTUNITIES

One variation of the model of Section 6 suggested by Merton (1973) is to introduce a new vector $X = (x_1, \ldots, x_N)$ of N state variables to replace the vector P of asset prices. X may include all, some, or none elements of P. It may include the parameters α_i in (35) which will themselves be assumed to satisfy the stochastic differential equations

$$d\alpha_i = a_i \, dt + b_i \, dq_i, \tag{59}$$

where dq_i are Wiener processes with unit variance. Let us write the stochastic differential equations for the elements of this new vector as

$$dx_i = f_i(X)dt + g_i^*(X)dq_i, \qquad i = 1, \ldots, N. \tag{60}$$

Let $E(dq_i \, dz_j) = \eta_{ij}$ and $E(dq_i \, dq_j) = v_{ij}$, dz_j being defined for (35), with $E(dz_i \, dz_j) = \rho_{ij}$. We further let the nth asset be "instantaneously riskless" in the sense of $s_n = 0$ and $\alpha_n = r(t)$ in (35), but $b_n \neq 0$ in (59) for $d\alpha_n = dr$.

Assume that each individual maximizes utility over time as in Section 6. The present variation, with $y = (W, X)$, leads to a slight modification of (40),

$$\mathcal{L}_y[V(y,t)] = \frac{\partial V}{\partial t} + \left\{ \left[\sum_1^m w_i(\alpha_i - r) + r \right] W - C \right\} V_w + \sum_1^N f_i V_i$$

$$+ \frac{1}{2} \sum_1^m \sum_1^m \sigma_{ij} w_i w_j W^2 V_{ww} + \frac{1}{2} \sum_1^N \sum_1^N g_i^* g_j^* v_{ij} V_{ij}$$

$$+ \sum_{i=1}^N \sum_{j=1}^m g_i^* w_j W s_j \eta_{ij} V_{iw}, \tag{61}$$

where $m = n - 1$ as before and V_i denotes partial derivative with respect to the ith element of X. Equation 43 becomes

$$WV_{ww} \sum_1^m \sigma_{kj} w_j + V_w(\alpha_k - r) + \sum_1^N g_j^* s_k \eta_{jk} V_{jw} = 0, \qquad k = 1, \ldots, m. \tag{62}$$

The solution of this linear system of equations for w_k yields

$$\hat{w}_k W = A \sum_{i=1}^m \sigma^{ki}(\alpha_i - r) + \sum_{i=1}^m \sum_{j=1}^N H_j g_j^* s_k \eta_{ji} \sigma^{ki}, \qquad k = 1, \ldots, m, \tag{63}$$

where $A = -V_w / V_{ww}$ and $H_j = -V_{jw} / V_{ww}$. The first term of this demand function is the same as given by (57). To interpret the second term, note that $V_w = U_c$ by (42) and hence $V_{ww} = U_{cc}(\partial C / \partial W)$ and $V_{jw} = U_{cc}(\partial C / \partial x_j)$, implying

$$H_j = -\frac{\partial C / \partial x_j}{\partial C / \partial W}. \tag{64}$$

If the jth state variable has a negative or unfavorable effect on consumption, that is, $\partial C/\partial x_j < 0$, H_j will be positive. Because $(g_j^* s_i \eta_{ji})$ is the covariance between dx_j and dP_i, the expression $H_j \Sigma_{i=1}^m (g_j^* s_i \eta_{ji}) \sigma^{ki}$ measures the investment in asset k to hedge against the unfavorable effect of state variable j acting through its correlation with P_i for all $i = 1, \ldots, m$.

Consider the special case when the vector X of state variables consists only of $\alpha_n = r$ which affects the mean rates of return $\alpha_i(X)$ of the assets $i = 1, \ldots, m$. Equation 63 becomes

$$\hat{w}_k W = A \sum_{i=1}^m \sigma^{ki}(\alpha_i - r) + H_r \sum_{i=1}^m \text{cov}(dr, dP_i/P)\sigma^{ki}$$

$$= Ag_k + H_r d_k, \qquad k = 1, \ldots, m, \tag{65}$$

and $\hat{w}_n = 1 - \Sigma_1^m \hat{w}_k$, where g_k and d_k are independent of the individual's utility function and wealth. Equation 65 is a generalization of the asset demand functions (56)–(57). Since there is an additional term H_r which depends on the individual's utility function and wealth, any individual's demand can be satisfied by *three mutual funds*. Let the first fund hold a fraction $\delta_k = ag_k$ of its value in asset k, $k = 1, \ldots, m$. Let the second fund hold only the "instantaneously riskless" asset n. Let the third fund hold a fraction cd_k in asset k. The demand functions (65) for any individual will be satisfied by investing proportions θ_1, $(1 - \theta_1 - \theta_3)$, and θ_3 in the three funds respectively, where

$$\theta_1 ag_k + \theta_3 cd_k = \frac{A}{W} g_k + \frac{H_r}{W} d_k, \qquad k = 1, \ldots, m,$$

or $\theta_1 = A/Wa$ and $\theta_3 = H_r/Wc$. Summing these equations over k, we get $\theta_1 + \theta_3 = \Sigma_1^m \hat{w}_k = 1 - \hat{w}_n$, which insures that the demand $\hat{w}_n$ for the "instantaneously riskless" asset n can be met by investing the remaining proportion $1 - \theta_1 - \theta_3$ of the individual's wealth in the second mutual fund. Comparison of (63) and (65) shows that if there are two state variables shifting the mean rates of return or investment opportunities which one would wish to hedge against, that is, $N = 2$ in the model, there will be one extra term in (65) and four mutual funds will be required.

This analysis provides a *theory of mutual funds*. The first type of funds holds a portfolio δ_k proportional to g_k in the demand function (65). The second holds an instantaneously riskless asset like a short-term government bond. Each of the remaining funds holds a collection of capital assets to hedge against one type of contingency. If there were no transaction costs, the individual could make up the collection himself. Because there are transaction costs, each fund provides a service in offering the required collection of assets.

This analysis also provides an equilibrium *theory of market prices of the m capital assets*, interpreted as securities of m firms. Let the demand functions (65) for asset k by individual i be written as

$$D_k^i = A^i \sum_{j=1}^{m} \sigma^{kj}(\alpha_j - r) + H_r^i d_k$$

$$= A^i g_k + H^i d_k, \qquad k = 1, \ldots, m. \tag{66}$$

The market demand for the asset of firm k is the sum of (66) over all individuals i, that is,

$$D_k = \sum_i D_k^i = \left(\sum_i A^i \right) g_k + \left(\sum_i H^i \right) d_k = A g_k + H d_k. \tag{67}$$

If we redefine w_k to be the ratio of the value of the assets of firm k to the total market value M of the assets of all firms, then in equilibrium $D_k = w_k M$. Given $D_k = w_k M$, we use (67) to solve for the equilibrium expected rates of return α for assets k, noting $g_k = \sum_{j=1}^{m} \sigma^{kj}(\alpha_j - r)$ in (67). The solution of these linear equations is

$$\alpha_k - r = \left(\frac{M}{A} \right) \sum_{j=1}^{m} w_j \sigma_{kj} - \frac{H}{A} \sum_{j=1}^{m} d_j \sigma_{kj}, \qquad k = 1, \ldots, m, \tag{68}$$

which provides an explanation of the expected rate of return of an asset k. Because $\sum_j w_j \sigma_{kj}$ is the covariance of the (instantaneous) rate of return of asset k and the aggregate of the rates of return of all assets in the market (i.e., the aggregate rate of the market portfolio), this covariance being known as the 'beta' of the kth asset in the finance literature, the first term of (68) requires a higher expected rate of return for asset k insofar as its price change varies with those of the entire collection of risky assets in the market. Recall that d_j represents the portfolio of the third mutual fund which can be used to hedge against the shifts in expected returns. $\sum_j d_j \sigma_{kj}$ is thus the covariance of the rate of return for asset k and the rate for this fund. The second term of (68) justifies a lower expected rate of return for asset k insofar as it serves the hedging function provided by the third mutual fund. For further discussion of equilibrium capital asset pricing, the reader may refer to Long (1974).

18.9 THE PRICING OF OPTIONS AND CORPORATE LIABILITIES

A call option, of the "European type," entitles the owner to purchase a share of a given stock at an exercise price c at time T. Its price w is certainly a function of the price P of the stock, which is assumed to follow a geometric Brownian motion,

$$\frac{dP}{P} = \alpha\, dt + s\, dz. \tag{69}$$

Black and Scholes (1973) derived this function $w(P, t)$ by observing that a hedged position consisting of one option long and $\partial w/\partial P$ shares of the stock short will be riskless. When the stock price changes by ΔP, the option price will change by $(\partial w/\partial P)\Delta P$, which is the same as the change in value of the $\partial w/\partial P$ shares of stock in the hedged portfolio. Such a portfolio should yield the riskless rate of interest r, that is,

$$\frac{dw - (\partial w/\partial P)dP}{w - (\partial w/\partial P)P} = r\, dt, \tag{70}$$

which provides a condition for determining the function w.

Using (69) and Ito's differentiation rule, we have

$$dw = \left(\frac{\partial w}{\partial t} + \frac{\partial w}{\partial P}\alpha P + \frac{1}{2}\frac{\partial^2 w}{\partial P^2}s^2 P^2 \right)dt + \frac{\partial w}{\partial P}sP\, dz, \tag{71}$$

which, together with (69), implies

$$dw - \frac{\partial w}{\partial P}dP = \left(\frac{\partial w}{\partial t} + \frac{1}{2}\frac{\partial^2 w}{\partial P^2}s^2 P^2 \right)dt. \tag{72}$$

Equations 72 and 70 yield the differential equation for $w(P, t)$,

$$\frac{\partial w}{\partial t} = rw - rP\frac{\partial w}{\partial P} - \frac{1}{2}s^2 P^2 \frac{\partial^2 w}{\partial P^2} \tag{73}$$

The solution of (73) will give the function w for the pricing of call options. The boundary condition of this problem is $w(P, T) = P - c$ for $P \geq c$ and $w(P, T) = 0$ for $P < c$, c being the exercise price.

As pointed out by Cox and Ross (1976), the solution can be obtained alternatively by assuming that there exist risk neutral investors, so that the price of the stock will follow (69) with $\alpha = r$. The option price at time t will be its expected price at time T discounted back to t, namely,

$$w(P, t) = e^{-r(T-t)} Ew(P, T). \qquad (74)$$

Let $X = \ln P$. Using (69) and Ito's differentiation rule, we have

$$dX = \left(\frac{d \log P}{dP} rP + \frac{1}{2} \frac{d^2 \log P}{dP^2} s^2 P^2 \right) dt + \frac{d \log P}{dP} sP \, dz$$

$$= \left(r - \tfrac{1}{2} s^2 \right) dt + s \, dz. \qquad (75)$$

Given $X_t = \log P_t$, (75) implies that the distribution of X_T is normal with mean $X_t + (r - \frac{1}{2} s^2)(T - t)$ and variance $s^2(T - t)$. The price of the option at time T will be zero if $P_T < c$, and it will be $P_T - c$ if $P_T \geq c$. Therefore, the expected price of the option at T is

$$Ew(P, T) = \int_c^\infty (P_T - c) \, \mathrm{pdf}(P_T) \, dP_T, \qquad (76)$$

where pdf stands for the probability density function.

Since the pdf of $X_T = \log P_T$ is normal with mean and variance given above, (76) can be written as

$$Ew(P, T) = \int_{\log c}^\infty (e^x - c) \frac{1}{\sqrt{2\pi} s \sqrt{T - t}}$$

$$\times \exp \left\{ -\frac{1}{2} \cdot \frac{\left[x - X_t - \left(r - \frac{1}{2} s^2 \right)(T - t) \right]^2}{s^2(T - t)} \right\} dx. \qquad (77)$$

Substituting (77) into (74) and simplifying, we obtain the solution

$$w(P, t) = e^{-r(T-t)} \int_{\log c}^\infty \frac{1}{\sqrt{2\pi} s \sqrt{T - t}}$$

$$\times \exp \left\{ -\frac{1}{2} \cdot \frac{\left[x - X_t - \left(r + \frac{1}{2} s^2 \right)(T - t) \right]^2}{s^2(T - t)} + X_t + r(T - t) \right\} dx$$

$$- e^{-r(T-t)} c \int_{\log c}^\infty \frac{1}{\sqrt{2\pi} s \sqrt{T - t}}$$

$$\times \exp\left\{ -\frac{1}{2} \cdot \frac{\left[x - X_t - \left(r - \frac{1}{2}s^2\right)(T - t)\right]^2}{s^2(T - t)} \right\} dx$$

$$= P_t N\left(\frac{\ln[P_t/c] + \left[r + \frac{1}{2}s^2\right][T - t]}{s\sqrt{T - t}} \right)$$

$$- ce^{-r(T-t)} N\left(\frac{\ln[P_t/c] + \left[r - \frac{1}{2}s^2\right][T - t]}{s\sqrt{T - t}} \right), \tag{78}$$

where N stands for the cumulative unit normal distribution function. Black and Scholes (1973) have pointed out that by considering corporate liabilities as combinations of options, the pricing formula (78) can be applied to corporate liabilities such as common stock, corporate bonds, and warrants.

18.10 OPTIMAL CONTROL OF A LINEAR SYSTEM WITH QUADRATIC LOSS

The continuous-time version of the optimal linear quadratic control problem assumes a linear model

$$dy = A(t)y\,dt + C(t)x\,dt + dv, \tag{79}$$

where $dv = S\,dz$ has covariance matrix $\Sigma\,dt = SS'\,dt$, z being a multivariate Wiener process with $I\,dt$ as its incremental covariance matrix, and a quadratic loss function

$$W(y,x,t) = \frac{1}{2}\left[(y - a_1)'K_1(t)(y - a_1) + (x - a_2)'K_2(t)(x - a_2)\right]$$

$$= \frac{1}{2}y'K_1 y - y'K_1 a_1 + \frac{1}{2}x'K_2 x - x'K_2 a_2$$

$$+ \frac{1}{2}a_1'K_1 a_1 + \frac{1}{2}a_2'K_2 a_2$$

$$= \frac{1}{2}y'K_1 y - y'k_1 + \frac{1}{2}x'K_2 x - x'k_2 + d(t). \tag{80}$$

The problem is to find

$$V(y,t) = \min_x E_t\left[\int_t^T W(y,x,t)\,dt + \frac{1}{2}y'(T)K_0 y(T) - y'(T)k_0 + d_0 \right]. \tag{81}$$

Applying the optimality condition derived from dynamic programming as stated in (24), we have

$$\min_{x} \left\{ \tfrac{1}{2}y'K_1y - y'k_1 + \tfrac{1}{2}x'K_2x - x'k_2 + d + \mathcal{L}_y[V(y,t)] \right\} = 0. \quad (82)$$

We use the differential generator (34) for $\mathcal{L}_y[\ \ ]$ in (82) to obtain

$$\min_{x} \left\{ \tfrac{1}{2}y'K_1y - y'k_1 + \tfrac{1}{2}x'K_2x - x'k_2 + d + \frac{\partial V}{\partial t} \right.$$

$$\left. + \left(\frac{\partial V}{\partial y}\right)'[A(t)y + C(t)x] + \tfrac{1}{2}\text{tr}\left(\sum \frac{\partial^2 V}{\partial y \partial y'}\right) \right\} = 0. \quad (83)$$

Differentiating the expression in curly brackets with respect to x yields

$$\frac{\partial\{\ \ \}}{\partial x} = K_2 x - k_2 + C'\frac{\partial V}{\partial y} = 0,$$

which implies the optimal control equation

$$x = -K_2^{-1}C'\frac{\partial V}{\partial y} + K_2^{-1}k_2. \quad (84)$$

When (84) is substituted for x in (83), we have

$$\tfrac{1}{2}y'K_1y - \frac{1}{2}\left(\frac{\partial V}{\partial y}\right)'CK_2^{-1}C'\left(\frac{\partial V}{\partial y}\right) - y'k_1 + \left(\frac{\partial V}{\partial y}\right)'CK_2^{-1}k_2$$

$$- \tfrac{1}{2}k_2'K_2^{-1}k_2 + d + \left(\frac{\partial V}{\partial y}\right)'Ay + \tfrac{1}{2}\text{tr}\left(\sum \frac{\partial^2 V}{\partial y \partial y'}\right) = -\frac{\partial V}{\partial t}. $$

$$(85)$$

The partial differential equation (85) is to be solved.

From knowledge of the solution for V in the discrete-time formulation of this problem, let us try the quadratic function

$$V = \tfrac{1}{2}y'H(t)y - y'h(t) + c(t). \quad (86)$$

The appropriate derivatives of (86) can be substituted into (85), giving

$$\frac{1}{2}y'K_1y - \frac{1}{2}y'HCK_2^{-1}C'Hy + y'HCK_2^{-1}C'h - \frac{1}{2}h'CK_2^{-1}C'h$$

$$- y'k_1 + y'HCK_2^{-1}k_2 - h'CK_2^{-1}k_2 - \frac{1}{2}k_2'K_2^{-1}k_2$$

$$+ d + \frac{1}{2}y'HAy + \frac{1}{2}y'A'Hy - h'Ay + \frac{1}{2}\text{tr}(\Sigma H)$$

$$= -\frac{1}{2}y'\left(\frac{dH}{dt}\right)y + y'\frac{dh}{dt} - \frac{dc}{dt}. \tag{87}$$

Equation 87 implies the following differential equations for H, h, and c:

$$-\frac{dH}{dt} = K_1 - HCK_2^{-1}C'H + HA + A'H, \tag{88}$$

$$\frac{dh}{dt} = HCK_2^{-1}C'h - A'h - k_1 + HCK_2^{-1}k_2, \tag{89}$$

$$\frac{dc}{dt} = \frac{1}{2}h'CK_2^{-1}C'h + h'CK_2^{-1}k_2 + \frac{1}{2}k_2'K_2^{-1}k_2 - d - \frac{1}{2}\text{tr}(\Sigma H). \tag{90}$$

These differential equations are to be solved with the boundary conditions $H(T) = K_0$, $h(T) = k_0$, and $c(T) = d_0$. Having found the parameters $H(t)$, $h(t)$, and $c(t)$ of V, we can evaluate $\partial V/\partial y$ for the optimal control equation (84) as $H(t)y - h(t)$.

CHAPTER 19

Optimum Use and Exploration of a Natural Resource

A classic paper of Hotelling (1931) deals with the optimum rate of consuming an exhaustible resource over time when the total reserve of the resource is known. This chapter attempts to find a solution to the optimum use and extraction of an exhaustible resource when the amount of the reserve is unknown.

19.1 SOLUTION IN THE CERTAINTY CASE

In the certainty case, let $x(t)$ be the rate of consumption and $y(t)$ be the known stock of reserves at time t. The differential equation is

$$dy = -x\,dt. \tag{1}$$

Given a utility function $u(x, t)$ the problem is to find

$$V(y,t) = \max_{x} \left\{ \int_{t}^{T} u(x,s)\,ds + B[\,y(T), T\,] \right\}. \tag{2}$$

By the method of dynamic programming, we need to solve

$$\max_{x} \left\{ u(x,t) + \frac{\partial V}{\partial t} - x\frac{\partial V}{\partial y} \right\} = 0. \tag{3}$$

Differentiation yields the first-order condition

$$\frac{\partial u}{\partial x} = \frac{\partial V}{\partial y},$$

(4)

which equates the marginal utility of consuming the resource at each point in time and the shadow price of the stock of reserve. Denoting the function $\partial u / \partial x = u_x$ by $G(x, t)$, we write the solution of (4) as

$$x = G^{-1}\left(\frac{\partial V}{\partial y}, t\right) = G^{-1}(V_y, t).$$

(5)

When (5) is substituted into (3), the resulting partial differential equation can be solved for $V(y, t)$.

To illustrate, let $u = e^{-\rho t}(x - \frac{1}{2}\beta x^2)$. This problem becomes a special case of the problem of Section 10 in Chapter 18, with $K_1 = 0$, $k_1 = 0$, $A = 0$, $C = -1$, $K_2 = e^{-\rho t}\beta$, $k_2 = e^{-\rho t}$, $d = 0$, and $\Sigma = 0$. The loss function W of (80) is $-u$. Therefore, if we redefine the function V to measure total expected utility instead of total expected loss, but retain the definitions for H, h, and c, we change the sign of the right-hand side of (86) of Chapter 18,

$$V(y, t) = -\frac{1}{2}H(t)y^2 + h(t)y - c(t).$$

(6)

By (88), (89), and (90) in Chapter 18 the differential equations for H, h, and c are

$$-\frac{dH}{dt} = -\beta^{-1}e^{\rho t}H^2,$$

(7)

$$\frac{dh}{dt} = \beta^{-1}e^{\rho t}Hh - \beta^{-1}H,$$

(8)

$$\frac{dc}{dt} = \frac{1}{2}\beta^{-1}e^{\rho t}h^2 - \beta^{-1}h + \frac{1}{2}\beta^{-1}e^{-\rho t}.$$

(9)

The terminal utility is assumed to be

$$-\frac{1}{2}y'(T)K_0 y(T) + y'(T)k_0 - d_0 = -\frac{1}{2}\lambda y^2(T),$$

(10)

with $K_0 = \lambda$, $k_0 = 0$ and $d_0 = 0$. We will let λ be extremely large to penalize any nonzero $y(T)$ and to insure that the resource is used up at a time T.

The solution to (7) is $H(t) = -\beta\rho(e^{\rho t} + \alpha)^{-1}$ where α is a constant of integration. To determine α, we use the condition $H(T) = K_0 = \lambda$, yielding $\alpha = -e^{\rho T} - \beta\rho/\lambda$. The solution to (7) is therefore

$$H(t) = \beta\rho(e^{\rho T} - e^{\rho t} + \beta\rho/\lambda)^{-1}. \tag{11}$$

Similarly, the solution to (8) is

$$h(t) = \rho(T - t)(e^{\rho T} - e^{\rho t} + \beta\rho/\lambda)^{-1}, \tag{12}$$

which satisfies the terminal condition $h(T) = k_0 = 0$. Having found the coefficients $H(t)$ and $h(t)$ of the quadratic function V, we can use (4) to obtain the optimum consumption function

$$x(t) = \beta^{-1}\{1 + e^{\rho t}[H(t)y(t) - h(t)]\}, \tag{13}$$

which is linear in the stock of reserve y. The shadow price of the reserve stock can be obtained as $\partial V/\partial y = h(t) - H(t)y$.

The above solution is provided partly to illustrate the method of Section 10 in Chapter 18. Note, however, that it ignores the restrictions that $y(t) \geq 0$. An alternative method of solving this problem is to utilize the optimality condition that the marginal utility of consumption should be the same at all time, that is

$$\frac{du}{dx} = k = e^{-\rho t}(1 - \beta x), \tag{14}$$

where k is constant through time and is chosen to exhaust all the resource at T. Hence the rate of consumption is

$$x(t) = \beta^{-1}(1 - ke^{\rho t}), \tag{15}$$

and total consumption from t to T is

$$\int_t^T x(s)\,ds = \beta^{-1}\left[T - t - k\rho^{-1}(e^{\rho T} - e^{\rho t})\right] = y(t), \tag{16}$$

yielding

$$k = \rho(e^{\rho T} - e^{\rho t})^{-1}[T - t - \beta y(t)],$$

and accordingly the optimal consumption function

$$x(t) = \beta^{-1}\{1 + e^{\rho T}\rho(e^{\rho t} - e^{\rho t})^{-1}[\beta y(t) - (T - t)]\}, \quad (17)$$

which agrees with (13). The function $V(y, t)$ can be obtained as $\int_t^T u[x(s)]ds$.

19.2 ASSUMPTIONS CONCERNING UNKNOWN STOCK OF RESERVES

When the total stock of reserves in the ground is unknown, a simple assumption is that it is distributed at random over the surface of the earth, with an expected number λ of hidden reserves per square mile. The reserves are assumed to take only discrete values. The quantity z to be discovered in n square miles is assumed to follow a Poisson distribution

$$f(z|\lambda, n) = \frac{e^{-n\lambda}(n\lambda)^z}{z!}. \quad (18)$$

The parameter λ is unknown.

To provide a model of learning about λ, let us consider for the moment that decisions on consumption and exploration of the resource are made in discrete time. We assume for analytical convenience that the prior distribution of λ_t at the beginning of period t is gamma with parameters s_t and r_t (time subscript to be omitted when understood),

$$g(\lambda|s, r) = \frac{e^{-s\lambda}\lambda^{r-1}s^r}{(r - 1)!}. \quad (19)$$

The conditional distribution of λ given z units being discovered in n squared miles is, by the Bayes theorem,

$$g(\lambda|z; s, r, n) = \frac{f(z|\lambda, n)g(\lambda|s, r)}{\int_0^\infty \text{numerator } d\lambda} \quad (20)$$

The marginal distribution of z is

$$\int_0^\infty f(z|\lambda, n)g(\lambda|s, r)d\lambda = \frac{n^z}{z!} \cdot \frac{s^r}{(r - 1)!} \cdot \int_0^\infty e^{-(s+n)\lambda}\lambda^{r+z-1}d\lambda,$$

or

$$\hat{f}(z|s,r,n) = \frac{n^z}{z!} \cdot \frac{s^r}{(r-1)!} \cdot \frac{(r+z-1)!}{(s+n)^{r+z}}.$$ (21)

Note that the function g given by (19) is a natural conjugate prior density function for the parameter λ of the Poisson distribution. The former distribution has parameters s_t and r_t. After n_t square miles are explored and z_t units of the resource are found, the posterior density function of λ as given by (20) has the same form, but has new parameters

$$s_{t+1} = s_t + n_t,$$ (22)

and

$$r_{t+1} = r_t + z_t.$$ (23)

Thus s_t and r_t can be interpreted respectively as the total number of square miles explored and the total quantity of the resource discovered up to time t. The marginal distribution function (21) of z, rewritten below, is a negative binomial distribution

$$\hat{f}(z|s,r,n) = \frac{(z+r-1)!}{z!\,(r-1)!} \left(\frac{n}{s+n}\right)^z \left(\frac{s}{s+n}\right)^r.$$ (24)

Having considered the problem of resource use and exploration in discrete time, we will reformulate the problem in continuous time by letting the time interval h between successive decisions become small. Let $x_2(t)$ be the number of square miles to be explored per unit time at time t. In a small time interval h, $x_2(t)h$ is the number n_t of square miles explored; n_t, is small compared with the total square miles s_t having been explored up to that point in history. According to (24) the probability of discovering no resource during the time interval h is

$$P(z=0) = \left(\frac{s}{s+x_2 h}\right)^r = \left(1 + \frac{x_2 h}{s}\right)^{-r} = \left[e^{x_2 h/s} + o(h)\right]^{-r}$$

$$= e^{-(r/s)x_2 h} + o(h) = 1 - \frac{r}{s}x_2 h + o(h).$$ (25)

The probability of discovering one unit of the resource during time h is, again by (24),

$$P(z = 1) = r\left(\frac{x_2 h}{s + x_2 h}\right)\left(\frac{s}{s + x_2 h}\right)^r$$

$$= r\left(\frac{x_2 h}{s} + o(h)\right)\left(1 - \frac{r}{s}x_2 h + o(h)\right)$$

$$= \frac{r}{s}x_2 h + o(h). \tag{26}$$

Thus in a very small time interval h, the probability of finding no resource is $1 - (r/s)x_2 h$; the probability of finding one unit of the resource is $(r/s)x_2 h$; and the probability of finding two or more units can be ignored. We have just specified a *Poisson process* dv with parameter $\lambda x_2 = (r/s)x_2$. This process generates an outcome "one" with probability $\lambda x_2 dt$ and an outcome "zero" with probability $1 - \lambda x_2 dt$ during a time interval $dt = h$ if an exploratory effort x_2 is applied.

19.3 THE OPTIMAL CONTROL PROBLEM FORMULATED

Our model so far has three state variables: the quantity $y_1(t)$ of known reserves in stock, the amount $s(t)$ of land already explored, and the total quantity $r(t)$ of the resource ever discovered up to time t. The two control variables are the rate $x_1(t)$ of consumption and the rate $x_2(t)$ of exploratory effort. We will replace the second state variable by $y_2(t) = L - s(t)$, where L is total explorable land; $y_2(t)$ thus denotes the amount of land as yet unexplored. The state variables satisfy the stochastic differential equations

$$dy_1 = -x_1 dt + dv,$$

$$dy_2 = -x_2 dt,$$

$$dr = dv. \tag{27}$$

The objective is to find

$$V(y, t) = \max_{x} E_t\left\{\int_t^T u(y, x, s)ds + B[y(T), T]\right\}, \tag{28}$$

where y denotes the vector of state variables and x the vector of control variables.

Since the stochastic differential equations involve the Poisson process dv, we will derive the optimality condition for a model of the form

$$dy = f(y,x,t)dt + g(y,x,t)dv, \qquad (29)$$

where f and g are vector functions. In the special case of the model (27),

$$f = \begin{bmatrix} -x_1 \\ -x_2 \\ 0 \end{bmatrix}, \qquad g = \begin{bmatrix} 1 \\ 0 \\ 1 \end{bmatrix}. \qquad (30)$$

By the method of dynamic programming, we need to solve

$$\max_x \left\{ u(y,x,t) + E_t\left(\frac{1}{h}dV\right) \right\} = 0, \qquad (31)$$

where

$$dV = V[\,y(t+dt),t+dt\,] - V[\,y(t),t\,]$$

$$= \frac{\partial V}{\partial t}dt + \left(\frac{\partial V}{\partial y}\right)' dy + o(dt)$$

$$= \frac{\partial V}{\partial t}dt + \left(\frac{\partial V}{\partial y}\right)' fdt + \left(\frac{\partial V}{\partial y}\right)' gdv + o(dt). \qquad (32)$$

Note that dv has probability $\lambda x_2 dt$ of being one (or being W in a more general formulation with W having some given probability distribution) and probability $(1 - \lambda x_2 dt)$ of being zero. Hence

$$E_t\left(\frac{1}{dt}dV\right) = \frac{\partial V}{\partial t} + \left(\frac{\partial V}{\partial y}\right)' f + \lambda x_2\{V[\,y(t) + g,t\,] - V[\,y(t),t\,]\}.$$

$$(33)$$

When (33) is substituted into (31) for our model (30), we have

$$\max_x \left\{ u(x,t) + \frac{\partial V}{\partial t} - x_1\frac{\partial V}{\partial y_1} - x_2\frac{\partial V}{\partial y_2} \right.$$

$$\left. + \lambda x_2[\,V(y_1 + 1,y_2,r+1,t) - V(y,t)\,] \right\} = 0. \qquad (34)$$

19.4   INVESTIGATION OF A SIMPLIFIED PROBLEM

We will study a simplified version of the problem (34) by ignoring the third state variable r which is the quantity of the resource discovered up to t. This state variable helps us construct the estimate $\lambda = r/s = r/(L - y_2)$. In other words, we are ignoring the possibility of active learning about λ in the future and utilizing only the current value of $\lambda(t)$ as if it would remain constant in the future. The problem (34) will then become

$$\max_x \left\{ u(x,t) + \frac{\partial V}{\partial t} - x_1 \frac{\partial V}{\partial y_1} - x_2 \frac{\partial V}{\partial y_2} + \lambda x_2 \Delta V_1 \right\} = 0, \qquad (35)$$

where $\Delta V_1 = V(y_1 + 1, y_2, t) - V(y_1, y_2, t)$. Compare (35) with (3).

If $u(x,t) = e^{-\rho t} u(x)$, ρ being the rate of discount, and if the planning horizon is infinite, we can write $V(y,t)$ as $e^{-\rho t} V(y)$ because the expected total utilities V for a given initial state y at two different points of time differ only by the discounting factor. Substituting $e^{-\rho t} u(x)$ for $u(x,t)$ and $e^{-\rho t} V(y)$ for $V(y,t)$ in (35) gives

$$\max_x \left\{ u(x) - x_1 \frac{\partial V}{\partial y_1} - x_2 \frac{\partial V}{\partial y_2} + \lambda x_2 \Delta V_1 \right\} = \rho V(y). \qquad (36)$$

We solve (36) by differentiation, using subscripts to denote partial derivatives

$$\frac{\partial \{\ \}}{\partial x_1} = u_1 - V_1 = 0, \qquad (37)$$

$$\frac{\partial \{\ \}}{\partial x_2} = u_2 - V_2 + \lambda \Delta V_1 = 0. \qquad (38)$$

V_1 and V_2 are the shadow prices of the known stock of reserves and of unexplored land respectively. The price $V_1 = p_1$ of the reserve is equated to its marginal utility. The price $V_2 = p_2$ of the unexplored land is equated to the sum of its marginal utility u_1 (actually the negative marginal cost of exploration per square mile) and the expected gain $\lambda \Delta V_1$ of discovering new resource. We can write $u(x)$ as the sum $u(x_1) - c(x_2)$ where $c(x_2)$ is the cost of exploring x_2 square miles of land per unit time. The marginal utility $u_1(x_1)$ is a decreasing function of x_1. Denoting the inverse of the function u_1 by u_1^{-1}, the solution of (37) is

$$x_1 = u_1^{-1}(p_1). \qquad (39)$$

The marginal cost $dc/dx_2 = -u_2(x_2)$ is assumed to be a nondecreasing function of x_2. The solution of (38) is

$$x_2 = -u_2^{-1}[-p_2 + \lambda p_1], \tag{40}$$

showing that the exploratory effort x_2 will increase as the price p_2 of land is lower, as the density λ of deposits is higher and as the value p_1 of the resource is higher.

To study the dynamics of the prices following the work of Arrow (1977), we differentiate (36) with respect to y_1 and y_2 respectively, obtaining

$$- x_1 V_{11} - x_2 V_{12} + \lambda x_2 [V_1(y_1 + 1, y_2) - V_1(y_1, y_2)] = \rho V_1, \tag{41}$$

$$- x_1 V_{12} - x_2 V_{22} + \lambda x_2 [V_2(y_1 + 1, y_2) - V_2(y_1, y_2)] = \rho V_2. \tag{42}$$

In differentiating (36) we treat the control variables x_1 and x_2 as constants. The reader can verify the results (41) and (42) by treating x_1 and x_2 as functions of y_1 and y_2 and utilizing the first-order conditions (37) and (38). Consider the price of the resource at time $t + dt$. It will depend on whether additional resource is discovered during the time interval dt because the argument of the function V_1 takes different values in the two cases:

$$V_1(t + dt) = V_1(y, t) + V_{11} dy_1 + V_{12} dy_2$$

$$= V_1(y, t) - V_{11} x_1 dt - V_{12} x_2 dt \quad \text{with prob.}\,(1 - \lambda x_2 dt)$$

$$V_1(t + dt) = V_1(y_1 + 1, y_2) \quad \text{with prob.}\,\lambda x_2 dt. \tag{43}$$

Using (41) to substitute $\lambda x_2 [V_1(y_1 + 1, y_2) - V_1(y_1, y_2)] - \rho V_1$ for $x_1 V_{11} + x_2 V_{12}$ in (43) one finds the expectation

$$E\left[\frac{V_1(t + dt) - V_1(t)}{dt}\right] = (1 - \lambda x_2 dt)[-x_1 V_{11} - x_2 V_{22}]$$

$$+ \lambda x_2 dt [V_1(y_1 + 1, y_2) - V_1(y_1, y_2)]/dt,$$

$$= \rho V_1 + (\lambda x_2)^2 [V_1(y_1 + 1, y_2) - V_1(y_1, y_2)] dt$$

$$- \lambda x_2 \rho V_1 dt. \tag{44}$$

By taking the limit of (44) as dt approaches zero, one finds that the expected proportional rate of increase in the price of the resource to be the rate of discount ρ. This conclusion generalizes a conclusion of Hotelling (1931) for the case with known quantity of the exhaustible resource.

19.5   EXPLICIT SOLUTION TO THE SIMPLIFIED PROBLEM

An explicit solution to this problem can be obtained if we assume a quadratic loss function and a finite time horizon T. Equation 35 then becomes

$$0 = \min_{x} \left\{ \tfrac{1}{2} y' K_1(t) y - y' k_1(t) + \tfrac{1}{2} x' K_2(t) x - x' k_2(t) + d(t) \right.$$

$$\left. + \frac{\partial V}{\partial t} + \left(\frac{\partial V}{\partial y} \right)' (Ay + Cx) + (\Delta V)' Dx \right\}. \tag{45}$$

Equation 45 is a formulation of the optimization problem that includes our problem of exhaustible resource as a special case if we assume

$$K_1(t) = 0, \quad k_1(t) = 0, \quad A = 0, \quad C = \begin{bmatrix} -1 & 0 \\ 0 & -1 \end{bmatrix},$$

$$\Delta V = \begin{bmatrix} \Delta V_1 \\ \Delta V_2 \end{bmatrix} = \begin{bmatrix} V(y_1 + 1, y_2) - V(y_1, y_2) \\ V(y_1, y_2 + 1) - V(y_1, y_2) \end{bmatrix},$$

$$D = \begin{bmatrix} 0 & \lambda \\ 0 & 0 \end{bmatrix}. \tag{46}$$

Finding the minimum of (45) by differentiation yields

$$\frac{\partial \{ \ \}}{\partial x} = K_2 x - k_2 + C' \left(\frac{\partial V}{\partial y} \right) + D' \Delta V = 0,$$

which gives the optimal feedback control equation

$$x = -K_2^{-1} C' \left(\frac{\partial V}{\partial y} \right) - K_2^{-1} D' \Delta V + K_2^{-1} k_2. \tag{47}$$

When (47) is substituted for x in (45) we obtain

$$\tfrac{1}{2} y' K_1 y - y' k_1 - \tfrac{1}{2} \left(\frac{\partial V}{\partial y} \right)' C K_2^{-1} C' \left(\frac{\partial V}{\partial y} \right) - \tfrac{1}{2} \Delta V' D K_2^{-1} D' \Delta V$$

$$+ \left(\frac{\partial V}{\partial y} \right)' Ay + \left(\frac{\partial V}{\partial y} \right)' C K_2^{-1} k_2 + \Delta V' D K_2^{-1} k_2$$

$$- \left(\frac{\partial V}{\partial y} \right)' C K^{-1} D' \Delta V + d - \tfrac{1}{2} k'_2 K_2^{-1} k_2 = - \frac{\partial V}{\partial t}, \tag{48}$$

which is a partial differential equation to be solved.

From the knowledge of linear-quadratic control theory, we can try a quadratic function for the solution,

$$V = \tfrac{1}{2}y'H(t)y - y'h(t) + c(t). \qquad (49)$$

The derivatives and difference of (49) are

$$\frac{\partial V}{\partial y} = Hy - h, \qquad (50)$$

$$\Delta V = Hy - h - h_d, \qquad (51)$$

where h_d is a vector composed of the diagonal elements of H, and

$$\frac{\partial V}{\partial t} = \tfrac{1}{2}y'\frac{dH}{dt}y - y'\frac{dh}{dt} + \frac{dc}{dt}. \qquad (52)$$

Substituting these derivatives into (48) and equating coefficients of the quadratic functions on both sides of the resulting equation, we obtain

$$-\frac{dH}{dt} = K_1 - H\big(CK_2^{-1}C' + DK_2^{-1}D' + CK_2^{-1}D' + DK_2^{-1}C'\big)H$$

$$+ HA + A'H, \qquad (53)$$

$$\frac{dh}{dt} = -k_1 + H\big(CK_2^{-1}C' + DK_2^{-1}D' + CK_2^{-1}D' + DK_2^{-1}C'\big)h - A'h$$

$$+ H\big(CK_2^{-1}k_2 + DK_2^{-1}k_2 + DK_2^{-1}D'h_d + CK_2^{-1}D'h_d\big), \qquad (54)$$

$$-\frac{dc}{dt} = -\tfrac{1}{2}h'CK_2^{-1}C'h - h'CK_2^{-1}k_2 - \tfrac{1}{2}(h' + h_d')DK_2^{-1}D'(h + h_d)$$

$$- k_2'K_2^{-1}D'(h + h_d) - h'CK_2^{-1}Ch - h'CK_2^{-1}D'h_d$$

$$+ d - \tfrac{1}{2}k_2'K_2^{-1}k_2. \qquad (55)$$

By introducing appropriate terminal conditions analogous to the ones given in the beginning of this section, one can solve these differential equations to obtain the function V of (49).

This chapter has illustrated the method of dynamic programming as applied to a continuous time model governed by a Poisson process. It has treated some useful methods that are applicable to the optimum use and exploration of an exhaustible resource, while leaving the discussion of many economic issues to be further explored.

Bibliography

Adelman, I., and Adelman, F. L. (1959), "The dynamic properties of the Klein-Goldberger model," *Econometrica*, **27** (4), 596–625.

Andersen, L. C., and Carlson, K. M. (1970), "A monetarist model for economic stabilization," *Federal Reserve Bank of St. Louis Review*, **52**, 7–25.

Andersen, L. C., and Carlson, K. M. (1972), "An econometric analysis of the relation of monetary variables to the behavior of prices and unemployment," in O. Eckstein, Ed., *The Econometrics of Price Determination* (Washington, D.C.: Board of Governors of the Federal Reserve System, pp. 277–308.

Anderson, P. (1979), " 'Rational' forecasts from 'nonrational models,' " *Journal of Monetary Economics*, **5** (1), 67–80.

Ando, A., and Palash, C. (1976), "Some stabilization problems of 1971–1975, with an application of optimal control algorithms," *American Economic Review*, **66** (2), 346–348.

Arnold, L. (1974), *Stochastic Differential Equations: Theory and Applications* (New York: John Wiley and Sons).

Arrow, K. (1977), "Optimal pricing, use and exploration of uncertain natural resource stocks," Paper presented at the Conference on Natural Resource Pricing, Wyoming.

Aström, K. J. (1970), *Introduction to Stochastic Control Theory* (New York: Academic Press).

Athans, M., et al. (1975), "Sequential open-loop optimal control of a nonlinear macroeconomic model," Paper presented before the 3rd World Congress of the Econometric Society, Toronto, Ontario, Canada, August 21–25.

Black, F., and Scholes, M. (1973), "The pricing of options and corporate liabilities," *Journal of Political Economy*, **81**, 637–654.

Bodkin, R. G. (1972), "Wage and price formation in selected Canadian econometric models," in O. Eckstein, Ed., *The Econometrics of Price Determination* (Washington, D. C.: Board of Governors of the Federal Reserve System), pp. 369–385.

Butters, E. J., and Chow, G. C. (1977), "Optimal control of nonlinear systems program: User's guide," (Princeton, New Jersey: Princeton University, Econometric Research Program, Research Memorandum 209). Reprinted as Chapter 5.

Chow, G. C. (1964), "A comparison of alternative estimators for simultaneous equations," *Econometrica*, **32**, 532–553.

Chow, G. C. (1973), "Effect of uncertainty on optimal control policies," *International Economic Review*, **14**, 632–645.

Chow, G. C. (1975), *Analysis and Control of Dynamic Economic Systems* (New York: John Wiley and Sons).

Chow, G. C. (1976a), "Control methods for macroeconomic policy analysis," *American Economic Review*, **65**, 340–345.

Chow, G. C. (1976b), "An approach to the feedback control of nonlinear econometric systems," *Annals of Economic and Social Measurement*, **5** (3), 297–309. Reprinted as Chapter 2.

Chow, G. C. (1976c), "The control of nonlinear econometric systems with unknown parameters," *Econometrica*, **44** (4), 685–695. Reprinted as Chapter 3.

Chow, G. C. (1977), "Usefulness of imperfect models for the formulation of stabilization policies," *Annals of Economic and Social Measurement*, **6**, 175–187. Reprinted as Chapter 11.

Chow, G. C. (1978), "Evaluation of macroeconomic policies by stochastic control techniques," *International Economic Review*, **19** (2), 311–320. Reprinted as Chapter 8.

Chow, G. C. (1980a), "Econometric policy evaluation and optimization under rational expectations," *Journal of Economic Dynamics and Control*, **2**, 1–13. Reprinted as Chapter 15.

Chow, G. C. (1980b), "Estimation of rational expectations models," *Journal of Economic Dynamics and Control*, **2**, 241–256. Reprinted as Chapter 16.

Chow, G. C. (1981), "Evaluation of econometric models by decomposition and aggregation," in J. Kmenta and J. Ramsey, Eds., *Methodology of Macroeconomic Models* (Amsterdam: North-Holland Publishing Company).

Chow, G. C., and Megdal, S. B. (1978a), "The control of large scale econometric systems," *IEEE Transactions on Automatic Control*, **AC-23** (2), 344–349. Reprinted as Chapter 4.

Chow, G. C., and Megdal, S. B. (1978b), "An econometric definition of the inflation-unemployment trade-off," *American Economic Review*, **68** (3), 446–453. Reprinted as Chapter 7.

Christ, C. F. (1975), "Judging the performance of econometric models of the U.S. economy," *International Economic Review*, **16**, 54–74.

Cooley, T. F., and Prescott, E. (1976), "Estimation in the presence of stochastic parameter variation," *Econometrica*, **44**, 167–183.

Cox, J. C., and Ross, S. A. (1976), "The valuation of options for alternative stochastic processes," *Journal of Financial Economics*, **3** 145–166.

Craine, R., Havenner, A., and Tinsley, P. (1976), "Optimal macroeconomic control policies," *Annals of Economic and Social Measurement*, **5** (2), 191–204.

Cruz, J. B., Jr. (1975), "Survey of Nash and Stackelberg equilibrium strategies in dynamic games," *Annals of Economic and Social Measurement*, **4** (2), 339–344.

De Menil, G., and Enzler, J. J. (1972), "Prices and wages in the FR-MIT-Penn econometric model," in O. Eckstein, Ed., *The Econometrics of Price Determination* (Washington, D.C.: Board of Governors of the Federal Reserve System), pp. 277–308.

Eckstein, O., Ed., (1972), *The Econometrics of Price Determination* (Washington, D.C.: Board of Governors of the Federal Reserve System).

Fair, R. C. (1974), "On the solution of optimal control problems as maximization problems," *Annals of Economic and Social Measurement*, **3** (1), 135–154.

Fair, R. C. (1976), *A Model of Macroeconomic Activity, Volume II: The Empirical Model* (Cambridge, Massachusetts: Ballinger Publishing Company, Cowles Special Publication).

Fair, R. C. (1978a), "The use of optimal control techniques to measure economic performance," *International Economic Review*, **19**, 289–309.

Fair, R. C. (1978b), "The sensitivity of financial policy effects to assumptions about the behavior of the Federal Reserve," *Econometrica*, **46**, 1165–1179.

Fair, R. C. (1978c), "An analysis of a macroeconometric model with rational expectations in the bond and stock markets." Unpublished manuscript (New Haven, Connecticut: Yale University).

Fischer, S. (1975), "The demand for index bonds," *Journal of Political Economy*, **83**, 509–535.

Friedlaender, A. F. (1973), "Macro policy goals in the postwar period: A study in revealed preference," *Quarterly Journal of Economics*, **87**, 25–43.

Friedman, B. M. (1973), *Methods in Optimization for Economic Stabilization Policy* (Amsterdam: North-Holland Publishing Company).

Garbade, K. D. (1975), *Discretionary Control of Aggregate Economic Activity* (Lexington, Massachusetts: D. C. Heath and Company, Lexington Books).

Gertler, M. (1980), "Uncertain lags and optimal monetary rules," Presented before the meetings of the Society for Economic Dynamics and Control at Princeton University on June 4, 1980.

Goldberger, A. S. (1959), *Impact Multipliers and Dynamic Properties of the Klein-Goldberger Model* (Amsterdam: North-Holland Publishing Company).

Goldfeld, S. M., and Quandt, R. E. (1972), *Nonlinear Methods in Econometrics* (Amsterdam: North-Holland Publishing Company).

Gordon, R. H., and Jorgenson, D. (1976), "The investment tax credit and counter-cyclical policy" in O. Eckstein, Ed., *Parameters and Policies in the U.S. Economy* (Amsterdam: North-Holland Publishing Company), pp. 275–314.

Green, D. W., and Higgins, C. I. (1977), *SOVMOD I, A Macroeconometric Model of the Soviet Union* (New York: Academic Press).

Hansen, L. P., and Sargent, T. J. (1980), "Formulating and estimating dynamic linear rational expectations models," *Journal of Economic Dynamics and Control*, **2**, 7–46.

Harvey, A., and Phillips, G. D. A. (1978), "The maximum likelihood estimation of autoregressive-moving average models by Kalman filtering," Working paper No. 3, S.S.R.S. supported Project on Testing for Specification Error in Econometric Models, University of Kent at Canterbury.

Hirsch, A. A. (1972), "Price simulations with the OBE econometric model," in O. Eckstein, Ed., *The Econometrics of Price Determination* (Washington, D.C.: Board of Governors of the Federal Reserve System), pp. 237–276.

Hirsch, A. A., Hymans, S. H., and Shapiro, H. (1978), "Econometric review of alternative fiscal and monetary policies, 1971–75," *Review of Economics and Statistics*, **60**, 334–345.

Holbrook, R. S. (1974), "A practical method for controlling a large nonlinear stochastic system," *Annals of Economic and Social Measurement*, **3** (1), 155–176.

Hotelling, H. (1931), "The economics of exhaustible resource," *Journal of Political Economy*, **39**, 137–175.

Hymans, S. H. (1972), "Prices and behavior in three U.S. econometric models," in O. Eckstein, Ed., *The Econometrics of Price Determination* (Washington, D.C.: Board of Governors of the Federal Reserve System), pp. 309–324.

Hymans, S. H., and Shapiro, H. T. (1973), "The Michigan quarterly econometric model of the U.S. economy," in *The Economic Outlook for 1973*, papers presented to the Twentieth Anniversary Conference of the University of Michigan (Ann Arbor, Michigan: University of Michigan).

Ito, K., and McKean, H. P., Jr. (1964), *Diffusion Processes and their Sample Paths* (New York: Academic Press).

Kalchbrenner, H. H., and Tinsley, P. A. (1976), "On the use of feedback control in the design of aggregate monetary policy," *American Economic Review*, **66** (2), 349–355.

Kalman, R. E. (1960), "A new approach to linear filtering and prediction problems," *Journal of Basic Engineering*, **82D**, 33–45.

Kmenta, J., and Smith, P. E. (1973), "Autonomous expenditures versus money supply: an application of dynamic multipliers," *Review of Economics and Statistics*, **55**, 299–307.

Kydland, F. (1975), "Noncooperative and dominant player solutions in discrete dynamic games," *International Economic Review*, **16**, 321–335.

Kydland, F. E., and Prescott, E. C., "Rules rather than discretion: The inconsistency of optimal plans," *Journal of Political Economy*, **85**, 473–491.

Long, J. B. (1974), "Stock prices, inflation, and the term structure of interest rates," *Journal of Financial Economics*, **1**, 131–170.

Loury, G. C. (1978), "The optimum exploitation of an unknown reserve," *Review of Economic Studies*, **45**, 621–636.

Lucas, R. E., Jr. (1976), "Econometric policy evaluation: A critique," *Journal of Monetary Economics: Supplement*, **1**, 19–46, and in K. Brunner and A. H. Meltzer, Eds., *The Phillips Curve and Labor Markets* (Amsterdam: North-Holland Publishing Company).

Marschak, J. (1953), "Economic measurements for policy and prediction," in W. C. Hood and T. C. Koopmans, Eds., *Studies in Econometric Method*, Cowles Commission Monograph 14 (New York: John Wiley and Sons), pp. 1–26.

McKean, H. P., Jr. (1969), *Stochastic Integrals* (New York: Academic Press).

Merton, R. C. (1969), "Lifetime portfolio selection under uncertainty: The continuous-time case," *Review of Economics and Statistics*, **51**, 247–257.

Merton, R. C. (1970), "Optimum consumption and portfolio rules in a continuous-time model," *Journal of Economic Theory*, **3**, 373–413.

Merton, R. C. (1973), "An intertemporal capital asset pricing model," *Econometrica*, **41** (5), 867–887.

Muth, J. F. (1961), "Rational expectations and the theory of price movements," *Econometrica*, **29**, 315–335.

Norman, A., Norman, M., and Palash, C. (1975), "On the computation of deterministic optimal macroeconomic policy," Federal Reserve Bank of New York, Research Paper 7507.

Pagan, A. (1975), "A note on the extraction of components from time series," *Econometrica*, **43**, 163–168.

Pagan, A. (1980), "Some identification and estimation results for regression models with stochastically varying coefficients," Australian National University, unpublished manuscript.

Phillips, A. W. (1958), "The relation between unemployment and the rate of change of money wage rates in the United Kingdom, 1861–1957," *Economica*, **25**, 283–299.

Rosenberg, B. (1973), "A survey of stochastic parameter regression," *Annals of Economic and Social Measurement*, **2**, 399–428.

Rosenberg, B., and Ohlson, J. A. (1976), "The stationary distribution of returns and portfolio separation in capital markets: A fundamental contradiction," *Journal of Financial and Quantitative Analysis*, **11**, 393–402.

Samuelson, P. A. (1969), "Lifetime portfolio selection by dynamic stochastic programming," *Review of Economics and Statistics*, **51**, 239–246.

Sant, D. (1977), "Generalized least squares applied to time-varying parameter models," *Annals of Economic and Social Measurement*, **6**, 301–314.

Sargent, T. J. (1978), "Estimation of dynamic labor demand schedules under rational expectations," *Journal of Political Economy*, **86**, 1009–1044.

Sargent, T. J. (1979), *Macroeconomic Theory* (New York: Academic Press).

Sargent, T. J., and Wallace, N. (1975), " 'Rational' expectations, the optimal monetary instrument, and the optimal money supply rule," *Journal of Political Economy*, **83**, 241–254.

Shiller, R. J. (1977), "Rational expectations and the dynamic structure of macro-economic models," *Journal of Monetary Economics*, **3**, 1–44.

Simon, H. A. (1956), "Dynamic programming under uncertainty with a quadratic criterion function," *Econometrica*, **24** (1), 74–81.

Smith, C. W., Jr. (1976), "Option pricing: A review," *Journal of Financial Economics*, **3**, 3–51.

Swamy, P. A. V. B. (1971), *Statistical Inference in Random Coefficient Regression Models* (New York: Springer-Verlag).

Swamy, P. A. V. B. (1974), "Linear models with random coefficients," in Paul Zarembka, Ed., *Frontiers in Econometrics* (New York: Academic Press), pp. 143–168.

Taylor, J. B. (1977), "Conditions for unique solutions in stochastic macroeconomic models with rational expectations," *Econometrica*, **45**, 1377–1385.

Taylor, J. B. (1979), "Estimation and control of a macroeconomic model with rational expectations," *Econometrica*, **47** (5), 1267–1286.

Theil, H. (1958), *Economic Forecasts and Policy* (Amsterdam: North-Holland Publishing Company).

Wallis, K. F. (1980), "Econometric implications of the rational expectations hypothesis," *Econometrica*, **48** (1), 49–73.

Index

309